ONT

EC

LA PROPRIÉTÉ

CONTRÔLEE

750 ml

EU" VOUVRAY (I&L) France

SAUMUR-CHAMPIGNY

CHATEAU DE CHAINTRES

Appellation Saumur-Champigny Contrôlée

B. de TIGNY, Propriétaire, DAMPIERRE-SUR-LOIRE (M. et-L.)

MISE EN BOUTEILLES AU CHATEAU

ALCOHOL 12,8 % BY VOL.

SELECTED BY
GERALD ASHER

SANCERRE

Domaine de la Mercy - Dieu

Appellation Sancerre Contrôlée

WHITE TABLE WINE

B. BAILLY-REVERDY
Viticulteur

75cl

à BUÉ
18300 Sancerre
FRANCE
Produce of France

CONTENTS 750 ML

Mis en bouteille à la propriété

IMPORTED BY THE MOSSWOOD WINE COMPANY, NEW-YORK, N.Y.

ON

CONTRÔLÉE

ignes

A DIOTERIE

IRE VITICULTEUR

TÉL. (47) 58.55.53

maine

ADET-PIOLA

ru Classé

MÉDAILLE D'OR PARIS 1867. GROUPE DES 1ERS CRUS
MÉDAILLE D'OR PARIS 1889

GRAND CRU CLASSÉ

CHATEAU FONPLÉGADE

SAINT-EMILION

APPELLATION SAINT-ÉMILION CONTRÔLÉE

1962

SOCIÉTÉ CIVILE DES VIGNOBLES A. MOUEIX PÈRE & FILS
PROPRIÉTAIRE A SAINT-ÉMILION (GIRONDE)

MIS EN BOUTEILLES AU CHATEAU

THE WINES OF BORDEAUX
AND WESTERN FRANCE

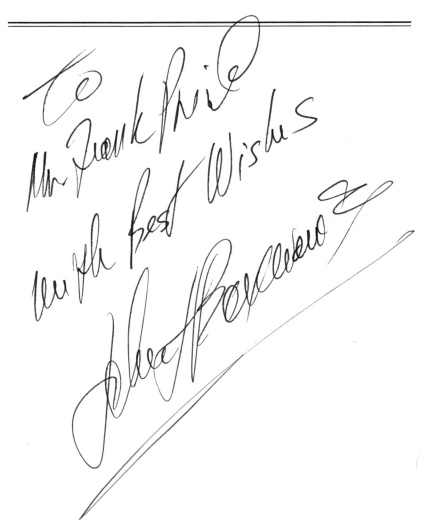

To Mr Frank Prial with best Wishes

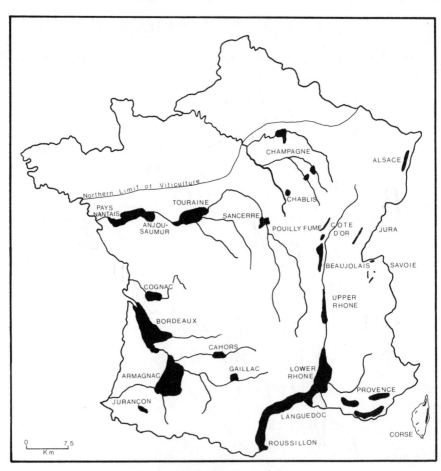

Major Wine Regions of France

THE WINES OF
BORDEAUX
AND WESTERN FRANCE

JOHN J. BAXEVANIS

ROWMAN & LITTLEFIELD
PUBLISHERS

TO JAMES

ROWMAN & LITTLEFIELD

Published in the United States of America in 1987
by Rowman & Littlefield, Publishers
(a division of Littlefield, Adams & Company)
81 Adams Drive, Totowa, New Jersey 07512

Library of Congress Cataloging-in-Publication Data

Baxevanis, John J.
   The wines of Bordeaux and western France.

   Includes index.
   1. Wine and wine making—France—Bordelais.
   2. Wine and wine making—France.   I. Title.
TP553.B28 1987   641.2′22′09447   87-4876
            ISBN 0-8476-7490-8

            87   89   91   90   88
              1   3   5   4   2

Printed in the United States of America

Contents

ILLUSTRATIONS

Tables

Figures

Plates

Note: Unless otherwise noted, illustrations were supplied by the
domaines.

FOREWORD

THIS volume owes its origins to a little-known but highly insightful book, *A Wine Tour of France,* first published in 1967, written by the erudite and highly competent Frederick S. Wildman, Jr. Although France and French wines were familiar to me before I read this interesting book, it soon proved to be an invaluable resourse, guide, and inspiration during my European "salad" days. As my sojourns and vinicultural interest intensified over the years, the seed for an expanded version of Wildman's book, written from a geographical perspective, soon took root.

This book surveys the viticultural regions of western France and briefly outlines the main historical, economic, and geographic characteristics of three of the country's major viticultural regions. The three vineyards encompass 19 major departments and collectively encompass 225,000 hectares, or approximately one-fourth of the national table-wine hectarage. Even more significant, the Loire, Bordeaux, and the Southwest produce about 40 percent of all AOC wine in France.

It is hoped that this modest volume will guide both casual and experienced wine lovers through the wide range of available wines, clarify major inquiries, explain others, and in the process simplify the cumbersome process of choosing wine. The book identifies each major wine region, highlights its major features, and describes many of the more prominent producers.

A few words on the quality of statistics, especially those pertaining to hectarage and production. Statistics published by central, regional, and wine- and grape-related agencies rarely concur and are therefore difficult to determine with precision. I have relied in large part on documentation from the Ministry of Agriculture and Commerce. In addition, and to be as accurate as possible, I have written to responsible parties for data, comments, and corrections on a good deal of the statistics herein. In the final analysis, I assume sole responsibility for any errors that may exist.

I should like to express my gratitude to the following persons, properties, cooperatives, and governmental offices who, over many years, have assisted my quest for reliable documentation.

First, I wish to thank the Office International de la Vigne et du Vin, the ministries of Agriculture and Commerce, l'Institut National Interprofessionel des Vins de Table, Jerome Agostini of l'Institut National des Appellations d'Origine des Vins et Eaux-de-Vie (INAO), and La Direction de la Consommation et de la Répression des Fraudes, all in Paris, for valuable statistical assistance.

I would like to express my appreciation to P. E. Poniatowski of Clos Baudoin, G. Huet of Le Huet-Lieu, Pascal H. Gitton of Gitton Père et Fils, and Chateau de Tracy, in the Loire.

For help concerning the Gironde, I would like to extend my appreciation to the late André Mentzenopoulos and to Corinne Mentzenopoulos-Petit of Chateau Margaux, Comte A. de Lur Saluces of Chateau d'Yquem, Chateau Troplong-Mondot, Malet-Roquefort of Chateau la Gaffelière, Alain Querre of Chateau Monbousquet, Chateau FourcasHosten, Chateau Pape-Clement, J. Borie of Chateau la Rivière, Chateau Cheval Blanc, Hubert Bouteiller of Chateau Lanessan, and J. B. Delmas of Chateau Haut-Brion.

Regarding the Southwest, I would like to acknowledge the assistance of Clos Triguedina, J. Chige of Cru Lamouroux, and J. Blaquière of Cave Coopérative des Grands Vins de Monbazillac et Bergerac.

I would like to take this opportunity to thank, in this country, Thierry Laloux, Commercial Attaché of the French Embassy, Washington, D.C.; and Alice Lubecon of Food & Wines of France, New York City. Special thanks for kind words and encouragement to Professor Harm de Blij of Miami University and the National Geographic Society and to Professor Frank Tancredi for his thought-provoking conversation; and to the East Stroudsburg University Research and Out-Service Training Fund. A special acknowledgement of gratitude to Mrs. B. Ash for her insightful comments, and the warmest of sincere thanks to Mrs. Cecile Daviduke for her ability to make sense of the French language; to Professor Ian Ackroyd-Kelly for his sagacity, patience, and graphic skills; and to my wife, Magda, who endured more than I care to remember when I was "in the office." Finally, I wish to acknowledge the assistance and advice of Mr. Martyn Hitchcock, the proficient editing of Mrs. Janet Johnston, and the support and patience of Mr. Paul Lee, all of Rowman & Littlefield.

PART I

THE WINES OF THE LOIRE

1

INTRODUCTION

E NCOMPASSING an area about four times the size of New Jersey, the Loire viticultural region lies southwest of Paris, east of Brittany, and south of Normandy. Well watered and fertile, the region's most prominent feature is the Loire River and its tributaries, including the Allier, Cher, Vienne, and Maine rivers. Originating in the Cévennes Mountains of southcentral France and draining nearly 20 percent of the nation's surface water, the Loire River, with a length of more than 1,000 kilometers, is the longest in the country. For most of its course it flows north to Orléans, where it suddenly and sharply veers westward to empty into the Atlantic near Nantes.

The Loire influences the economy and social life of more than 10 million people throughout its course. Geographically, the Loire valley is divided into four separate viticultural regions: from the Atlantic inland they are Muscadet, Anjou-Saumur, Touraine, and Sancerre-Pouilly. The 60,000 hectares of vine grown along the entire length of the river account for about 6 percent of the entire French vineyard. Figure 1.1 shows the vineyards and hectarage of western France.

The entire region is recognized for at least 55 different appellations producing more than 2.5 million hectoliters of wine, of which more than 50 percent is white, slightly less than a third rosé, and the remainder red and sparkling. The wines are of special interest because about 57 percent of total production is classified as AOC or VDQS in quality.* In terms of national comparisons, the Loire is responsible for 13 percent of all AOC wine, 8.2 percent of all red AOC, and 21.2 percent of all white AOC wine.

The Loire is a vast, slow-moving, and magnificent river with extraordinary scenery, thin slivers of forest, rich, green gardens, and vine-clad hills. While the northern and eastern portions sometimes deviate from

---

*French wine place origins are graded by a complex *appellation contrôlée* system, which ranks the top-grade as Vin d'Appellation d'Origine Contrôlée (AOC); the second tier as Vin Délimité de Qualité Supérieure (VDQS); and the third as Vin de Pays. A fourth type, Vin de Table, is a blended wine that is marketed without regional origin. The entire system, administered by the Institut National des Appellations d'Origine (INAO), regulates vineyard and fermentation practices, grape varieties, the yield per hectare (one hectare equals 2.47 acres), bottle labels, and more.

Figure 1.1
WINES GRAPES PLANTED BY DEPARTMENT, IN WESTERN FRANCE,
IN HECTARES, 1979*

Region	Department	Hectares	Region	Department	Hectares
Loire:			Southwest:		
1	Loire-Atlantique	17,979	13	Dordogne	13,858
2	Maine-et-Loire	20,292	14	Lot-et-Garonne	8,859
3	Indre-et-Loire	10,250	15	Lot	4,503
4	Loir-et-Cher	10,878	16	Tarn-et-Garonne	6,379
5	Cher	2,043	17	Tarn	17,006
6	Nièvre	609	18	Haute-Garonne	5,029
7	Vendée	3,442	19	Pyrénées-Atlantiques	1,81 2
8	Deux-Sèvres	1,286	Total		57,446
9	Vienne	2,481			
10	Indre	867	Total:	Western France	226,528
11	Loiret	162			
Total		70,289	Total:	France	998,715
Bordeaux:			Western France:	Percent of Total	22.7
12	Gironde	98,793			

*Does not include wine grapes destined for distillation and other minor producing areas.

Table 1.1 Loire AOC Wine Production, 1980

Producing region	Hectoliters	Percent of total
Pays Nantais	477,177	28.3
Anjou-Saumur	699,204	41.52
Touraine	413,271	24.6
Sancerre, Pouillly, others	94,328	5.6
Total production	1,683,980	100.0

Source: French Ministry of Agriculture.

the norm, the region between Nantes and Blois is lovely country, immaculately cultivated, fat, rich, comfortable, and oozing with agricultural delights. It is interesting that it is a primary production area for fruit, tobacco, mushrooms, and asparagus, and vines cover only a minor portion of all tillable land. With its extensive stockrearing, the region is also the largest producer of beef in France. The area is peppered with several dozen magnificent Renaissance châteaux of a majesty and opulence found nowhere else in the world. Along with Alsace and the areas north and east of Paris, the Loire is one of the wealthiest agricultural regions of the country (see Figure 1.2).

Except for Nantes in the west, the entire valley is virtually untouched by modern technology. Few cities approach the status of metropolitanism, and there are few smokestacks, oil or gas refineries, big factories, or

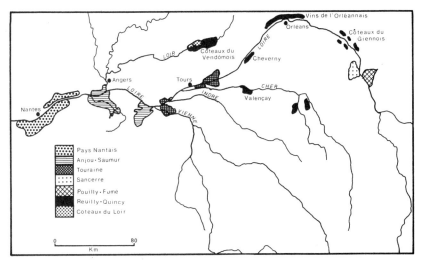

Figure 1.2 Major Vineyards of the Loire

miles of railroad track. With many small but productive holdings, it has long been known as the "Jardin de France," and it was the favorite retreat of French kings and nobility. The Touraine vineyard, known as "the boulevard of kings and the gallery of masterpieces," boasts the "purest" French.

The economic and social history of the Loire is long and, unlike many other regions of France, quite peaceful. Paleolithic and Neolithic settlements were widespread, and Celtic settlements served as subsequent bases for Roman legions. Winemaking, almost continuous for at least 1800 years, is often considered, by the many small growers, an important cash crop to more lucrative farm products destined for the capital and the industrial regions of northern France. Medieval barons, Plantagenet kings, religious orders, Dutch hydrographers, English merchants, and the insatiable thirst of Paris have all played their roles in cultivating what is considered one of the most stable and durable of French vineyards.

Because of its size and orientation with reference to prevailing winds and topographical features, the Loire is not homogenous in terms of climate and soil. Climatic variations grade from maritime influences in Muscadet, along the western fringes of the Loire, to relatively mild continental features in Sancerre, in the eastern portions of the valley. In general, however, the overall weather regime is surprisingly free of extremes. Spring is early, long, and mild, marred only by an occasional burst of frost; summers are bright, long, and warm; autumn is dry and lingering; and winter is known for its benign and unassuming character.

The average seasonal variations of monthly temperatures for Nantes range from 5.5° C. in January to 19° C. in July. While cloudiness and strong, persistent westerly winds are standard in Muscadet, Sancerre experiences less fog, more sunlight, and a greater range of annual temperature variation. Generalities aside, local weather peculiarities do occur throughout the region. Snow is more prevalent in the east, and while the entire Loire valley does not experience abnormal precipitation, the western margins are hampered by poorly drained soil. Sudden autumn storms accompanied by hail are more prevalent in Sancerre, while Chinon and Bourgueil, protected by a small plateau from cold northerly winds, enjoy the mildest climate in the entire region. A bad vintage in the Loire is the result of less sun, more rain, and lower temperatures, which produce thin, colorless, acidic wines.

The soil, like the diverse climatic patterns, varies immensely, and most grape variations are chosen for their microclimatic-pedologic affinities. In portions of Muscadet the soil, composed of schist rock high in potassium and magnesium, is sandy in texture and very acidic. In Vouvray and Sancerre the soil changes to limestone mixed with sand, gravel, marl, and wind-blown material called *limon*. Throughout that region the heavy, alluvial soil of the Loire and its former terraces produces undistinguished wine of quality scarcely above the level of *vin ordinaire*. Limestone and/or well-drained soil on hilly terrain enjoy the best reputations.

In the final analysis, the type of wine produced is a function of soil and the ability of weather to produce high sugar levels. Muscadet, with its schistous soil, experiences a high incidence of fog, which prevents the full maturation of grapes and results in wine that is nearly all white, light in alcohol, body, and extract. In a continental climatic setting, Sancerre, on the other hand, with a base of hard limestone overlaid with *limon,* is able to produce fuller, deeper-flavored wines with higher alcohol levels. More than 75 percent of all red wine is produced in the warmest areas of the Loire (usually on limestone soil) in the Chinon–Bourgueil region and areas immediately to the east and west. Between the Touraine and the eastern margins of Muscadet, the marginal-quality rosé regions of Anjou and Saumur produce more than 80 percent of the regional total.

Of the ten major departments bordering the Loire vineyard, four— Loire Atlantique, Maine-et Loire, Loire-et Cher, and Indre-et-Loire—are responsible for 90 percent of the total hectarage and 95 percent of the AOC hectarage. The two largest vineyards, the south bank of the Loire at Angers and Muscadet to the west, contain more than 50 percent of the entire hectarage of the Loire.

2

THE WINES OF THE PAYS NANTAIS

THE Pays Nantais, with 26 percent of the AOC wine in the entire Loire basin, is the second-largest wine producer of the Loire region. Its three AOC wines are Muscadet de Sèvre-et-Maine, Muscadet, and Muscadet des Coteaux de la Loire (see Table 2.1). The two VDQS wines are Gros Plant du Pays Nantais, and Coteaux d'Ancenis. In addition, approximately one-tenth of regional production is *Vin de Pays*—a wide assortment of wines produced throughout the area, and particularly in the Loire-Atlantique department. The most important are Vin de Pays de Retz and Vin de Pays des Marches de Bretagne. The Vendée, south of Nantes, is known for Vin de Pays des Fiefs Vendéens, principally red and rosé wines with a reputation for high acid levels and a bitter finish.

All of Muscadet and portions of Anjou are regions of *bocage,* a checkerboard pattern of hedges and trees enclosing small fields devoted to cattle grazing. Granite, schist, and sandstone form the base for the varied soils of the region and ultimately determine its land use. The viticultural portions of the region are all part of the geologic *faluns sea* that contains fewer rock outcrops, more organic material, and significantly more clay; its verdant and fertile character stands in stark contrast with the poorer interior regions of Brittany, to the north, and Vendée, to the south.

The vine-growing area covers a narrow strip of floodplain, terraces, and foothills on the north bank; across the river to the south, the vineyards

Table 2.1   Pays Nantais AOC Wine Production, 1980

Appellation	Hectoliters	Percent of total
Muscadet de Sèvre-et-Maine	425,186	89.1
Muscadet	35,855	7.5
Muscadet des Coteaux de la Loire	16,136	3.4
Total production	477,177	100.0

Source: French Ministry of Agriculture.

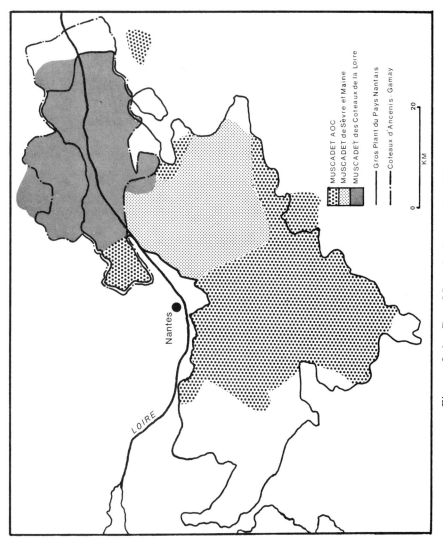

Figure 2.1   Pays Nantais: Major Appellations

spread to the southwest, almost to the Atlantic margins. Most of the vines are planted on hillsides at modest altitudes of 50 meters to take advantage of the sun, the best sites being oriented toward the south and west (see Fig. 2.1).

With the ocean less than 50 kilometers away from the center of the region, the temperature regime is more temperate than either Anjou and Touraine. The abundance of fog and less extreme seasonal variations promote the growth of magnolias, laurel, and occasional pine. Precipitation is evenly distributed, with only October, November, and December experiencing a slight increase from the normal. June, July, and August are the driest, sunniest months. The critical "wine-quality-influencing" months are August and September. If they are sunny, dry, and hot, the grapes ripen fully and produce exceptional vintages.

If the climatic patterns exhibit a degree of uniformity, the complex geology of the region has produced chaotic soil configurations. While the soil composition of Sèvre-et-Maine, for example, is composed mainly of sand (derived from gneiss) with varying amounts of alluvium, pebbles, and *limon,* the communes of Vertou, Maisdon, and Monnières are dominated by micaschist. Gorges, Clisson, and Tillières are underlain by gabbro rock; le Loroux-Bottereau and St.-Crespin are influenced by gneiss and sand; and Vallet, Mouzillon, and Pallet are a mixture of gneiss, sand, and gabbro rock. Deep pebble formations of alluvial origin are found in sections of la Haie-Fouassière, Haute et Basse-Goulaine, le Landreau, and le Lorou-Bottereau.

Throughout the entire area the schist, gabbro, and gneiss rock is close to the surface. Because it is dense, contains few fissues, and is resistant to the vertical movement of water, there are numerous small lakes, swamps, and poorly drained, low-lying areas. As a consequence, the best viticultural sites are located on top of the minor plateaus and sandy hillsides that are found throughout the area. In general, soils are wet and highly acidic.

History

As in many other areas of France, the first traces of vinegrowing in the Nantes region go back to Roman times. Caracalla (alias Marcus Aurelius) not only built straight roads, but encouraged winemaking and was the first to allow the indigenous population to own vineyards and produce wine. During the next thousand years, however, viticulture encountered many setbacks from both natural and political events.

During the Middle Ages, viticulture suffered from numerous floods, cold winters, invasions, and economic uncertainty. Beginning in the 6th century, monastic orders, especially those in Vertou and Nantes, did much to foster viticulture, and by the 11th century they were the largest owners of vine hectarage. In the 16th century a good deal of the real estate in the lower Loire was drained by Dutch hydrographers who, with time, stimulated, organized, and controlled a lively trade in wine. A happy combination of lower taxes and the presence of a light, acidic wine suitable for distillation soon enabled this region to further augment its export market. By 1568 the port of Nantes alone exported 99,000 hectoliters, an impressive amount for that time. The trade was further amplified by the British who shipped woolen textiles in exchange for wine.

During this period the dominant grape varieties were Chenin Blanc, Folle Blanche, and Meslier, the latter an indigenous vine. The Muscadet, or Melon grape, introduced to Nantes from Burgundy during the Middle Ages, was a minor variety until the first half of the 17th century. As a series of bad winters and late-spring killing frosts had taken a heavy toll on the then-predominant red-skinned grapes, it was decided in 1639 to replace such vines with Muscadet. The greatest impetus to the diffusion of the Muscadet vine occurred in 1709 during the coldest winter on record, when nearly all vines were destroyed except the Muscadet. As a consequence, the Muscadet wine trade prospered, and for a short period of time the Pays Nantais produced more wine than the department of Aude in the Midi. In 1731 new plantings were forbidden in an attempt to maintain prices, and since red grapes were outlawed, the dominance of white grapes has continued to this day. During the period 1878–92, *phylloxera* reduced hectarage by one-half and production by two-thirds.

After the *phylloxera* epidemic, the production area stabilized at around 7,000 hectares with an output of barely 300,000 hectoliters, half its present yield. Until 1920, the city of Nantes consumed the whole of production, but during the heyday of the lively 1920s, Paris "discovered" Muscadet and demand sky-rocketed to such high levels that hectarage in the Nantes area increased to more than 44,000 hectares. Both hectarage and production declined during the Great Depression and World War II, so that by 1950 the planted area had been reduced to 36,000 hectares. Since then, uninterrupted farm abandonment of former marginal vineland has reduced the total to 17,000 hectares by 1979. With the rise of the white wine craze in the 1960s, Muscadet was "discovered" once again, this time by Americans, Germans, and Englishmen—and its rise to prominence enjoyed a success similar to that of Beaujolais. Specifically, the rise of tourism since 1955 and the development of direct sales at the vineyard to English, Dutch, Belgian, and German visitors has brought Muscadet out of obscurity. Since the wine is much cheaper than Chablis, more consistent than Mâcon Blanc, and more predictable in quality and less expensive than Sancerre, it has become a popular wine for casual occasions. Its light, dry taste, which complements most light dishes and seafood, also helped enormously. It is still known as a "petit vin," but is no longer thought of as inexpensive carafe wine.

The formation of appellation status began in 1919, and by 1925 several growers had begun to label their bottles "Muscadet Grand Crus de Sèvre-et-Maine." By 1933 the area was demarcated, and AOC status was awarded in 1936. The two VDQS appellations, Gros Plant du Pays Nantais and Coteaux d'Ancenis, were not officially delimited and legally conferred until 1954. Today, all appellation hectarage is almost exclusively planted in Muscadet, followed by Gros Plant, the local name for Folle Blanche. Other varieties include the obscure Chambourcin, Grolleau, Cabernet Franc, and Colombard. Approximately 9 percent of the hectarage, one of the highest percentages in France, is planted in hybrids, mostly in the outlying, colder, windier portions of the hilly northern and western coastal regions.

Of the more than 24,000 growers, 61 percent are part-time farmers who cultivate less than one hectare, 28 percent own between one and three hectares, and fewer than 1 percent own more than ten hectares. As a consequence, the wine is mainly in the hands of large negociants who control two-thirds of the distribution business. The only cooperative in the entire Pays Nantais is a minor element in the production and distribution of wine. Less than 15 percent of the wine is the product of estate production. But the price of Muscadet has escalated in recent years, and the process of farm consolidation is now proceeding at full force, so the number of "domaine" wines is expected to proliferate in the near future.

Prior to 1920 (when fewer than 40,000 hectoliters of Muscadet were produced), little was shipped outside the region and little was exported. Now more than 60 percent of the harvest is bottled, direct sales account for one-quarter of all sales, and negociants make, buy, and distribute more than two-thirds of production. Exports of wine currently amount to more than 150,000 hectoliters, or approximately 20 percent of production. This is expected to increase in the coming years despite the fact that exports to Common Market countries are being hurt by serious Italian competition. As expansion of the producing area is limited by desirable space, projected shortages are expected to be filled by the export of Gros Plant, a wine that is similar to Muscadet.

Two-thirds of all exports are destined for Great Britain, Belgium-Luxembourg, and Holland (see Table 2.2). It should also be noted that while the overwhelming percentages of exports to the United States, Holland, Belgium-Luxembourg, Switzerland, West Germany, and Canada are bottled Muscadet, the mass of exports to Great Britain are bulk sales. In the United States, Muscadet offers exceptional value since the domestic market offers no equivalent.

Grape Varieties and the Taste of Muscadet

The Muscadet vine (with a big wide trunk and a heavy bark with short canes and big buds) is well adapted to the climate and soil of the Nantais.

Table 2.2   Muscadet Exports, 1981

Country of destination	Percent of total	Country of destination	Percent of total
Great Britain	39.5	Canada	2.3
Belgium-Luxembourg	17.4	Denmark	2.1
Holland	11.0	Ireland	1.8
West Germany	8.6	Switzerland	1.6
United States	8.1	Other	7.6
		Total exports	100.0

Source: Ministry of Agriculture.

It tolerates frost and winters in which the temperature may drop below −5°C. Further, the large and long leaves protect the berries from rain and wind damage. The Gros Plant (Folle Blanche), a more vigorous vine, yields well and is able to grow in extremely acidic soil such as that derived from locally dominated gabbro, schist, and granitic rocks.

The Muscadet grape, dominating departmental hectarage, represents 94 percent of all national plantings. It is followed by Folle Blanche and a host of hybrids, all of which are in rapid regression, falling from 61 percent of all plantings in 1940 to less than 11 percent in 1984. As with all viticultural regions in the northern fringes of the country, marginal vine hectarage is being reduced by uprooting hybrid vines no longer considered economically and viticulturally important.

The best sites for vineyards are along hills and the small plateaus within the region. In lower areas with less sand, fewer stones, and a more poorly drained soil, the vines are coarse and unyielding. The biggest enemy, humidity, is most common in bottom land. When vines are planted on poorly drained land, ditches must be dug to channel water away. Historically, vines were pruned and trained in the gobelet method, but due to the high humidity of the region, most of them are now cordon-trained to facilitate air movement.

Muscadet differs significantly from Gros Plant, its chief competitor, in that it contains at least 1 percent more alcohol, while its density, extract, and fixed and volatile acidity are markedly lower. Gros Plant, in other words, is not the light-weight cousin of Muscadet in terms of substance, and in good years it can be equal or better than the finest Muscadet. Unfortunately, its major drawbacks are high acid levels and a lack of depth in flavor.

The appellation abounds with regulations. Soil is subject to analysis prior to AOC status and restricted only to the Muscadet vine; hybrid vines are totally forbidden on soil designated for AOC Muscadet production. The juice for plain Muscadet is obliged to contain sugar levels of at least

163 grams per liter and at least 9.5 percent alcohol.* Muscadet des Coteaux de la Loire and Muscadet de Sèvre-et-Maine contain a must density of at least 170 grams per liter and an alcohol content of 10 percent.

For all types of Muscadet, the maximum yield per hectare is supposed to be 40 hectoliters, a figure that is easily and regularly modified by authorities, depending upon the quality and quantity of the harvest. In reality, the yield often exceeds 75 hectoliters to the hectare, one of the highest yields of any AOC region in France. Anything in excess theoretically should be declassified into the next lower appellation, but more common are the bad habits of back-blending the wine with weaker vintages or storing it to regulate the next harvest—both practices being neat, legal, widely practiced, and tempting to irreversible abuse. Yet quality, especially for exportable wine, has remained rather stable, perhaps because, since 1971, a chemical analysis is done and a tasting panel reviews all wine and issues a certificate of authenticity.

Historically, Muscadet was little known and much cheaper in price than other white wine from the Loire. With the escalation of prices since 1960, a number of fraudulent practices have appeared. The first, and potentially the most serious, is overproduction, a vexing complication that may seriously tarnish the image of Muscadet. Overproduction beyond allowable appellation limits is handled through a laborious and complicated system of "commercially permissible percentages," the excess being subjected to "blocking," only to be "unblocked" as demand picks up after a vintage. It is therefore possible to find as much as one-third of the wine originating from a vintage other than that stated on the label.

The second major issue in Muscadet today is the use of the expression "Mis(e) en bouteilles sur lie," an unregulated designation of quality that stands for "bottled on sediment or deposit." Despite the phrase's presence on the label, the process is rarely followed because it is very costly. Ideally, "sur lie" means that the wine is in contact with the yeast deposits after fermentation takes place, that it will not be racked, and hence it will develop a peculiar "yeasty" fragrance and taste. It is also not filtered, thus conserving nearly all the precious little extract that is available. There is no question that "sur lie" adds a prodigious dimension of essence and taste to the wine, helps preserve its youthful spirit, and adds an extra measure of fragrance. The expression suggests that the bottled wine should be more flavorful and fragrant, although there is no guarantee.

Muscadet de Sèvre-et-Maine

About 90 percent of all Muscadet is made in this district on the south bank of the Loire southeast of Nantes. It takes its name from two small

*Alcohol is usually (and incorrectly) expressed as a percent. With the Gay-Lussac principle, pure alcohol has a strength equal to 100 *degrees*. Nevertheless, this book will follow the more common usage.

rivers, the Sèvre and Maine, that join just south of Vertou and empty into the Loire 2 kilometers downstream. The best sites are located on the interfluvial slopes on well-drained, sandy soil. Four important cantons all produce distinctive wine. The canton of Clisson, located in the southern margins of the appellation, consists of hilly slopes along the Sèvre River and the important communes of Clisson, Gorges, Monnières, and St.-Lumine-de-Clisson. The canton of Loroux-Bottereau, in the northern portion of the producing area, consists of the communes of le Loroux, le Landreaux, la Chapelle-Basse-Mer, and St.-Julien-de-Concelles. Because the land is rather flat, vineyards face stiff competition from vegetable farms and orchards. The important canton of Vallet, in the southeastern portion of the area, consists of Vallet, Mouzillon, le Pallet, la Chapelle-Heulin, la Regrippière, Tillières, and St.-Crespin-sur-Maine, all of which border the Anjou appellation. Across the river from Nantes is Vertou, the most important producing district. It consists of la Haie-Fousassière, Châteauthébaud, Haute-Goulaine, Basse-Goulaine, and St.-Fiacre, the latter being considered the focal point of Muscadet due to the high concentration of hectarage devoted to the production of wine. In terms of quality, the irregular, well-drained zone between St.-Fiacre, Vallet, Mouzillon, and la Chapelle-Heulin enjoys the best reputation for wine that is supple, fragrant, and zesty—the three essential elements of good Muscadet. The wines of the 270-hectare St.-Fiacre vineyard are particularly well scented and delicate.

Since fewer than 20 percent of all growers are full-time vignerons, negociants control, directly or indirectly, more than 50 percent of all hectarage and production and at least 60 percent of total distribution. The number of labels and firms doing business staggers the imagination, and it is nearly impossible to memorize labels, holding companies, and *sous marques*. In the late 1960s a special long-necked and numbered "Nantaise" bottle was created by a small group of growers of Muscadet and Gros Plant in an attempt to raise and maintain standards. This reliable, though small and, as yet, not very influential organization, guarantees quality as well as authenticity. Of the many growers who use the "bouteille Nantaise" and its special label, Gabriel Thébaud, André Vinet, Guilbaud Frères, and Gilbert Bossard are considered among the very best.

Of the many firms within the Muscadet and surrounding appellations, the following are above average: *Ch. Noë* is one of the largest and most imposing estates. It produces full-bodied, fragrant, yeasty and supple wines bottled "sur lie" that are extraordinary, expensive, and offer excellent value. *Dne. des Herbanges* is a fair-sized, 20-hectare property known for yeasty, fruity, fresh-tasting wines with a good nose.* The small, little-known *Dne. de la Forchetière* produces first-quality, full-bodied, complex wine. *Louis Métaireau* enjoys a superlative reputation for

---

*Wines or estates are italicized to highlight them.

Plate 2.1   Ch. Noë

the best that Muscadet is able to produce. His wines have a good dose of complexity and finesse and are always well balanced. He heads a small syndicate of fine producers who offer a certain share of their production to Métaireau to be sold under his label. Carefully selected and always in limited supply, these wines are sold to a select list of hotels, restaurants, and retail outlets. The house has several labels, all above average and quite expensive. Métaireau is also part owner of one of the largest and finest estates, *Dne. du Grand-Mouton,* the source of incomparable Muscadet.

One of the largest growers with a wide following in the United States, Robert, the 11th Marquis de Goulaine, produces wine under his title, which enjoys a similar stylish reputation. The house bottles a wide range of wines; its usual "sur lie" is crisp, fruity, and has enough refinement to be called "classy"; a premium label, "Cuvée du Millenaire," is considered one of the top three wines of Muscadet. Equally important is *Clos des Rosiers,* a small firm with a superlative reputation located near the sleepy commune of Vallet. In a similar vein is the medium-sized house of *Joseph Hallereau* in Vallet. The wines are always first class, full-bodied, with character and style.

The relatively large firm of *Chéreau-Carré* distributes wines of several estates that are known for their longevity, unusual taste, color, and body. The estates have an established reputation for cultivating old vines, meticulous care, and a tradition of not filtering their wines. As a consequence, the wines appear in limited quantities, are expensive and hard to find, but are well worth the effort to seek them out, particularly *Grand Fief de la Cormeraie, Ch. Chasseloir, Moulin de la Gravelle, Ch. du Coing de St.-Fiacre, Ch. de l'Oiselinière,* and *Dne. du Bois-Bruley. Clos de Roches Gaudinières* is a fair-sized property that makes exceptionally flaverful wine, light in color, with perfect balance and a supple, soft, satisfying taste. *Guilbaud Frères* is known for the well-made, branded Muscadet "Le Soleil Nantes"; the house also distributes a number of estate wines, all with established reputations.

On the outskirts of St.-Fiacre is the well-managed *Ch. de la Cantrie,* known for eminently quaffable wines that are light, fragrant, well balanced, and consistently good. *André Vinet,* one of the biggest multiple-brand negociants, is a grower, winemaker, broker, and distributer of wine from small estates. Within his stable of properties and labels, the wines range from the superlative to the "tired," thus careful selection is necessary.

Considered among the top five growths, *Ch. du Cléray* is a superlative, clean, stylish Muscadet of classic proportions. The firm maintains several labels of which "Dne. de l'Aurière" and "Cardinal Richard" are above average. *Ch. de la Galissonnière* and *Ch. Jannière* both belong to *Pierre Lusseaud* and enjoy a superlative reputation for wines with outstanding and distinctive bouquet and balance. The former estate, owned by the Marquis de la Galissonnière, the 18th-century governor-general of Canada, has a distinctive flavor and a darker color than most Muscadet. One of the most important firms owning land, producing wine, and engaged in a thriving negociant business is that of *Gabriel Thébaud.* His *Dne. la Hautière* is above average, but not as distinctive as other estate wines. The negociant firm of *Marcel Sautejeau* is known for three above average estates: *l'Hyvernière, Clos des Orfeuilles,* and *Dne. de la Batinière,* the first being widely available in the United States and easily recognized by its distinctive bottle.

Dne. de la Haute Maison, a 20-hectare 17th-century property first established by a Dutch family, produces above average wines from several properties, of which *la Bourdelière* and *les Chamboissières* are particularly good. The wines of *Dne. des Dorices* are full-bodied, fragrant, and capable of improving past their first year. *Dne. de la Batardière* is a popular label in the United States, especially in the French restaurant trade. The wines are soft, reliable, but rarely memorable. Equally important are *Dne. Francis Viaud la Fevrie, Ch. de la Turmelière, Ch. de la Ragotière, Ch. Plessis Brezot, Dne. des Mortiers-Gobin, Dne. de la Martinière,* and *La Folliette.*

Two very good estates are *Dne. des Moulins* and *Dne. des Hauts Pemions,* the former wine usually fresh, the latter almost always fuller and darker in color than most Muscadet. Mild, fruity, uncomplicated wines are made by *Dne. de la Débaudière* and *Ch. la Berrière. Dne. de Grand Maison,* a label owned in part by *Bollinger,* is light, crisp, and found on many restaurant lists. The following three negociants enjoy above average reputations in the production of a full range of Muscadet: *Gautier Audas, Marcel Martin,* and *Martin-Jarry.* The only cooperative in the Nantes region, *Cave Coopérative La Noëlle,* controls 5 percent of the total Muscadet hectarage and produces a full line of average quality wines, most of which are disposed of through negociant firms.

Muscadet des Coteaux de la Loire

Of the three Muscadet appellations, Muscadet des Coteaux de la Loire, the smallest in total area, produces less than 4 percent of all Muscadet. The producing areas, straddling both sides of the Loire north of Nantes, roughly coincide with the boundaries of Coteaux d'Ancenis and the western fringes of Anjou. Since vines find it hard to compete with more productive agricultural crops along the north bank of the river, the 400 hectares of Muscadet grapes are expected to decrease in the future, with the eventual demise of the appellation not too far away.

Because the soil contains chalk, the wines of this appellation are more austere, harder, unyielding, contain high acid levels, and are characterized by a muted nose. They are also lighter in alcohol, drier, less fruity and less yeasty than those from the south bank. Those vineyards sited on granitic soil have an agreeable mineral taste and appear to be more supple. The principal producing areas are Ancenis, Carquefou, Champtoceaux, Ligné, St.-Florent-le-Veil, and Verades. *Dne. de la Cassarderie* and *Dne. des Genaudières* are two above-average quality producers.

Muscadet

The "Muscadet Appellation Controlée" region is the second largest after Gros Plant du Pays Nantais in terms of land area. It covers any part of the area of Muscadet production that does not benefit from either the Sèvre-et-Maine or the Coteaux de la Loire designations. More than half comes from Longne, Boulogne, and from the area of Herbauges in the district of Bouaye, which lies just to the north of lake Grand Lieu. It is the source of some of the cheapest and poorest-quality Muscadet because the vines are located on flatter, poorly drained land. The wine, softer and somewhat neutral in taste, is decidedly inferior to that originating on more hilly terrain.

Gros Plant du Pays Nantais

Geographically, Gros Plant du Pays Nantais is the largest appellation in the western Loire. With 2,500 hectares, 63 percent of all wine, and 89 percent of total white wine, it is the largest VDQS production appellation in the entire Loire, and the second largest in the nation after Corbières in

Languedoc. Despite its wide territory, the center of production is centered in Herbauges, Logne, and Boulogne.

The wine is made solely from the Gros Plant, a vine that dominated hectarage in the entire region 200 years ago by a factor of ten to one, but has been steadily declining since *phylloxera*. With the rise of Muscadet in the past 90 years, it has been relegated a secondary position in the Nantais, being usually found on poorly drained and highly acidic schistous soil. Regulations allow a maximum of 50 hectoliters to the hectare and a minimum alcohol content of 9 percent. In the past, the wine lacked an element of charm, was overly acidic, and was often marred by a bitter aftertaste and high variability. Within the past twenty years, new forms of fermentation techniques and equipment have improved its quality and, as a consequence, the Gros Plant is currently a "hot" wine with hectarage and production increasing at a rate comparable to Muscadet.

In exceptional years the vine manages to produce quality wine comparable to AOC status. The best comes from the following producers, all of which are major players in Muscadet: *Joseph Hallereau* (considered the epitomy of fine Gros Plant), *Marquis de Goulaine, Dne. de Bois-Bruley, Dne. de la Forchetière, Louis Métaireau, Antoine Guibaud, Clos des Rosiers, Dne. de la Haute Poeze, Ch. de la Ragotière,* and *Dne. Guy Charpentier.*

Coteaux d'Ancenis

Located barely 30 kilometers northeast of Nantes is the captivating VDQS wine district of Coteaux d'Ancenis, named after the medieval town, and the site of the Brittany Parliament during the 17th and 18th centuries. It produces approximately 10,000 hectoliters of red, rosé, and white wine from fewer than 195 hectares. Rarely exported, they form the daily fare of practically every restaurant and inn throughout the district.

Very similar in price to the wines of Anjou and Saumur, the wines are suprisingly good, supple, and ideal as carafe wines. Made principally from Gamay, Cabernet Franc, and Cabernet Sauvignon, the red is light in color, fruity, fragrant, and low in tannin. White wine constitutes less than 10 percent of total production; it is made from Muscadet, Gros Plant, Chenin Blanc, Sauvignon Blanc, and several local eccentricities— Verdelho and Malvoisie. Considered an interesting specialty, the wine is pleasant yellow in color, often pétillant, pleasing on the palate, certainly different in flavor, but offers little value.

Despite its small hectarage, the district is widespread and roughly coincides with the boundaries of Coteaux de la Loire. It embraces small portions of real estate around the following districts on both sides of the river; the largest producer is the regional cooperative mentioned previously. Two private producers of local repute are *Jacques Guindon* and *Auguste Athimon,* both of whom produce interesting red wines.

3

THE WINES OF ANJOU-SAUMUR

L YING to the east of Muscadet, the viticultural region of Anjou-Saumur is found principally in the department of Maine-et-Loire and portions of Vienne and Deux Sèvres. Nearly the whole of the vineyard, confined along the Layon, Argenton, and Thouet tributaries, is located along the southern bank of the Loire (see Fig. 3.1). The highland areas of the north bank are (with only one exception) too windy and cold for good vinegrowing. Because the producing regions are protected by highlands on the north, the microclimate is warm for the latitude, with nearly 2,000 hours of sunshine, and relatively dry, with less than 600 mm. of rain annually. The area also experiences a mild autumn and winter.

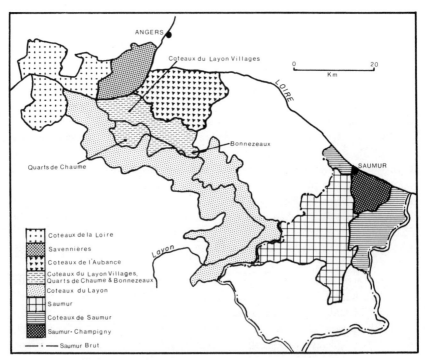

Figure 3.1   Anjou-Saumur: Major Appellations

The soils of the region are divided into three broad zones: the highland section is hard schistous rock with only a thin layer of topsoil; the western portion of Angers is a highly mottled collection of alluvial, wind-blown sand and schist with no definitive pattern; the eastern zone of Saumur is merely the western extension of the Touraine limestone belt and quite homogeneous. Throughout the western section, soil and microclimate seem to have combined to produce highly diverse viticultural patterns.

Anjou-Saumur is one of the most-productive agricultural regions of France—rich in orchards, garden crops, pastureland, and beef. Viticulturel throughout the southern portions of the Loire competes effectively only on higher, well-drained ground with a peculiar aspect conducive to grape maturation. The department of Maine-et-Loire is the largest vineyard in the Loire. Just barely ahead of Loire-Atlantique, it is responsible for more than 44 percent of all AOC and 27 percent of all wine, respectively, in the valley. It is also the largest in terms of appellations—at least 22 AOC, many of which are obscure and unimportant (see Table 3.1). Approximately 20,000 hectares of vineland are in the department, half of which are AOC, employing 30,000 growers with (unlike Nantes-Atlantique) only a negligible amount of VDQS wine.

Despite its northerly location, the Anjou-Saumur district has had a lively viticultural history dating back to the days of the Romans. The monks of Angers did much to stimulate production during the early medieval period, and numerous manuscripts indicate that a meaningful export trade with England existed as early as the 4th century. For a short time the Plantagenet kings not only gave their blessing to the industry, but advocated and encouraged exports. The greatest impetus, however, occurred during the French Renaissance when the French court considered the middle Loire the most important of all regions in the kingdom and stimulated the construction of elaborate châteaux. Production and hectarage increased throughout the 18th and 19th centuries up to the time of the *phylloxera* disaster. The boom was propelled by the popularity of Saumur Mousseux and the sweet white wines of the Layon district. Land planted to the vine in 1870 stood at 42,000 hectares, the all-time high figure for the region, but has declined since.

From the "belle époque" of the 1890s until the world depression of the 1930s, the industry shifted to rosé as well as sweet wine and Mousseux. As economic conditions improved during the post–World War II period, marginal vineland began to be supplanted by more productive uses and, as a consequence, total hectarage has declined by one-third, with the probability that it will reach the 14,000-hectares figure by 1995. This reduction, if it occurs, will represent a drop of more than 59 percent from the post–World War II high of 34,000 hectares in 1949.

Although the Anjou-Saumur vineyard is a highly diversified region whose wines show a wide range of style and color, the finest wines are the semi- and sweet wines of Chenin Blanc or Pineau de la Loire. It is the

Table 3.1   Anjou-Saumur Wine Production by AOC
Appellation, 1980

Appellation	Hectoliters	Percent of total
Rosé d'Anjou Rouge	180,597	26.0
Cabernet d'Anjou Rouge	128,665	18.5
Anjou Rouge	71,179	10.2
Anjou Blanc	68,895	9.9
Anjou Gamay Rouge	6,851	1.0
Anjou Coteau de la Loire Blanc	1,313	
Saumur Mousseux Blanc	92,041	13.2
Saumur Mousseux Rouge	5,900	.9
Saumur Blanc	21,904	3.1
Saumur Rouge	12,262	1.7
Saumur Champigny Rouge	26,635	3.9
Cabernet de Saumur Rouge	1,185	
Coteaux de Saumur Blanc	78	
Crémant de Loire Blanc	15,544	2.1
Crémant de Loire Rouge	93	
Rosé de Loire Rouge	18,768	2.7
Coteaux du Layon Blanc	42,134	6.0
Quarts de Chaume Blanc	776	
Savennières Blanc	1,449	
Bonnezeaux Blanc	861	
Coteaux de l'Aubance Blanc	2,074	.3
Total production	699,204	100.0

Source: French Ministry of Agriculture.

most important vine in terms of quality of wine made, as well as the most
common grape. While more important fifty years ago than today, it
remains the dominant white grape of the region because of its versatile
wine styles and its ability to adapt to different soils.

The wine is always fruity and fresh, and because it is able to maintain
high acidic levels as it ages, it manages to produce the longest-lived white
wines of northern France. With a rather neutral taste in its youth, it is the
base for all Mousseux wine of the region.

Despite its historic popularity, Chenin Blanc is just barely ahead of
Cabernet Franc in terms of area cultivated. The rise of Cabernet Franc
from 14.3 percent in 1968 to 26.4 percent in 1978 is a reflection of the
fickle nature of the consumer, who demands more red table, sparkling,
and fruitier rosé wines, and less sweet white wine. Grolleau, with 19.3
percent of total hectarage, is the third most widely planted vine.
Combined, these three grape varieties are responsible for nearly three-
quarters of the entire planted area. Gamay and Cabernet Sauvignon are

Table 3.2   Major Grape Varieties Planted in the Department of Maine-et-Loire, 1968 and 1979

Grape variety	1968 Hectares	1968 Percent	1979 Hectares	1979 Percent	Percent of national total, 1979
Chenin Blanc	7,000	26.2	5,400	26.6	56.8
Cabernet Franc	3,800	14.2	5,300	26.1	23.5
Grolleau	3,900	14.6	3,900	19.2	67.2
Gamay	500	1.9	1,000	4.9	
Cabernet Sauvignon	400	1.5	800	3.9	
Melon	500	1.9	500	2.4	
Plantet	1,600	5.9	400	2.0	
Chambourcin	100	.4	400	2.0	
Villlard Noir	500	1.9	300	1.5	
Folle Blanche	300	1.1	300	1.5	
Pinot d'Aunis	100	.4	200	1.0	
Bacot Noir	1,200	4.5	100	.5	
Sauvignon Blanc	100	.4	100	.5	
Rayon d'Or	400	1.5	100	.5	
Others	6,300	23.6	1,500	7.4	
Total hectarage	26,700	100.0	20,300	100.0	

Source: French Ministry of Agriculture.

the next most popular varieties. As in all areas of the Loire throughout the 20th century, the percentage of land devoted to hybrids has steadily declined.

Fashion has always dictated production in the region. Medieval wines were primarily sweet; before World War I, more than three-quarters were white and sparkling; by 1925 more than 65 percent were rosé; and in 1980, 46 percent of production was rosé, 20 percent white, 18 percent red, 14 percent Mousseux, and 2 percent Crémant. With fashion and taste always changing, red and sparkling wines are gaining, while semi- and sweet white wines and rosé are declining. Today, nearly two-thirds of production is composed of Rosé d'Anjou, Cabernet d'Anjou, Saumur Mousseux Blanc, and Anjou Rouge. As a consequence and in an attempt to lessen risks, medium and large-scale producers make a large number of different wines.

THE ANJOU APPELLATIONS

Anjou refers to a small historic region and a former duchy that eventually produced the powerful counts of Anjou. The small metropolitan city of Angers, the capital and main commercial center, is known for two medieval dynasties, a famous cathedral, and an imposing castle overlooking the city. The surrounding region, mainly to the south and west, has given its magical name of Anjou to six appellations of varying degrees of importance. They are, in terms of production: Rosé d'Anjou, Cabernet d'Anjou, Anjou Rouge, Anjou Blanc, Anjou Gamay, and Anjou Coteaux de la Loire Blanc. In addition, there are minor non-AOC and VDQS wines, the most significant being Anjou Mousseux and Anjou Pétillant. Collectively, these constitute about two-thirds of all AOC wine from the entire Anjou-Saumur vineyard.

Rosé d'Anjou

Rosé d'Anjou is the prototype of the carafe rosés. Fresh, light, semi-sweet, sprightly, and thirst-quenching, it is the most popular and cheapest of all rosé from northern France. With 26 percent of production, or more than 2 million cases of wine each year, this is the largest and single most-important wine appellation of the middle Loire (making as much as one-third of all wine in a prolific year).

Two production elements create the prospect for a wide range of wine styles. Although the law allows the use of Cabernet Franc, Cabernet Sauvignon, Gamay, Pineau d'Aunis, and Malbec, the grape that dominates the encépagement is the Grolleau. Since there is no formula for the allocation of each variety, it stands to reason that overall wine character, as well as quality, will vary enormously. The second factor is geography. Although the official production region encompasses nearly the entire Anjou-Saumur vineyard, three principal places of production each produce totally different wines: the Tigné district in the extreme southern portion near Thouars, the Saumur region north and west of the city of Saumur, and the Brissac region near Quince. The first area contains clayey soil, and the wines are not very exceptional; the Saumur wine is "harder" and "fuller" on the palate; and those wines from Brissac are considered the best and most heavily scented.

Rosé d'Anjou is said to be the most gentle and feminine of all rosés produced in France. Its charm is first encountered in its clear bottle, which highlights an attractive color. It is soft on the palate, light in body, pleasant, medium-dry to semi-sweet, and can be both flat and refreshing. It has been very popular for at least 100 years and is widely distributed within France and abroad. As good and as popular as it is, Rosé d'Anjou, inferior to Cabernet d'Anjou and Cabernet de Saumur, is a poor value in overseas markets. Due to the prevailing fashion for drier and fuller rosé, Rosé d'Anjou suffers competition from domestic production as well as from Italian, Portuguese, and American wines. Two modest producers with above average reputations are *Dne. des Quinze Deniers* and *Robert Lecomte-Girault*.

Cabernet d'Anjou

Cabernet d'Anjou is made principally from Cabernet Franc, with only minor infusions of Cabernet Sauvignon. As a result, the wine is much fuller, purplish-pink in color, has a higher alcohol content,has greater extract and a longer, more satisfying finish than Rosé d'Anjou. Most important, it is made semi-dry instead of semi-sweet, and its higher acid content makes it capable of aging several years while retaining much of its freshness. A good portion is made quite dark in color, preserving its refreshing lightness and, at the same time, intensifying its bouquet.

The finest wine comes from limestone, shale, and gravelly soil in a much narrower production region than Rosé d'Anjou—mainly Chalonnes, Brissac, Tigné, Doué-la-Fontaine, and Martigné, the latter considered the most delicate and the center of the appellation. The fact that Cabernet d'Anjou is mainly produced from non-clayey soil and a much smaller number of producing communes gives the appellation a better grip on quality control. As a result, the wines are decidedly better, firmer, more stylish, and made with fewer imperfections than Rosé d'Anjou.

Production, now 60 percent of Rosé d'Anjou, or roughly 19 percent of all output in the district, is increasing rapidly at the expense of the larger appellation. In 1950, it represented less than 5 percent of all wine made in Anjou-Saumur. Because of its recent popularity, the wine is widely immitated throughout the middle Loire.

The third type of rosé is Rosé de Loire, a regional AOC appellation that straddles both sides of the Loire river and encompasses the Anjou vineyard. Production, however, is less than 3 percent of regional production. What makes this appellation different is that it was created in 1974, and its wine is made *dry* with just a trace of residual sugar. Cabernet grapes are at least one-third of the cépage, with Grolleau, Pinot Noir, Gamay, and Pineau d'Aunis allowed with no particular guidelines. As a result, the final product differs markedly from producer to producer. When compared with Rosé d'Anjou and Cabernet d'Anjou, this wine falls somewhere in the middle in terms of substance, and hence offers very little value. *Dne. des Maurières* and *M. Aguilas-Gaudard* are two above-average producers of white and red wines.

Anjou Rouge and Anjou Gamay

Of all the wines under the Anjou appellation umbrella, red wines are increasing most rapidly. Two legal names are recognized. Anjou Gamay, made solely from the Gamay Noir à Jus Blanc grape, is a lightweight, Beaujolais-type wine distinguished by fresh fruit, but marred by a grassy taste, instability, and an unreliable track record. The grape manages to produce an acceptable wine only when the vine grows on slate and gravelly soil and the vintage is above average.

Anjou Rouge, from Cabernet Franc, Cabernet Sauvignon, Pineau d'Aunis, and Malbec, is the better wine by a wide margin. A darker, more complex wine than simple Gamay, it is capable of bottle improvement over a period of two to three years. Yet both wines offer little value, and when compared with the finer, more superior Champigny, they are decidedly inferior. Five excellent producers are *Dne. de Beillant, Dne. des Charbottières, Richou Père, Dne. de Sainte-Anne,* and *Dne. des Hauts-Perrays.*

Anjou Coteaux de la Loire Blanc, Anjou Blanc, and Savennières

Anjou Blanc was the historic wine of the region until the *phylloxera* epidemic of the 1870s changed the mix of grape varieties in the area. Imitating the superior libations of Vouvray, it was meant to be as sweet as possible. The tendency since 1950 has been to make it drier and to increase its appeal by adding as much as 20 percent Chardonnay and Sauvignon Blanc to the Chenin Blanc. The final product is fragrant, mouth-filling, high in acidity, but lacking finesse and balance. When purchasing Anjou Blanc, care must be taken to select bottles with appropriate residual sugar; and although there may be indications on the label, the reputation of the producer most often is the only guide. Anjou Blanc offers little, if any, value in export markets. The production area is widespread, with the sweeter wines coming from the Layon district and the drier from the Saumur eastern section. Although declining, output, presently about 10 percent of regional total, is rather considerable.

The Anjou Coteaux de la Loire appellation lies mainly along the north bank of the Loire west of Angers to the eastern border of the Coteaux d'Ancenis district. Dominated by Chenin Blanc, the wines are all white, acidic, somewhat flavorless, and so common that fewer than 2,000 hectoliters are produced under the appellation banner, the overwhelming portion being blended and used in other appellations.

The finest white wine of this region is that of Savennières, located southwest of Angers near the small village of the same name and including the two small communes of Bouchemaine and la Possonnière. This appellation, an enclave of the Coteaux de la Loire region, contains fewer than 360 hectares, of which only 100 are planted in vines. The best sites face southwest overlooking the Loire and are on gravelly terraces composed of weathered volcanic rock, slate, and schist.

Four elements differentiate this small area from the surrounding countryside—aspect, soil, steepness of the terrain to facilitate drainage, and a well-sheltered situation from northerly winds—all of which combine to produce the best dry white wine of the entire Loire valley. Pale gold, full-bodied, clean, with intense floral and vinous fragrances, it is substantive and satisfying. Its flavor is multidimensional, complex, and absolutely exceptional in every detail.

Savennières must be produced solely from Chenin Blanc, possess 12.5

percent alcohol, and its yield be restricted to 20 hectoliters to the hectare. The best-known site from a historical perspective is La Roche aux Moines, whose vineyards were planted by monks of Saint Nicholas d'Angers in the 12th century. The largest vineyard in the appellation, it is subdivided among several owners, all of whom make above-average Savennières— bright yellow, refreshing, supple, and well balanced.

Very much in demand is Coulée de Serrant, a walled estate of 25 hectares of which only 5 are planted with vines carrying the Savennières appellation. This wine, by wide margin the acknowledged leader of all Savennières and hence the entire Loire valley, is known for its elegant, smooth, well-balanced taste and long, lingering, satisfying finish. It is a honeyed wine with no trace of bitterness and is silky and mellow in texture and flavor, all features that are often described as extraordinary.

One single element is recognized as being responsible for the unique wines of Coulée de Serrant—a microclimate so unusually warm that it is capable of producing grapes with the highest sugar levels in all of northern France, thus raising alcohol levels to unparalleled limits. The grapes, never destemmed, are allowed to ferment slowly in wooden vats. Filtered and bottled in late spring following the vintage, the wine is racked several times during the next seven months and is hard, unyield-ing, and nearly unpalatable for the next five years. At its best at least ten and sometimes twenty years later, it is one of the longest-lived dry white wines in France today.

Equally good, the 18-hectare, highly fragmented *Domaine de la Bizolière* estate makes wine that is perhaps just as elegant, but is lighter in alcohol and hence matures earlier. Similar in style are the classic wines of *Clos du Papillon, Ch. d'Epiré, Ch. de Chamboureau, Clos de Coulaine,* and *Dne. du Closel.* Despite miniscule annual production, the price of Savennières has remained comparatively low, thus offering outstanding value.

Coteaux du Layon Blanc, Coteaux du Layon–Villages Blanc, Bonnezeaux Blanc, and Quarts de Chaume Blanc

Thirty years ago, Coteaux du Layon was the second-largest appellation in the Anjou region, but today it produces fewer than 45,000 hectoliters (6 percent of total regional output) from 1,400 hectares of vineland. Established in 1950, the appellation straddles both banks of the Layon River and includes at least twenty communes. The wine is mainly the product of the Chenin Blanc, with minor amounts of Chardonnay and Sauvignon Blanc grapes added. Despite a viticultural history that spans more than sixteen centuries, the wines remain relatively obscure.

The wines of the Coteaux du Layon are white and vary from the half-dry, to the moelleux, to the very sweet. The maximum allowable yield per hectare is 30 hectoliters, but a significantly larger yield is attained almost every year. The wine is pale yellow, fresh on the palate, and fragrant, but often unbalanced. It suffers from intense competition from less expensive, similar wines of the Loire, and is simply outclassed by Vouvray, Sauternes, and Barsac, as well as by some other libations of the Gironde. Moreover, it is subject to a poor image problem, high prices in relation to quality, and a marketplace that no longer demands sweet white wine in large quantities.

In poor years the wine is ready to drink almost immediately, but in great years it manages to improve for ten to as long as twenty years. Bottle bouquet usually does not develop until the second year for mediocre vintages, and only after the fourth for exceptional years. While it lacks the concentration and richness of Sauternes and the freshness and balance of Vouvray, Coteaux du Layon can be surprisingly good when all the elements capable of producing great wines come into play and reach their peak in a great year. Although local custom serves it as an aperitif, it is at its best with fresh fruit and light desserts, and the less-sweet versions with fowl and fish.

Although the Layon River stretches for more than 50 kilometers with varying amounts of vineyards along its course, the heart of the district extends only 15 kilometers inland from the Loire. The valley is warm, relatively dry, sheltered from excessive wind, and attracts *botrytis cinerea,* a fungus that produces distinctly flavored sweet wines. The best sites are located on the right bank of the Layon near its confluence with the Loire. Soil varies with commune: sand and schist at Martigné and Charagnes, marl in Bonnezeaux, Faye d'Anjou, Beaulieu, Saint-Aubin, and Quarts de Chaume. Near Aubance, Brissac, Soulaines, Mûrs, Mozé, Denée, and part of the Coteaux de l'Aubance appellation, the soil is schistous and marl. Along the left bank, the soil is poorly drained and less good for quality wine. Throughout the length of the right bank, schist, limestone, gravel, sand, and marl form a varigated pattern.

Since 1955, nearly one-third of the producing communes have been given the elevated status of "Coteaux du Layon–Villages" to set them apart from the less privileged. Their wines must contain at least one degree more alcohol and be produced from sandy and gravelly soils. After thirty years, however, few growers in the area insist on the use of this higher appellation, preferring to maintain the more familiar designation.

The following seven communes are considered the best in the area: Beaulieu-sur-Layon, Faye d'Anjou, Rablay-sur-Layon, Rochefort-sur-Loire, Saint-Aubin-de-Luigné, Saint-Lambert-du-Lattay, and Chaume. Appellation laws allow all the forementioned to be added to the label including individual *lieu-dit* (individual vineyard site) names. Chaume, with its more concentrated and consistent wines, is considered the best, even though, unlike the rest, it lies mainly on clayey soil. The commune of Saint-Lamber-du-Lattey contains about 36 percent of all the vines in the "Villages" appellation.

Very little Coteaux du Layon wine is exported to the United States, hence it is relatively unknown. While England imports about 10 percent of the total exported, Holland and Belgium account for more than 50 percent of all exports. It should also be noted that the wines of Anjou and Saumur are the most exported after Bordeaux, Burgundy, and the Côte du Rhône. Three-quarters of all wine exported is rosé.

The wines of Joseph Touchais, varying from dry to sweet (the latter sold under the banner of *Moulin Touchais*), are superlative, extraordinary, and capable of aging as long as forty years with little deterioration, a remarkable achievement for any Loire wine. With more than 200 hectares, the house is one of the largest property owners making a complete line of rosé, red and dry white wines, all of which are not in the same league as sweet wines made from Chenin Blanc. The brand name *Moulin Touchais* is reserved exclusively for outstanding wines of the harvest and from the finest sites of Anjou, most specifically Layon. The wines are meticulously made, the must being racked before fermentation, which may last for weeks. The most expensive in the Loire, the wines are considered to be the most "fruited" and to rival the finest from Sauternes.

Located near Beaulieu-sur-Layon, *Dne. de la Soucherie,* a small producer of Chenin Blanc and Sauvignon Blanc, makes delicate, fruity, well-balanced wines. *Dne. des Rochettes* is a small estate that produces above-average, fruity white, rosé and red wines. The firm of *Aubert Frères* is known for red Cabernet, a wine of some complexity and appeal, in addition to other less distinguished wines. *Dne. de Montchenin* is the label of a number of vinegrowers making above-average white wine from Chenin Blanc and Chardonnay.

Dne. des Baumard is a medium-sized, well-established and respected house that owns the largest share of Quarts de Chaume, portions of Savennières, and other fine vineyards, as well as a number of less distinguished sites. All wines are above average and offer considerable value, although occasionally wine made in a "fresh," stainless steel manner can be inconsistent. The "Clos Saint Catherine" is outstanding in good vintages. Equally good are the wines of *Ch. de la Guimonière,* maker of one of the finest sweet Layon wines—well balanced, with a pronounced bouquet, and a strong lingering finish. *Dne. de la Motte,* like *Guimonière,* enjoys a superlative reputation. *Ch. la Fresnaye, Ch. de la Roulerie, Ch. de Tigné; Dne. de Pierre Bise, Jacques Beaujeau, Vignoble Diot-Antier, Jean-Pierre Chene,* and *Clos des Ortinières* are all highly regarded for above-average wines.

Dne. de Champteloup, a small firm, enjoys a superlative reputation for a stylish, pale, Cabernet Franc–Cabernet Sauvignon rosé. Well-made wines are consistently produced at *Ch. de Parnay* and *Clos de l'Aiglerie. Ch. de Passavant* is known for supple, dark-red wine from Caberent Franc and Cabernet Sauvignon; the house of *Henri Métaireau* enjoys a good reputation for a well-balanced and fruity rosé. *Dne. de Marzelle,* a shipper's blend

Plate 3.1   Harvesting Chenin Blanc along the Layon River in Quarts
de Chaume (courtesy Jean Baumard)

of white and rosé wines of average quality, is often encountered in
America but offers little value.

While Coteaux du Layon appears to be the most common sweet wine of
Anjou-Saumur, there are two smaller and more prominent vineyards—
Quarts de Chaume and Bonnezeaux. Quarts de Chaume, AOC since
1954, is a 45-hectare site within the village of Rochefort-sur-Loire.
Located on the protected slopes of the south bank of the Layon, it enjoys
an unusually warm microclimate, enabling grapes to mature fully two
weeks sooner than all other sites in the valley. *Chaume* is not only a place
name, but the name of the wine, which is exclusively from Chenin Blanc.
Along the Savannières, the iron-rich, stony, schistous and sandstone soil
of *Chaume* dictates the lowest yields of any Loire appellation.

The wines, made by a handful of producers, are all sweet and ideally
only from *botrytized*-infected grapes. The classic bottles are pure berry
selections, fermented slowly, and matured in the bottle rather than in
cask. The wine is well balanced and fruity without being cloying, and has
at least 12 percent alcohol and a golden color that deepens with age. The
flavor is most memorable, with hints of honey, peaches, pear, flowers, and
an elegance that is absolutely staggering. The wine is little known,
neglected, almost forgotten and, as a result, offers extraordinary value
when compared with other, similar wines. By Loire standards it is always

expensive and always scarce. *Dne. Baumard,* the largest owner of Chaume, is considered the standard. Equally good is *Ch. de Belle Rive,* a 17-hectare property that consistently outperforms many of its neighbors. Other quality producers include the house of *Laffourcade, Ch. de l'Echarderie, Dne. du Logis, Guy Gousset, Dne. des Maurières, Ch. de Plaisance, Ch. Montbenault,* and *Dne. de la Pierre Blanche.*

An AOC appellation since 1961, Bonnezeaux, less famous than Quarts de Chaume, is located upstream and named after a small crossroads of a site near the commune of Thouarce on the edge of the Coteaux du Layon appellation. Here the soil differs from that of Quarts de Chaume by containing large concentrations of marl, schist, slate, and clay. The appellation covers about 125 producing hectares that are subdivided and widely scattered on rather steep slopes. The wine, made entirely from Chenin Blanc, is more variable and less intense than its more famous neighbor to the north. In good years, however, it has a penetrating bouquet and considerable elegance, is well structured, perfectly balanced, and full-bodied. Sometimes it is made half-dry with a slightly bitter aftertaste. Production, limited to about 10,000 cases, is about 30 percent greater than that of Quarts de Chaume. Located within the commune of Thouarce and considered the leader in the production of quality Bonnezeaux, *Ch. de Fesles,* known for its rich golden color and somewhat drier aftertaste, gives excellent value. *Dne. du Petit Val, Dne. de la Croix-de-Mission, Dne. de la Croix-des-Loges, René Renou,* and the house of *Raimbault* are all above-average producers.

Coteaux de l'Aubance

This formidable white AOC region, extending from the outer margins of Quince to the Layon River, takes its name from a small stream. The terrain is gently rolling to flat, and the soil is a mixture of schist and sandstone mixed with alluvial material. This varied soil mixture is well drained and usually very dry, giving the white wines a peculiar *gout de terroir* flavor—a significant and unusual difference from those areas immediately to the west and south.

The principal estates with some degree of renown are *Dne. St.-Melanie, Dne. Soulaine, Dne. Vauchrétien,* and the house of *Gerard Chauvin.* The largest single producer in the appellation and the entire region is the large, 500-member Caves de la Loire Cooperative, located in Brissac.

THE SAUMUR APPELLATIONS

Extending along the south bank of the Loire, the vineyards of Saumur are sandwiched between those of the Touraine in the east and Anjou in the west. Saumur, a city one-sixth the size of Angers, is a medieval settlement and, as one of the oldest Huguenot centers of the 16th and 17th centuries, it is the locus of one of the most historic and productive regions in the entire Loire valley. The city's four dozen magnificent Renaissance châteaux, Roman ruins, cavalry school, profusion of mushroom caves, and castles and museums too numerous to mention radiate history.

Approximately one-fifth of all wine from the Anjou-Saumur vineyard emanates from the Saumur district, an overwhelming amount of which is white and sold under a large number of confusing names and appellations. Approximately 60 percent of the wine is sparkling and dominated by Saumur Mousseux Blanc, followed by Champigny and Saumur Blanc.

Although 93 communes contain commercial vineyards along the Chouet and Thouet Rivers, the heart of the producing district, known as the "Coteaux," is higher in elevation than the surrounding countryside and is composed of a 100-meter-thick layer of chalk. Because Saumur contains larger amounts of limestone, its wines are higher in acidity, lighter in color, livelier and drier in taste, and have a more pronounced *goût de terroir* than those of Anjou. Since Saumur is considered part of Anjou, its wines can be marketed either as Saumur or Anjou, while those of Anjou can be sold only as Anjou—an important consideration when one attempts to determine geographic origin.

Saumur Mousseux

The sparkling wine of Saumur is sold either as Saumur Mousseux Blanc, Saumur Mousseux Rosé, Pétillant, Crémant de la Loire Blanc, or Crémant de la Loire Rosé. They are differentiated only by the amount of froth they produce: lowest for pétillant and highest for mousseux. They are all bottle-fermented according to appellation laws and exhibit sharp differences in style, color, and taste from their two principal competitors, Vouvray and Champagne. Approximately 115,000 hectoliters of Saumur sparkling wine is produced annually, one-eighth the output of Champagne but double the production of Vouvray, its most formidable rival in the Loire valley.

The proportion and type of grapes vary markedly by producer but, in general, the Chenin Blanc dominates the encépagement. Chardonnay and Sauvignon Blanc are limited to 20 percent, with the remainder coming from a wide assortment of black grapes—Cabernet Franc, Cabernet Sauvignon, Malbec, Grolleau, Pinot Noir, and Pineau d'Aunis—with appellation requirements limiting black grapes to 60 percent of the encépagement. Most interesting is the fact that the number of grapes legally allowed in the production of sparkling wine is greater for Saumur than for any other sparkling wine region in all of France.

Although all vineyard sites are required by law to be located on limestone formations, the thickness of chalk and its composition with other mineral matter in the soil profile are not specified. As a result, the producing region is widespread, with more than 85 communes providing grapes ultimately destined for sparkling wine production. This diversity, plus the non-standardization of the encépagement, accounts in part for the wide style variations among the many producers. The sites locally acknowledged to be the best are Parnay, Turquant, Montsoreau, Souzay, and Dampierre.

Appellation laws specify a minimum alcoholic strength of 9.5 percent and that the wines be aged at least nine months from the time the *liqueur de tirage* is added to the *dégorgement* stage. It is interesting to note that in Saumur, appellation regulations severely limit the property holdings of large sparkling wine houses. As a result, most of the larger producers buy the base wine from small growers and then re-ferment in the bottle. In 1978, a number of Saumur-Champigny negociant houses formed a syndicate to promote their sparkling wines. They promulgated the use of the phrase "Saumur d'Origine" on the label to distinguish the wines of Saumur from those of Anjou.

Sparkling Saumur is not the same as Champagne in terms of intensity of bouquet, size and persistency of carbonation, overall complexity and body. Good Saumur is fresh, zesty, simple, and far cheaper than good Champagne. It is at its best in the second year and rarely improves after its third birthday. Furthermore, it is invariably less delicate and far more variable than sparkling Vouvray. Nevertheless, it often provides excellent value in overseas markets and almost always in the area of production.

Less than 5 percent of all Saumur Mousseux is made into rosé, a wine with eye appeal but little else, since the pigmentation and taste of Cabernet Franc interferes with the delicacy of the Chenin Blanc grape. Its production varies widely to reflect prevailing fashion for color as well as taste—a very important aesthetic consideration in the sale of sparkling wine. The pétillant style is pleasant but a minor element in total production.

Sparkling Saumur, first made by Belgian banker Jean Ackerman in 1811, has had a turbulent history. The wine was neglected, remained relatively obscure, and was sold as Champagne until AOC laws were promulgated in 1908. In 1860 no more than 2 million bottles were produced, in 1880 1.5 million, and in 1900 7 million bottles. The world economic depression and competition from Champagne took a heavy toll and, as a consequence, total output declined by half in 1938 from the peak production figure of the late 1890s. Production in recent years has grown rapidly—8 million bottles in 1970, 9 million in 1977, and 13 million in 1981—with expectations that if the current sparkling boom continues, production will rise to 25 million bottles by 1995.

Saumur Mousseux was not exported until the 1890s, did not really become popular until the 1920s, and only recently has become a noticeable export commodity. Today, about 2.5 million bottles are exported, with nearly two-thirds going to England and the Low Countries, and the remainder to Germany, Switzerland, and the United States.

While, historically, nearly all was demi-sec, three-quarters of current production is made brut to satisfy contemporary tastes.

Among the many sparkling houses of Saumur, the following are known for quality and consistency: Ackerman-Lawrence, the largest producer of sparkling Saumur, sells more than 3.5 million bottles each year (or about one-quarter of total production) under several quality-grade labels, of which "Cuvée Privée," made both Blanc and Rosé, is exceptional. The firm produces less than 6 percent of all grapes needed and exports approximately one-third of total output. The wines are cleanly made, emphasizing the flavor and body of the Chenin grape. Production is currently stable at around the 4 million-bottle range. The region's second-largest firm with 20 percent of all sparkling Saumur is *Veuve Amiot,* an old but recently rejuvenated house that makes more than 3 million bottles of sparkling Saumur. Like all major houses, it makes a complete range of wines, but unlike all others, it exports less than one-fifth of total output. The wines, with an emphasis on lightness of flavor and fragrance, are well made and consistently good.

Gratien Meyer, Bouvet-Ladubay and *Compagnie Française des Grands Vins* each produce approximately 10 percent of total sparkling Saumur. Of the three, Bouvet-Ladubay, a traditional house, exports more than 50 percent of production. The wines are above average to excellent, of which Brut, made entirely from Chenin Blanc, offers outstanding value. Equally good are the wines of *Gratien Meyer,* but they are heavier in flavor and body from those of *Bouvet-Ladubay* and *Veuve Amiot.* Less consistent, the wines of *Compagnie Française des Grands Vins* are known for their lightness, neutral flavor, and early maturing character.

With nearly 1 million bottles made annually, *De Neuville* is the sixth-largest producer. The wines, containing less Chenin Blanc and more Cabernet, are characterized by delicacy, finesse, and a pronounced bouquet. The *Cave Coopératives des Vignerons de Saumur* produces more than 1 million bottles of sparkling Saumur in addition to vast quantities of Saumur Blanc and Rouge, its primary business. The wines are modestly priced and sell well.

Among the smaller producers, *Rémy-Pannier* exports more than 50 percent of its good to above-average production of 300,000 bottles. A traditional firm with an excellent reputation, *Langlois-Château,* owned by *Bollinger,* is known for superb "Blanc de Blancs" non-vintage, vintage, and Crémant. This fine house also distributes excellent quality Saint-Florent Saumur Blanc and Rouge, Muscadet, Chinon, St.-Nicolas de Bourgueil, Saumur-Champigny, Sancerre, and Pouilly-Fumé. *Ch. de Montreuil-Bellay,* a huge estate with a postage-stamp vineyard, makes a full-bodied rosé, one of the best in Saumur. *Ch. de Parnay,* a small producer of sparkling wine, *Ch. de Beaulieu,* and the negociant houses of *Albert Bescombes* and *Sylvan Maimfray* are all reputable.

Crémant de Loire Blanc and Rosé

Crémant de Loire is a comparatively new (1975) regional appellation incorporating not only the sparkling wines of Saumur, but those of Anjou and the Touraine as well. It is made from Chenin Blanc, Cabernet Franc, Cabernet Sauvignon, Pineau d'Aunis, Pinot Noir, Chardonnay, and Menu Pineau—all of which must be at least 70 percent of the total encépagement. Grolleau and other grapes are considered supplementary to the total encépagement.

Yield per hectare and production methods differ significantly from Saumur Mousseux. The grapes, for example, are pressed whole, the must is the product of the first pressing, and vinification occurs over a two-to-three month period. The wine receives a minimum of one year bottle-aging from the time the *liqueur de tirage* is added to the *dégorgement* stage. Finally, grapes must originate from "approved soil regions" considered above average in the production of the fragile Crémant. As a consequence, the Crémant de Loire appellation is a more delicate product than Saumur Mousseux. The Blanc style is pale yellow, fragrant, smooth, frothy, and absolutely refreshing. The rosé, showing less elegance and refinement, is not produced in large quantities.

Crémant de Loire, within a very short time, has become a popular wine with demand outpacing production. From nearly insignificant levels twenty years ago, production has grown to more than 25,000 hectoliters and is increasing rapidly. *Gratien Meyer* and *Perry de Maleran,* both located in Amboise, have the best reputations. Their wines are not cheap, but are well worth the effort and experience.

Saumur-Champigny

Saumur-Champigny, with an output of 30,000 hectoliters (or 4 percent of regional AOC production) is the region's largest and highest-quality red wine appelation. The entire vineyard is centered around the hamlet of Champigny, located southeast of Saumur on soil that contains high levels of limestone, sand, and very little clay. The best sites are along the small Thouet River and include the communes of Dampierre, Parnay, Chacé, St.-Cyr-en-Bourg, Montsoreau, and Varrains. The small village of Chaintres, surrounded by some of the finest growths, is the nucleus of the producing zone. Fewer than 600 hectares produce approximately 4 million bottles annually.

The wine, made almost entirely from Cabernet Franc (with small infusions of Cabernet Sauvignon), is of medium color and has a fragrance of raspberries and strawberries; its long finish can be quite impressive. It generally needs 12 months in wood and at least two years of bottle-aging to come around, although a good vintage has the ability to prolong its ageing potential to ten years. Although it is considered the best that

Anjou-Saumur has to offer, Saumur-Champigny, no matter how good it may appear, is never the equal of fine Bourgeuil, Chinon, or St.-Nicolas-de-Bourgeuil, its next-door neighbors to the east.

The reputation of the finest Champigny belongs to the firm of *Paul Filliatreau,* maker of full-bodied, highly concentrated, sturdy wines with plenty of depth and character under two different labels. More consistent and often the better wine is the 10-hectare *Dne. des Roches Neuves.* The well-made wines are rich, full-bodied, well-flavored, and age gracefully beyond the third year. *Dne. des Varinelles* and *Ch. de Chaintres,* two major producers located in Dampierre, enjoy above-average reputations for early maturing and supple wines. *Claude Daheuiller* is known for soft, light-colored, and supple Champigny with little concentration and staying power. *Ch. de Villeneuve,* a medium-sized estate, enjoys a reputation for soft and fragrant wine in addition to interesting Saumur Blanc. The highly reputable firm of *Couly-Dutheil* makes lightweight Champigny, always above average and consistently good.

Saumur Blanc and Rouge

These two appellations account for less than 4 percent of the regional output, of which 90 percent is white, mostly dry, early maturing, and quite appealing as carafe wine. Saumur Blanc is primarily made from Chenin Blanc, with Sauvignon Blanc and Chardonnay contributing as much as, but not more than, 20 percent of the finished product. When made solely from Chenin Blanc, it is usually softer and more agreeable than the blended versions. While it appears to be delicate, often "pearling" with a lively froth that both enlivens the bouquet and the flavor, it is, in the main, undistinguished and offers no extraordinary value. *Rémy Pannier, Cave des Vignerons de Saumur, Ch. de Brézé, Jean Douet,* and *Ch. de. Villeneuve* are five of the biggest producers of Saumur Blanc. *Caves des Vignerons de Saumur, Ch. de Targe, Ch. de Saint-Florent,* and *Clos de l'Abbaye* are major producers of Saumur Rouge.

Small quantities of red wine are produced in Turquant, Montsoreau, and Montreuil-Ballay. Made primarily from Cabernet Franc, Cabernet Sauvignon, and Pineau d'Aunis, the wines are generally light, fragrant, with little tannin or extract, and slightly above *vin ordinaire* quality levels.

Cabernet de Saumur

Cabernet de Saumur, a very fresh, usually well-balanced wine, was first produced in 1977 after the local producers petitioned for AOC status in 1974. Prior to that time, the wine was simply known as "Rosé de Saumur" and treated as a local curiosity. Fewer than 3,000 hectoliters are produced each year with the potential for substantial increases. The wine, very pale, dry, and made primarily from the Cabernet Franc with minor additions of Cabernet Sauvignon, is considered superior to Cabernet d'Anjou.

Coteaux de Saumur

Made in minute quantities, Coteaux de Saumur wines are white with the capacity to mellow with age, and although good to above-average in quality, they do not seem to compare favorably with equivalents from Layon and Vouvray. The wine is essentially a Chenin Blanc from the communes of Bizay, Brézé, Parnay, Turquant, and Dampierre. Since it does not sell well under its official appellation banner, vignerons use the Saumur Blanc appellation name instead. The wine, usually half-dry, light in body, and yellow in color, is otherwise undistinguished.

Other Wines

Along the southern margins of the Anjou-Saumur vineyard are two VDQS wines that are receiving considerable attention. The most interesting of the two is Vins de Haut-Poitou where the *Cave Coopérative du Haut-Poitou,* located in Neuville-de-Poitou, makes nearly the entire production of surprisingly good white and red wines. Poitou Blanc made primarily from Sauvignon Blanc and Chardonnay is the wine with a reputation from this little-known area. It is fresh on the palate, dry, fruity, and substantial in body and character. Because the wine is little known, its current low price does not reflect true quality. Less good is the minuscule red wine production from varying quantities of Gamay, Pinot Noir, and Cabernet Sauvignon.

Centered around the town of Thouars, a small region, are the Vins du Thouarsais, the usual assembly of Chenin Blanc–dominated white wines, with small quantities of red and rosé. All are unremarkable except for the minute quantities of red wine from the commune of Noir.

4

THE WINES OF THE TOURAINE

THE Touraine, often referred to as the "Jardin de France," is a remarkable region of fertile valleys, splendid castles, and an easy, fat life that is most atypical of the rest of the country. The peaceful landscape is dominated by the medium-sized but lively city of Tours, formerly *Urbs Turonum,* of Roman fame. It is a city of fine restaurants, haphazard but pleasant medieval streets, and a good touch of lethargy. In Tours, the center of the province, history, romance, and politics have firm footholds. Tours sheltered medieval kings and nurtured the Plantagenets. Charles VII spent his exiled years in Tours, which established a tradition for French royalty building luxurious chateaux along the Loire. The city is also the site of the final days of Leonardo da Vinci and the famous "School of Amboise" founded by Charles VIII. Most important, it is the locus of the finest red wine in the Loire River valley.

The climate is a happy combination of maritime and continental influences characterized by mild winters, warm summers, and spectacular equinoxes. Spring and summer are known for brilliant sunshine, the lowest amount of precipitation, and the greatest amount of degree days of any area in the Loire. Fall, on the other hand, can be unfavorable for proper grape maturation, as the number of degree days are reduced by 60, and the number of sunshine hours by 100. Although the temperature can fall as low as $-10°C$ for several days at a time, the biggest environmental hazard is hail, particularly in June and July. Therefore, the elements that determining microclimatic site selection are a reduced incidence of rainfall and the maximization of average annual and fall temperatures.

The vineyards, dating back to the 6th century, form a thin, intensively cultivated ribbon along both banks of the Loire River (see Fig. 4.1), and stand in sharp contrast to the surrounding uplands, which are drier, cleared of forest, and given less intense use. North of Blois is the plateau of Beauce, a deserted, treeless, windswept area mainly devoted to cereal cultivation. The core of the producing district stretches from Saumur to Blois, covering three departments and a multitude of small river valleys, the most important of which are the Loire, Indre, Vienne, and Creuse. The most famous appellations are Vouvray, Chinon, Bourgeuil, and Montlouis. There are several other outlying vineyards, of which Touraine Mesland, Coteaux du Loire, and Jasnières are the most important, and three minor VDQS districts.

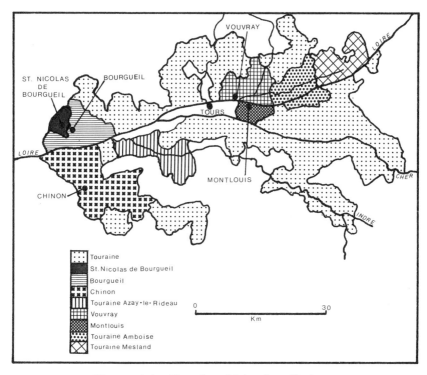

Figure 4.1   Touraine: Major Appellations

Historically, the Touraine was known as a white wine region which produced semi-sweet and sweet wines from the Chenin Blanc and Folle Blanche grapes. Its most celebrated wine was Vouvray, both still and sparkling, with the best sites located along a small limestone region east of Tours along the north bank. Since 1960, however, red wines have increased their share of total production, with Cabernet Franc alone accounting for nearly 30 percent of all plantings. Red and rosé wines collectively constitute more than half the total production, the highest such figure in the entire valley.

Viticulture has been on a steady downward trend for the past ninety years with hectarage declining from 62,800 in 1900 to 8,000 in 1980. Production for the same period declined from 1 million hectoliters to 400,000 (see Table 4.1). Fortunately for the wine lover, nearly all the abandoned areas occurred on marginal land, and the quality wine regions have largely remained unaffected.

Touraine Nature Blanc, Rouge and Rosé, and Mousseux Blanc

Although Vouvray, Chinon, and Bourgeuil are well-known names, few are familiar with the "Touraine" appellation (formerly known as "Coteaux de Touraine"), the largest in the producing region. With an annual

Table 4.1   Touraine Wine Production by AOC Appellation, 1980

Appellation	Hectoliters	Percent of total
Touraine Nature Blanc	121,394	29.4
Touraine Rouge	94,442	22.9
Vouvray Nature Blanc	47,361	11.5
Chinon Rouge	38,214	9.3
Chinon Blanc	262	
Bourgeuil Rouge	33,494	8.1
St. Nicolas de Bourgeuil Rouge	20,031	4.9
Vouvray Mousseux	25,865	6.3
Montlouis Blanc	5,609	1.4
Montlouis Mousseux	5,146	1.2
Touraine Amboise Rouge	5,207	1.3
Touraine Amboise Blanc	4,142	1.0
Touraine Mesland Rouge	7,555	1.8
Touraine Mesland Blanc	1,594	.4
Touraine Azay-le-Rideau Rouge	907	.2
Touraine Azay-le-Rideau Blanc	1,279	.3
Total production	412,502	100.0

Source: French Ministry of Agriculture.

production of more than 200,000 hectoliters, it is second in size after Muscadet de Sèvre-et-Maine. The more than 4,000 hectares in the appellation are widely scattered on all manner of soil along the Loire, Indre, Cher, Choisille, and Brenne rivers. Although known for a variety of red, rosé, still, and sparkling white wines, only minute amounts are considered distinctive enough to be called a "Sunday wine."

Red wine is largely made from Cabernet Franc, Gamay, Cabernet Sauvignon, and Malbec; rosé largely from two indigenous vines, Grolleau and Pineau d'Aunis; white wines from Chenin Blanc, Folle Blanche and, recently, from increasing amounts of Sauvignon Blanc and Chardonnay. Sauvignon de Touraine, often called the "poor man's Sancerre," appears to be the best. Its crisp taste and flavor, with a short finish, make it a far better value at half the cost of mediocre Sancerre. It has therefore grown in popularity, and production is increasing rapidly. One of the leading producers is *Ch. de Breuil,* owned by Patrick Ladoucette of Sancerre-Pouilly. Made exclusively from Sauvignon Blanc, the crisp, fruity, and balanced wine is marred only by the presence of vegetal-grassy flavors that detract from an otherwise very pleasant experience. Superb Sauvignon Blanc and blended wines are made by *La Croix de Mosny, Dne. Joel*

Table 4.2   Major Grape Varieties Planted in the Department of Indre-et-Loire, 1968 and 1979

Grape varieties	1968 Hectares	Percent	1979 Hectares	Percent	As percent of national total in 1979
Cabernet Franc	2,300	12.2	3,000	29.1	13.3
Chenin Blanc	3,700	19.8	2,800	27.2	29.3
Grolleau	3,800	20.3	1,100	10.7	19.0
Plantet Noir	1,600	8.5	800	7.8	20.0
Gamay Noir	1,000	5.3	700	6.8	
Gamays Teinturiers	50	.5	200	1.9	
Cabernet Sauvignon	50	.5	200	1.9	
Malbec (Cot)	600	3.1	200	1.9	
Folle Blanche	500	2.6	100	1.0	
Villard Noir	200	1.1	100	1.0	
Seinoir	300	1.6	100	1.0	
Rayon d'Or	200	1.0	50	.5	
Others	4,400	23.5	950	9.2	
Total	18,700	100.0	10,300	100.0	

Source: French Ministry of Agriculture.

Delaunay, Gerard Gabillet, Ch. de Launay, Jackie Masnière, Jacques Preys, Gaec Sauvete and Le Vieux Chai.

Equally good are the wines of Vignoble des Corbillières Aimé Boucher. Two small but exceptional producers known for dry, full, well-scented and flavored Sauvignon Blanc are Dne. de la Charmoise and Dne. du Grand Moulin, both of which offer outstanding value. Unusual and most distinctive in character, the "Sauvignon Touraine," by the Confrérie des Vignerons de Oisly et Thesee, is rare and expensive, but well worth the effort and cost.

Because of the size and diversity of the producing region, red wines exhibit incredible variety in color, body, and longevity. The best from a bewildering number of styles appears to be Gamay, a grape that shows a special affinity to the Amboise region, where it is often referred to as the "best Beaujolais of France." Light in color and body, it is almost Beaujolais in character, but more grassy and less bitter in taste. Offering a surprisingly full-bodied wine with concentrated flavor and staying power, Dne. de la Charmoise appears to be the finest producer of Gamay. The Dne. des Corbillières is also known for above-average Gamay, but not anywhere near the quality of "Baronnie d'Aignan," the brand name of the Confrérie des Vignerons de Oisly, whose wine is made from an intriguing blend of Gamay and Malbec and is one of the best from the appellation.

The leading producers of Cabernet Franc are *Jean Louet* and *Le Clos Neuf des Archambaults*, followed by *Dne. Joel Delaunay, Guy Deletang, Jean-Marie Duvoux, Gaec Sauvete,* and *Dne. des Echardières.*

Amboise, Azay, and Mesland

In an attempt to distinguish their wines from the general "Touraine" appellation, a number of growers in Amboise, Azay, and Mesland append the name of their locality to the Touraine appellation. Their combined production is approximately 5 percent of total Touraine output, a figure that is expected to drop appreciably in the near future. Mesland, with 250 hectares and a yearly output of 11,000 hectoliters of red, rosé and white wine is considered the best of the three subregions. The small, 100-hectare Azay subregion produces 4,000 hectoliters of thin, crisp, unappealing red, rosé and white wines. Significantly better than the wines of Azay, Amboise encompasses slightly less than 200 hectares, and produces more than 6,000 hectoliters of wine in all three colors, the finest of which is red, particularly when made from Malbec.

Vouvray

Vouvray, lying 10 kilometers east of Tours on the north bank of the Loire, has long been known as the wine of Rabelais and Hemingway. It is strictly a white wine region that produces nearly 18 percent of the total output in the Touraine. Average production is 60,000 hectoliters, of which 40,000 is "nature," while the remainder is mousseux. The historic reputation was based on sweet wine mainly for local and regional consumption. Exports were limited to England, Belgium, and Holland, the latter being the most important export market for 400 years. Since the wine was a favorite of the French aristocracy, many kings, including Henry IV, owned vineyards in the producing region. While the practice of making sweet wine has continued, its share of total production has declined, and the majority is now made moelleux, half-dry, or dry.

Vouvray for centuries sought a prominent place in the litany of fine sweet wines but unfortunately never managed to captivate the public's attention for any sustained length of time. During the 1920s it gained a good measure of popularity when its name filled the literary pages of American expatriate writers in Paris, but its short-lived fame was quickly extinguished by the world depression of the 1930s. Although often referred to as the "taffeta wine" because of its delicacy, it lacked the intensity of Chaume, the elegance of Sauternes, and the bouquet and flavor of fine Mosel, Rheingau, and Tokay. Nevertheless, Vouvray was one of the very first viticultural regions to attain AOC status in 1936.

Produced solely from the Chenin Blanc grape, Vouvray is known not only for its fragrance and fruitiness, but for its freshness. At its best, it is eminently balanced without being cloying on the palate. Whether dry, semi-sweet, or sweet, alcohol content is rarely excessive, usually between 10 percent and 12 percent. Only in exceptionally hot years, when grapes are infected by *botrytis* do sugar levels rise to heights that ultimately produce alcohol levels greater than 12 percent. The happy combination of high acid, sugar, and alcohol levels of exceptional years enables Vouvray to age for more than ten years, and often for as many as twenty-five. Though rare, these vintages produce wines of exceptional color, fragrance, and silky texture that are good enough to rival any other in the Loire, including Chaume. The very best are superb and offer outstanding value. At their worst, however, a good portion of sweet Vouvray is often thin, flat, and overly sulfured, offering little value and doing nothing to enhance the reputation of the appellation. Vouvray Sec, on the other hand, is a loosely applied designation that can have considerable residual sugar, but when truly dry and well balanced is very refreshing, especially when fully matured.

Production of Vouvray reached an all-time high during the middle 1920s and then slowly declined to a low point of less than 10,000 hectoliters during the immediate post–World War II period (see Fig. 4.2). Despite the fact that consumer demand shifted from sweet white wine to dry, total AOC hectarage increased from 1,022 in 1949 to more than 1,500 in 1952, fluctuating within a narrow range until the middle 1970s, when it again showed renewed vigor. Generally, the amount of mousseux produced is indirectly related to the quality of the nature vintage; the higher the sugar content of the latter, the lower the total quantity of grapes available to produce sparkling wine. Problems of grape availability notwithstanding, Vouvray Mousseux, enjoying the popularity of contemporary fashion for sparkling white wine, is currently a "hot item" in the Loire. It increased its share of regional Touraine output from .1 percent in 1947 to 6.4 percent in 1980. Vouvray nature, on the other

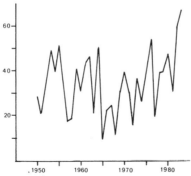

Figure 4.2 Vouvray Nature:
Wine Production, 1949–1983
(in thousands of hectoliters)

hand has had its share of total regional production reduced to levels approaching 10 percent. Anywhere from one-fifth to one-quarter of total Vouvray production is exported, nearly all of it "nature."

The physical elements of climate and soil determine the quality of Vouvray. The lack of consistency of weather conditions from one season to the next confronts and frustrates growers. Over the past fifty years the number of sunshine hours during the three critical stages of budding, growth, and final maturation has varied by as much as 500 hours, precipitation by 250mm, and degree days in Centigrade by as much as 1,100. Because the vagaries of nature are more pronounced on the plateau or northern section of the producing region, viticulture has been replaced by cattle raising. Most vineyards are still located on south-facing lime-stone bluffs to mitigate the severity of north wind, trap as much heat as possible, and reduce the incidence of frost. This favorable but precarious microclimate is also augmented by morning fog called *brumes,* which helps reduce the incidence of frost during the budding stage. In the fall, the *brumes* helps to promote the development of *botrytis,* producing moelleux and sweet wine. As a consequence, there is no typical or standard Vouvray. The wine, depending on the nature of the vintage, is highly impulsive and capricious; full-bodied, and sweet; sometimes well scented, flavorful, and soft; and occasionally light in body, fruity, and dry. Nearly always it is mouth-filling, flavorful, and pleasant on the palate.

Eight important parishes dominate hectarage: Saint-Radegonde, Ro-checorbon, Vouvray, Vernou, Noizay, Chançay, Reugny, and Parçay-Meslay. The last three are located on the plateau overlooking the Loire, while the rest are sited on superior south-facing exposures on a large bed of chalk overlain by *limon* and a thin mantle of surface gravel. Of the nearly fifty *lieu-dits* more than half are located within the confines of Vouvray: Clos l'Auberdière, Clos des Barguins, Clos la Barre, Clos Baudoin, Clos Bel Air, Clos des Bidaudières, Clos du Bois-Rideau, Clos le Bouchet, Clos du Bourg, Clos de l'Epinay, Clos Dubois, Clos de la Lucassière, Clos le Marigny, Clos Moncontour, Clos le Mont, Clos le petit Mont, Clos les Gués d'Amant, Clos le Gaimont, Clos des Girradières, Clos Saint Mathurin, Clos Vaufuget, Clos les Verneries, Clos le Vigneau, Clos le Paradis, Clos St.-Côme, Clos des Roches, Clos de Nouis. The commune of Rochecorbon contains the important *lieu-dits* of Clos des Armuseries, Clos des Bâtonnières, Clos de la Bourdonnerie, Clos de la Chasse Royale, Clos de Bellevue, Clos Château Chevrier, Clos Martin, Clos l'Olivier, Clos des Pentes, Clos de Sens, Clos de la Tainerie, and Clos de Vaufoynard. The commune of Vernou contains Clos Cosson, Clos de Chaillemont, Clos du Fougeray, Clos du Pouvray, Clos des Thierrières, and Clos de Vaux, and Ste.-Radegonde, located in the extreme western portion of the appellation, contains Clos de la Hallotière. Fermenting and storage capacity is nestled in the soft tufa rock at the base of the plateau, including the numerous "troglodite" houses of the growers.

Vouvray Nature

For Vouvray to be competitive and to offer exceptional value, it must be the product of careful berry selection, be well balanced, and be affected by *botrytis*. The wines, locally called "tranquille," are usually labeled sec, demi-sec, and moelleux, have an alcohol content that varies between 10 percent and 12 percent, and a yield of 45 hectoliters to the hectare. The better wines carry a vineyard name, locally called *lieu-dit*. The very best can be outstanding, hard to find, and well worth the effort for those with a sweet and delicate tooth. Fresh, intensely flavored, and scented, they are fruity on both the palate and nose.

Of the many producers, the following are considered the most important: the house of *Gaston Huet* makes superlative sec, demi-sec, and moelleux wines from three outstanding sites. Le Haut-Lieu ("manor of the high place") consists of 8 hectares and is known as a superb *lieu-dit*. Clos du Bourg is an 8-hectare site entirely enclosed by a wall that was once owned by the Abbey of St. Martin of Tours and the king of France. The "Le Mont" vineyard consists of 7 hectares and produces less delicate wine than the others. The first two wines are made from select berry pickings, are consistently good, and have excellent balance. In the same category as Gaston Huet, the 23-hectare estate of *Clos Baudoin,* which dates back to 1707, is owned by Prince Poniatowski. The flagship label is "Le Clos Baudoin," a 4-hectare site composed of solid chalk that produces classic, honeyed, well-scented moelleux wines. The "Aigle Blanc" label is a less fine and decidedly drier wine; "Aigle d'Or" is the label for an above-average Vouvray Mousseux; and under the Touraine AOC appellation, the estate produces a rosé sparkling wine made from 100 percent Cabernet Franc. The wines, very rare and expensive, often offer exceptional value. Three additional producers with outstanding reputations are *Pierre Lothion, Sylvain Gaudron,* and *Jean-Pierre Freslier.*

A complete range of wines is also made by *Marc Brédif,* owned by Ladoucette of Pouilly-Fumé. The moelleux is inconsistent, but in exceptional years it rises above all others in the producing region. The firm makes an interesting pétillant Vouvray that is one of the best in all France. *Dne. de la Rochère* is a small estate with impeccable credentials. Along the same line are *Clos de l'Avenir, Dne. des Barquins, Clos Baudinand, Jean-Pierre Gilet, Bernard Courson, Clos Dubois, Dne. de Bidaudière, André Fouquet, Bernard Bongars, Lionel Gauthier, D. Lefevre, Dne. des Clos Naudin, Jean-Pierre Laisement, Daniel Jarray,* and *Vigneau Chevreau. Ch. de Moncontour* is inconsistent, the house of *Monmousseau* above average, and *Maison Mirault* is known for robust, refreshingly tart wines.

Vouvray Mousseux Blanc

Vouvray Mousseux Blanc, constituting more than 6 percent of total wine production in the Touraine, represents half the output of still Vouvray. It is also the second-largest sparkling wine appellation in the entire Loire vineyard. Minimum alcohol content is 9.5 percent, but unlike other sparkling Loire wines, the mousseux of Vouvray has the capacity to age past its third birthday. Production in 1980 exceeded 25,000 hectoliters, a figure that has increased fivefold since 1945 and is expected to achieve parity with still Vouvray by the end of the century.

Commonly referred to as "Blanc de Blancs," it is made solely from the Chenin Blanc grape. Always made with meticulous care, the wine, rarely completely dry, is rich in flavor, has an expansive bouquet and a delicate, lingering fragrance, and is closer to Champagne in style than Saumur Mousseux. Although it lacks the depth of flavor and fullness of a first-rate Champagne, it offers exceptional value among the many French sparkling wines. Plain Vouvray Mousseux Blanc may contain varying quantities of Petit Pinot or "Menue Pinot," and is not as good as the "Blanc de Blancs." All Vouvray Mousseux is made by the "méthode Champenoise."

Among the many producers, *Blanc Foussy* is a popular and widely distributed brand made by the largest house in Rochecorbon. *Bouvet Ladubay* and *Jean Ackerman* of Saumur both make respectable, well-priced Vouvray known more for consistency and reliability than for outstanding quality. Among premium producers, *A. Foreau,* a small but unusual house (Clos Naudin) makes remarkable mousseux, placing it on the market only after extended cellar ageing. It is always expensive but of good value. *Gaston Huet* makes first-class, very reliable mousseux, as do *Aimé Boucher, Ch. des Bidaudières, Bernard Bongars, Chevreau-Vigneau, Bernard Courson, Alain Ferrand, Jean-Pierre Freslier, Jean Vrillon, Sylvain Gaudron, Maison Mirault, Claude Metivier,* and *Prince Poniatowski. J. M. Monmousseau* makes more than 100,000 cases of mousseux a year, which are mostly light, agreeable, and early maturing. *Girault-Artois* in Amboise and *Ch. de Vaudenuits* in Vouvray are both above-average producers.

Montlouis

Until 1938, when Montlouis was given appellation status, the wines of Montlouis were sold as Vouvray. But unlike Vouvray, which is located on solid chalk along the north bank, Montlouis and its two sister communes of Lussault and St.-Martin-le-Beau lie along the south bank about 70 meters above the river on a mixture of sand and gravel, with only a little chalk in the subsoil. In addition, the aspect differences in Montlouis places the appellation at a disadvantage. While the best sites in Vouvray are located along south-facing exposures, Montlouis does not benefit from solar intensity. As a consequence, although the wines are made entirely from the Chenin Blanc by methods identical with those of Vouvray and are similar in style, they differ qualitatively from the superior Vouvray: they are slightly lighter in body, earlier maturing, somewhat more acidic, less complex, and thinner on the palate.

Production of still and mousseux wines is approximately 11,000 hectoliters, or about one-seventh the output of its more famous neighbor across the Loire River. As the demand for semi-sweet and sweet wines has steadily deteriorated within the last fifty years, production and hectarage have both diminished. In 1950, hectarage stood at an imposing 1,450 hectares, only to decline to less than 300 in 1983. In an attempt to revive the sluggish market, producers have increased production of mousseux to still wine levels, and there are indications that it will continue to increase in the near future. It should also be noted that the still wines of Montlouis are made less sweet than they once were.

Among the two dozen producers, more than half are centered in Montlouis. The house of *Dominique Moyer,* considered the standard, makes above-average wines that are noticeably less sweet than most. *Dne. de Saint Martin* is well regarded and makes interesting demi-sec wines that offer good value. Six additional, above-average producers are *Claude Boureau, Jean Chauveau, Daniel Mosny, Marcel Lelarge, J. and M. Courtemanche,* and *Guy Deletang et Fils,* the latter considered one of the finest in the appellation. Also of note are *Clos de la Freslonnerie, Clos de la Gravelle,* and the house of *Latouche-Renard.*

Chinon, Bourgeuil, and St.-Nicolas-de-Bourgeuil

Just as the famed Chambord stands as an architectural masterpiece of the French Renaissance, Chinon and its two neighboring appellations represent the supreme red wine sites of the entire Loire River. The three areas, all clustered west and south of Tours, produce not only the most expensive red wine of the entire valley, but one-third of total output in the Touraine as well.

The extraordinary red wines of the region are due to a combination of exemplary microclimatic and pedologic conditions. The protection of a forested plateau along the north bank, and the higher temperatures and lower precipitation than any other region of the Loire, enable the production of high-sugar must levels.

Wine quality within the three producing districts varies significantly due to the wide diversity of soil and aspect. From the sandy and gravelly deposits along the Vienne and Loire rivers come *vins de sables* or "sand wines," light, fruity, and early maturing. The *vins de plateau,* from soils that contain more clay with pockets of gravel, are wines high in alcohol but with considerable scent and extract. The *vins de coteaux,* or "hill wines," from areas located not only on slopes, but on the edge of the plateau with a favorable southern aspect and containing larger quantities of limestone fragments, are round, dark wines that are full-bodied, rich in extract, and highly flavored and scented.

While the Cabernet Franc grape is widely distributed in western France, it is considered a minor variety in the southwest, in Graves, and even in the Médoc. Yet its importance increases with latitude. It thus assumes a prominent position in both Saint Emilion and Pomerol, and totally dominates red wine production in the Touraine (where it is locally known as the "Breton") due to its ability to attain high sugar levels. With the exception of Champigny, the Cabernet Franc grape is vinified as rosé throughout the rest of the valley.

The Cabernet Franc produces spicy, fruity, herbal-type wine of moderate color and alcohol. It lacks the astringency, tannin, and complicated flavor of Cabernet Sauvignon and, if not given extensive barrel-aging, is usually early maturing. The wine, which is made from destalked grapes, experiences a relatively long vatting, followed by a long and cool fermentation in limestone cellars. Alcohol is moderate, varying between 10.5 percent and 12 percent and rarely exceeding 12.5 percent. All three regions make minor amounts of rosé (the quantity rising in poor years), and only Chinon is allowed to make small quantities of white wine under its own appellation. The resulting wine is free of astringency, bitterness, and excessive tannin; and although there are subtle differences between all three producing regions, the final product is always fragrant, tasty, supple, and free of any rough edges. Aggregate production for the Chinon, Bourgeuil, and St.-Nicolas-de-Bourgeuil appellations has grown steadily over the past 40 years; it was a mere 13,485 hectoliters in 1937, 45,259 in 1944, 72,717 in 1960, 88,901 in 1970, 91,481 in 1980, and 141,407 in 1982, of which nearly half comes from Chinon (see Fig. 4.3).

The wine of Chinon takes its name from the charming, quaint medieval city of the same name that is, perhaps, the cleanest and neatest in the entire Loire basin. Attractive spots for visitors are the Chinon castle overlooking the entire city, the Wine Museum, beautiful promenades, and the Sainte Radegonde Chapel. The city is the center for the local wine industry that produces approximately 45,000 hectoliters, or four times the average output of the early 1950s. The 1,400-hectare vineyard, located southwest of Tours along the south bank of the Loire and the lower course of the Vienne River, is the largest of the three red wine–producing districts. The grapes used to produce Chinon came from eighteen communes that encompass a vineyard whose hectarage has tripled since 1950 and is currently increasing by 50 each year, a rather unusual phenomenon in the Touraine.

Along the south bank of the Vienne River are the communes of Anche, Cinais, la Dervinière, L'Ile-Bouchard, Rivière, la Roche-Clermault, Sazilly, Ligré, and Tavant. The most important communes located along the north bank are Avoine, Avon-les-Roches, Beaumont, Chinon, Cravant-les-Coteaux, Crouzilles, Huismes, Panzoult, and Savigny.

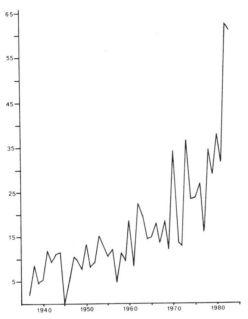

Figure 4.3   Chinon Rouge:
Wine Production, 1937–1983
(in thousands of hectoliters)

With more than one-third of total production, Cravant-les-Coteaux, with little limestone but more gravel in the soil, is the largest producing commune. The best individual vineyards are La Vauzelle, Rochette-Saint-Jean, les Clozeaux, la Rochelle, Saint-Louans, Clos de l'Echo, Clos-du-Parc, and Clos de l'Olive, all superlative sites, located on solid chalk. Downstream, from Chinon to Rabelais on a stretch known as "Le Pays Veron," are the excellent *lieu-dits* of la Roche Honneur, Château de Dauzany, and les Pouilles. Upstream and along the south bank of the Vienne are the important sites of Saute-aux-Loups, la Noblaie, les Rosettes, les Roches Saint-Paul, and le Vau Breton.

Vineyards are small throughout the Chinon appellation, but consolidation efforts are proceeding at a rapid pace. With a few large estates, more than two-thirds of all Chinon is the product of negociant houses. But since the Chinon vineyards are more widespread than those of Bourgeuil and St.-Nicolas-de-Bourgeuil, wine quality is highly variable and less predictable than its two neighbors. Depending on the nature of the vintage and the type of soil on which the grapes are grown, it is possible to produce early or late maturing, light- or dark-colored wines, thus defying easy generalizations. They are all magnificently colored, with a pronounced scent, and refreshingly outstanding in every way. Good Chinon has an alluring aroma of violets and raspberries, often with a good dose of refinement, and is probably the most underrated red wine of

France. Locally it is referred to as the "wine of intellectuals" because at one time it was the preferred red wine of the satirist Rabelais and the author Ernest Hemingway. In the United States, because of its relative obscurity, it offers extraordinary value.

Although Cabernet Sauvignon, Grolleau, Gamay, Malbec, and Meunier can be added in minor quantities, the finest Chinon contains a minimum of 95 percent Cabernet Franc. Alcohol content varies between 11.5 percent and 12.5 percent, and while the wine prior to World War II was aged in wood for three years, it rarely receives more than 18 months in cask today. The appellation also makes a dry rosé from a wide assortment of grapes, and although it is far better than the lighter and sweeter equivalents of Anjou, it is not in the same league as the red. Since fewer than 2,000 hectoliters of Chinon Blanc are made, and only made from the Chenin Blanc grape, the wine is rare and hard to find. Its popularity has fluctuated widely: prior to 1944, production exceeded 1,000 hectoliters, output then dropped steadily to 53 hectoliters in 1977, but then recovered by 1983 when 1,186 hectoliters were made. The wine is dry, fruity, rather austere with a slight bitter finish, and will not age.

Among the finest Chinon, the house of *Charles Joguet* enjoys a sterling reputation, especially for the "Cuvée du Clos de la Diotere," considered to be one of the finest, most delicate, fruity, and balanced wines of the entire district. The firm of *Couly-Dutheil*, said to be the largest grower and negociant in Chinon, makes average to above-average wines, and holds major positions in Champigny and Bourgeuil as well. All wines are consistently above average, meticulously made by long and cool fermentations, and well aged. "Le Clos de l'Echo," Le Clos de l'Olive," and "Le Clos des Caves Voutées de l'Hospice" all produce, dark, full, well-structured wines that require five years to reveal their complex subtle flavor, aroma, and nuance. *Dne. René Couly*, part of *Couly-Dutheil*, hails from the clay and sandy plateau soils of Louans and yields well-rounded, supple, yet firm wines that are ideal for extended aging. "Barommie Madeleine," a special selection of superior cuvées, is considered by many to be the finest wine made. "Les Garous" of the *Dne. du Turpenay*, located on gravel and sandy soil along the slopes of Cravant, is fruity, light, supple, and can age for as long as seven years. Equally good are the consistent and expertly made wines of *Olga Raffault, Dne. Raffault, Guy Caille, Dne. du Roncee,* and *Dne. de la Noblaie.*

Plouzeaux et Fils is another fine negociant firm known for above-average Chinon under the "Cuveé Bellamour" label. *Serge Sourdais, Guy Lemaire,* and *Aimé Boucher* all make above-average Chinon. *Dne de la Perrière, Ch. de Dauzay,* and *Les Picasses* are all excellent and difficult to find, but well worth the effort. One of the very best estates is *Dne de la Chapellerie,* whose wines are aged in wood and possess a distinctive, full, well-balanced and flavorful character. *Dne. de Pallus Beauséjour,* a meaty, succulent, early maturing wine with lots of class and style, is not only outstanding but reliable as well. *Ch. de le Grille,* owned by the Gosset family, is a superlative, wood-aged wine that rivals the best in the appellation. The negociant firm of *Audebert et Fils* offers consistently good Chinon from purchased grapes and wine, as well as from two excellent vineyards, "les Marquises" and "Grand Clos" in neighboring Bourgeuil. Excellent but hard-to-find estate-bottled Chinon comes from the following: "Clos du Parc" by *Farou,* "Clos Saint-Martin" by *Vazereau;* "Clos de la Haie-Marte" by *Desserre-Boue;* "Vignoble du Grand-Jardin" by *Rouzeau;* and "Clos de Cement" by *de Graeve.*

Bourgeuil, located west of Tours and along the north bank of the Loire, became viticulturally important only after the 11th century when a Benedictine abbey was established. Here the monks introduced the Cabernet Franc, the most distinguished red grape of the valley, in what was to become the Mecca of red wine in the Loire. The surviving vineyards, Clos de l'Abbaye and Grand Clos, are a living testimony to 800 years of winemaking in the area.

Vineyards are protected from north winds by a small, densely forested rise that shields Bourgeuil from cold air and produces a microclimate characterized by mild temperatures and sparse precipitation. Not only are the south-facing slopes warmer and drier than surrounding areas, but they are bathed in brilliant sunshine. As a consequence, the entire region is part of the true "Jardin de Paris," one vast truck-farm producing some of the finest vegetables of France—leeks, onions, asparagus, and berries.

The appellation is limited to eight communes: Bourgeuil, St.-Nicolas-de-Bourgeuil (the wines of the latter may be sold as plain Bourgeuil despite the separate appellation), Restigné, Ingrandes-de-Touraine, St.-Patrice, Benais, la Chapelle-sur-Loire, and Chouzé-sur-Loire. The 38,000-hectoliter, 1,300-hectare vineyard is only slightly smaller than Chinon. Approximately 10 percent of production is rosé, higher quality than most in the Loire, but still a rather nondescript product and treated as a minor entity in the region. Within the appellation confines, Cabernet Franc constitutes nearly the whole of the planted area. The average vineyard is small, and most vignerons are part-time farmers who live in modest houses.

The difference between Chinon and Bourgeuil is one of personal taste. Chinon has an element of finesse and elegance, while Bourgeuil is earthier, fruitier, more acidic, and often fuller, with a duller color and a spicier taste and bouquet. It also ages longer than Chinon. When made lighter, it loses a good dose of its body, hence the tendency for the more meticulous producers to bottle it between 12 and 18 months after the vintage. Alcohol content varies between 11 percent and 12.5 percent, and the yield is 40 hectoliters to the hectare. Unlike Chinon, Bourgeuil produces no white wine.

The best sites are le Clos de la Gardière, Clos de Perrières, les Galuches, la Salpetriere, la Chevalerie, les Brosses, and Restigné, all located on slopes that contain considerable amounts of limestone, and all producing coarse but long-maturing wines. Clos de l'Abbaye, a first-rate vineyard, produces classic wines that are fruity, complex, and well worth the effort to seek them out. In sharp contrast, the la Chapelle and Chouzé vineyards, located along an alluvial terrace of gravel and sand, produce lighter, supple, early maturing wines.

Among the five dozen local producers with a reputation, *Clos de l'Abbaye* and *Audebert et Fils* hold a primary position in the district. The above-mentioned vineyards produce wines that are well structured, tannin-rich, and require at least five years to mature fully. *Lamé-Delille-Boucard, Marc Delaunay, Dne. de la Chateleuserie, Paul Maître, Paul Poupineau, Dne. des Ouches, Dne. Hubert, Pierre Gregoire, Marc Mureau,* and *Raphaël Galteau* are all known for above-average, dark, exquisitely balanced wines. *Dne. Jacques Morin* is also highly recommended for its "Clos de la Henry." Excellent but hard-to-find estate-bottled Bourgeuil are "La Salpetrierre" by *Causeret,* "la Valate" by *Guillon-Gouffier,* "Clos des Geslets" by *Juteau,* and "Les Sablons" by *Ruesche.*

The third and smallest of the red wine districts of the Touraine is St.-Nicolas-de-Bourgeuil. It lies to the west of Bourgeuil, contains 500 hectares, or less than half the hectarage of Bourgeuil, and makes approximately 20,000 hectoliters of first-class wine. This underrated appellation contains a large percentage of high-quality plateaus and slopeland, the former containing sand and gravel, the latter being a mixture of stone, clay, and fine limestone. The entire district is sandier and less productive, as its soils are more porous than either Chinon or Bourgeuil. While the maximum yield is limited to 40 hectoliters in Chinon and Bourgeuil, it remains 35 in St.-Nicolas de Bourgeuil. As a consequence, the wines are not only fruitier, softer, and earlier maturing, but more delicate and refined than those of its more immediate neighbor, Bourgeuil. The best vineyards are le Vigneu, Clos de la Gardière (which it shares with Bourgeuil), Clos de l'Epaisse, and Les Fondis, le Fresne, la Contrie, le Bourg, le Moulin Neuf, la Martelliere, and Chezelles le Vau Renou.

Among the few estates is *Clos de la Contrie,* a superlative estate making unfiltered wines excellent in color, full in flavor, and quite distinctive in taste. Very similar are the wines of *Claude Amirault* of *Clos du Quarterons,* an exceptional wine that should not be missed. In addition to *Audebert et Fils,* a quality-oriented firm and the largest within the appellation, other producers known for quality wine production include *Boireau, Jean-Paul Mabileau, Joel Taluau,* and *Pierre Jamet,* the latter known for his excellent *Clos du Vigneau.*

Minor Wine-Production Districts

North and west of Touraine, widely scattered over three departments, are two small AOC and three larger VDQS vineyards that collectively contain

1,600 hectares of vines and produce 24,000 hectoliters of wine annually. The largely white wine region of Cheverny, characterized by libations that lack bouquet and suppleness, are unappealing and offer little value. The most interesting is Romorantin, made from an indigenous grape found nowhere else in France, very unusual and well worth the effort of seeking it out. There are few large independent producers, and more than three-quarters of production is sold to negociants. Valençay, the second largest VDQS region, makes white, rosé and red wines, of which the latter, made from a wide assortment of vines, is the most important. North of the Touraine in the department of Sarth lie the three viticultural regions of Coteaux Vendômois, Jasnières, and Coteaux du Loir, the last two being AOC appellations, and part of a much wider area of vine abandonment that has been underway throughout this century. While the wines of Jasnières are largely white and made from Chenin Blanc, those of the much larger Coteaux du Loir come in all three colors. The wines of the Coteaux du Vendômois, an obscure appellation of 225 hectares, produces unappealing, coarse, thin and overly acidic red, rosé and white wines.

5

THE WINES OF THE UPPER LOIRE

THE upper Loire viticultural region is a widely dispersed vineyard located on both sides of the Loire River in the Cher, Nièvre, and Loiret departments of north-central France. Its reputation rests on white wine, particularly Sancerre and Pouilly-Fumé, and to a lesser extent those of Reuilly and Quincy.

The Loire in central France flows north and stands in sharp contrast to that portion of the river flowing west of Orléans. It is less green, more windswept, has great expanses of denuded landscape, is poorer in agriculture, has more extensive goat-grazing activities, and possesses no large city. In this area of chronic outmigration (similar to Chablis just 70 kilometers northeast), close to 4,000 hectares and 3,000 growers produce fewer than 250,000 hectoliters of wine. As slightly more than one-third is AOC, and only a minor portion is classified as VDQS, the majority of the output is *vin ordinaire.*

Because the producing area is quite large, soils vary widely but, in general, good viticultural land lies on hilly terrain containing varying amounts of clay, limestone, and gravel. Quality, full-bodied, and long-lived wine is produced from vines growing in limestone and stony soils, while gravel soil yields supple, fragrant, and early maturing wines. The climate is the most continental of all the Loire vineyards: winters are cold, and summers are hot and dry. During the fall season, frequent morning fog and brilliant afternoon sun allow the grapes to mature fully and to attain high sugar levels.

The dominant grape, Sauvignon Blanc, was first introduced in the Quincy region by Cistercian monks. Although the grape is native to the Gironde region, it has adapted somewhat differently here, losing its "Graves grassy grip" and acquiring a more rounded, fuller, mineral character. It constitutes the only AOC white grape in all the best appellations—Reuilly, Sancerre, Pouilly-Fumé, and Quincy—and has become synonymous with quality dry white wine from the Loire. It differs sharply in terms of style from the Chardonnay-dominated wines of Chablis and Champagne, both of which are located northeast and north of Sancerre.

In comparison to other hardier vines, the Sauvignon Blanc matures relatively early, hence its prominence as the preferred grape on first-class sites. The Sauvignon Blanc AOC wine is the best of the region—dry, robust, eminently refreshing, and sometimes blessed with consonant character. Not as round and balanced as Chablis, nor as elegant and fine as good Meursault, it can upon occasion offer excellent value over these two overpriced competitors. Chasselas has been given to inferior locations, where it produces acidic, single-dimensional carafe wine.

AOC wine production by specific appellation is given in Table 5.1. The dominance of Sancerre with 54 percent of all white AOC and 12 percent AOC red is evident. Pouilly-Fumé, with 23 percent of all AOC white, is the second most important appellation. The widely diffused areas of Quincy, Ménétou-Salon, Reuilly, and Pouilly-sur-Loire contribute less than 10 percent of the total AOC wine output of the entire Loire River valley.

Sancerre

Sancerre, a picturesque medieval town of 4,000 people, sits on a mountain of chalk that overlooks the Loire. It is located downriver from Pouilly-sur-Loire, and has lent its name to two appellations: Sancerre Blanc, made solely from the Sauvignon Blanc grape (AOC 1936), and Sancerre Rouge/Rosé (AOC 1959), both made entirely from Pinot Noir.

Although settled by Romans, the region did not become a major viticultural center until the Austin friars arrived with the necessary expertise to lay the groundwork that eventually made this area famous. Production eventually exceeded local demand so that, by 1040, surplus wine was exported to Paris and beyond central France. The initial success encouraged other religious orders to migrate into the area, and by the middle of the 12th century, the Abbey-Satur owned a good deal of the Sancerre vineyard. The vineyards were never extensive, however; not until 1621, when the city's fortifications were destroyed and political tranquility established, did viticulture grow in prominence. The wines at that

Table 5.1   Wine Production in the Sancerre, Pouilly Region, 1980

Wine appellation	Hectoliters	Percent of total	Wine appellation	Hectoliters	Percent of total
Sancerre Blanc	50,970	54.3	Pouilly/Loire Blanc	2,728	3.2
Pouilly-Fumé Blanc	22,131	23.4	Ménétou-Salon Blanc	2,110	2.1
Sancerre Rouge	10,615	11.7	Reuilly Blanc and Rouge	1,067	1.0
Quincy Blanc	3,785	4.3			
			Total production	93,406	100.0

Source: French Ministry of Agriculture.

time were nearly all red and made from Pinot Noir. Religious control of wine production continued until the democratic zeal of the French Revolution secularized and subdivided the large viticultural estates.

By 1850 hectarage exceeded 3,000, and the *phylloxera* crisis of the 1870s produced significant changes in the character and style of Sancerre. Production shifted from red to white wine, and grape varieties changed from Pinot Noir to the hardy Chasselas and hybrids. Recently, the emphasis has reverted back to the Sauvignon Blanc and Pinot Noir. Today, white wine outnumbers red and rosé by four to one, while in 1959 it was forty to one. Hectarage, which began to decline after *phylloxera*, reached a low of 180 hectares in 1945, increased rapidly to 1600 by 1983 and, in response to the current popularity of dry white wine, is expected to double that amount by 2010.

As of 1981, there were 547 vignerons, 374 of whom cultivated less than three hectares, 103 between three and five hectares, and the remainder more than five hectares. It is important to note that only three growers owned more than 35 hectares of vineland. It is estimated that there are about 7,200 individual parcels of vine plots. Despite this highly fragmented pattern of ownership of limited-size vineland, farm consolidation is proceeding at a rapid pace.

The production of quality Sancerre wine occurs in four types of soil: *caillotes, terres blanches, silex,* and clay. The first is a dry chalk made up of limestone and clay that produces early maturing wine with good fruit and suppleness. The *terres blanches* soil found in higher elevations is derived from solid limestone and produces wines characterized by firmness and pronounced "steely" taste. The wines are round, slow to develop, and come primarily from the upper slopes of Sancerre and Chavignol. The *silex* ("flint") soils, minor outcroppings found throughout the area, produce "hard," mineral-tasting wines used to improve those that are bland and weaker in constitution. The clay soils of low-lying areas produce bland, coarse, early maturing wines.

The best sites are found along southerly or westerly exposures and along any slope protected from the cold, northerly winds. In all instances, the superior vineyards are found on well-drained middle slopes that contain a mixture of the Kimmerdgian chalk of the *terres blanches* and the dry chalk of the *caillotes*. All other soils are unsuitable for the production of quality wine. The best sites are approximately 100 to 350 meters in elevation (low-lying areas are subject to poor drainage and frost). The Chasselas grape is grown in the extreme southern portions of the appellation, where the percentage of clay and sand increases.

Covering an area of 1,600 hectares, the vineyards are unevenly distributed among the following communes: Thauvenay, Veaugues, Verdigny, Vinon, Amigny, Bué, Crézancy, Ménétou-Ratel, Ménétréol, Montigny, Chavignol, St.-Satur, St.-Gemme, Sancerre, Sury-en-Vaux, and Maimbray. The best Sancerre comes from Bué, Chavignol, Amigny, Verdigny, and Sury-en-Vaux. Crézancy, Sancerre, Verdigny, Bué, and Sury-en-Vaux contain more than 1,100 hectares, or more than two-thirds of the appellation's total hectarage. The highest concentration of vines, more than 500 hectares, occurs around the sleepy village of Bué. Of the many vineyard sites, 19 are considered above average in the production of quality wine. The most important in Chavignol are les Monts Damnés, les Bouffants, les Chasseignes, and Cul de Beaujeau; in Amigny, St.-Martin, Beau Regard, l'Epée, and le Grande Côte; in Bué, Chêne Marchand, Chemarin, and la Poussie; in Verdigny, les Montachins, les Cris, and la Côte; in Champtin, Côte de Champtin and Clos du Roy; in Sury-en-Vaux, Denisottes, les Godons, and Demalées.

The harvest begins sometime after the middle of September and continues for the next three to four weeks. Grapes are pressed uncrushed, vinification is quick, and aging occurs in glass or steel containers for a variable period of time. Barrel-aging is very rare, as most producers wish to highlight the fresh and fruity character of the Sauvignon Blanc grape. Historically low at 20 to 25 hectoliters to the hectare, yields have recently doubled and are expected to increase still further. Although there are exceptions, nearly the whole of production is bottled young to preserve freshness and to accentuate the wine's zesty taste.

At its best, the wine is known for its penetrating fragrance and mineral flavor of limestone, has a pleasing "asparagus" taste, and a medium body that is delightfully tart. Excellent Sancerre is always assertive, spirited, and mouth-filling. At its worst, however, it cannot be described as "tender" because it can be thin, "grassy" on the palate, austere, highly acidic and, in poor years, almost unpalatable. Compared with Pouilly-Fumé, it is less elegant, lighter in body, less "flinty," and severely overpriced. Recently, the practice of deacidification has progressed to dangerous levels and is threatening wine quality.

Although the very best can last as long as six years, Sancerre matures earlier than Pouilly-Fumé, rarely develops complexity with age, and oxidizes relatively fast. The wine should be consumed before its second birthday, sometimes the third, but seldom after the fifth. Its clean and crisp taste make it an excellent aperitif and a wise choice with seafood. The *vin ordinaire* of Sancerre, made principally from the Chasselas grape, is marketed as Pouilly-sur-Loire.

Sancerre Rouge and Rosé originate from the less protected and least desirable sites. Once thought to be less than second-class citizens, they now account for one-fifth the annual amount of Sancerre Blanc. Production increased sharply from an insignificant 600 hectoliters in 1959 to 4,100 in 1971, 14,500 in 1979, and to the all-time high of 23,500 in 1982.

Sancerre Rouge is very vinous in taste, not well balanced or fragrant. It is one-dimensional, overrated, and always a poor value—even in Sancerre. The very dry rosé, because of its higher alcohol and extract content, it is one of the better rosés of the Loire. Firms that specialize in the production of Pinot Noir are *Jean Vacheron, Lucien Picard, Lucien Crochet, Dne. Paul Prieur et Fils, Jean Reverdy, Dne. de St.-Pierre, Serge Laloue, Paul Cotat, Marcel Gitton,* and *André Dezat.*

Sixty percent of all Sancerre is made by growers, 18 percent by cooperatives, and the remainder by negociants. It is interesting to note that while thirty years ago less than 50 percent of all Sancerre was bottled, about 90 percent of production was bottled in 1982. For the 1983 vintage, 10 percent of production was sold as bulk, 40 percent was handled wholesale by negociants, and 50 percent was sold directly by growers to retail outlets, restaurants, hotels, and private customers. Approximately 5 percent of production is consumed locally, and 45 percent in Paris and northern France. The remainder is exported to Belgium, Holland, Switzerland, England, and the United States.

Of the four dozen major growers and negociants of Sancerre, the following are considered the most important: *Alphonse Mellot* is regarded as the biggest negociant and the largest estate owner in Sancerre. His *Dne. de la Moussière,* considered a rising star in classy restaurants in and out of France, contains a degree of finesse, is very fruity and well rounded, has a pronounced nose, and can offer considerable value. In the same league, "Grand Chemarin" by *Jean Max Roger* is considered by many as the prototype of fine Sancerre. Another firm with a fine reputation, the house of *Lucien Crochet* is known for stylish Sancerre, particularly "Clos du Chêne Marchand." The equally superb house of *Lucien Picard* is known for outstanding "Clos du Chene Marchand" and "Clos du Roy", both of which are full, flavorful, and satisfying. Another excellent firm whose wines are hard to find but offer good value is *Gitton Père et Fils,* also a large grower (of 16 hectares, all located on steep slopes) with a reputation for consistency and honesty. The house uses multiple labels, each reflecting the individuality of different vineyard sites. "Les Montachins," "Les Romains," and "Belle Dames" are particularly good. The house makes distinctive, full-bodied wines with character and individuality that should not be missed. It also owns vineland in Puilly-Fumé (Clos Joanne D'Orion) and in the Pouilly-sur-Loire appellation. *Paul Cotat,* a good-sized grower, makes full, round, hearty Chavignol under a number of labels, of which the "La Grande Côte" and "Monts Damnes" are outstanding.

Jean Vacheron et Fils is a leading grower (19 hectares) known for highly sophisticated wines that are very expensive but rarely as good as their advanced billing. "Domaine les Romains," "Le Clos des Roches," and "Le Paradis" are all clean, fresh, mouth-filling, and early maturing. *Dne. des Villots,* by *Jean Reverdy,* is a rich-flavored wine, consistently well made and expensive. *Comte de la Perrière, Comte Lafond,* and the wines of *Dne. de la Mercy-Dieu* are all fresh, highly polished, and stylish, but inconsistent and expensive. Although not outstanding, "Clos de la Poussie" by *Cordier* is consistent, refreshing on the palate, and with enough fruit and character to earn it a place high on the list of fine values. The house of *Pierre Archambault,* a good-sized grower and negociant firm, is known for attractively priced white, red, and rosé wines.

Among the many small growers with above-average reputations are *Jean Vatan,* known for acceptable white, red, and rosé; *Lucien Thomas,* for sprightly white and a small amount of red; *André Dezat,* for superlative, full, delicate white; *Domaine du Nozay,* a new estate making stylish, soft wines; *Paul Prieur,* known for unspectacular but smooth, soft wines; *H. Bourgeois et Fils,* for well-balanced wine with few rough edges; *F & P Cotat,* a tiny concern making outstanding wine—hard to find, but well worth the effort; *Philippe de Benoist,* known for well-rounded, sound, full-flavored wines; *Ch. de Maimbray,* for soft and supple wines; *Ch. Sancerre,* for smooth and soft wines, often offering good value; *Michel Girard,* for sound and consistent wines; *Dne. des Garmes,* for supple, often full wines; *Dne. Sarry,* for soft and appealing wines; and *Dne. des Rotins,* for full, firm, yet early maturing wines that are moderately priced. Three others are *Dne. des Trois Pressoirs, Vincent Delaporte,* and *Bernard Ballardet Fils.* The Cave Coopérative des Vins de Sancerre enjoys a good reputation and sells under numerous labels.

Quincy, Reuilly, and Ménétou-Salon

Located west of Sancerre, the three minor AOC wine districts of Quincy, Reuilly, and Ménétou-Salon collectively produce 10 percent of all AOC wine in the upper Loire vineyard from fewer than 950 hectares. Vineyards are located on a plateau along the south bank of the Cher, 70 kilometers from Sancerre.

Of the three, Quincy, east of Reuilly, is the largest, with 550 hectares, and most important in terms of quality and production. Often neglected and scorned by wine writers (it lies in the midst of dull country, with no major road nor tourist attraction), Quincy was nevertheless the second vineyard in France, after Châteaueuf-du-Pape, to be honored with AOC status in 1936. The vineyard, founded by Cistercian monks during the Middle Ages, is clustered around the town of Quincy and the neighboring hamlets of Gravoches, Chavoches, and Cornançay, all of which lie on a minor plateau north of the town.

The producing area is covered with a thick bed of alluvial gravel lying on top of a limestone base that provides the foundation for white wine production. Left behind by an old geologic river, the limestone gravel, in some places about 8 meters thick, provides a perfect medium for excellent root penetration. The best sites, Rimonet, la Victoire, and Crèvecoeur, have a long history and are the only vineyard names to appear on the hard-to-find bottles from Quincy.

The appellation produces white wine only from the Sauvignon Blanc and represents a sound alternative to the high-priced Sancerre and Pouilly-Fumé. While it lacks the fragrance of Sancerre, it is softer, rounder, well balanced, less "steely" and more supple than either Reuilly or Pouilly-Fumé. Its light, refreshing, and flavorful character allows for early consumption, and it is an ideal companion to seafood. Because Quincy is so little known, its value is superior to any other white wine produced in the upper Loire.

The wines of *Pierre Mardon,* the largest grower, are known for their pronounced bouquet, clean taste, brilliant color and, in exceptional years, considerable character. The wines of *Raymond Pipet* are always considered superb and are often the best within the appellation. *Claude Houssier, Marcel Fragnier,* and the house of *Meunier-Lapha* also enjoy a good reputation.

Reuilly is located along the small Arnon River slightly to the west of Quincy. In existence as an AOC appellation since 1937, this old, historically rich, and important region is little known in America, Europe, or even within France. It is mainly centered around the village of Reuilly, despite the fact that the appellation encompasses six additional, widely dispersed hamlets and communes; about half of the 200 hectares is AOC. The soil is excellent for winemaking, as it includes limestone and chalk similar to that found in Chablis.

The finest wine is white and made entirely from the Sauvignon Blanc. It is a robust, full, alcoholic libation similar to Sancerre but with a more pronounced and prominent mineral taste. It is dry, austere yet appealing and, despite the absence of superior soil and exposure, often better than the wine of Sancerre in terms of taste while as durable as that of Pouilly-Fumé. An underrated wine, it almost always sells at half price of average Sancerre. Along with Quincy, it offers excellent value.

Small amounts of *vin gris* are made from Pinot Noir. Very attractive, light in alcohol, fruity and enjoyable, but with limited production, it is found only within the regional confines of the producing area. Minor amounts of red wine are also made, chiefly from Pinot Noir with some inclusion of Pinot Gris, known locally as Beurot. Of the 1,200 hectoliters of wine produced each year, fewer than 300 constitute red and rosé. Among the handful of producers in the appellation, *Robert Cordier, Didier Martin, Claude Lafond,* and *Henri Beurdin* are foremost in quality and consistency of product.

The small white and red wine region of Ménétou-Salon produces approximately 4,000 hectoliters of Savignon Blanc and 3,000 hectoliters of red wine from Pinot Noir. Both wines are good, consistent in quality, and deserve to be better known. The appellation, established in 1959 with fewer than 40 hectares, has grown to 99 in 1983, with expectations that by the end of this century the total will rise to 500. The vineyards are fragmented and widely dispersed over an additional nine communes: Morogues, Soulangis, Humbligny, Aubinges, Parassy, Vignoux-Sous-les-

Aux, St. Céols, Pigny, and Quantilly. The soil, mainly limestone with considerable gravel, is well drained, with the best sites confined to Morogues and Ménétou-Salon.

The white wine is fresh and has a mild, lingering bouquet with an element of depth. It lacks only the steeliness and strength of a better Sancerre or Pouilly-Fumé. The red and rosé, both rare and not readily found even within the producing region, are above average in quality and often a good value. The white wine of repute is made by *Dne. de Chatenoy;* the red and rosé wines of *J. Teiller, Jean-Paul Gilbert,* and *George Chavat* are also above average in quality.

The Wines of Nièvre and Pouilly-Fumé

The department of Nièvre, a widely dispersed vineyard of 1,000 hectares and 2,000 growers, produces about 100,000 hectoliters of wine each year, 25 percent of which is AOC. One hundred years ago, production and hectarage were three times the present level. Because contemporary fashion demands more white than red wine, a good portion of the department will no doubt be replanted in the near future.

White wines, outproducing red by a factor of three to one, are considered vastly superior, especially the wines of Pouilly-Fumé. Robust and hard, Pouilly-Fumé often lacks suppleness; yet it keeps well while acquiring a more consonant character, not as round and balanced as Chablis, but nearly always better than the wines from the neighboring department of Cher. The color is light yellow with a greenish tinge. Larger quantities of Chasselas-based white wine are made, but it is decidedly less good and is mainly consumed as a carafe wine. In addition to Chasselas (the most widespread white grape) and Sauvignon Blanc (the finest in the production of quality wine), Aligoté, Chardonnay, Melon, and Pinot Blanc are cultivated. The dominant red grape is Gamay, followed by Pinot Noir and a host of hybrids. Red wine (from Pinot Noir), made around Pouilly-sur-Loire, is considered the best in the upper Loire (although the producers of Sancerre claim the accolade for themselves). Among the best vineyard sites are Tannay, Cours, Livry, Germigny, Devay, Bona, Tronsanges, and Pougues.

The Pouilly-Fumé wine district lies upriver from Sancerre on a series of hills overlooking the right bank of the Loire. Although the area produces red, rosé, and white wines, its reputation rests on one particular wine—Pouilly-Fumé, which can also be sold as Blanc Fumé de Pouilly or Pouilly-Blanc-Fumé. The name should not be confused with Pouilly-sur-Loire, made from the inferior Chasselas grape, which is consumed locally and rarely encountered outside the region.

Despite the fact that hectarage (715) is half that of Sancerre, vineyards are not contiguous (and hence, the appellation boundaries are much larger) but mainly confined to the hilly terrain of seven communes: St.-

Martin-sur-Nohain, Mesves-sur-Loire, St.-Laurent, Loges, Tracy-sur-Loire, Pouilly-sur-Loire, and St.-Andelain, the last three being considered superior to the others. The soil in the best producing areas, less gravelly than that of Sancerre, contains more marl, chalk, and sand.

The first-class vineyards in Pouilly-sur-Loire are les Chaumiènnes, les Foltières, Lausserie, les Bernadats, les Chênes, les Chaumes, les Cornets, la Prée, and Côtes des Nues. In the hamlet of Loges, located on terraces overlooking the Loire, Champs des Pierres and Champs de Billons produce rugged, masculine wines that are good for laying down. To the east of Pouilly-sur-Loire in the tiny settlement of le Bouchot are les Fouinelles, Corps-Sabots, Champ de la Maison, le Vaurigny, and le Champ du Bas Coin. The superb commune of St.-Andelain and its surroundings contain a number of vineyards with a wide following: le Champ du Clou, les Bois, la Charnoie, la Renardière, Château de Nozet, les Pres, and les Berthièrs. On outstanding exposures, the commune of Tracy-sur-Loire contains some of the finest vineyards, particularly those of Côte des Girarmes, Château de Tracy, Les Froids, and le Champ Billard.

Pouilly-Fumé, like Quincy, Reuilly, and Sancerre, was an enological fossil until the white wine boom of the 1960s revitalized hectarage and production. Although AOC status was conferred in 1937, hectarage declined from 1,100 in 1905 to less than 200 in 1945. Suddenly, demand rose and it became chic to sip "Fumé" in New York and Paris. As a consequence, hectarage and production have tripled within the past twenty years, with expectations that total output will exceed 50,000 hectoliters by the end of the 1980s.

Pouilly-Fumé is solely the product of Sauvignon Blanc. It is an assertive grape, full of pungency, fruit, and acid, and all its natural properties are maximized and its faults minimized in the Pouilly district. The vine is grown in three major areas in France—Graves, Sancerre, and Pouilly—for the production of average to above-average dry white wine, but only in Pouilly does it produce the longest aging, fullest, and most memorable libation. At its best, Pouilly-Fumé is a wine of distinction: spicy, round, complex, and with a hint of "smoke." It is second to Savennières in terms of quality and overall longevity in the entire Loire region. When compared with Sancerre, its more famous neighbor to the west, it has a better acid balance and is more complex, drier in taste, darker in color, more round, and it keeps better. Because it is less famous, it is less likely to subjected to counterfeit operations. Yet comparative tastings indicate vintage fluctuations. The wine can also be heavy, lack delicacy, and be marred by high alcohol levels. In addition, because of limited supplies, good Pouilly is rarely seen in the United States, suffers from a low turnover, and is usually past its prime when purchased.

The largest producer of Pouilly-Fumé is Patrick de Ladoucette, the owner of a 160-hectare medieval estate, *Château du Nozet*. (He also has other vineyards within the appellation, in Sancerre, and in the Touraine).

His reputation rests on the current popularity for fresh and succulent white wines known for balance and fruit. The firm is export-minded and owns a multitude of labels, practically all of which are marketed at the upper end of the price scale. A plain "Fumé" constitutes the firm's regional wine of excellent (but inconsistent) quality. This is followed by the prestigious "Baron de L." label, the most distinctive Pouilly-Fumé made, the product of a superlative cuvée from yielding vines and extraordinary harvests. The middle range, a simple Pouilly-Fumé, is bone dry with sharp flavors that do not always marry well after a year of bottle confinement.

Château de Tracy, the most-celebrated estate within the appellation, is an old-fashioned Pouilly-Fumé—darker than most in color, wood-aged, complex, and full on the palate. Two small hillside properties with outstanding reputations are *Dne. du Buisson-Menard* and *Dne. des Coques,* both of which are widely recognized for full-bodied, generous, and complex wines. Equally good is the outstanding Pouilly-Fumé *Les Berthièrs,* a 5-hectare property known for full, highly flavorful, fragrant, and balanced wines. *Domaine Saint-Michel,* the label of a prominent Burgundian firm, is a lightweight, quaffable wine subject to inconsistency. "Les Bascoins," from the *Domaine Masson-Blondelet,* is modestly priced and of good quality. *Michel Redde,* with 26 hectares, makes full, fresh, assertive and fruity wines, the best bottled is "La Moynerie." *Domaine Guy Saget* is a large, aggressive, 150,000-case negociant house that owns 17 hectares of vineland in Pouilly-Fumé and Sancerre. The firm, historically engaged in the production of table grapes, has grown markedly over the past fifteen years, first bottling its wines in 1970 and now exporting 50 percent of total sales. The house makes excellent Pouilly-Fumé, Sancerre, and Pouilly-sur-Loire. The latter, an extraordinary wine and a specialty of the house, is made from eighty-year-old Chasselas vines from a small plot. "Les Roches," one of the finest Fumés in the apppellation, is a prestige label also made from old vines.

Other producers and negociants with an above-average reputation are *Serge Dequeneau, Monsieur Blanchet, Robert Pabiot et Fils, Robert Penard, Jean Claude Guyat, La Loge Aux Moines, Paul Figeat, Marcel Gitton,* and *Paul Mollet.* The following are also good but more variable: *Aimé Boucher, Marcel Langoux, Robert Pesson, J. Chatelain, Maurice Bailly, Dennis Père et Fils, George Guyot,* and *René Michot.* The Cave Coopérative Pouilly-sur-Loire is responsible for more than one-fifth of regional production and between 10 and 15 percent of AOC Pouilly-Fumé.

The VDQS Wines of the Upper Loire River

The approximately 2,000 hectares of vineyards in the departments of Loire, Puy-de-Dome, and Allier produce more than 100,000 hectoliters of wine annually, half of which is *vin ordinaire.* Of the seven VDQS

appellations involved, five are intimately associated with the Loire River
and the other two with the Cher and the Allier rivers. The greater portion
of the producing regions lies adjacent to the Loire, its headwaters, and
two tributaries west of Burgundy. It includes the vineyards of Forez,
Roannaise, Côtes d'Auvergne, Puy-de-Corent, and St.-Pourcain-sur-
Sioule. Red, rosé, and white wines are made from the usual assortment of
vines. The principal red wine is made primarily from Gamay and
resembles the lesser wines of Burgundy and Beaujolais.

Châteaumeillant, located next to the Cher, is a minor, 3,000-hectoliter
red and *vin gris* wine district. The wines, primarily from Gamay and Pinot
Noir grapes, are light in body, coarse, and known more for their
inconsistency than anything else. Lying along the Loire between Pouilly
and Gien, Coteaux du Giennois, half the size of Châteaumeillant, is much
better in the production of red wine from the same varieties. The quality
center appears to be Gien, where several minor growers have established
local reputations. Other communes include Thou, Beaulieu, Bonny-sur-
Loire, Braire, and Chatillon-sur-Loire. White wines, superior to the red,
are made from a wide assortment of grapes—Sauvignon Blanc, Melon,
Chardonnay, Remorantin, and Auvernant Blanc.

The Vin d'Orléannais vineyard, a tiny 120-hectare site, is similar to
Jasnières and a number of other peripheral vineyards that are diminishing
in importance. It lies in a region with a harsh continental climate,
scattered woodland, wheat farms, windswept hilltops, and extensive
sheep grazing. Soils in the best locations are composed of limestone,
limon, and rich alluvial material. It produces 5,000 hectoliters of red wine
and only minor amounts of white. The former are from Gamay and the
latter from Chardonnay, Sauvignon Blanc, and Romorantin, and both are
undistinguished, common, and overrated. The cities of Orléans, Borges,
and Vierzon are peripheral to the producing areas.

PART II

THE WINES OF BORDEAUX

6

INTRODUCTION

THE wines of Bordeaux are all produced within the confines of the Gironde department, which is the most populous and important within the historic Duchy of Aquitaine.* The Gironde lies to the north of the sparsely populated, pine-studded Landes, west of the Dordogne and Lot-et-Garonne departments, and south of the Charente and Charente Maritime departments. It encompasses the lower margins of the Dordogne and Garonne rivers, in addition to both banks of the 70-kilometer Gironde estuary.

The Gironde, a pleasant region of rounded, verdant hills and shallow productive valleys, is intensely cultivated and supports one of the highest rural populations in France. Of the nearly 1.2 million hectares, about 550,000 are in forests, 200,000 are in pasture, and fewer than 400,000 are cultivated. Of this total less than 25 percent is devoted to the vine, the single most-valuable and important cultivated plant that contributes more than 50 percent of the department's gross agricultural product. Approximately 15 percent of the department's 1.5 million residents are engaged in agricultural endeavors, half of them employed in viticultural pursuits and the rest in the dynamic wine trade.

Of the 49 major wine-producing departments in the country, the Gironde, with 98,000 hectares or 10 percent of the national total, ranks third in size after Hérault and Aude. Wine output varies between 4 and 7 million hectoliters, or approximately 5 to 10 percent of total national output. Yet its modest size by national standards does not readily reveal the fact that the region consistently produces between 20 and 30 percent of all AOC wine in France. In terms of exports, the Gironde is responsible for 9 percent of all white and 17 percent of all red wine. Because of its ability to produce high-quality wine consistently, it is the largest and single most-important quality viticultural area of France, if not the world. Its annual production exceeds that of Algeria, Greece, Austria, Bulgaria, Australia, and New Zealand. Hungary, West Germany, and Chile are basically on the same productivity levels, while only eight countries produce more wine than the Gironde: Argentina, the United

*The name is derived from the Roman *Aquitania*, the "land of waters," a description that appropriately defines an important river system as well as the humid climate.

States, the Soviet Union, Spain, Yugoslavia, Romania, Portugal, and Italy.

The point of convergence of the Gironde wine trade is Bordeaux, the fourth-largest metropolitan city in the nation and the site of a superb natural harbor that serves as the economic nerve center of the Southwest. In terms of employment and wine exports, it is the largest wine city in the world. According to export statistics, not only is wine big business in Bordeaux, it is the only concern of this regional capital that really matters. Of the $2 billion Bordeaux wine trade, nearly 45 percent of the total is earned through exports—a substantial sum. Because of its importance as the locus for quality wine exports, the wines of the Gironde have long been referred to as those of "Bordeaux" and will be referred to here in the same manner. Bordeaux includes all types of white, rosé, and red, but the latter, considered the very finest, generates the largest interest. Over the centuries, but particularly since 1950, Bordeaux has become the Mecca of the wine world. Not only has it set the standard for quality red wine, but its busy quay, negociant offices, and cellars act as a crossroad and magnet for countless wine lovers who arrive to pay homage to this interesting corner of southwest France.

Bordeaux lies on the Garonne 100 kilometers upstream from the northern tip of the Médoc, 600 kilometers southwest of Paris, and 300 kilometers south of Nantes. In Roman times it was known as *Burdigala*, the city on the "water's edge." The population of the central city is slightly more than 250,000 while that of the metropolitan area now exceeds 1 million. It is considered the second-oldest port in France, and its sprawling metropolitan fringes have spread over considerable distances north, west, and south of the original urban boundaries. To the north and south are three of the finest vineyards in the Gironde: the Médoc, Graves, and Sauternes-Barsac.

History

Although human settlement in the Gironde dates back to the Neanderthal period and wild grapes are known to have existed during the early Neolithic era, effective cultivation did not occur until the first century A.D. when the Romans occupied the region. The meager plantings were subject to repeated ravages by Visigoths and by other invaders between the 5th and 8th centuries, including Moorish incursions into southern France. Nevertheless, small increments of viticultural progress continued throughout the Dark Ages. King Clovis subdued the Visigoths in 507 in the battle of Vouille and brought some measure of stability to the region. After a period of new invasions and the defeat of the Moors, nearly all of Aquitaine fell to Charlemagne, who encouraged the establishment of vineyards, especially along the north bank of the Gironde. Vassale de Montviel, coming from Quercy in the 8th century, introduced the Pressac grape to the region and was instrumental in promoting vinegrowing in St.-Emilion.

The gradual founding of religious orders during this medieval period was responsible for the spread of vineyards. By the middle of the 10th century, fourteen religious settlements were firmly established, and by the end of the 12th century they had planted more than seventy vineyards, with the highest concentration in St.-Emilion, Pomerol, the Médoc, and Graves. The most important and aggressive of these orders were the Benedictines, Templars, and Knights of Malta, followed by the Cistercians, Carmelites, Dominicans, Franciscans, and Ursulines. After the 11th century when the powerful counts of Poitiers took control of the area from the Normans and put an end to rival feudal conflict, the region assumed a good measure of tranquility and economic prosperity.

A most significant event in the history of the Gironde and western France took place in 1152 when Eleanor of Aquitaine married Henry Platagenet, bringing nearly half of France as a dowry. In addition to a good portion of the Loire and southwest France, the greatest prize was the Gironde, the jewel of Eleanor's possessions. Henry, as count of Anjou, soon came to control nearly all western France. The Gironde remained English for three centuries until John Talbot was defeated in the battle of Castillon in 1453.

During the reign of the Plantagenets, a lively and considerable wine trade developed with England. Bordeaux embarked upon a wine career when the Gironde was incorporated with England in the 12th century. In earlier times, medieval duty barriers in the interior provinces and poor transportation had curtailed a wine market elsewhere on the continent. Wine merchants were given favorable concessions in the Gironde and particularly in Bordeaux, which eventually led to a royal-near monopoly in the export of wine. A *banlieue,* also known as a *sénéchaussée privilégiée,* was established around Bordeaux (a protected area stretching from the Blanquefort jalle to the city of Martillac in Graves) that gave special rights and privileges to those merchants headquartered there and to no others. Exports were allowed only through Bordeaux and landed duty-free in London and Bristol. No other wine was to be shipped and exported through Bordeaux until the stocks of resident merchants were sold first, thus squelching competition from the "high country" of the Garonne and Dordogne. During this period of English domination, wine exports were second to wool throughout western France *except* in the Gironde, where the English monopoly fostered the creation of a viticultural monoculture, a condition that exists to this day. Wine exports grew rapidly and by 1347, more than 25,000 hectoliters were sold to England and other countries. The wine at this time was light in color and body, early maturing, and called "claret," a name that has endured for 700 years.

During the period of the Hundred Years' War, which ended in 1453, vineyard hectarage, production, and export of wine were severely reduced. But the three centuries of English domination had established a loyal following, and soon after the resolution of military conflict, vine cultivation and wine production picked up, and exports again began to increase. In an effort to encourage the industry, Louis XI extended merchant privileges, a development that attracted a number of Dutch, Belgian, and German merchants.

The 16th century was a period of mixed blessings. Aquitaine was a frequent battlefield during the Wars of Religion, but after the Edict of Nantes granted freedom of worship to the Protestant minority in designated places (of which Bordeaux was one), it enjoyed a brief interval of unprecedented prosperity. When the treaty was revoked in 1685, many Protestants left western France, thereby leaving many provinces depopulated and contributing to economic decline. During this time, a number of Dutch hydrographers arrived and drained a small portion of the Médoc, thus making available for the first time what would eventually become the prime wine-producing region of Bordeaux. For a short period, Holland replaced England as the primary export market.

Although Dutch influence continued well into the 18th century, the future wine-producing regions of the sparsely populated Gironde were isolated, small, and underdeveloped. Containing less than 10,000 hectares of vineland, the Gironde was heavily wooded in the interior but marshy along the coast and river floodplains. The development of the coastal and river marshes of the Médoc, portions of the north bank of the Gironde and Dordogne, the left bank of the Garonne south of Bordeaux, as well as portions of Entre-Deux-Mers had to wait for further Dutch reclamation. Over the course of the next hundred years, the Dutch not only increased arable land along coastal and river courses, but deepened and enlarged the numerous jalles that lace a good portion of the Médoc and Graves. This helped drain the interfluves and created some of the Médoc's most celebrated wine estates. Along with the numerous minor and major *croupes*, these sites have remained the preferred vine areas of the Médoc, Graves, and Sauternes appellations.

The events of the 18th and 19th centuries significantly influenced the city of Bordeaux, its people, and the status of viticulture. Industrialization and urbanization during the middle of the 18th century in England and the Low Countries raised disposable income dramatically, thereby resulting in strong demand for increased wine production and exports. Commercial bottle production and the introduction of the cork led the way to the proper maturation of fine wine—developments that further augmented demand for premium wine. Another important factor to increased consumption was the development of "la grande cuisine," with its elegant ambiance, multiple courses, and elaborate preparations. Two other important 18th-century developments were French overseas colonization efforts and the beginning of a long, sustained emmigration of foreign merchants to Bordeaux. Overseas colonies needed large quantities of wine, particularly red wine, and only Bordeaux had the ability to produce and supply this market cheaply and efficiently through the growth of large negociant houses.

Political events also proved fruitful for the growing wine industry. While the French Revolution, and the subsequent French-English military and political conflict in the first decade of the 19th century, temporarily gave the wine industry a pause, Bordeaux and the Gironde prospered enormously after the restoration of Louis XVIII. A good portion of Bordeaux proper was restored and expanded, stately mansions began to line broad boulevards, and wealthy bankers bought vine estates in the Médoc, Graves, and Sauternes. While the landed gentry had accumulated large estates in the previous century, after the defeat of Napoleon at Waterloo, the rise of the industrialist and the middle class set the stage for the present pattern of large-scale wine production. Part of the genre of time was to own vineland; in short order the area planted to vines increased from less than 40,000 hectares in 1725, to 135,000 in 1788, to 188,000 in 1873, the highest figure ever recorded. The industry was further encouraged by the construction of the Bordeaux–Paris railroad. In 1860 William Gladstone lowered the duty on French wine imports to England, and within two years exports tripled. It is easy to see why the period between 1845 and 1880 is commonly referred to as the "golden years of Bordeaux."

The effects of *oidium* and *phylloxera* on hectarage and production since 1850 are shown in Figure 6.2.* While the effects of *oidium* were short

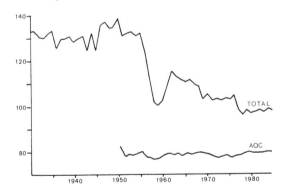

Figure 6.1   Gironde: Vine Hectarage, 1930–1985
(in thousands of hectares)
Note the sharp decline in hectarage after the 1956 frost.

*Also known as powdery or true mildew, *oidium* is a serious fungus disease indigenous to the United States that was introduced to Europe in the middle of the 19th century. By 1855, it reduced wine production in France by more than 20 percent. *Phylloxera*, a burrowing vine louse indigenous to the United States, was introduced in France in the 1860s and destroyed more than 1 million hectares of *vinifera* vines during the period 1868 to 1885.

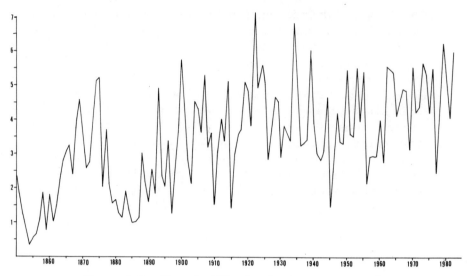

Figure 6.2   Gironde: Wine Production, 1850–1984
Note the decline in production due to *oidium* (1850s), the effect of *phylloxera* in
the 1870s and 1880s, the effects of overproduction in the first two decades of this
century, World War II, and the frost of 1956 (in millions of hectoliters).

lived, wine output declined by more than 75 percent within a five year
period; thirty years later, *phylloxera* caused production to decline from
more than 5 million hectoliters to 1 million. Except for periodic bouts of
frost, wine production, thanks to improved viticultural techniques, has
recovered and maintained output between 4 to 7 million hectoliters ever
since. It is interesting that in 1873, vineland, with 188,576 hectares, was
second in area to pineland, followed by 168,000 additional hectares of
arable land and 90,000 hectares of pastureland. Vine hectarage during the
1880–1955 period fluctuated between 148,000 and 117,000 hectares;
since the disastrous *gelée noir* (or "black frost") of 1956, it has declined to
less than 99,000, the lowest figure in the past 200 years. As a result,
vineland as percentage of total arable land within the Gironde has
declined from 34 percent in 1929 to less than 23 percent in 1985, and it
is expected to continue downward. The areas of major decline have been
in the marginal non-AOC regions, and in Bourg, Blaye, Entre-Deux-
Mers, Coutras, Guitras, and portions of the Landes.

The first half of the 20th century provided negative impacts. Overproduction of French wine in the first decade, two world wars, a major world
economic depression, American prohibition legislation, and a series of
autarkic economic policies with high import duties in central and
northern Europe acted to circumscribe the market for high-quality
Bordeaux. Beer and spirits, not wine, were the primary alcoholic prefer-
ences in the United Kingdom, the United States, and most other central
and north European countries. Furthermore, the industry was plagued by

a number of fradulent bottling scandals that aggravated and prolonged existing market conditions. Bordeaux in 1945 was in a dismal state: prices were low, vineyards were neglected, and bottles, corks, and equipment were scarce.

Since 1960, a number of internal and external forces have raised the consumers' awareness of Bordeaux wines. One of the most important factors was the escalating rise in the price of Burgundy while its quality was allowed to deteriorate. At the same time, the quality of Bordeaux improved steadily, and its price increased at much lower rates than that of Burgundy. The new wine consumer of the 1960s also found Bordeaux easier to understand, buy, and store. Other factors contributing to the popularity of Bordeaux in the past twenty-five years are increased disposable incomes, a general world wine boom, and the ascendency of West Germany, the United States, and Japan as principal markets for quality wine. As a consequence, exports as percent of total sales have increased from 5 percent in 1947 to 28 percent in 1984, and the percent of AOC wines for the same time period has tripled from 12 to 37 percent.

Over the past twenty-five years, total exports increased from 323,000 hectoliters to more than 1.6 million in 1984. Most of this extraordinary growth has occurred during the past fifteen years despite a number of scandalous revelations of fraudulent practices by prominent shippers in 1973. The controversy concerned the alleged sale of AOC wine under "false papers" by one of the most revered and hitherto impeccable negociant houses. It led to arrests, convictions, and a celebrated suicide. Since then, the industry has regrouped, restructured, and corrected its abuses. At no time in the history of Bordeaux has there been a more impressive series of above-average vintages, firm prices, and ever-expanding exports as in the past twenty years.

The foregoing is not difficult to understand. As the planted area declined from 132,000 hectares in 1955 to 96,000 hectares in 1980, the number of growers declined—from 56,000 to 24,000. As a consequence, land consolidation has accelerated and AOC hectarage has remained stable despite the overall reduction of marginal vine-bearing land. Equally important has been the use of viticultural and vinification technologies to improve the quality of both red and white wine production. The Gironde has become the leading area in the use of mechanical harvesters, which now pick more than 70 percent of the grapes in Entre-Deux-mers and the Médoc. They are 60 percent cheaper than hand pickers and can pick at optimal grape ripeness at night and in a much shorter time. Even on large estates the entire crop can be harvested within days, rather than weeks.

Climate and Soils

The Gironde is located on the Bay of Biscay along the same latitude as the middle Rhône vineyard. Situated too far poleward to be dominated by the dry influence of the subtropical oceanic high-pressure cells, it lacks southern France's summer dry months. Even more significant, a severe dry-cold winter condition is extremely rare, because the prevailing westerly maritime winds move west to east across the region. The average monthly temperature varies between 11°C. and 21°C. in the warm months, and between 4.7°C. and 8.7°C. in the coldest months. The cool air temperatures reduce evaporation and promote cloud cover. The Gironde therefore enjoys a moist, temperate climate year-round, mild in winter and warm in summer, without the harsh continental extremes of the upper Loire and Burgundy. Only 100 kilometers away, to the east of the Massif Central, the moist atmosphere is replaced by cold winters and hot, dry summers.

Annual precipitation, which averages 814 millimeters, is well distributed throughout the year but shows a distinct reduction during the summer months. The maximum occurs during the months September–December, and often interferes with the harvest during the two critical months of September and October. Heavier-than-normal autumnal precipitation also brings above-average morning fog that often lingers into the early afternoon. Meterological and vintage records demonstrate the singular fact that vintage quality rarely coincides with a late vintage. A late spring, which retards the flowering period, almost always means a late harvest to produce sufficient sugar levels. If warm and sunny weather lasts through the middle of November, the vintage, despite a cold and wet spring, can usually be saved, but this is a rare event. In addition to late-season precipitation, frost in low-lying areas and in frost pockets in the plateau on the north bank of the Gironde can be a major problem. As a result of weather fluctuations, vintages three years in ten will be above average in quality, one exceptional, four below average, and two poor. These weather fluctuations are clearly reflected in the Bordeaux vintage chart as well as in the output of wine production throughout the Gironde.

When compared with other vine-growing areas, Bordeaux is much warmer than Tours, Dijon, Mâcon, Chablis, Reims, and Colmar, and slightly cooler than Montpellier and Orange. Bordeaux has more days with temperatures above 10°C. than any vineyard north of Avignon, and has less rainfall during April–September than Orange, Dijon, Mâcon, and Chablis. In relation to its latitude, however, Bordeaux attains fewer hours of sunshine from April to September and fewer degree days than most other vineyards (see Fig. 6.3).

While climatic patterns are rather uniform throughout the Gironde, vineyards everywhere depend on the incidence of well-drained soils. They are not found on sandy or alluvial bottomland rich in organic material, but are restricted to a narrow belt in the eastern portion of the Médoc, Entre-Deux-Mers, below Bordeaux along the left bank of the Garonne, and along the protected south-facing hilly slopes on the north bank of the Gironde and Dordogne. The somewhat flat plateau north of St.-Emilion

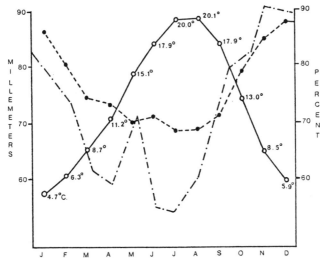

Figure 6.3   Bordeaux: Monthly Rainfall, Temperature, and Relative
Humidity
(As the temperature begins to drop in August, precipitation and humidity rise,
thus interfering with the harvest)

and Pomerol is wind-swept and subject to frost; along the eastern section
of the department, the soils are too fertile for quality wine production;
and along the west, the sandy soils of the Landes support a huge, man-
made pine forest that produces 25 percent of the nation's pulp and timber,
but no vineyards of any consequence.

Land planted in vines within the Gironde region is divided into five
major categories.

1. *Palus,* alluvial material in low-lying valleys next to rivers and along
the Gironde estuary, is an amalgam of gravel, sand, silt, clay, and organic
matter. In general, *palus* is very fertile but is poorly drained due to a high
water table. As a result, wines produced from grapes grown in *palus* (less
than 4 percent of the total land area of the Gironde) are considered second
rate and lack sufficient alcohol, delicacy, balance, and flavor. After the
outbreak of *phylloxera,* the *palus* soils of the Gironde were heavily planted
due to their resistance to aphid infestation, but today they mainly produce
large quantities of less-expensive wine, without AOC status.

2. Gravel and sand soils, discontinuous in location, are excessively
drained (and thus dry out during droughts) and are good for vines only
when the subsoil contains a clay layer.

3. Sand and clay soils comprise approximately 50 percent of the
Gironde, with the largest single concentration in the Entre-Deux-Mers
region. Elevated land with a mixture of clay and limestone in the subsoil
is well suited for vine cultivation. When clay dominates, drainage is
reduced and the resulting wines are coarse and unappealing. Only
marginally better are very compact, sandy subsoils that promote disease

and produce wines with the marked taste of "earth." In general, a loosely bound sandy surface and subsoil, while permitting excellent root penetration, produces wine that lacks color, body, and suppleness.

4. Hillsides comprise approximately 18 percent of the total land area of the Gironde. The best sites contain limestone and stony soils, are well drained and produce wines with considerable depth of flavor and aging potential. The finest vineyards lie along an irregular belt between Blaye and Côtes de Castillon along the north bank of the Gironde and Dordogne and, to a lesser extent, the Premières Côtes de Bordeaux appellation in the western portion of Entre-Deux-Mers. These areas are above average in the production of wine, and nearly all of it is red.

5. Gravel soil, particularly that found in the Médoc, Graves, and Sauternes regions, comprises nearly 10 percent of the total land area of the Gironde and is exceptionally good in the production of quality wine. The very best sites are well drained and contain an iron-oxide-bearing subsoil that gives the wine an outstanding color and bouquet. The gravel varies widely in its physical composition, depth, and relationship to subsurface material. The depth of gravel (up to a meter in thickness) and the size of the actual rock fragments is greater in the Médoc and Graves regions on little hillocks called *croupes*. While all gravel sites are above-average wine-producing regions, the incidence of clay, limestone, and iron in the subsoil determines the color, flavor, and other important constituents of fine Bordeaux.

Grape Varieties

Table 6.1 indicates the principal grape varieties planted in the Gironde by hectare and as percent of departmental and national total for the two latest agricultural censuses. It is interesting to note that during the intercensal period, the red : white ratio has changed from 52 percent white : 48 percent red, to 35 percent white : 65 percent red. It also indicates a sharp reduction of hybrid plantings from approximately 8 percent to slightly more than 1 percent.

Merlot Noir leads the list with 49 percent of total red grape plantings, followed by Cabernet Sauvignon, Cabernet Franc, and Malbec. Among white grape varieties, the leading vine (with nearly 49 percent of total plantings) is Sémillon, followed by Ugni Blanc and Colombard. Very surprising is the fact that Sauvignon Blanc and Muscadelle each account for 7 percent of total white grapes planted. The Gironde is also the principal area of concentration (95 percent of rational total) for two obscure grape varieties—Petit Verdot and Merlot Blanc. Slightly less, but still impressive are Merlot Noir (83.3% of national total), Cabernet Sauvignon (75.1%), Sémillon (71.4%), Muscadelle (65%), Colombard (62%), and Sauvignon Blanc (34.3%).

Table 6.1 Major Grape Varieties Planted in the Department of Gironde, 1968 and 1979

Grape varieties	1968 Hectares	Percent	1979 Hectares	Percent	Percent of national total, 1979
Merlot Noir	22,200	19.6	31,900	32.3	83.3
Cabernet Sauvignon	10,800	9.2	17,200	17.4	75.1
Sémillon	22,900	19.6	16,700	16.9	71.4
Cabernet Franc	9,400	8.0	9,800	10.0	43.4
Ugni Blanc	8,700	7.4	6,400	6.5	
Colombard	7,700	6.6	3,600	3.6	62.0
Sauvignon Blanc	5,100	4.4	2,400	2.4	34.3
Muscadelle	3,600	3.1	2,400	65.0	
Malbec (Cot)	4,900	4.2	2,100	2.1	44.0
Merlot Blanc	3,400	2.9	1,800	1.8	95.0
Bouchalès	1,700	1.5	400	.4	
Petit Verdot	250	.2	400	.4	90.0
Villard Noir	2,200	1.9	300	.3	
Villard Blanc	1,400	1.2	100	.1	
Others	12,550	10.8	3,399	3.4	
Total	116,800	100.0	98,899	100.0	

Source: French Ministry of Agriculture.

The Merlot Noir, a delicate vine whose grapes are difficult to pick, is very sensitive to frost and cold weather. Today, more than 35 percent of the vine hectarage of the Gironde is devoted to this vigorous and consistent producer. Merlot matures before and yields more than Cabernet Sauvignon, is moderately resistant to disease, but is extremely sensitive to *coulure* (the dropping of flowers and berries during the early stages of growth) and rot and is affected adversely by cold and humid growing conditions. It is absolutely outstanding in good vintages, producing wine that is comparatively high in alcohol, rounder, and much softer than Cabernet Sauvignon. While 83 percent of all Merlot plantings in France are found in the Gironde, their distribution varies considerably within the department, with the highest concentration in Pomerol, St.-Emilion, Fronsac, Bourg, and the Premières Côtes de Bordeaux appellations. Over the past fifteen years, Merlot has become the most important variety in a number of properties in the northern Médoc and is increasing its hectarage share in all other communes as far south as Graves.

Cabernet Sauvignon (historically called Vidure Savignonne), the second most widely planted red grape in the Gironde, remains the dominant vine in the production of classic Médoc and red Graves. It is a thick-skinned, small, firm, deeply colored grape that produces tannic, astringent, aggressive wine that is harsh, austere, and strapping when young. The wine softens with time, and subtle nuances in bouquet and flavor develop into one of the longest-lived and most-memorable red wines available anywhere. Cabernet Sauvignon, over the past twenty-five years, has doubled its hectarage share of red grape plantings from less than 8 percent in 1968 to 17 percent in 1979, and is projected to increase to perhaps as much as 19 percent by 1990. Although it has declined along the north bank of the Gironde, Dordogne, and Entre-Deux-Mers, it remains strong in the Médoc and Graves regions where it dominates hectarage in the finest classified properties. As a percentage of total vines planted, it varies dramatically from property to property, from high levels in such well-regarded estates as *Ch. Mouton Rothschild* and *Ch. Pédesclaux,* to low percentages in *Ch. Coufran* and *Ch. Marquis-de-Terme.*

Cabernet Sauvignon is very hardy, resists rot and *couloure* well, and is capable of withstanding summer and fall rain as well as heavy downpours of hail—unlike the more fragile Merlot. With Petit Verdot, it is the last grape to be picked and responds poorly to weather extremes. High temperatures obliterate its varietal character and produce wine that is unbalanced and coarse, while cold, moist, and cloudy conditions prevent full berry maturation and produce green, thin, astringent wine. But in years of climatic perfection, the wine is second to none, and because it ages slowly, it is judiciously blended with other varieties to soften and broaden its intrinsic qualities. At its best, it is a true *vin de garde* wine known for its intense flavor, aroma, bouquet, and *sève.*

Cabernet Franc, a less hardy but more prolific vine than Cabernet Sauvignon, is the third most important producer, and is second to the Merlot in Pomerol and St.-Emilion, its two main areas of concentration. Although it has an excellent nose, its poor color, less-intense flavor, and reduced body and tannin content place it in a marginal position to its bigger, and far superior, Cabernet cousin in the Médoc. Despite its often dull, flat taste, it blends well with Merlot, and due to its high-yielding character, hectarage has increased from fewer than 9,000 hectares in 1960 to 10,100 in 1986. Approximately 43 percent of all national plantings are concentrated in the Gironde.

Malbec, also known as Cot Rouge, Pressac, and St.-Emilion (especially along the north bank of the Gironde and Dordogne), is a low-alcohol, low-acid grape that is the first to ripen in the Gironde (followed by Merlot, Cabernet Franc, and Cabernet Sauvignon). Vinified alone, it produces an ordinary quaffing wine with little character; but when blended with Cabernet Sauvignon, Merlot, and Cabernet Franc, it imparts softness and roundness. Malbec's concentration in the Gironde is 44 percent of national plantings. But because the grape is subject to the same diseases and yields less than Merlot, it has declined from 4.2 percent of total Gironde plantings in 1968 to less than 2 percent in 1985. Its main attraction, other than its ability to blend well with more acidic grapes, is its ability to produce fruit from shoots on old wood when normal shoots are frost-damaged. If the trend continues, as many in the Gironde think it will, the Cahors region in the department of Lot will become the single largest area of Malbec vines in the country.

Historically more important, Petit Verdot (also known as Petit Vidure) is an extraordinary grape contributing far more than its small percentage first suggests. It needs a long hot summer to produce wine that is dark in color, alcoholic, and tannin-rich. Because it imparts firmness, longevity, and structure when properly blended, it has long been considered an essential ingredient in the production of true *vin de garde* wine. Vintages characterized by a long, moderately hot growing season produce wine that is deep and rich in color, with a superb aroma, bouquet, and flavors that are absolutely outstanding in the production of "classic" Bordeaux. But because aging is no longer an important quality to the contemporary market, the percentage of Petit Verdot is steadily decreasing, and fewer than 10 percent of all growers cultivate it along the south bank of the Gironde. Another reason for its demise is that the finest clone is extremely delicate and subject to disease, hence difficult and expensive to grow. As a consequence, only the largest and most prestigious properties in the production of old-fashioned *vin de garde* wine maintain hectarage at levels above 5 percent of total plantings.

The last of the important red grape varieties is Carmenère, an obscure, low-yielding, temperamental vine (but otherwise excellent grape) that makes luscious wine. Fewer than 100 hectares exist, planted only by row, and only on those estates that can withstand the cost of production. Because it has excellent color, a full, rich, flavorful character, and aging potential, it is a fair substitute for Cabernet Sauvignon.

Among white grapes, Sémillion is the most distinguished vine for the production of sweet and semi-sweet white wine. It is a very vigorous, high-yielding grape that is subject to *botrytis* and yields luscious, well-flavored, glycerine-rich, sweet wine. Its historical importance has declined since the post–World War II switch to drier, fresher, early maturing white wine.

Sauvignon Blanc, the most important variety in the production of quality dry white wine, is very aromatic and pungent, with high acid levels. Although yields are much lower than all other white grape varieties, the wine is of medium body, well flavored, fruity, and currently very much in vogue. Muscadelle, historically more prominent in the production of sweet wine, is now declining rapidly as demand for sweet wine has diminished. Although it has a pronounced taste and is well scented, it ages rapidly. Colombard and Ugni Blanc collectively account for 10 percent of total vine hectarage in the Gironde. As non-premium grape varieties, they are the workhorses of the generic Bordeaux white wine trade. They are concentrated mainly in Blaye, Bourg, and Entre-Deux-Mers.

The Wines of Bordeaux

Bordeaux, the largest producer of AOC wine in France, is a region of 57 major appellations whose 1980 wine production by color is shown in Table 6.2. Table 6.3 shows wine production by appellation. In terms of volume, the most important wines are the large number of generic Bordeaux appellations whose combined total exceed 70 percent and 50 percent of total and AOC wine production, respectively. In short, Bordeaux produces a veritable sea of inferior and mediocre red and white wine, more than half of which is made in Entre-Deux-Mers, the single largest vineyard in the Gironde department.

Bordeaux is known for three basic types of wine: common to superlative dry red; common to superlative sweet white, and common to average dry white. In the first two categories, Bordeaux's best equals or exceeds the finest wines of any other region in the world. The finest dry white wines, however, rarely equal those from the Loire, Chablis, and the Côte d'Or. Red Bordeaux varies from the most common generic form to sterling-quality estate-produced wine—the former representing everyday drinking wine, and the latter expressing the most exciting viticultural and enological practices. This wine, approximately 10 percent of departmental output, is the basis for Bordeaux's international fame. The approximately 500,000 hectoliters represent between 4 and 5 million cases produced annually.

Dry white production in the Gironde has benefited the most from viticultural and vinification improvements. In the past, the problem of

Table 6.2   Bordeaux AOC and Non-AOC Wine Production by Color, 1980

Variety	Hectoliters	Percent of total
AOC Red	2,050,000	56.0
Vin de Table, Red	190,000	5.0
AOC White	870,000	24.0
Vin de Table, White	550,000	15.0
Total production	3,660,000	100.0

Source: French Ministry of Agriculture.

gray rot led to an oxidized condition requiring the heavy use of sulfur. Today, controlled and low-temperature fermentation has yielded intensely flavored and scented wines. With a minimum or no wood-aging, the wines are fresher, light-bodied, and significantly crisper than in the past. The Gironde, with an annual production of nearly 2 million hectoliters, is the nation's single-largest producer of still white AOC wine. White Bordeaux represents between one-quarter to one-third of all AOC wine production by volume, or about 20 percent by value. When non-AOC white production is added to this figure, the total represents 40 percent of departmental wine output, with approximately 55 percent of all growers making some white wine. Production of sweet white wines has fallen below pre–World War I levels, because demand for all other than from the handful of excellent producers has been declining.

The style of red wine has also changed in recent years. Prior to the 18th century, red Bordeaux, made from a wide variety of red and white grapes, was pale red in color, light-bodied, early maturing, and notoriously unstable. In the 19th century, the wine was made darker, fuller, and spent at least 24 months in wood before bottling. The post-1950 trend is to destem the grapes, reduce the time of maceration, ferment in stainless steel, and limit barrel-aging to 12 months. The resulting wine is fruitier, less astringent, early maturing, and very appealing to contemporary tastes. More important, most of the antiquated vineyard, vinification, and distribution practices have disappeared. Winemaking is no longer considered an art, but a science: guesswork and intuition are replaced by chemical analysis, and the vintage, no matter how dismal, cannot resemble the failures of 1965 and 1968. Needless to say, more good wine is available now than ever before.

The wines of the Gironde are divided into four specific geographic categories: departmental (Bordeaux or Bordeaux Superieur), district (Premières Côtes de Blaye), communal (Margaux), and single-vineyard (*Ch. Petrus*). In general, the grape yield is lower and the quality of the wine higher as the geographic unit gets smaller. The various types and their characteristics are as follows:

1. Wines without the AOC label are likely to be below average in quality. Served in local cafés and third-rate restaurants, they form the basis for everyday fare throughout the region. They are harsh, coarse, and lack individuality, and are consumed immediately after fermentation.

2. With approximately 55 percent of total output, Bordeaux and Bordeaux Superieur (collectively described as "generic Bordeaux") are the two largest AOC appellations. When compared with communal and classified properties, these two appellations are "grassy" in flavor, acidic, less concentrated, highly variable, and coarse on the palate. The basis of negociant jug wine, nearly all lacks color intensity, depth of flavor, and bouquet. Yet by historic standards, it is much improved, and over the past fifteen years, quality differences have narrowed to the point that they

are now virtually indistinguishable. The Superieur designation, considered the better wine, contains half a percent more alcohol and is the product of a slightly lower yield than plain Bordeaux. Red wine, usually acidic and thin, rarely will improve in the bottle past its first year. Generic white is generally more variable in quality, flavor, and style.

Table 6.3   Bordeaux Wine Production, by AOC Appellation, 1980

Appellation	Hectoliters	Percent
TOTAL GIRONDE	2,894,518	100.0
Bordeaux Rouge	692,969	23.9
Bordeaux Rouge, Côtes de Castillon	475	
Bordeaux Rouge, Côtes de Francs	6,469	
Bordeaux Blanc	528,491	18.2
Bordeaux Blanc Côtes de France	556	
Bordeaux Supérieur Rouge	284,168	9.8
Bordeaux Supérieur Côtes de Castillon Rouge	75,686	2.6
Bordeaux Supérieur Blanc	11,586	
Bordeaux Clairet Rouge	2,572	
Bordeaux Rosé	4,626	
Bordeaux Supérieur Rosé	55	
Bordeaux Mousseux Rouge		
Bordeaux Mousseux Blanc		
Blaye Rouge	111	
Blaye Blanc	12,124	
Premières Côtes de Blaye Rouge	68,292	2.3
Premières Côtes de Blaye Blanc	282	
Bourg or Côtes de Bourg Rouge	86,721	3.0
Bourg or Côtes de Bourg Blanc	5,960	
Entre-Deux-Mers Blanc	102,049	3.5
Côtes de Bordeaux St.-Macaire Blanc	4,049	
Graves de Vayres Rouge	5,452	
Graves de Vayres Blanc	12,796	
Premières Côtes de Bordeaux Rouge	41,723	1.4
Première Côtes de Bordeaux Blanc	33,605	1.2
Ste-Foy-Bordeaux Rouge	2,136	
Ste-Foy-Bordeaux Blanc	4,044	
Médoc Rouge	95,106	3.3
Haut-Médoc Rouge	94,323	3.3
Listrac Rouge	15,298	.5
Margaux Rouge	34,512	1.2
Moulis Rouge	11,322	
Pauillac Rouge	32,733	1.1
St.-Estèphe Rouge	40,904	.8
Total Médoc	347,788	12.0

3. Bordeaux Clairet, a light (almost rosé)-colored wine, is the product of a short vinification process. Meant to be consumed young, it rarely improves in the bottle and offers little value.

4. Bordeaux Nouveau, despite the name, is not at all similar to Beaujolais. Although fruity and capable of bottle improvement for six

Table 6.3 *Continued*

Appellation	Hectoliters	Percent
St.-Emilion	187,070	6.5
Lussac-St. Emilion Rouge	32,847	1.1
Montagne-St. Emilion Rouge	43,632	1.5
Parsac-St. Emilion Rouge		
Puisseguin-St. Emilion Rouge	22,519	.8
St.-Georges—St. Emilion Rouge	5,724	
Sables-St. Emilion Rouge		
Total St.-Emilion	291,792	10.1
Graves Rouge	62,098	2.1
Graves Blanc	22,551	.9
Graves Supérieurs Blanc	21,714	.8
Total Graves	109,363	3.8
Pomerol Rouge	23,283	.8
Lalande de Pomerol Rouge	24,249	.8
Néac Rouge (sold as Lalande de Pomerol)		
Total Pomerol	47,532	1.6
Barsac Blanc	13,739	.5
Sauternes Blanc	26,899	.9
Cérons Blanc	7,407	
Total Sauternes and Cérons	48,045	1.7
Canon-Fronsac Rouge	10,951	
Fronsac Rouge	25,833	.9
Total Fronsac	36,784	1.3
Cadillac Blanc	2,551	
Loupiac Blanc	9,739	
St.-Croix du Mont Blanc	13,927	
Total Rive Droite	26,217	.9

Source: French Ministry of Agriculture.

months, overall quality is below that of other similar wines and rarely offers value.

5. Bordeaux Rosé, like Clairet and Nouveau, contains less than 11 percent alcohol, and while fresh on the palate, it does not compete well with similar wines from other areas.

Suggestions for Buying Bordeaux

Purchasing a bottle of Bordeaux for an occasion requires time for deliberation in addition to a reasonable amount of acquired knowledge. The following salient features are a guide to rational consumer selection.

1. *Know the name of the property and its specific location.* For example, approximately 72 properties in 54 communes have names beginning with "Vieux," 100 begin with "Tour," 80 with "Saint," 25 with "Petit," 162 with "Haut," 82 with "Grand," 61 with "Croix," 7 with "Lamothe," 6 with "Lagrange," and 5 with "Plaisance." Furthermore, each of the 12 properties named *Ch. Bellevue* is found in as many appellations. It is quite possible for even a knowledgeable oenophile to confuse one bottle with another.

Since 10 percent of all property names in the Gironde are hyphenated, the similarities in spelling add to the confusion. There are, for example, *Ch. Laffitte-Carcasset-Padirac, Ch. Lafite-Rothschild, Ch. Laffitte, Ch. Laffitte-Canteloup,* and a *Ch. Lafitte-Laguens,* as well as seeming random use of Clos, Domaine, and Château, as in *Clos Lacoste* and *Domaine de Lacoste,* or *Ch. Lafleur* and *Domaine de Lafleur.* The nearly three dozen Bel-Airs are preceded by *Château, Clos, Cru, Château de,* and *Domaine.* It is also easy to confuse a Bordeaux property with another of the same name elsewhere in France as in the case of the *Moulin-à-Vent* appellation in Beaujolais and *Château Moulin-à-Vent* in Néac.

Finally, the consumer should be aware of the important distinctions between blended regional or communal wine and that of a single vineyard. "Chevalier de Lascombes" is a blended wine, but *Ch. Lascombes* is not; "Mouton Cadet" is not the equivalent of *Ch. Mouton-Rothschild.*

2. *Be aware of comparative value.* A blended Médoc, St.-Emilion, Pomerol, etc., selling at the same price as an estate-bottled Cahors, Chinon, Bourgueil, or a good Médoc Bourgeois growth, is invariably a poor buy.

3. *Know vintages and significant variations from commune to commune.* The nature of the vintage determines the character or style of the wine, its quantity, and price. The trade and vignerons classify vintages as *Les Grandes Années* (the most expensive), *Les Années Moyennes* (less expensive), and *Les Petites Années* (below-average quality years, the cheapest). The cost of producing all three is essentially the same, but the price between a "Grande" and a "Moyenne" vintage may vary by a factor of 10 or more. Those with a limited budget are advised to buy Bourgeois growths of *Les*

Grandes Années and classified growths of *Les Années Moyennes* and *Les Petites Années* vintages. There are always buying opportunities and undervalued stocks. At the time of writing, vintages from the 1970s offer superb values, especially those from 1976, 1977, 1978, and 1979.

4. *Avoid the top growths* (perhaps 100 properties at most). They are immensely expensive and offer the poorest return: their asking price rarely reflects their quality and value.

5. *Build a wine collection on a good assortment of Bordeaux* (particularly Médoc, Graves, Pomerol, and St.-Emilion wines). The knowledgable wine collector always has a small cache of liquid funds to draw upon when an attractive buying opportunity arises. There are more sales in the course of one year than is widely believed, particularly in California, New York, and Washington, D.C.

6. *Purchase half-bottles whenever possible* to taste critically with food; then buy larger amounts in various sizes, by the case.

7. *Be aware of current events in the world of wine.* Bordeaux wine is a commodity and its price fluctuates directly with the nature of the vintage, available stocks, the size of the previous two vintages, overseas demand, competition from California, Italy, Australia, etc., the strength of the American dollar, and French domestic politics. For the "serious" investor/ collector (e.g., cellars valued at $5,000 or more) "keeping up" with current happenings in the world of wine is absolutely imperative.

8. *Be aware of "second labels."* Second labels on wines from higher-quality properties in the Médoc imply a lower-quality, less-expensive wine made from a higher percentage of *vin de presse,* younger vines, infected fruit, or lower-quality cuvées (see Table 6.4). In the past, this wine was marketed in bulk to negociants to be sold as regional wine. A number of Bordeaux estates also sell wines to different importers under various names for purposes of exclusivity. The "second label" movement, like chateau-bottling, is a rather recent development: as the size of properties has grown during the past thirty years, so has the amount of wine that is not worthy of the primary label. Growers have come to realize that they can charge higher prices for the second label than if it were sold under the less-expensive communal or regional appellation names. Second labels can also be confusing and misleading. In many instances, the wine shown on the second label is not from the same vineyard. For instance, the second label of a prominent St.-Estèphe growth is not necessarily from the same property, but is from a neighboring estate that does not enjoy the same classification as the primary label. Invariably, second labels are good business for château owners but not for the consumer.

9. *Store fine Bordeaux properly* to protect it as it ages. Particularly if the vintage warrants ten or more years of aging time, it is imperative that the wine be stored at a uniform temperature in a moderately humid, dark place free of vibration (from a furnace or washing machine, for instance) and odor. For optimum or near-optimum aging potentials for fine

Table 6.4   Selected Bordeaux Second Labels

Property	Second label
Ch. d'Angludet	Bory
Ch. Brane-Cantenac	Notton, Dne. de Fontarney
Ch. Cap-de-Mourlin	La Rose Faurie, Mayne-d'Artugon
Ch. la Cardonne	Romefort
Ch. Cissac	De Martigny
Ch. Côte-Baleau	Des Roches Blanches
Ch. Coufran	Les Gravilles de Ch. Coufran
Ch. Cos d'Estournel	De Marbuzet
Ch. Couvent des Jacobins	Beau-Mayne
Ch. Ducru-Beaucaillou	Clos la Croix
Ch. Duhart-Milon-Rothschild	Moulin de Duhart
Ch. Duplessis-Hauchecorne	La Morène
Ch. Durfort-Vivens	Dne. de Curé Bourse
Ch. Gloria	Peymartin, Dne. de la Croix, Haut-Beychevelle-Gloria
Ch. Grand-Mayne	Beau-Mazerat, Cassevert
Ch. Grand-Puy-Ducasse	Artigues-Arnaud
Ch. Grand-Puy-Lacoste	Lacoste-Borie
Ch. Gruaud-Larose	Sarget de Gruaud-Larose
Ch. Hanteillan	Larrivaux-Hanteillan
Ch. Haut-Brion	Bahans-Haut-Brion
Ch. Lafite-Rothschild	Moulin des Carruades
Ch. la Lagune	Ludon-Pommies-Agassac
Ch. Lanessan	Comaine du Ste.-Gemme
Ch. Larmande	Des Templiers
Ch. Lascombes	La Gombaude
Ch. Latour	Les Forts de Latour
Ch. Léoville-las-Cases	Clos du Marquis
Ch. Léoville-Poyferré	Moulin-Riche
Ch. Lynch-Bages	Haut-Bages-Avérous
Ch. Margaux	Pavillon Rouge
Ch. Marquis-de-Terme	Les Gondats
Ch. Montrose	Demereaulemont
Ch. de Pez	La Salle de Pez
Ch. Pichon-Longueville-Comtese-de-Lalande	Réserve-de-la-Comtesse
Ch. Pontet-Canet	Les Hauts de Pontet
Ch. Potensac	La Salle
Ch. Prieuré-Lichine	Clairefont
Ch. Poujeaux	La Salle de Poujeaux
Ch. Siran	Bellegarde
Ch. Talbot	Connétable Talbot
Ch. Tertre-Daugay	Moulin du Biguey
Ch. la Tour-de-By	La Roque-de-By
Ch. la Tour-Carnet	Sire de Camin
Ch. Villemaurine	Maurinus, Beausoleil

Bordeaux, store *Les Petites Années* for one to five years, *Les Années Moyennees* for five to ten years, and *Les Grandes Années* for fifteen to twenty years.

10. *Consider the Bordeaux price escalation.* Bordeaux prices over the past twenty years, especially for classified growths, have increased much faster than the American Consumer Price Index. It is time to consider the merits of a $50 bottle of wine with a $10 steak.

11. *Beware of "expert opinion."* Often, so-called "experts" own vineyards or are otherwise employed by the industry. Wine writers are often entertained by wine syndicates, and large property owners. How objective the written words are when the expert's airplane ticket and week's vacation are paid by the evaluated property is anyone's guess.

12. *Be aware of discounts.* Bordeaux wine is a commodity and its price is subject to negociation. Because retail mark-ups can be greater than 100 percent and are subject to seasonal fluctuations (more than 50 percent of all classified growth sales occur during November and December), the consumer is in a comparatively strong position to "mark down" the price of case lots during February, March, and April. Generally, the more expensive the wine, the larger the discount.

13. *The uninitiated should be wary of "futures" buying,* in which the consumer pays for the wine about six months after the vintage and takes delivery three years later. The practice began on a large scale after the 1973 Bordeaux scandal weakened the power and influence of a number of Bordeaux negociants, a situation compounded by rising interest rates. The large growers of the Médoc began to offer *tranches* (literally "slices" of their current vintage) to negociants in Bordeaux and to foreign importers and specialty retailers, which came to be known in the United States as "futures buying." After the arrival of the wine three years after the vintage, prices are usually higher than the "opening" futures offering. The consumer who buys "futures" is thus betting on the availability of his favorite growth and its appreciation in value, and is cheating prevailing interest rates.

Exports

Bordeaux has had a long tradition as an article of commerce to the United Kingdom, Holland, Belgium, and portions of Scandinavia. While it was a major export item during the Plantagenet reign, exports fluctuated widely with the political and economic circumstances of the times. Exports climbed steadily after the defeat of Napoleon, and by the eve of the *phylloxera* epidemic in the middle of the 1870s, they had reached a peak of nearly 1.6 million hectoliters. Soon after, a combination of political, social, and economic forces reduced overseas demand, and exports declined steadily over the next five decades to fewer than 200,000 hectoliters during the 1930s. If the period just prior to *phylloxera* can be described as Bordeaux's "golden years," the period after 1950 can be termed the "resurrection." Over the past thirty-five years, between one-

Table 6.5 BORDEAUX VINTAGE CHART

1985 Promises to be an above-average vintage. Hot and dry summer—small grapes with thick skins and no rot. Wines are tannin-rich, well concentrated, with excellent color.

1984 Uneven flowering and late rain—a variable vintage: best in Graves,
10–16* average in the Médoc, below average north of the Gironde-Dordogne. A Cabernet year that turned out better than expected; harvest at least 40 percent below 1982–83 levels. Above-average acid and tannin levels assure longevity at the expense of elegance; white wines much better than red.

1983 Classic, tannin-rich vintage that will take time to mature fully. Hot
13–18 and humid July and August produced rot. Wines leaner, firmer, less fruity, and longer lived than those of 1982.

1982 Second-largest vintage on record, the product of a prolonged
14–20 drought and high temperatures. Well-colored red wines with low acid levels and exceptionally high alcohol levels; vintage favored the Merlot grape. Vintage produced (a) average, low-acid wines, supple and early maturing; and (b) tannin-rich, higher-acid wines that will mature after A.D. 2000. Generally high overall quality, with wines rich in extract, spicy, fat, savory, well structured. Perhaps the best red Graves since 1961.

1981 Vintage characterized by hot, dry August, followed by heavy rain
12–15 and rot—a variable harvest. The very best, in northern Médoc, will mature after 10 years, the rest before 1990. Wine soft, accessible, lacking depth and, in some cases, color.

1980 Late spring and fall rains, small harvest; thin, early maturing, low
4–9 tannin and extract wines. The very best are from the Médoc and attractively priced; a few are quite supple in character.

1979 Huge harvest, the product of a wet spring, good but chilly growing
12–16 conditions, hot September, rainy October. Highly variable vintage, but outstanding in St.-Julien, Pauillac, Pomerol, and St.-Emilion. The best are well colored, flavored and scented; the middle lack concentration and will mature early.

1978 With 1970 and 1975, the top three vintages of the decade. Wretched
13–18 spring and summer, perfect September and October produced successes, particularly in the Médoc and Graves. Very best will continue into the 1990s. Wines have an elegant nose, excellent color, are relatively foreward, but may lose ripe fruit flavor early.

Table 6.5 *Continued*

1977
3–7
Late flowering, wet summer, and several frosts – small and late harvest of poor, thin, acidic wines with few redeeming features. Quality highly variable, with wines of Graves and Médoc the best, and north of the Gironde and Dordogne less successful.

1976
11–16
Above-average year: hot spring, dry June–August, wet and cold September, above-normal harvest the earliest since 1945. Wines span the entire spectrum – from thin and poorly concentrated to substantial and well structured. More successful vintage in the Médoc and Graves than north of the Gironde and Dordogne.

1975
15–20
Cool spring and warm/dry summer produced a small harvest of classic, Cabernet-type wine – deeply colored, tannin-rich, astringent, requiring at least 10 years for Bourgeois quality to mature. In almost all regions, wines loaded with extract, scent, and color; quality lately downgraded by some writers and experts. Will mature in the mid-1990s.

1974
3–9
Dry summer and rainy September – large harvest of diluted, often-unbalanced, early maturing wines that are better than the dismal '73s. Before the late '70s many properties, particularly in the Médoc and Graves, showed fruitiness and charm; almost all are now astringent and drying out.

1973
4–10
Large, highly variable harvest produced fruity, early drinking wines that required careful selection. Overall rating higher than 1974, but bulk of wines of poorer quality.

1972
1–3
Late spring, cold/wet August and September – worst vintage since 1968. In general, wines thin, astringent, lacking in fruit and suppleness.

1971
12–16
Uneven growing condition from spring through fall produced above-average wine in Graves, variable north of Gironde and Dordogne, less than good wine in Médoc. Nearly all had matured by 1985, but the very best Graves and Médoc continue to improve.

1970
15–20
One of the best vintages and largest harvests in 50 years. Above-average quality from nearly all producing districts. Vintage well colored, full in body and extract, concentrated, well flavored and scented. Very best is still maturing.

*In ratings following year, 20 = best, 0 = worst.

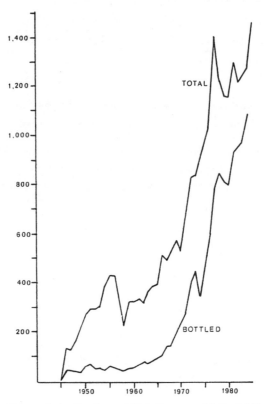

Figure 6.4   Bordeaux Wine Exports, 1945–1985
(in thousands of hectoliters)

third and one-half of total production has been subject to export. For the country as a whole, red Bordeaux exports represent 17 percent of all red wine exported and 33 percent of total export value. On the other hand, the export of white Bordeaux accounts for just 9 percent and 8 percent of total volume and value, respectively.

Figure 6.4 shows the evolution of Bordeaux wine exports since 1945. The dramatic acceleration is directly attributable to higher disposable incomes in western Europe and Anglo-America, increased tourist traffic into the producing region, and the spectacular rise of the American, West German, Swiss, Japanese, Hong Kong, and "specialty" markets, such as overseas resorts. Equally important is the fact that while Bordeaux wine prices are at historically high levels, their rise has been more moderate than that of Burgundian wines.

Since 1950, the principal foreign markets have been Belgium, Holland, West Germany, the United Kingdom, Canada, and Denmark. The neighboring countries of Belgium, Holland, West Germany, and Switzerland account for 45 percent of total exports, the United Kingdom for 12 percent, and the United States and Canada for 25 percent. It is interesting that despite the international fame of the Gironde as the Mecca of the fine red wine, the above-mentioned countries consistently represent approximately 85 percent of all imports. The United States wine-importing profile for the year 1982 shows a number of interesting features: 44 percent of all imports consisted of dry white; 25 percent, red generic Bordeaux; 17 percent, red Médoc and Graves; 8.8 percent, red wine from the north banks of the Dordogne and Gironde; and sweet white wine, only 3.4 percent of total imports. While all of the above-named wines change substantially from year to year, the following are long-established national patterns: Switzerland specializes in the importation of Médoc and Graves, Holland imports large quantities of white Bordeaux, and Belgium imports large quantities of Pomerol and St.-Emilion (see Table 6.6). Due to a strong dollar and insatiable demand, the United States during the period 1983–86 became the largest market for Bordeaux in terms of volume, value, and the percent of total-bottle sales.

In 1982, of the nearly 1.2 million hectoliters of Bordeaux wine exported, 759,000 hectoliters, or 64 percent of the total, was red. Leading the list by appellation was generic Bordeaux, followed by Bordeaux Supérieur (see Table 6.7). The premier-quality–oriented communal and district appellations collectively accounted for 25 percent of total exports. The export of white wine is mainly generic Bordeaux, followed by Entre-Deux-Mers. Among quality-oriented districts and communes, the combined total of Graves and Graves Supérieurs amounts to only 12 percent, and the sweet wines of Sauternes, Barsac, and Cerons account for less than 4 percent of total white wine exports. While generic Bordeaux dominates the volume of red and white wine exports, it is important to note that the prestigious communal appellations export much larger percentages of their production. For 1982, among red wine production communes, Pauillac exported 17 percent of its production, Margaux 66 percent, St.-Julien 61 percent, and Pomerol 50 percent.

Table 6.6 Bordeaux Exports, 1982

Country	Percent of volume	Percent of value	Country	Percent of volume	Percent of value
Belgium	18.2	18.0	Denmark	6.3	5.3
Holland	15.8	11.1	Canada	5.9	4.9
United States	15.1	20.6	Others	16.5	18.9
United Kingdom	12.7	12.4			
West Germany	9.5	8.8	Total exports	100.0	100.0

Source: Conseil Interprofessionnel du Vin de Bordeaux.

Table 6.7   Export of Red Bordeaux by Appellation, 1982

Appellation	Hectoliters	Percent	Appellation	Hectoliters	Percent
Bordeaux	302,222	39.8	Graves	18,780	2.5
Bordeaux Supérieur	83,312	11.0	Pauillac	17,644	2.3
St.-Emilion	67,637	8.9	Premières Côtes	17,324	2.3
Médoc	48,996	6.5	de Blaye		
Haut-Médoc	36,039	4.7	Others	139,873	18.4
Côtes de Bourg	27,257	3.6	Total exports	759,084	100.0

Source: Conseil Interprofessionnel du Vin de Bordeaux.

Among white wine communes and districts, Graves exported more than 70 percent of production, Graves de Vayres 57 percent, and Sauternes 53 percent.

The Châteaux of Bordeaux

The average property size of all Bordeaux vineyards, at the time of the 1979 viticultural census was 3.5 hectares—twice the size of 100 years ago, but still small by American standards. Averages, however, do not give a complete picture. While the average property that bottles, ages, and exports wine is about 15 hectares, sixteen large property owners, with nearly 3,000 hectares of vineland, own about 3.5 percent of the total vine hectarage of the Gironde. Two hundred additional proprietors, whose holdings vary between 20 and 50 hectares, own 8 percent of total vine hectarage in the department. If all family hectarage holdings are included, then approximately 20 percent of the hectarage is owned by less than 2 percent of all proprietors—and perhaps more. In Burgundy the vineyards are divided into small parcels, often as small as one row of vines, and each one is owned by a different individual. The Gironde, long a bastion of Protestantism and rigid customs adhering to primogeniture, is thus an area of relatively large productive units belonging to one owner. The average size of vineyards has been increasing throughout the last eighty years and is expected to continue to do so as long as the price of vineland is less than the economies of scale realized through capital inputs. Some of the largest property owners are: Société Louis Eschenauer, Domaine Cordier, Société de France, Société Mestrezat-Preller, André Lurton, La Société de Gaston des Domaines Baron de Rothschild, Vignobles Rocher-Cap-de-Rive, Vignobles Aubert, Lucien Lurton, Jean Faure, A. Moueix & Fils, Vignobles Jean Milhade, Baron-Mouton-Rothschild, Jean Medeville, Vignobles Bayle-Carreau, and Vignobles Rollet. The illusion of large size is created by constant reference to "château," a concept limited to the small number of large classified growths in the Médoc, Graves, and Sauternes appellations. In the Gironde, the word "château" does not refer to a castle or fortification, but to an entire estate consisting of a main house, vineland, woodland, productive facilities, workers' houses and, according to Hugh Johnson, to "microclimate and philosophy" as well. It definitely implies large size, a touch of class, and above-average-quality wine production. The growth of large estates began late in the 17th century and accelerated after the fall of Napoleon. The tradition began in Graves, gradually infiltrated the Médoc, where it exhibits the highest density, and is found only in scattered areas along the north bank of the Dordogne and the Gironde estuary. Its significant physical dimensions have had important implications. Large size allows more-efficient distribution of resources and provides the necessary incentives to maintain and, often, to improve and sustain high-quality standards. In the classic châteaux of the Gironde, the wine is not only made and stored, but the label, which is for all intents and purposes a trademark, is a guarantee of authenticity, despite the fact that wine quality varies enormously by location, size, and local winemaking traditions. Of the 4,000 "châteaux" or "domaines" with more than 10 hectares of vineland, the *crème de la crème* numbers about 200.

Legally, "château" is a highly restrictive term that refers to the existence of a real vineyard that is entitled to AOC status. One of the most significant aspects of its nomenclature is "château bottling." While a few châteaux grew grapes, vinified, aged, and bottled wine on their premises in the 19th century, the large-scale practice known as "château bottling" is a recent phenomenon. In the 1920s Baron Philippe de Rothschild began to perform all operations at his property, in the process bypassing negociants and thereby reducing the possibility of fraudulent practices. Château bottling became standard practice only after the mid-1950s and is considered a guarantee of quality. The term "mis en bouteille par l'acheteur" (bottled by the purchaser) was used until 1980 to distinguish between those firms bottling purchased wine and those claiming to be authentic "château."

The expression "petit château" refers to any producing unit that is not classified and lacks a well-established international reputation. It can be a stately country mansion with 200 hectares under vines or a fragmented 2-hectare vineyard. Their number exceeds 3,000, and because they are marginal to the more celebrated growths in terms of location and familiarity, they offer, when the buyer selects carefully, exceptional value, especially in good vintage years.

The Bordeaux Negociant

The Bordeaux negociant (from the Latin *negotiari* "to transact business," itself derived from "nec otium," lack of leisure), a veritable institution over the course of the past three centuries, was a powerful clique of wine merchants who dominated the entire Gironde wine industry by developing domestic and foreign markets, blending and bottling wine for specific markets and aging and bottling "château" wines of all ranks. The negotiant was a landowner, wholesaler, distributer, public relations officer, and banker. Ever since the Plantagenet kings offered privileges to merchants engaged in foreign trade with southwestern France, foreign merchants have been permanent members of the Bordeaux commercial community. The foreign dependency on the export of Bordeaux wine has produced an abnormally large number of non-French negociants historically known as "dynastie du bouchon," of which Cordier and Eschenauer (Alsace), Barton (England), Kressmann (Germany), Schröder & Schyler (Germany and Holland), Mahler-Besse (Holland), Alexis Lichine (United States), Johnston (England), and Cruse (Denmark) were among the largest and most important.

Negociants began to proliferate late in the 17th century in response to sustained overseas demand for Bordeaux wine in the Low Countries, England and northern Europe. A large number of merchants who had settled in Bordeaux, the principal French port in the 18th century, to engage in coffee, sugar, spice, and indigo trading, gave up their principal business to concentrate on wine. First acting as middlemen between vignerons and retailers, they formed a minor element in the commercial life of Bordeaux. Because they were foreigners and Protestants, they were ostracized within Bordeaux city limits and lived north of the city in the "faubourg of Chartrons," a densely built-up area that became the center of the vast storage and underground wine cellars known as the "Quai de Chartrons." They prospered, purchased vineyards, intermarried; their descendants continued to assemble and export wine. They became powerful under Louis XVIII and, by the second half of the 19th century, virtually dominated the social, economic, and political life of the Gironde. Collectively they monopolized more than 85 percent of all foreign sales emanating from the Gironde, and nearly all wine from the various departments of the Southwest.

Over the past two centuries, about two dozen large houses have dominated the market through skillful and sophisticated business tactics. They would buy *sur souche* (a portion of the entire crop prior to harvesting) or *en primeur* (a portion of the crop after the wine was made). Negociants also acted as exclusive agents in the distribution for small growers who lacked the means to properly age, filter, and bottle their own wine. They assembled wines originating in different appellations as "blends" which, in the final analysis, were more complete wines and definitely more marketable. These "generic" blended wines in time represented more than three-quarters of the total wine handled (commonly called "shippers wines"). A related development was the negociant's uncanny ability to develop particular blends for specific markets. He perfected the art of blending to give one overseas market light wines in terms of color, tannin, and alcohol content, while offering a different wine under the same label in a neighboring country.

Over the past fifty years the power and influence of the large negociant houses have diminished appreciably for a variety of reasons. The first, and most important, is the ascendency of cooperatives during and after the 1933–45 period. Due to governmental subsidies, cooperatives today perform less expensively the same functions as negociants once did, and they distribute at least a third of all wine historically handled by negociants. Second, because they were family-owned and warped with nepotism, succeeding generations of negociants have lacked the energy and commitment to pursue what is a very demanding business. Third, the Bordeaux scandal in 1973 and the demise of the houses of Cruse and Ginestet (two of the oldest and most venerable of the "old guard" negociant houses) and others over the next several years did much to undermine the power and influence of the "big houses". Fourth, the increase of chateau bottling in the late 1950s replaced one of the negotiants functions. Today the trade is mainly in bottle, and while a good deal of Bordeaux and Bordeaux Supérieur is handled in bulk, cooperatives dominate this segment of the industry. Fifth, direct sales now account for at least one-third of total annual turnover, which leaves less wine in negociant hands. At least half of all direct sales are to tourists, followed by private clients who represent restaurants, hotels, etc., and foreign wholesalers who import direct. Finally, the growth of the "futures" market (primarily after the 1975 vintage in the U.S. and U.K.) has reduced the quantity of wine normally handled by negociants.

Despite the diminished negociant influence over the past fifty years, they still handle collectively, more than 60 million cases annually, or about 40 percent of total Bordeaux production, and provide employment to more than 10,000 people. The negociants themselves number about 190, down from 600 in 1950. Some of the largest have "retrenched" by selling part of their business and vineyards, others have merged, and in nearly all cases, the quality of the final product has been improved by the introduction of the latest technology. Finally, foreign or domestic multinational corporations have take over a substantial portions of the negociant business. Barton and Gustier, for example was taken over by Seagrams, Delor is now part of Allied Brewers, Eschenauer is part of Holt, Alexis Lichine belongs to Bass Charrington, and de Luze is part of Remy Martin. The following negociant houses handle more than 50 percent of all exports, *Établissment Cordier, Castel Frères, Société Mestrezat-Preller, Société Distribution Vins Fins, Jean-Pierre Moueix, Consortium Vinicole de Bordeaux et de Gironde, Louis Eschenauer, Schröder & Schyler, Borie-Manoux, Maison Ginestet, Alexis Lichine, Yvon Mau, Mahler-Besse, La Baronnie, D. Milhade & Fils, W & A Gilbey, Calvet & Cie, Cruse & Cie, de Luze & Cie, Dubos Frères, Nathaniel Johnston, Maison Sichel, Barton & Gustier, Dourthe Frères, Les Fils de Marcel Quancard, Vintex S. A., De Rivoyre & Diprovin, Michel Querre, Lebeque & Cie,* and *Établissement Menjucq.*

7

THE WINES OF THE NORTH BANK OF THE GIRONDE-DORDOGNE

THE WINES OF BLAYE AND BOURG

CONTAINING 8 percent of total hectarage, Bourg and Blaye are two of the largest vineyards in the Gironde (see Fig. 7.1). The region is hilly, very windy, and agriculturally far more productive than the areas along the south bank of the Gironde. The Plantagenet kings used the area as the center of their defensive strategy for several centuries. Bourg was once the summer residence of archbishops, and it is one of the oldest wine-producing regions in the Gironde. A century ago hectarage was more extensive, and wine output was triple present levels. In this century, it has been an ignored viticultural region and is considered by many to be third rate.

Today the area is primarily a red wine region. The fruity, soft, early maturing, and very appealing red wines (which are 90 percent of total production) are, due to high yields, lighter in color and body than those from the more famous neighboring appellations to the east and south. The tendency at present is to make wine in the "nouveau" manner by reducing skin contact to impart suppleness and to heighten fruitiness. The red and white wines of Bourg are on a higher plane than those of Blaye: they keep better, have an older and finer reputation, and appear to be making a formidable comeback.

With rising demand and improved prices, interest in the two regions has increased since 1960. Increases in the average size of the producing unit and investments in plant and equipment have improved the quality of the wines in both regions, thus reducing the percentage of "generic" Bordeaux produced. The wines, once considered the "poor man's Bordeaux," are now assuming a "serious" position in the Bordeaux hierarchy. Approximately one-third of total AOC output is exported to Great Britain, Holland, Belgium, and Scandinavian countries.

For marketing purposes, the all-encompassing "Les Côtes de Bordeaux" is now the semi-official name for the wines of Côtes de Castillon, Côtes de Bourg, Côtes de Blaye, Côtes de Franc, and Premières Côtes de Bordeaux. Despite the fact that all five areas lie mainly on hilly terrain, are red wine regions, and plant the same family of vines, their wines are not all that

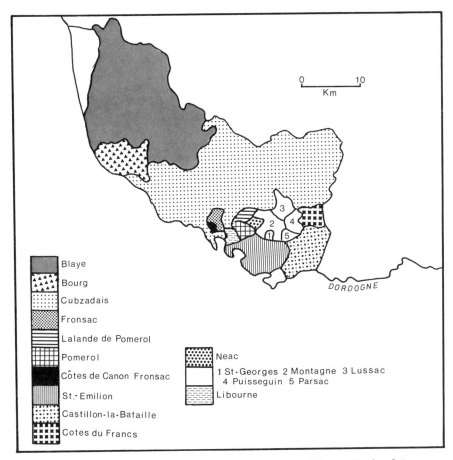

Figure 7.1   AOC Wine Appellations along the North Bank of the
Dordogne and Gironde

similar in character. While considerably better than Bordeaux Supérieur,
they lack, for the most part, the elegance, finesse, and consistency of
Médoc, St.-Emilion, Pomerol, and Graves wines. With few exceptions,
the properties, commonly called "petit château," are small family affairs
with little pretence of grandeur. Nevertheless, the syndicat's efforts to
improve exports have been successful.

The Wines of Blaye

The principal red grape varieties are Cabernet Franc, Cabernet
Sauvignon, Malbec, Merlot Rouge, Bouchalès, and Petit Verdot. Wine
containing a minimum of 10.5 percent alcohol and made entirely from
Cabernet Sauvignon, Cabernet Franc, Merlot Rouge, and Malbec is better
than plain Blaye or Blayais and assumes the Premières Côtes de Blaye

appellation name. The distinctions between the appellations are obscured by the fact that the actual encépagement varies dramatically throughout the region. The best sites are restricted to the well-drained hillsides north of Blaye, which are very similar to those of Bourg. For both appellations the yield is limited to 50 hectoliters to the hectare.

The main distinctions between the three white appellations are subtle, but important. For the Blaye or Blayais Blanc appellation, the wine is made from Sémillon, Sauvignon Blanc, Muscadelle, Merlot Blanc, Folle Blanche, Colombard, Chenin Blanc, and Ugni Blanc. Minimum alcohol content is 10 percent, and the yield is restricted to 45 hectoliters to the hectare. For the Côte de Blaye appellation, the alcohol content is raised by half a degree, the yield is reduced to 42 hectoliters, and the grape varieties are confined to Sémillon, Sauvignon Blanc, Muscadelle, Merlot Blanc, Folle Blanche, Colombard, and Chenin Blanc. For the Premières Côtes de Blaye appellation, the requirements are identical to the previous except that the encépagement is limited to only three grape varieties—Sémillon, Sauvignon Blanc, and Muscadelle. All the above is very confusing to the consumer in view of the fact that some of the finest white wine is made entirely from Sauvignon Blanc and carries the Blaye appellation name. The two principal villages for the production of white wine are St.-Vivien, and St.-Ciers.

The Premières Côtes de Blaye appellation is reserved for the "pick" of the very best vineyards. The wine is not as full nor as aromatic as the best from Bourg, but good, nevertheless, as quality has recently shown dramatic improvement. Cooperatives account for more than 60 percent of production. Of the nearly 400 properties that produce respectable wine, the following, listed by commune, are considered average to above-average in quality.

With its 4,000 residents, the city of Blaye is located in a valley surrounded by a plateau. It contains 70 hectares of average-quality vineland and approximately one dozen growers of which the following are the most important: *Ch. le Cône-Taillasson-de-Lagarcie, Ch. les Moines, Ch. la Grange, Ch. Loumède,* and *Ch. La Tonnelle.*

In the extreme southern appellation margins, the small village of Berson, with 785 hectares of vines, is the largest individual vineyard in Blaye. While the best sites contain limestone, the majority of the planted area rests on sand accumulations. Of the more than seventy growers, the following are the most important: *Dne. de Florimond-la-Brède;** *Ch. Peyredoulle; Ch. Bourdieu; Ch. Loumède;* and *Ch. le Chay.* Located north of Berson and east of Blaye, Cars, with 707 hectares of vineland, is the second most important village in the appellation and the site of several above average growths: *Ch. Crusquet-Sabourin, Ch. Sociondo, Ch. Crusquet-de-Lagarcie, Ch. Barbé, Ch. Clairac, Ch. Peybonhomme, Ch. les Videaux, Ch.*

---

*As in the rest of this book, the listings in each geographical area are by quality of the wine and/or historical importance of the producer.

Mayne-Boyer-Chaumet, Ch. l'Escarde, Ch. Pardaillan, Ch. des Petits-Ar-nauds, Ch. Magdeleine-Bouhou, Ch. Peymelon, and *Ch. Chante-Alouette-la-Roseraie.*

Lying north of Cars on the Bourg road, St.-Paul is known for one above-average growth: *Ch. la Rivalerie.* In the neighboring hamlet of Mazion, *Ch. la Bretonnière* enjoys a good reputation for full-bodied, substantial red wine. Just south of Blaye the small village of Plassac contains nearly 300 hectares of vineland located mostly on fertile plateau soil. Among the forty growers, the following enjoy a good reputation: *Ch. Bellevue-Gazin, Ch. Bellevue, Ch. Ricaud, Ch. Monconseil,* and *Dne. du Grand-Barrail.* The importance of the small village of St.-Martin-Lacaus-sade is reflected in its name, Lacaussade, which was derived from the Latin name for limestone. Although it contains 153 hectares of vineland, and twenty-two growers, the quality of wine made is impressive. The following six growths are particularly good: *Ch. Lacaussade-St.-Martin, Ch. Cap-St.-Martin, Ch. Labrousse, Ch. Charron, Ch. Mazerolles,* and *Ch. Peyreyre.*

Lying immediately north of Blaye, the small village of St.-Genès-de-Blaye has about twenty-five growers, and one excellent property with a good average reputation: *Ch. Pérenne.* The small village of St.-Androny contains 200 hectares of vineland and three properties with established reputations: *Ch. la Tour-Gayet, Ch. la Menaudat,* and *Ch. Lamanceau.* Located east of Eyrans, the hamlet of Fours contains 160 hectares and thirty-six growers, of which five enjoy a good reputation: *Ch. Haut-*

Plate 7.1   Ch. la Rivière, Fronsac

Canteloup, Ch. les Chaumes, Ch. la Girouette, Dne. du Chay, Ch. Bel-Air.
The small hamlet of Campugnan, with eighteen growers and 175
hectares, contains two growths with outstanding reputations for full-
bodied, fleshy, *vin de garde* wines: *Ch. Morillon* and *Ch. la Botte.*

The Wines of Bourg

Separated from Blaye by the small stream of Brouillon, Bourg takes its
name from Bourg-sur-Gironde, the principal port and village of the
region. It is an area of three distinct topographic features: a thin sliver of
coastal alluvial soil; a gently undulating plateau in the interior; and
overlooking the Gironde, a series of deep valleys and steep hills high
enough to enable the local Chamber of Commerce to label Bourg the
"Switzerland of the Gironde." The series of hills ("côtes") that parallel the
estuary are very verdant, productive, and the site of the best appellation
growths. The narrow belt of alluvial material, while good for pasture, is
less than marginal for the production of quality wine. The low-lying areas
within the plateau are somewhat better, while the better drained, upper
sections of the numerous knolls approach the quality character of the
"côtes."

Throughout, the area is essentially underlain by limestone mixed with
clay, sand, and gravel. The soils, much richer in natural fertility than the
gravelly areas of the Médoc and Graves, support a much denser, mixed
agricultural population, particularly in the production of potatoes. In
addition, the entire region is honeycombed by caves supporting a thriving
mushroom industry.

As in the rest of the appellations along the northern bank of the
Dordogne and Gironde, Merlot dominates the encépagement, followed by
Cabernet Franc, Cabernet Sauvignon, Malbec, and Petit Verdot, the
latter virtually extinct. Between 90 and 95 percent of the wines are red
and characterized by a beautiful color, clean and penetrating bouquet,
fruity flavor, and with an ability to age well. At their best, they tend to be
fuller and bigger than most from the Médoc; however, they lack the
elegance, finesse, refinement, and multilayered scents of their more-
illustrious neighbor along the south bank of the Gironde. If the large and
influential estates can resist the temptation to produce nouveau-type
wine, Bourg will certainly become more popular in the future, as its
wines offer excellent value and consistency.

While Bourg has a number of appellations, the Bourg and Côte de
Bourg designations are widely considered the finest in the region,
especially in the production of red wine. Minimum alcohol for both is
10.5 percent, and the yield is limited to 50 hectoliters to the hectare, a
figure that is exceeded routinely. White wines, made primarily from
Sémillon, Sauvignon Blanc, Muscadelle, Merlot Blanc, and Colombard,
are produced along the northern and eastern portions of the producing

region. Their minimum alcoholic percentage and yield are identical to the red. The wines, although dry and fresh on the palate, are not the equal of the red and have declined dramatically within the past fifty years. They are marketed as Bordeaux Blanc, Bordeaux Blanc Sec, and Bordeaux Supérieur Blanc. To assist the consumer in selecting the finer wines of the region, the Syndicat Vinicole des Côtes de Bourg has introduced a "Certificat d'Aptitude au Vieillissement" for those wines capable of aging, or which have been tested for soundness and palatability by an official commission. Selected bottles are numbered and have a special capsule identifying their special quality status.

About 900 growers (more than half are part-time farmers) cultivate nearly 3,900 hectares of vineland. Properties are small and, as a result, the five cooperatives (Tauriac, Gauriac, Pugnac, Bourg, and Lansac) produce more than 60 percent of the total output. The largest, located east of Bourg in Tauriac, boasts the largest wood-aging cellars in the Gironde. This innovative cooperative makes use of the Portuguese autovinification, or "rapid extraction" method, in which color and tannin extraction time is reduced by as much as 75 percent.

Of the fifteen main producing communes, those of Bourg, Tauriac, Bayon, Gauriac, and Villeneuve enjoy the finest reputations and produce about 40 percent of the appellation's total output.

Bourg-sur-Gironde, the main center for the appellation, is the largest settlement, with 2,300 residents and 550 hectares of vineland. It is an ancient, fortified town whose best vineyards lie on hilly terrain composed of gravel and limestone soils. The commune contains about seventy producing units, of which the following are the most important: *Ch. du Bousquet* is a 62-hectare estate making about 35,000 cases of red wine a year. One of the few highly mechanized estates equipped with temperature-controlled, stainless steel fermentation tanks, it currently is making superb-quality wine characterized by smoothness and flavor. *Ch. Lalibarde* is a 10,000-case estate marvelously located on the edge of a bluff overlooking the Gironde. The wine is well made, hard to find, but well worth the effort. *Ch. de la Grave,* a 40-hectare property, is part of a medieval walled property. The entire producing area is located on sloping ground, and the wines, very popular in the United States and England, are dark, full-bodied, consistently good, and age well. *Ch. de Lidonne,* an 18-hectare property, is currently making excellent well-balanced, fruity and flavored wine. *Ch. Moulin d'Eyquem,* located on a bluff overlooking the Gironde, makes firm, robust wine from a high percentage of Cabernet Sauvignon. *Ch. la Nègre, Ch. le Clos du Notaire,* and *Ch. Caruel* produce expertly made, well-balanced, and flavorful wine offering outstanding value. *Ch. Croûte-Courpon* is an 11-hectare estate in the process of replanting and expansion. Its grand 19th-century mansion sits magnificently on an old Roman settlement, and the wine is expertly made. *Ch. Camponac* an estate of less than 20 hectares, enjoys a good reputation for supple, well-structured, long-lived wines. *Ch. de la Plantonne* is a small 7-hectare estate with a reputation for soft, supple, consistently well-made wine. *Ch. de la Clotte-Blanche,* a small estate of 8 hectares, is known for dark, tannin-rich, somewhat robust wines. Other properties include *Ch. Lagrange, Tour Camillac, Ch. du Marquisat,* and *Ch. Haut-Gazin.*

Located east of Bourg overlooking the Cubzadais, the small town of Tauriac, with 400 hectares of vineland, is the second most important vineyard within the Bourg appellation. It is a quality-wine region, with seven excellent growths and one big, above-average cooperative. *Ch. Haut-Macô,* a 4-hectare estate, makes well-structured, firm, well-scented wines that offer outstanding value. *Ch. Brulesecaille,* a 15-hectare estate whose soil contains large quantities of gravel and limestone, makes firm, outstanding wine that is widely exported. *Ch. Guerry* is a 22-hectare estate whose supple and flavorful wines are widely exported to Belgium and the United Kingdom. Other properties include a *Le Piat, Ch. la Barde. Ch. Laroche,* and *Ch. Haut-Nodoz.*

Lying on the northernmost margins of Bourg just below Blaye, the large hamlet of Villeneuve overlooks the Gironde. It is a quality-wine commune with four above-average growths: *Ch. de Barbe,* considered among the top five estates in Bourg, is known for full-bodied, dark, Médoc-type wine, offering substantial value. *Ch. Mendoce* is a beautiful 14th-century country manor house whose vineyards date back to the 9th century. The wines are soft, supple, well made and early maturing. *Ch. Escalette,* located on the plateau and recently improved, makes soft, fruity, early maturing wine. *Ch. Cana,* ranking among the top five growths in Bourg, sits on a hillside with a magnificent aspect. Also above average in quality are *Ch. Sauman, Ch. Plaisance,* and *Pey Chaud Bourdieu.*

Located south of Villeneuve along the Gironde, the small town of Gauriac contains 200 hectares of vineland, one major cooperative, and several above-average properties: *Ch. Laurensanne, Ch. Blanquie, Ch. de Thau, Ch. Poyanne, Ch. Peyror, Ch. Bujan,* and *Ch. Lacouture.* The town of Bayon is sandwiched between Gauriac and Bourg along the coast and faces Margaux across the Gironde. It contains nearly 200 hectares of vineland and twenty-five growers, of which five enjoy a good reputation. *Ch. Eyquem,* the largest property in the commune, is well situated on a bluff and known for hard, firm, astringent wines that require time to soften. *Ch. Falfas,* dating back to the 14th century, is known for superb, soft, fruity, early maturing wines. *Ch. de la Croix-Millorit,* a large property of 26 hectares, makes excellent wood-finished wine that offers outstanding value. *Ch. Nodot,* a tiny property, makes absolutely superb wine.

Located northwest of Tauriac, Lansac, with 350 hectares, ranks as the third-largest wine commune in Bourg. It contains nearly thirty growers, of which the following are the most important. *Ch. la Croix-Davids,* well situated on high ground, is an expertly run property dating back to the 11th century. *Ch. Lamothe,* a 22-hectare property, is considered one of the better estates of Bourg. *Ch. Guionne*, a 14-hectare estate, makes full-bodied, solid, well-structured wine. *Vieux-Domaine-de-Taste*, a small, meticulously maintained estate, makes full-bodied, robust, well scented and magnificently flavored wine. Other important growths include *Ch. Pillot*, *Ch. Donis*, *Ch. Civrac*, and *Ch. Bégot*. Containing 200 hectares, the small hamlet of Samonac supports nearly twenty-four growers, of which three enjoy outstanding reputations. *Ch. Rousset*, a 25-hectare estate making about 10,000 cases of exceptional wine, ranks among the top five growths in the appellation. Full-bodied yet supple, this highly consistent wine ages magnificently and offers outstanding value. *Ch. Macay*, a 28-hectare property, makes soft, fruity, early maturing wine. *Ch. Beaulieu*, one of the oldest properties in Bourg, makes small quantities of widely sought-after wine. Other excellent properties include *Ch. Haut-Castenet*, *Ch. Castenet*, *Ch. Gravette-Samonac*, and *Tour de Tourteau*.

Located in the center of the producing district, the small but important village of St.-Ciers-de-Canesse contains 350 hectares of vineland and nearly thirty-five growers, of which fifteen are important: *Ch. Haut-Rousset*, *Ch. la Grolet*, *Ch. les Tours-Séguy*, *Ch. Rousselle*, *Ch. les Heaumes*, *Ch. Bélair-Coubet*, *Ch. Bélias*, *Ch. la Tuilière*, *Ch. Nicoleau*, *Ch.Montaigut*, *Les Hommes Cheval Blanc*, *Ch. de Canese*, *Ch. Haut-Guiraud*, and *Ch. Guiraud*. Located northwest of Bourg, the hamlet of St.-Suerin-de-Bourg contains 134 hectares of vineland and thirteen growers, four of which enjoy a national reputation: *Ch. Tayac*, *Ch. les Rocques*, *Ch. Camblanne*, and *Ch. Bel-Air*. Located in the north central portion of the appellation, Teuillac, a small, productive village contains nearly 300 hectares of vineland and thirty growers. Approximately 20 percent of production is white wine, and there are seven important growths: *Ch. Peuchaud*, *Ch. Grand-Launay*, *Ch. Haut-Launay*, *Ch. du. Haut-Mousseau*, *Ch. la Cottière*, *Ch. le Pont de la Tonnelle*, and *Ch. les Grands Bertins*. The village of Prignac, located in the southernmost portion of the appellation, contains four properties with a reputation: *Ch. Grand-Jour*, *Ch. Cantegrit*, *Ch. De Grissac*, and *Ch. Hourtou*.

THE WINES OF THE CUBZAGUAIS, GUITRES AND COUTRAS, FRONSADAIS, FRONSAC AND CANON-FRONSAC, AND OF THE LIBOURNAIS

The Wines of the Cubzaguais

Lying between the Fronsadais and Bourg is the obscure, but significant, 2,000-hectare viticultural region of Cubzac. Twice the size of Fronsac, the 100,000-hectoliter vineyard is known primarily for its red wines and an Eiffel bridge. The producing region consists of a narrow river plain and a succession of hilly ridges that stretch beyond the Fronsadais to the equally obscure Guîtras and Coutras vineyards. The soils along the Dordogne are rich in alluvium and not suitable for quality-wine production. Limestone dominates the character of the soils along the first series of ridges, which are planted in red grapes. Toward the north and east, the interior section is sandy and planted mainly in white grapes. Of the nine producing communes, St.-André-de-Cubzac, Salignac, St.-Gervais, and Aubie-et-Espessas account for nearly 75 percent of total hectarage.

All the wine is sold as Bordeaux or Bordeaux Supérieur, with hardly any appearing with the name of Cubzaguais on the label as most of it is marketed to negociants for blending. More than three-quarters of production is nothing better than café-quality wine. The very best, from a limited section of hilly terrain overlooking the Dordogne, commonly referred to as "côtes" wine, is almost always herbal in flavor, somewhat coarse, light in body, and early maturing. The "grassy" flavor sets it apart from the better Bourg and Fronsac wines, and although widely exported, the wines seldom offer any value. White wines, produced in the eastern and northern portions of the producing district, are characterized by excessive acidity, coarseness, and a tendency to fade quickly.

With more than 5,000 residents and more than 558 hectares of vineland, St.-André is the largest settlement and vineyard in the Cubzaguais. Of the nearly fifty growers cultivating more than 5 hectares, seven enjoy a regional reputation. *Ch. Timberlay,* with 20 percent of the district's total vineland, is the largest producer of red and white wine, a good deal of which is sold in the United States. Although the attractively priced red is better than the white, the wine offers little value. *Ch. du Brouilh* is an old, 55-hectare estate that makes a full-bodied red wine with some character. Other properties include *Ch. le Peuy-Saincrit, Dne. de Peneture, Dne. de Beychevelle,* and *Ch. la Joye.*

In the commune of Salignac the principal properties are *Ch. Tarreyrots* and *Dne. Lauberterie.* In the medieval town of St.-Gervais the principal estates are *Ch. des Arras, Ch. St. Ygnan,* and *Ch. du Mass.* In Cubzac the largest estate is *Ch. de Terrefort-Quancard,* a property with a reputation for sound, well-made red and white wines.

The Wines of Guîtres and Coutras

North of Fronsac and Lalande-de-Pomerol is the hill country of Guîtres and Coutras, a forest and agricultural region where scattered vinegrowing has occurred since the 11th century, when several Benedictine orders established vineyards. As most of the alluvial soil is too rich for viticulture, hectarage over the past fifty years has declined by more than 50 percent. There are nearly 2,000 hectares of vineland distributed in two dozen villages, of which St.-Denis-de-Pile, St.-Martin-du-Bois, St.-Ciers-d'Abzac, St.-Martin-de-Laye, Maransin, and Lagorce contain more than 60 percent of the total. Slightly more red wine is made than white; nearly all is sold as plain Bordeaux, with only miniscule amounts marketed under the higher appellation of Bordeaux Supérieur. More than 90 percent of the growers are part-time farmers and belong to cooperatives, which bottle more than 95 percent of total output. As a result, there are few private producers with a reputation.

The Wines of Fronsadais

The substantial 100,000-hectoliter vineyard of Fronsadais lies between Fronsac and Cubzac. Nearly 2,300 hectares of vineland are distributed among six major and twelve minor villages, all of which produce nothing higher than Bordeaux-quality wine. Despite the influence of the church in the production of wine as early as the 11th century, the quality of wine has remained wanting due to the poorly drained soil and the incidence of killing frosts.

Approximately one-third of the hectarage produces white wine, most of which is common, fruity, often bitter, and nearly always unbalanced. White wine hectarage, limited to villages located in the northern portion of the district, is declining rapidly in favor of red wine production. The latter, though light in body, coarse on the palate, and acidic, is far better, with the best sold as Bordeaux Supérieur. It originates mainly on the hilliest sites of the producing district.

Four villages—Cadillac, Galgon, Villegouge, and Lugon—all clustered together north and west of Fronsac, contain more than half of the hectarage in the appellation. Galgon contains 400 hectares and sixty-two growths, of which the following are the most important: *Ch. Mayne-Vieil, Ch. Recougne, Ch. Jalousie-Beaulieu, Ch. Tour-de-l'Espérance,* and *Ch. Pascaud.* The most important growths in the village of Villegouge are *Ch. Vieux-Moulin, Dne. de Reindart, Ch. la Croix-Moulinet,* and *Ch. Tour-Bellegarde.* In Cadillac, hectarage is dominated by the magnificent, walled property of *Ch. de Cadillac.* In Lugon, the principal growths are *Ch. de Pardaillan, Ch. Mouton, Ch. de la Grande-Chapelle,* and *Ch. Rochet-Bosgramont.*

Fronsac and Canon-Fronsac

The charming medieval countryside of Fronsac lies just to the west of Libourne and Pomerol on a series of limestone bluffs and plateaus. Along the coast, the plateau edge is steep and verdant with spectacular views of the Dordogne and Entre-Deux-Mers. The region is studded with remnants of Charlemagne's 8th-century fortifications, along with numerous churches and castles that date from the 12th century. Consisting of two appellations scattered over six villages, the viticultural hectarage and total output of wine are slightly larger than Pomerol.

Fronsac is a 50,000-hectoliter red wine region whose wines enjoyed widespread notoriety in the 18th century when the Duke de Richelieu popularized them within the Gironde and in Paris. Until recently, the wines were *très forte*—big, powerful, well-flavored and scented libations that required far more time to mature than the now-more-famous Médocs. Today, lacking the elegance and finesse of the finest Pomerols and Saint-Emilions, they are made more supple, fruity, with less tannin, and are intended for early consumption. The wines differ from surrounding areas due to the high concentration of Cabernet Franc and Cabernet Sauvignon. Containing less Merlot and Malbec, the wines of the better producers have more spirit, firmness, richness, and tannin. Because they are well made, full on the palate, flavorful, reliable, and distinctive, they offer considerable value.

Production for the two appellations has steadily increased to nearly triple the output of the immediate post–World War II period, and it is expected that output may rise to 90,000 hectoliters by the end of this century. Hectarage, which declined after *phylloxera,* now exceeds 1,200 and is expected to double in the near future. While the average holding among the 245 growers is barely 5 hectares, the laborious process of land consolidation is occurring at a feverish pace. Approximately one-third of production is exported. While the wines are little known in the United States, they have been widely distributed in Holland and Belgium for centuries, and to a lesser extent in the United Kingdom.

The soils are highly variable: alluvial material dominates the coastal margins, while clay and sand covers the hillsides and the plateau sections. The best cities are associated with the limestone bluffs of the "tertre de Fronsac" and "tertre de Canon," and within portions of the plateau that is an extension of Pomerol. Making ordinary wine at best, the coastal plain with its *palus* soils resisted *phylloxera* during the epidemic of the 1870s and 1880s. The wine of the *palus* gave the area a poor reputation in the first half of the century and tarnished its former image. Accelerating Fronsac's recent renaissance in popularity, today's finest sites all lie on the upper portions of the *côtes* and on the plateau.

The area is divided into two seperate and distinct wine appellations: Canon-Fronsac, located near the Dordogne, and Fronsac, on the plateau. The former is considered the better of the two, although the quality differences are not as distinct today as they once were. The Canon-Fronsac appellation contains fewer than 400 hectares of vineland, all restricted to hilly sites and southern exposures overlooking the Dordogne within the confines of the communal boundaries of Fronsac and St.-Michel-De-Fronsac. The Fronsac appellation, with more than 800 hectares of vineland, is the larger of the two and includes the interior plateau region north of Fronsac.* Due to soil and exposure differences, the wine is fruity, but less intense, and lighter in body than the richer wines of Canon-

*The old appellation names of Côtes de Canon-Fronsac and Côtes de Fronsac are slowly being eliminated from bottle labels.

Fronsac. For both appellations, the authorized grape varieties, in order of preference, are Cabernet Franc, Cabernet Sauvignon, Malbec, and Merlot Rouge. The minimum alcohol content is 11 percent, and the minimum yield per hectare is 42 hectoliters. This appellation also makes small quantities of white wine, all of which must be sold as plain Bordeaux.

The historic medieval town of Fronsac contains approximately one-fourth of total hectarage and more than twenty major properties producing wine under the Canon-Fronsac and Fronsac appellations. The following are among the more prominent: *Ch. Canon* (with less than 2 hectares, is considered by many to be standard in the production for full-bodied, dark, and consistently good wine); *Ch. Canon de Brem* (a 9-hectare, newly refurbished property by J. P. Moueix, makes supple, well-flavored wine); *Ch. de la Dauphine* (with a magnificent chateau built by Victor Louis, often produces the finest wine in the commune); *Ch. la Valade* (known for consistency and outstanding value); *Ch. Gagnard* (located in the center of the plateau region, makes excellent *vin de garde* wines); *Ch. Junayme* (with 16 hectares and an output of 7,000 cases, is the largest producer in the commune); *Ch. Belloy* (a 6-hectare property with a magnificent chateau, ranks among the top six producers); *Ch. Vrai-Canon-Bouche* (a 12-hectare property located on very stony soil, makes firm, well-structured wine); *Clos Toumalin* (a 3-hectare property, makes full-bodied, robust wine); *Ch. Haut-Panet* (a 4-hectare property, makes robust, spicy, well-flavored wine); *Ch. Barrabaque; Ch. du Gaby; Ch. Bodet; Ch. du Pavillon-Gros-Bonnet; Ch. Haut-Gros-Bonnet; Ch. Toumalin; Ch. Pey-Labrie; Ch. Moulin-Pey-Labrie; Ch. la Marche-Canon; Ch. Comte; Ch. la Croix; Ch. Pontus; Ch. Arnauton; Ch. Roullet; and Ch. Coustolle.*

The small village of St.-Michel-de-Fronsac contains 200 hectares and at least forty growers. The better sites contain larger amounts of stone and are located on the plateau portion of the producing district. There are thirteen principal properties with above-average reputations: *Ch. Canon* (a 9-hectare property known for consistency); *Ch. Mazeris* (known for supple, fruity wines); *Ch. Termaline* (makes full-bodied, strapping, well-flavored wine); *Ch. Grand-Renouil* (known for well-aged, distinctive wines); *Ch. Lariveau* (excellent, dark, plummy, well-flavored wines); *Ch. Vray-Canon-Boyer; Ch. Cassagne-Haut-Canon; Ch. Haut-Mazeris; Ch. Mazeris-Bellevue; Ch. Vray-Canon-Bodet-la-Tour; Ch. Combes-Canon; Ch. Mausse,* and *Ch. Haut-Ballet.*

The largest producer of "Fronsac" appellation wine is Saillans, a village of 230 hectares and eight good properties: *Ch. Mayne-Vieil* (a 70-hectare estate dating back to the 15th century, considered the standard in the commune); *Ch. de Carles* (a 25-hectare, above-average-quality property); *Ch. Puyguilhem* (a little-known property that consistently makes above-average quality wine); *Ch. Dalem; Ch. Villars; Ch. la Vieille-Croix; Ch. la Vieille-Cure;* and *Ch. Moulin-Haut-Laroque.* With 200 hectares of vineland and six major growths, St.-Aignan is the second most-important "Fronsac" wine village. While *Ch. Jeandeman, Ch. Plain-Point, Dne. Vincent,* and *Ch. du Tasta* make full-bodied, well-structured, long-lived wines, *Ch. Lambert* and *Ch. les Tonnelles* are known for the production of supple, fruity, early maturing wines.

La Rivière is a small village with 120 hectares of vineland and approximately two dozen growers producing Fronsac, Bordeaux Supérieur, and Bordeaux appellation wines. The finest in the Fronsac appellation are as follows: *Ch. la Rivière,* the showpiece in Fronsac, is the largest property with a most-magnificent chateau that supposedly sits on a Charlemagne site. Located on high ground with excellent aspect, the limestone soils produce inconsistent quality wine, but those of excellent vintages are long-lived, well structured, and often offer outstanding value. Other properties include *Ch. Musseau-et-Bellevue, Ch. Renard, Ch. Tour-Bicot,* and *Ch. Ripeau.* The last remaining "Fronsac" village, St.-Germain-la-Rivière, contains only 100 hectares of vineland and two growths: *Ch. Rouet* and *Ch.les Abories-de-Meney.*

Libournais

With 24,000 residents, Libourne is the largest city along the north bank of the Dordogne. An old English stronghold named after Roger de Leyburn, it was a very historic port during the Plantagenet occupation of the region. For a good portion of its history, the city enjoyed a formidable reputation as the marketing center for Pomerol, St.-Emilion, and other wines emanating from the northern portion of Entre-Deux-Mers and the Dordogne.

The city of Libourne and eight other villages contain roughly 1,200 hectares of vineland producing 60,000 hectoliters of wine, nearly all of which is red wine used in the production of innocuous blended wine sold under the plain regional appellation of Bordeaux. The very best, perhaps 5 percent of total production, is sold as Bordeaux Supérieur. The particularly poor soils, alluvial in character with heavy accumulations of clay, are located on rich bottomland with poor drainage. Hectarage has declined by more than 50 percent within the past forty years, and a number of growers are essentially part-time farmers.

With more than 400 hectares of vineland, Libourne is the principal producing commune. The principal properties are *Ch. du Pintey, Dne. du Galet, Dne. Charruaud,* and *Dne. de la Paillette.* The principal growths of St.-Terre are: *Ch. de Lavagnac, Ch. Guillemin-de-Gorre, Ch. de la Nauze,* and *Dne. Feuchette.* The major growths in the village of Les Artigues-de-Lussac are *Ch. Trocard, Ch. des Grands-Jays, Ch. de Faize,* and *Ch. Haut-Colas-Nouet.*

8

THE WINES OF POMEROL,
LALANDE-DE-POMEROL, AND NEAC

THE WINES OF POMEROL

POMEROL, a small 3-by-4 kilometer vineyard of 735 hectares, produces 35,000 hectoliters, or about 4 million bottles of red wine annually. The official boundaries are the Barbanne stream in the north, St.-Emilion in the east, Libourne and the valley of the l'Isle toward the southwest and west. Although a theoretical ceiling of 795 hectares can be used to produce wine entitled to the Pomerol apellation, urban encroachment and other land uses have left little room for the possible expansion of this world-famous vineyard. It produces as much wine as St.-Julien in the Médoc, and less than 1 percent of total AOC Bordeaux. Its motto in recent years has been "the smallest of the greatest," a fitting testament to its popularity and the high prices it almost always attains.

Although grapegrowing dates back to the time when Pomerol was a Roman military outpost, its modern viticultural history began in the 12th century when the Templars and the Knights of St.-John of Jerusalem established orders near Libourne. Because Pomerol was a waystation for crusading pilgrims, the Knights of St.-John constructed a commanderie, church, and hospital—and in keeping with Roman and medieval traditions, they cultivated vines, which attracted a large number of pilgrims.

Vineyards, devastated and abandoned by the decimated population during the turbulent Hundred Years' War, were not completely replanted until the end of the 18th century. The wines remained obscure even longer, until the district was granted a separate identity in 1923. The wines continued to be ignored and prices remained low until *Ch. Petrus* began its meteoric rise in New York City in the early 1950s. The region today ranks in the highest echelons of quality-wine producers, along with the Médoc, St.-Emilion and the Côte d'Or.

Figure 8.1 indicates the growth of production since 1949. Not only has output doubled over the past forty years, but total hectarage has increased from less than 300 hectares in the middle 1920s to 735 in 1983. Today, due to high and stable prices, vines are planted to the total exclusion of any other agricultural crop. Of the total hectarage, approximately 62 percent, or 470 hectares, is found in the top forty properties. Although the maximum yield is limited to 40 hectoliters to the hectare, overcropping, as in other vine-growing regions of France, is a regular practice. As a result, an ever-increasing proportion of the wine appears to be less concentrated in extract and less intense in flavor than it was twenty-five years ago. Many in the district are of the opinion that wine quality may have peaked as recently as 1975.

The pedology of the region has been studied intensely. Although local experts disagree, the soils are divided into three major categories:

1. Clay and gravel soils are found along the St.-Emilion border and in a small but irregular region containing many of the top growths, such as *Ch. Trotanoy, Ch. Petrus, Ch. Petit-Villages, Ch. l'Evangile,* and *Vieux-Château-Certan,* and a number of lesser growths, principally *Ch. St.-Pierre, Ch. Mairie,* and *Ch. Lagrange.* Nevertheless, this region is not uniform in the depth and composition of its clay/gravel mixture. It varies from almost pure clay in *Ch. Petrus* (an unusual phenomenon) to more gravel in *Ch. Trotanoy.* This area of the producing region is considered the finest section for the production of "fleshy" or "meaty" wines that improve markedly with bottle age.

2. Sand and scattered gravel is the next best section; it too is irregular in shape and surrounds the clay/gravel soil area mentioned above. Although the ratio of sand and gravel varies significantly, this zone includes at least thirty well-known growths, such as *Ch. Gazin, Ch. Lafleur-Gazin, Ch. Clinet, Ch. Lafleur,* and *Ch. Beauregard.* Here the gravel-dominated soils produce wines that are leaner and more refined, but not as long-lived as the clay/gravel soils mentioned previously.

3. A wide belt of sand, the largest portion of the appellation, surrounds the clay/gravel and the sand/gravel sections, totally dominating

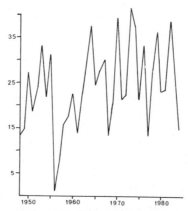

Figure 8.1   Pomerol: Wine Production, 1949–1984
(in thousands of hectoliters)

the southern and western sections of the appellation. It includes what the local aficionados call the lesser wines of Pomerol—growths known for fruity, light-to-medium-bodied wines that mature relatively early. A small but important enclave of gravel outcrop occurs in *Ch. l'Enclos* and *Ch. Clos-René,* both located in the western portion of the district and known for the production of above-average wines, particularly the former growth.

Although many experts maintain that these three soils determine *the* character of the wine, a number of additional variables come into play to alter this idealistic picture. These variables include a wide belt of iron oxide inbedded in the clay (called *crasse de fer* and widely considered the key contributing factor in the production of the pronounced bouquet of Pomerol), and degree of drainage, aspect, encépagement, and vineyard and vinification practices. For these reasons, three growths—*Ch. de Sales, Ch. Ferrand,* and *Ch. Taillefer*—while essentially located on sand-dominated soils, do not produce the same type of wines. The first is thinner, low in extract, with less flavor and bouquet than the firmer, more-fragrant and more intensely flavored wines of the latter two. Moreover, the next property to the east of *Ch. de Sales, Ch. Moulinet,* exhibits a greater intensity of flavor, color, and bouquet, in part because of improved drainage and superior aspect. Similarly, the north-facing properties of *Ch. Rouget* and *Ch. le Gay* (located on sand/gravel soil) vary significantly in terms of concentration and depth of flavor from the south-facing growths of *Ch. Beauregard, Ch. Nenin, Ch. la Croix,* and *Ch. le Caillou.* Finally, the superiority of *Ch. Petrus* in comparison with *Ch. St.-Pierre* is attributed to a combination of more clay, more Merlot (this grape likes to grow in cold, wet soils), a thicker vein of *crasse de fer,* and more gravel in the subsoil.

As in St.-Emilion, the wines of Pomerol are made principally from the Merlot (usually between 50 and 60 percent of the encépagement), followed by Cabernet Franc, Cabernet Sauvignon, and Malbec; the latter, called Pressac, is declining in importance. The minimum alcohol content is 10.5 percent, and the yield is limited to 40 hectoliters to the hectare.

Pomerol wines are supple, generous, fat (or *gras*), more delicate, but lower in alcohol than those of neighboring St.-Emilion. At their best, they have a deep ruby color, a rich taste, and a penetrating "truffle" bouquet; at their worst, they are light, acidic, bitter, thin, and harsh, with unsavory "grassy" flavors and odors. Due to a higher glycerine content, they feel substantial on the palate, but because of lower tannin levels, they fade and dry up sooner than equivalent Médocs. In above-average to excellent vintages, the top growths are at their peak between seven and fifteen years.

Although there are several exceptions, Pomerol vineyards, more modest in size than those of the Médoc, exhibit little of the grandeur of the 19th century typically found along the south bank of the Gironde. The "chateaux" are humble houses, and the average property size is only 6 hectares, compared with 20 in the Médoc. Only *Ch. Gazin, Ch. la Pointe, Ch. Nenin,* and *Ch. de Sales* cultivate more than 20 hectares of vineland. At least 50 percent of all growers own less than 3 hectares, and one-fifth cultivate a mere *barail,* a mini-vineyard of less than 1 hectare. With such small producing units, it is highly unusual not to find a cooperative in Pomerol, Neac, and Lalande-de-Pomerol.

Over the past forty years the price of Pomerol has escalated to dizzying heights, a development largely caused by the minascule amounts of wine available to the apparently insatiable demand. Direct sales at the property siphon between 20 and 30 percent of total production. Although negociants still dominate export distribution channels, their share of total wine handled has decreased from 80 percent prior to 1950, to less than 50 percent in 1982. Table 8.1 indicates the nature of internal consumption and export destination of Pomerol wines for the year 1982. (By contrast, wine exports from Lalande-de-Pomerol, including Neac, were 6,000 hectoliters out of a total available pool of 24,557 hectoliters for the same year, or approximately 25 percent of the total. Exports by country of destination appear to be the same as for Pomerol, except that the United States imports very little.)

The principal properties are as follows:

Ch. Petrus is an 11-hectare estate located in the northeastern portion of the producing region near the St.-Emilion border. Its wine made from nearly 100 percent Merlot, is outstanding in every way and is the most expensive in the Gironde. The estate's key to success lies in meticulous care, low yields, and old vines. Although production rarely exceeds 4,200 cases, this truly magnificent wine is a must for those with sufficient funds. Eighty percent of production is sold in the United States. *Ch. Conseillante* is a highly regarded 13-hectare estate producing 5,300 cases of wine annually. The long-lived wines lack the *gras* of many Pomerol's, but are always full-bodied, somewhat austere, smooth with a pronounced bouquet, and marred only by a lack of consistency. *Ch. Trotanoy,* lying on the

Table 8.1   Sale of Pomerol, 1982

Sale	Hectoliters	Percent	Sale	Hectoliters	Percent
Belgium	4,565	41.5	Denmark	536	4.9
United States	1,745	15.8	Other	623	5.7
Switzerland	1,623	14.7	Total exports	11,006	100.0
West Germany	803	7.3			
Holland	561	5.1	France	11,018	50.0
United Kingdom	550	5.0	Total sales	122,024	100.0

Source: Conseil Interprofessionnel du Vin de Bordeaux.

edge of the plateau north of the hamlet of Catusseau, consists of 7 hectares producing 3,200 cases of wine annually. It is a reliable and absolutely magnificent wine—a complex, mouth-filling, chewy, and well-made libation that rivals the best in the Gironde. The property contains a large proportion of old vines that produce first-rate wine in good vintages, and while less concentrated than *Ch. Petrus,* it offers exceptional value. *Ch. l'Evangile,* a medium-sized propery producing 5,000 cases of fruity and elegant wine, is located next to the St.-Emilion border. The very best wine is absolutely stunning, meticulously made, complex in flavor and bouquet. Along with *Ch. Petrus,* it is one of the most reliable of the first-class vineyards in the Gironde. *Ch. la Fleur-Pétrus,* a 7-hectare property located next to *Ch. Petrus,* makes about 3,000 cases annually. The wine— dark in color, round, complex, well structured, loaded with fruit and oak flavors—is constantly in demand and should not be missed, as it offers excellent value. *Ch. Lafleur,* an above-average estate, is located on hilly terrain overlooking the Barbanne stream in the northern portion of the producing district. The wine is full-bodied, delicate, and absolutely first class but, due to a minascule output of less than 2,000 cases, very hard to locate. *Ch. Latour-Pomerol,* located in the north-central portion of the producing district, makes dark, fragrant, flavorful, muscular, and well-balanced wine with a good finish that requires at least ten years to mature fully. Overall quality is high but its rustic character is somewhat below that of the top growths. *Vieux-Château-Certan,* a rather large 14-hectare property well situated on the edge of the plateau, contains a low proportion of Merlot and, hence, produces one of the longest-lived and least-fruity of all the major Pomerol growths. Over the past twenty years the wine has been overrated and overpriced, offering little value. *Ch. Beauregard* is a 14-hectare estate that sacrifices production for quality. This little-known property makes rich, mouth-filling, well-flavored, but somewhat austere wine that warrants many years of patience before it fully matures. *Ch. le Gay,* overlooking the Barbanne stream along the northern portion of the producing district, contains 8 hectares of very old vines. The wine, impeccably made by the owners of *Ch. Lafleur,* is firm, elegant, with a penetrating bouquet and a lingering finish. *Ch. la Grave-Trigant-de-Boisset,* located in the northcentral portion of the producing district, is a 6-hectare Moueix property that consistently makes first-class wine. This little-known and highly promising property makes deep-colored wine with a penetrating bouquet and satisfying, mouth-filling flavors. Production of less than 3,000 cases is hard to find and expensive, but well worth the effort. *Ch. le Bon Pasteur,* located on the St.-Emilion border, is a 6-hectare property and one of the most consistent of all Pomerols. The wine is rich, supple, fruity, and overpowers the palate with complex flavors. Productin exceeds 2,500 cases and offers exceptional value.

   Ch. Rouget, an 18-hectare property well situated on hilly terrain overlooking the Barbanne, is one of the better Pomerols—dark in color, highly concentrated in flavor and bouquet, long-lived (due to a high percentage of Cabernet Sauvignon), and often austere on the palate, it offers exceptional value. *Clos l'Eglise* is a 6-hectare property that makes 2,500 cases of above-average wine, much improved in recent years. *Ch. Petit-Village,* located on a rise, is an immaculate 11-hectare property that makes first-class wine only in above-average vintages. *Ch. de May* is a small, 2,000-case, 5-hectare property making firm, elegant, and fruity wine that offers good value. *Ch. de Dne. de l'Eglise,* a 7-hectare property recently acquired by the Casteja family, makes solid, round, full-flavored wine that offers excellent value. *Ch. Gazin,* a 22-hectare property founded by the Templars, is currently known for inconsistent and overpriced wine. Although much lighter in body than it once was, it has maintained one of its excellent attributes—a long, lingering, penetrating bouquet. In 1969 it sold 5 hectares of its best land to *Ch. Petrus. Ch. la Pointe,* a large 25-hectare property with a distinguished history, is located on the northeastern margins of Libourne and annually makes more than 8,500 cases. Although marred by inconsistency, it often produces outstanding wine that offers excellent value. *Ch. Clos-René,* a 10-hectare property located in the western portion of the producing district, makes above-average wine in good years, but is somewhat inconsistent in average vintages. *Ch. l'Enclos* contains 11 hectares and produces more than 3,500 cases annually. After two decades of mediocre vintages, quality appears to be on the rise. *Ch. Nenin,* a 17-hectare property located along D21 east of Libourne, produces more than 7,000 cases. Although inconsistent, the wine has recently been improved. *Ch. Clinet* is a small 6-hectare property currently making hard *vin de garde* wine that is mouth-puckering, rustic, and chewy. Undervalued, it almost always offers excellent value. *Ch. Feytit-Clinet* is a little-known property of 4 hectares that makes 2,000 cases of rustic, full-bodied, tannin-rich, brawny-type wine that offers excellent value.

   Ch. l'Eglise-Clinet is a little-known, 5-hectare estate currently making 2,000 cases of full-bodied, complex wine. *Ch. la Croix* is a well-regarded, 17-hectare property currently making full-bodied, rustic wine that requires patience. *Ch. Vraye Croix de Gay,* an obscure, 4-hectare property located next to *Ch. Lafleur,* makes outstanding, intense, and powerful wine. The libation is distinctive, as the proportion of Merlot rarely exceeds 50 percent. Production rarely exceeds 1,500 cases, so the wine is very rare and sought after. *Le Pin,* an obscure, postage-stamp sized property, makes above-average, meaty wine nearly impossible to find. *Ch. Certan-Giraud* is a 6-hectare property known for full-bodied, round, and well-structured wine. A small amount is sold under its former name of *Ch. Certan-Marzelle. Ch. Lagrange* is an underrated 9-hectare property that is currently making above-average, supple, eminently drinkable wine. *Ch. de Sales,* with 48 hectares and a magnificent chateau, is the largest property in the appellation. The wine, at one time early maturing and quite thin, has recently improved and offers excellent value. *Clos du Clocher,* a little-known 6-hectare property, is currently making under-rated, fruity, supple, expertly made wine. *Ch. la Croix-de-Gay* is a little-known property of 9 hectares making 4,000 cases of above-average, well-structured wine, offering excellent value. *Ch. Taillefer,* located east of Libourne, is a 20-hectare Moueix property known for the consistent production of soft, above-average, eminently drinkable wine that offers excellent value. *Ch. la Cabanne* is a popular 10-hectare property located on the plateau that makes above-average fruity, early maturing wine.

Ch. Bourgneuf-Veyron is a 9-hectare estate making 4,200 cases of excellent and distinctive, but often inconsistent wine. *Ch. la Commande-rie,* a 6-hectare property located in the southern portion of the producing district, makes 2,200 cases of pleasant, supple, and early maturing wines. *Ch. Ferrand,* a 15-hectare property founded by the Templars, is known for early maturing, supple, and well-scented wine. *Ch. Moulinet,* an 18-hectare property located next to *Ch. de Sales,* makes light, pleasant wine that is modestly priced. *Ch. la Violette,* a small 3-hectare property in the southeastern portion of the producing region, makes fewer than 1,500 cases of fragrant, supple and early maturing wine. *Ch. Guillot,* a 5-hectare property, makes 2,500 cases of flavorful but rustic wine. *Ch. la Croix-St.-Georges,* an obscure, rarely seen wine in the United States, is known for average quality despite its location in the midst of better-known proper-ties. *Ch. le Caillou* is a recently improved 8-hectare estate that makes above-average, full-bodied, yet supple wine that offers good value only in good vintages. *Ch. Bel-Air* is located in the central portion of the producing district. One of the largest properties, it currently produces more than 5,000 cases of good, firm, flavorful, and well-scented wine that offers excellent value in good vintages and requires patience for full maturation. *Ch. Plince* is an 8-hectare property producing more than 4,000 cases of supple, fruity, but otherwise undistinguished wine. *Ch. Fleur-du-Gazin,* a small property, currently makes above-average-quality wine that offers good value.

In addition to the above-listed properties, approximately 70 obscure growers have a more-limited distribution and reputation. Of these, the most important are *Ch. Moulinet-Lasserre, Ch. Chêne-Liège, Ch. de Valois, Ch. Rocher-Beauregard, Ch. de la Nouvelle-Eglise, Ch. de la Gravette, Ch. le Commandeur, Ch. Monregard-Lacroix, Ch. la Fleur-des-Rouzes, Ch. Franc-Maillet, Ch. Mazy, Ch. Grange-Neuve, Ch. Lafleur-du-Roy, Ch. la Ganne, Ch. de Bourgueneuf, Ch. Haut-Maillet, Ch. Mazeyres, Ch. St.-Pierre, Ch. Grate-Cap, Ch. Rève-d'Or, Ch. la Croix-Toulifaut, Ch. du Tailhas,* and *Ch. la Croix-du-Casse.*

LALANDE-DE-POMEROL

Slightly larger than Pomerol, the flat-to-undulating region of Lalande-de-Pomerol adjoins and is nearly twice the size of Néac. It is a fertile, rural region of 1,000 arable hectares that contains considerable amounts of forest, cattle grazing and cereal growing. Annual production exceeds 45,000 hectoliters, a figure comparable to the total output of Pauillac.

The 530 hectares of vineyards occupy mainly sand/gravel and gravelly soils along the Néac and Pomerol borders, and exhibit only a minor concentration along the sand/clay soil regions of the western and northern portions of the appellation. As the soils are heavy and poorly drained, the wines are coarser, with traces of bitterness and less finesse than the better Pomerols. The very best growths, however, rival the second-tier Pomerol properties in terms of a sweet bouquet, suppleness, full flavor, and a rich *gras* feeling on the palate. At their worst, they tend to be grassy in flavor, acidic, and not well balanced. Alcohol content, yield, and grape varieties, for both Lalande-de-Pomerol and Néac, are identical with the Pomerol appellation.

The viticultural history of Lalande is also similar to and for a long time was more renowned than that of Pomerol. Although a number of commanderies were established by crusading orders in the 12th century, vine hectarage grew rapidly only after the arrival of the Hospitalers in the 13th and 14th centuries. The growth of viticultural hectarage was augmented by numerous bequests from the landed gentry of Castillon, Grailly, and Barbanne. Because of high and stable wine prices during the past twenty-five years and the inability of Pomerol to extend hectarage, during the same period the Lalande vineyard nearly doubled and production tripled. Since the wines are so little known, they are less expensive than surrounding communes and hence offer excellent value.

Of the 122 separate exploitations, forty-six produce fewer than 1,000 cases, fifty-six between 1,000 and 4,000 cases, eighteen between 4,000 and 11,000 cases, and only two produce more than 11,000 cases. Of the total, approximately twenty properties make quality wine. *Ch. Bel-Air* is an old 12-hectare property that makes more than 5,000 cases of good, solid wine offering considerable value. *Ch. Perron,* lying on the sand and gravel plateau near Pomerol, is a 12-hectare property making approximately 5,000 cases that are widely distributed in Belgium. *Ch. des Tourelles,* a 17-hectare Janoueix property, has recently produced a series of excellent, full-bodied, well flavored and scented wines. *Ch. des Annereaux,* one of the oldest properties in the commune, is well known in the region and widely available in export markets. The 22-hectare estate produces more than 11,500 cases of well-made, deeply colored, moderately priced wine with good balance. *Ch. de Viaud* is a 12-hectare property producing more than 7,300 cases of robust, tannin-rich wine capable of aging gracefully beyond ten years. *Ch. Laborde* is a 6,500-case property that makes sound, well-balanced wine, more than half of which is exported. *Ch. des Moines* is a 10-hectare property known for light but delicate wine, widely exported to Belgium. *Ch. de la Commanderie,* an 18-hectare property on the site of a 12th-century Commanderie, currently makes

8,000 cases of good, solid, well-colored wine with considerable depth of flavor.

Clos de l'Eglise is a 9-hectare property that makes 3,800 cases of soft yet firm, concentrated, well-balanced wine that ages well. *Ch. la Croix-Bellevue,* a small Moueix property lying next to the Pomerol boundary, makes 3,100 cases of full-bodied, dark, and robust wine capable of extended cellaring. *Ch. la Croix-des-Moines,* part of a stable of vineyards, is a very old property that makes 3,000 cases of average to above-average-quality wine that is well structured, robust, and alcoholic. *Ch. Bourseau* is a little-known 10-hectare property that makes light, vinous, early maturing wine. *Dne. de Musset,* a large property of 175 hectares, produces fewer than 3,000 cases from 6 hectares of vineland; the wines are very reliable and offer excellent value. *Ch. la Marechaude* is a small property making fewer than 2,700 cases of good, reliable, well-balanced wine. *Ch. Sergant,* one of the largest producers in Lalande, makes more than 9,000 cases of average, fruity, early maturing wine. Other, less well known properties include *Ch. Grand-Ormeau, Ch. les Cruzelles, Clos de Templiers, Clos des Moines, Cha. la Gravière,* and *Ch. la Mission.*

NEAC

Although the region was merged with Lalande-de-Pomerol in 1954 and its wines are marketed under the "Lalande-de-Pomerol" banner, Néac remains a distinct viticultural region. It is bordered on the west by Lalande, on the south by Pomerol, and along the northern and eastern sections by Montagne-St.-Emilion. Néac, containing 350 hectares of vineland, produces more than 17,000 hectoliters of red wine annually. Undergoing steady and continuous expansion, the planted area over the past forty years has grown by more than 100 hectares, and is one of the few areas in the Gironde where small farmers are growing grapes as a cash crop. This area of small holdings contains seventy-one properties, of which eighteen produce less than 1,000 cases and only ten are large enough to make more than 5,000 cases.

Representing two distinct styles of wine made, the vineyards are concentrated along either the Pomerol or the Montagne border. The area close to Pomerol produces soft, more delicate wine, while the Montagne portion makes wine that is considerably more rustic, firmer, and alcoholic. Because the wines are so little known, they offer excellent value, particularly in good vintages. The principal properties are: *Ch. Garraud, Ch. Tournefeuille, Ch. Belles-Graves, Ch. Chevrol-Bel-Air, Ch. du Bourg, Ch. Teysson, Ch. Moulin-à-Vent, Ch. Vieux-Chevrol, Dne. de Grand-Ormeau, Ch. Haut-Surget, Ch. de Marchesseau,* and *Ch. la Fleur-St.-Georges.* Along the Montagne side of Neac, the principal properties are as follows: *Ch. Siaurac, Ch. Moncets, Ch. les Chaumes, Ch. Haut-Chaigneau, Ch. de Bertineau,* and *Ch. la Croix-St.-André.*

9

THE WINES OF ST.-EMILION, COTES DE CASTILLON, AND COTES DE FRANCS

THE WINES OF ST.-EMILION

St.-Emilion, one of the finest viticultural districts of France, lies east and north of Libourne and is centered on the medieval town of St.-Emilion, a charming settlement of 3,200 people that, in addition to its fame for wine and leisurely living, is also known for the production of macaroons. On a series of côtes and along the rolling interior plateau stretching to Pomerol are 5,100 hectares of vines that produce more than 200,000 hectoliters of wine, or five times the annual output of St.-Julien in the Médoc. With 6.5 percent of total production, St.-Emilion is the largest single wine commune appellation responsible for 10 percent of all AOC wine in the entire Gironde. Furthermore, the surrounding five communes, commonly referred to as the "satellite towns" (Lussac, Montagne, Parsac, Puisseguin, and St.-Georges), produce an additional 100,000 hectoliters of red wine, nearly all of which is AOC.

Despite the fame of St.-Emilion, the town and surrounding countryside are rural backwaters—quiet, unspoiled, and seemingly untrodden by the numerous summer and fall tourists. There are no large factories, no superhighways, and no large blocks of high-rise apartments. Unlike the Médoc, Graves, and Sauternes regions, there are also few chateaux in the "grande" manner surrounded by extensive vineyards, pasture, horses, and parkland. Although there are occasional exceptions, most vineyards are small by Bordeaux standards—between 2 and 10 hectares, with the largest established by wealthy businessmen and politicians only within the last 100 years.

Although viticulture dates back to the Romans, it seems to have been a secondary activity until Vassale de Montviel arrived from Quercy in the middle of the 8th century and introduced the Pressac grape. Until that time, St.-Emilion had been a fortified town and the countryside in continuous disarray, due to the periodic ravages of Visigoths and other invaders. Such was the dismal state of affairs until the 11th and 12th centuries, when religious orders began to establish priories, abbeys, and monasteries. Of the fifty major vineyards founded by religious orders in

Plate 9.1   The medieval town of St.-Emilion

the entire Gironde, nineteen are found in St.-Emilion, exhibiting a level of concentration second only to Burgundy. While the ten religious Pomerol properties were mainly the product of Templar and Knights of Malta efforts, those of St.-Emilion were significantly more varied. One of the largest and most important was the Ursuline order, which developed *Ch. le Couvent, les Demoiselles, la Grâce Dieu-des-Prieurs, l'Hermitage,* and *l'Hermitage Mazerat.* The Dominicans founded *Ch. Couvent-des-Jacobins, Clos des Jacobins, Clos des Moines,* and *Clos des Religieuses.* The Fransiscans developed *Ch. le Prieuré, Clos des Cordeliers,* and *Tauzinat l'Hermitage;* the Benedictines, *le Prieure St.-Emilion;* the Templars, *Ch. Montdespic;* and the Cistercians, *Ch. la Tour-Ségur* and *Ch. la Barbe-Blanche.*

After the English occupation of a good portion of western France, King John granted extensive privileges to the "Jurade" of St.-Emilion to collect taxes, administer civil affairs, and establish a court system. The Jurats, elected officials representing all the neighboring communes, became in time synonymous with the region's most famous industry—winemaking. As a consequence, wine exports (mainly to England) grew steadily and in 1309 reached the staggering figure of 15,000 tons. Not only did the Jurade delineate the boundaries of the producing district (intact to this day), but it issued harvest proclamations, devised viticultural and vinification practices, and prosecuted those suspected of fraud. It also devised an iron seal that was stamped on each oak barrel exported from the region. Today, as its legal and legislative position has been stripped, it is supported solely by winegrowers.

With the departure of the English from western France, viticulture lost its stable and primary market. Compounded by the devastation wrought by the religious conflict between Catholic and Protestant, an uncertain economic climate was produced that lasted until the second half of the 18th century, when a short-lived revival attracted investment and the establishment of two prominent properties—*Ch. Soutard* and *Ch. Canon.* The construction of the Bordeaux–Paris railroad in the middle of the 19th century prompted a new interest in St.-Emilion and Pomerol and the infusion of new investment capital. This short-lived period was ended by two of the deadliest vine enemies known to man—*oidium* and *phylloxera,* which collectively reduced hectarage almost in half by 1875.

Between 1890 and 1914 much rebuilding occurred, and expansion of vineyard properties was impressive, particularly *Ch. Pavie, Ch. Gaffelière, Ch. Ausone, Ch. la Tour-Figeac,* and *Ch. Haut-Sarpe.* But by the end of World War I, demand for red wine dropped, prices tumbled, and economic depression became a way of life. During the interwar period (1920–40) the wines of St.-Emilion and Pomerol, because they were little known, sold at prices at or below Médoc Cru Bourgeois levels. The economic climate did not improve until the late 1950s, and over the past thirty years the region has enjoyed an unprecedented period of extraordinary prosperity. Properties have expanded hectarage, and cellar, vineyard, and vinification improvements have been steady and very progressive. By 1985, nearly all available land for vine growing was utilized, to the near exclusion of all other agricultural crops. By stretching all appellation restrictions, the local syndicate estimates that only 360 possible hectares are available for vinegrowing in the following areas: St.-Emiliom 140, St.-Christophe 33, St. Hippolyte 15, St.-Etienne 29, St.-Laurent 22, St.-Pey 23, St.-Sulpice 47, and Vignonet 31. Most important, only 11 hectares are available for future expansion in Premier Grand Cru Classé sites: 37 in Grand Cru Classé sites, and 92 in Grand Cru sites. With so little room for expansion, any increase in demand will have a tendency to drive prices upward, much in the Burgundian manner. When one realizes that a similar situation exists in Pomerol, it is apparent that the areas of "discovery" in the near future will be Fronsac, Bourg, Graves, and the Côtes-de-Castillon regions. See Figure 9.1 for thirty-year wine production of St. Emilion.

Small by historical standards, the average viticultural exploitation over the past thirty years has been steadily rising and the number of growers declining. The pressures of meeting the efficiencies generated by economies of scale will enlarge a number of growths and severely reduce those

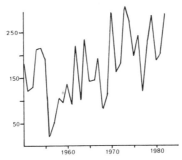

Figure 9.1   St.-Emilion: Wine Production, 1950–1982
(in thousands of hectoliters)

producing less than 3,000 cases. Of the 1,000 growers in St.-Emilion (200 fewer than in 1945), 22 percent cultivate less than 1 hectare, 27 percent between 2 and 4 hectares, 30 percent between 4 and 8, 15 percent between 9 and 15, and only 6 percent more than 15 hectares. Only two properties contain more than 44 hectares of vineland, and both are located in St.-Christophe. Nearly two-thirds of all growers work their own properties; the rest lease and work under various arrangements of the *métayage* system. As of 1970, at least 40 percent of all growers did not vinify their grapes, and 65 percent did not bottle their wine.

The wines of St.-Emilion are so much in demand that the pace of consolidation has risen to unprecedented levels. Land speculation and the dramatic increase in multiple ownership are now commonplace and threaten price stability by limiting quality-wine production to fewer and fewer hands. As of 1985, approximately 100 properties were owned by negociant houses and corporations, and another 125 by other chateaux. This is a rather recent development, as local ownership was the rule prior to 1955. Yet this tendency is slowly succumbing to market pressures, emphasizing economies of scale and distribution capability.

Exports of St.-Emilion wine rose from fewer than 20,000 hectoliters in 1946 to more than 78,000 in 1981, the latter figure representing 41 percent of all available stock of 190,170 hectoliters. In 1982, two-thirds of all exports were destined for Belgium, the United States, and the United Kingdom (see Table 9.1).

St.-Emilion lies 30 kilometers east of Bordeaux and north of the much flatter Entre-Deux-Mers vineyard. Not a homogeneous area in terms of topography, soil, or climate, it varies significantly from the above-mentioned areas, particularly the Médoc. The climate, more continental than the Médoc, exhibits larger annual and diurnal temperature fluctuations; winters are colder, summers are warmer, and the incidence of humidity and cloud cover is significantly less. Unfortunately, frost is also more prevalent, effecting especially the frost-sensitive Merlot along the plateau section of the producing district. When compared with St.-Estèphe, the northernmost of the four important Médoc communes,

Table 9.1 Sale of St.-Emilion, 1982

Sale	Hectoliters	Percent	Sale	Hectoliters	Percent
Belgium	19,543	28.9	Canada	1.458	2.2
United States	11,743	17.4	Other	5,823	8.6
United Kingdom	8,873	13.1			
Holland	4,694	6.9	Total exports	67,637	100.0
Switzerland	8,471	12.5			
West Germany	4,487	6.6	France	125,190	
Denmark	2,545	3.8	Total sales	192,827	100.0

Source: Conseil Interprofessionnel du Vin de Bordeaux.

annual precipitation is at least 10 percent less, and a minimum of 25 percent less in the critical months of August, September, and October. Nevertheless, total wine production does pulsate in a dramatic fashion with the vagaries of nature, as indicated in Figure 9.1.

In order of decreasing importance, the six generalized soils of St.-Emilion are (a) the limestone plateau (commonly called St.-Martin); (b) the limestone "côtes" that surround a good portion of the limestone plateau; (c) the gravel/clay soils of the extreme northwestern portion near and on the Pomerol boundary; (d) the clay/gravel/sand soils of the northcentral portion of the plateau; (e) the sand soils of the central plateau; and (f) the alluvial soils of the Dordogne.

The limestone portion of the plateau is a small, irregular area that contains ten of the twelve Premier Grand Cru Classé properties. All are located on the outer edges of the plateau, overlapping onto the "côtes," with only one growth located to the east of the town of St.-Emilion. In this area of fewer than 225 hectares, the limestone rises to the surface, and because it is soft, easily worked, and heavily fissured, allows for good root penetration and the production of full-bodied, well-scented wine with admirable aging potential. The medieval town of St.-Emilion lies on the margins of the large limestone escarpment, locally called "côte calcaire," facing south on a gentle incline toward the Dordogne. The vineyards along the southern aspects are not only protected from frost, but experience exceptional air drainage, which reduces the incidence of frost and fungus diseases.

The "côte calcaire" is considered by many to be superior to the limestone plateau because of its better air drainage, stonier soil, and more favorable southerly aspect. The soils are skeletal and contain far less clay than those of the limestone plateau. Soft limestone dominates, and water and air drainage are excellent, yields are low, and the easterly, westerly, and southerly aspects combine to produce the most generous, fragrant, and longest-lived of all St.-Emilions. Throughout this irregular area are varying concentrations of iron oxide and potassium, and, along the lower slopes, sand accumulations, the latter particularly evident in *Ch. l'Arrosée* and *Ch. l'Angelus*. On the higher slopes, the soils are very stony (colluvial) in origin, and by far the best of all the "côtes" sites.

The gravel/clay soils of the western plateau section are synonymous with *Ch. Cheval Blanc* and *Ch. Figeac,* and to a lesser extent *Ch. la-Tour-du-Pin-Figeac, Ch. la Marzelle, Ch. la Dominique,* and *Ch. Ripeau,* among others. The soil of this rather small section contains little or no limestone, but more gravel, clay, and sand. The wines are known for their deep color, pronounced flavor, and enormous bouquet.

The extreme northern portion in and around the cluster of Corbin properties, which contains less gravel but more clay and sand, is marginally more productive than the gravel/clay region farther west. Although long-lived and above average in quality, the wines are a bit coarser and lack the refinement of *Ch. Cheval Blanc.*

The sand belt of the central plateau encompasses approximately 40 percent of the commune of St.-Emilion, but contains few important properties. Wine quality varies widely and, although there are numerous Grand Cru growths, more than half of total output is sold as generic St.-Emilion.

The *palus,* the recently deposited material near the Dordogne, contains little limestone and is composed mainly of silt, clay, and gravel. It is in general poorly drained, with numerous stretches of stagnant water on its surface. Vines from this soil produce incredibly high yields, but the wine lacks bouquet, flavor, and color and is coarse on the palate. Farther inland are a number of older terraces that contain less organic matter, but more gravel, stone, and sand. These areas produce marginally better wine with good color. The wines of the *palus* cannot be sold under the commune name, although those close to the lower foothills are able to market their wines under various communal appellations.

The Vines and Wines

As in Pomerol, the most important grape is Merlot, followed by Cabernet Franc, Cabernet Sauvignon, and Malbec. Despite its susceptibility to frost and fungus diseases, Merlot shows a high degree of concentration in cold, wet, and acidic soils. It yields large berries that are easily crushed to produce soft, fleshy, supple, and early maturing wine. The second most-important grape, Cabernet Franc, when added in judicious amounts to Merlot seems to impart firmness and structure but, when the proportion increases beyond 35 percent, tends to produce coarse and often dull wine. Cabernet Sauvignon faces a number of formidable problems in St.-Emilion. It does not like limestone soil heavy in clay, nor one that is overly fertile—a combination of features that leads to the production of coarse and acidic wine with limited aging possibilities. Malbec is considered the insurance grape because it is very productive and yields early maturing and low-acid wine, the latter feature most important in balancing the overly tannic, acidic, and astringent wines of wet, cloudy, and cool vintages.

Although the yield for all St.-Emilion is restricted to 42 hectoliters per hectare, overcropping is a common and disturbing feature throughout the region. In general, the yield is highest in the richer soils of St.-Pey and lowest in St.-Emilion, highest for the generic St.-Emilion appellation and lowest for the Premier Grand Cru Classé properties, a feature that is partly related to the average age of the vines. For example, while the St.-Emilion appellation contains nearly 46 percent of total hectarage, it has 61 perent of all vines under fifteen years of age; Premier Grand Cru Classé and Grand Cru Classé properties, with nearly 19 percent of all hectarage, contain only 13.5 percent of all vines under the age of fifteen.

The wines of St.-Emilion are noted for their richness, suppleness, fine color, luscious fruity flavor, and a slight trace of pleasing bitterness. Although less austere than most Médocs, they have a lingering fruity aroma, are a shade more powerful, and are more readily accessible. In theory at least, they are said to mature sooner than equivalents from the Médoc and Graves. Their only flaws when compared with fine Médoc are the lack of a long lingering finish, the classic "cigar box" aroma, and their inability to acquire the same complex character with extended bottle age. The very finest, however, along with the best from Pomerol, do acquire a good measure of finesse and elegance after fifteen years. In the final analysis, recent vinification techniques have improved to the point that major disapointments are few. Small quantities of white wine, mainly from Sauvignon Blanc and Merlot Blanc grapes, are also made. Nearly all is above average in quality, very agreeable on the palate, and surprisingly fresh and complex in flavor.

The Union de Producteurs de St.-Emilion is an above-average-quality cooperative and the largest for a single appellation in the Gironde. Founded in 1934, it produces more than 50,000 hectoliters, or between 20 and 30 percent of appellation total, and at least 20 percent of all Grand Cru wine. The cooperative has nearly 400 members and controls 1,000 hectares. It markets its wine under the labels "Les Palmes," "Le Clocher," "Roche d'Emilion," and "Monolithe." It has a fermenting capacity of 200,000 hectoliters, stocks a minimum of 3.5 million bottles, and sells 3 million annually, one-third of which are exported.

The St.-Emilion Classification

The vineyards of St.-Emilion were classified for the first time in 1954 into four specific categories: Premier Grand Cru Classé, Grand Cru Classé, Grand Cru, and generic St.-Emilion (see Table 9.2 for comparative sizes). The first group consisted of twelve properties, and the second seventy-two

Table 9.2   Vine Hectarage and Wine Production in
St.-Emilion, 1982

Appellation category	Hectarage	Percent of Total Wine Production
Premier Grand Cru Classé	4.0	3.0
Grand Cru Classé	14.5	12.0
Grand Cru	36.0	32.0
St.-Emilion	45.5	53.0

Source: Syndicate Viticole de St.-Emilion.

(see Table 9.3). The numbers of the third group, subject to annual review, varied, while the rest were lumped into one large mass of anonymous St.-Emilion. In 1958 the list was fine-tuned to separate the Premier Grand Cru Classé properties into "A" and "B" divisions; the former include *Ch. Ausone* and *Ch. Cheval Blanc,* while the second tier includes the remaining ten. The twelve Premier Grand Cru Classé estates cover approximately 225 hectares and produce about 1 million bottles of wine annually. The Grand Cru Classé properties encompass 742 hectares and produce about 2.5 million bottles annually. The 200 Grand Cru properties embrace nearly 1,900 hectares and produce nearly 8 million bottles. At the base of the pyramid are 750 large and small properties whose total land area is more than 2,200 hectares and which produce more than 11 million bottles, of which nearly 40 perent is made by the appellation's only cooperative.

In the fall of 1969, the list was revised again. While the Premier and Grand Cru Classé rankings remained the same, the syndicat set in motion a system of compulsary tasting before an estate is awarded its rank in a periodic ten-year evaluation, thus assuring, at least in theory, a method by which properties are given an opportunity to move up or down in their ranking. For the Grand Cru, a blind annual tasting is compulsory for that particular property to attain its status for a specific vintage. If it has earned its rank for at least ten consecutive years, it has the right to apply for Grand Cru Classé status; during the past ten years, only *Ch. Berliquet* has achieved this objective. The wines are either accepted, adjourned, or rejected; when the latter occurs, the decision is final and the wine can be sold only as St.-Emilion AOC. The total number or properties with the rank of Grand Cru varies annually according to the quality of the vintage, and it is important to remember that the wine is classified, not the property.

The classification was again revised in 1985 with a number of significant changes. *Ch. Beauséjour-Bécot,* because it had not requested permission to combine several neighboring plots, was demoted to the rank of

Table 9.3 The 1954 St.-Emilion Classification

Premiers Grands Crus Classés

Ch. Ausone	Ch. Beauséjour (Duffau)	Ch. Clos Fourtet	Ch. Magdelaine
Ch. Cheval Blanc	Ch. Bélair	Ch. Figeac	Ch. Pavie
Ch. Beauséjour (Bécot)[a]	Ch. Canon	Ch. la Gaffeliere	Ch. Trottevielle

Grands Crus Classés

Ch. L'Angelus	Ch. la Clusière	Ch. Grand-Mayne	Ch. Pavie-Macquin
Ch. L'Arrossée	Ch. Corbin Michotte	Ch. Grand-Pontet	Ch. Pavillon-Cadet
Ch. Balestard la Tonnelle	Ch. Côte Baleau (Baleau)[f]	Ch. Grandes-Murailles[g]	Ch. Petit-Faurie-de-Soutard
Ch. Bellevue	Ch. la Couspaude[g]	Ch. Guadet-St.-Julien	Ch. le Prieuré
Ch. Bergat	Ch. Coutet[g]	Ch. Haut-Corbin	Ch. Ripeau
Ch. Berliquet[b]	Ch. Couvent des Jacobins	Ch. Haut-Sarpe	Ch. Sansonnet
Ch. Cadet-Bon[g]	Ch. Croque-Michotte	Ch. Jean Faure[g]	Ch. St.-Georges-Côte-Pavie
Ch. Cadet-Piola	Ch. Curé-Bon	Ch. Laniote	Ch. Soutard
Ch. Canon-la-Gaffelière	Ch. Dassault	Ch. Larcis-Ducasse	Ch. Terre Daugay
Ch. Cap-de-Mourlin[c]	Ch. la Dominique	Ch. Lamarzelle	Ch. la Tour-du-Pin-Figeac (Giraud)
Ch. Chapelle-Medeleine[d]	Ch. Faurie-de-Souchard	Ch. Larmande	Ch. la Tour-du-Pin-Figeac (Moueix)
Ch. la Carte[e]	Ch. Fonplegade	Ch. Laroze	Ch. la Tour Figeac
Ch. le Chatelet	Ch. Fonroque	Ch. La Serre	Ch. Trimoulet
Ch. Chauvin	Ch. Franc-Mayne	Ch. Matras	Ch. Trois-Moulins [e]
Ch. Clos des Jacobins	Ch. Grand	Ch. Mauvezin	Ch. Troplong-Mondot
Ch. Clos la Madeleine	Barrail-Lamarzelle-Figeac	Ch. Moulin-du-Cadet	Ch. Villemaurine
Ch. Clos St-Martin[f]	Ch. Grand Corbin-Despagne	Ch. l'Oratoire	Ch. Yvon-Figeac
Ch. la Clotte	Ch. Grand Corbin	Ch. Pavie Decesse	

[a]Demoted to Grand Cru Classé in 1985.
[b]Elevated from Grand Cru in 1985.
[c]Two properties now joined into one.
[d]Incorporated with Ch. Ausone.

[e]Incorporated into Ch. Beauséjour (Bécot) and demoted to Grand Cru in 1985.
[f]Incorporated into Ch. Grandes-Murailles and demoted to Grand Cru in 1985.
[g]Demoted to Grand Cru in 1985.

Grand Cru Classé, and ten additional properties either merged or were demoted to the rank of Grand Cru.

THE GROWTHS OF ST.-EMILION

Premier Grand Cru Classé

The twelve Premier Grand Cru Classé vineyards contain fewer than 225 hectares of vineland and produce about 9,000 hectoliters of wine, or 4 and 3 percent of appellation totals, respectively. The wine is considered superior to all other growths because of its structure, color, bouquet, and flavor. These properties also contain older vines, whose wines are carefully made and aged. With only *Ch. Belair* and *Clos Fourtet* as possible exceptions, the standard of quality is exceptionally high, offering outstanding value especially when compared with Burgundy and first-growth Médoc.

Ch. Ausone, the foremost property of St.-Emilion, consists of 7 hectares that produce fewer than 3,200 cases from comparatively old vines. One of the oldest in the Gironde, the property sits on a Roman site first settled and planted in vines in the 4th century. At least 5 hectares lie on a thick bed of soft, well-drained limestone, locally referred to as "la Magdelaine." During the period 1962–80, the wine was notoriously inconsistent, expensive, and early maturing; fortunately, recent vintages are much improved. Although less robust than most St.-Emilions, the wine is known for its long, lingering finish, finesse, and stylish character. *Ch. Cheval Blanc,* located on clay (with iron-bearing subsoil) on the gravel portion of the producing district, has better keeping qualities than *Ch. Ausone,* although it is second to *Ch. Pavie* in production and shares many features with the finer Pomerol properties. It is one of the top twenty-five properties in the Gironde and is widely considered by some to be the finest growth in St.-Emilion. The wine is firm yet round, elegant, big, full-bodied, well-flavored, tannin-rich, and known for its pronounced and lingering aroma. The vineyard was nearly destroyed in the 1956 frost, which makes the bulk of the vines less than thirty-five years old, but as they age, wine quality will continue to improve. The property consists of 37 hectares producing 11,500 cases of wine. Very unusual is the fact that Cabernet Franc, not Merlot, is the dominant grape.

Ch. Canon, a 17-hectare property located on the limestone plateau, produces more than 8,000 cases of absolutely marvelous wine. An excellent, old-fashioned estate, it is currently making full-bodied, long-lived, powerful, complex, firm, and highly reliable wine that takes at least fifteen years to mature fully and offers outstanding value. *Ch. Figeac* is a large 34-hectare property lying on gravel/clay soils next to Pomerol. Because of iron in the subsoil and an unusually high percentage of

Plate 9.2   Ch. Cheval-Blanc

Plate 9.3   Ch. la Gaffelière

Cabernet Sauvignon, this estate makes tannin-rich wines that require patience. Although not as supple as other growths, the wine is old-fashioned: dark, firm, multidimensional in flavor, rich, and substantial on the palate. When completely mature it is characterized by delicacy, a complex nose, and considerable elegance. Offering outstanding value, the output exceeds 17,000 cases. *Ch. Magdelaine* is an 11-hectare property that makes 5,000 cases of wine. Containing one of the highest percentages of Merlot among the top growths, its wine is relatively early maturing, silky, elegant, supple, and delicate. *Ch. Trottevieille* is a 10-hectare estate that makes 5,000 cases of wine known for its dark color, fullness, and great depth of flavor and bouquet. The property has not been producing wine up to its true potential in recent years, and in general offers value only in good vintages. *Ch. Pavie* is a 37-hectare property superbly situated on the "côtes" that makes more than 16,000 cases of stylish, supple, fruity and, in good vintages, intensely flavored and scented wine. Notoriously inconsistent during the past twenty-five years, the property has recently made changes with marked improvement in the wine. This estate is the most prominent in a small but good stable of properties. *Ch. la Gaffelière,* a 24-hectare property located on the "côtes" downslope from *Ch. Belair,* produces more than 10,000 cases. The medieval-looking estate, well situated along a south-facing slope, is well managed and makes supple, plummy, fruity, and fleshy wine—highly consistent, though often dull and not as firm as other neighboring properties. *Ch. Beauséjour* (Duffau), along with *Ch. Ausone,* is the smallest of the Premiers Grands Crus Classés. Historically very popular, it now produces a hard, firm wine that takes at lest ten years to soften. The property, located on the west-facing "côtes," consists of 7 hectares and makes approximately 3,500 cases. *Ch. Bélair,* on the limestone edge of the plateau south of the town of St.-Emilion, is a 14-hectare property that has one of the most spectacular exposures in the entire appellation. Although the wines have shown signs of improvement, they remain lighter than most, inconsistent, and not up to potential. Output is approximately 4,500 cases. *Clos Fourtet* is a 15-hectare property lying on the limestone plateau along the western margins of the town of St.-Emilion. Although in good vintages the wines are dark and full-bodied and require at least fifteen years to mature fully, they are usually dull and awkwardly made and require careful selection. Annual output is approximately 6,000 cases. *Ch. Beauséjour*-Bécot, the larger of the two Beauséjours, consists of 18 hectares producing nearly 10,000 cases. The wine during the past twenty years has been rather thin, variable, and early maturing. It was purchased in dismal condition by Bécot in 1969 and has since been restored to its historical place among the twelve supreme sites of St.-Emilion. In 1979, the owner acquired and incorporated *Ch. la Carte* and *Ch. les Trois Moulins* without permission from the local commission; as a consequence, it was demoted in a very emotion-charged decision to Grand Cru Classé status in 1985.

Grand Cru Classé

The more-numerous Grand Cru Classé properties contain nearly 750 hectares and produce 36,000 hectoliters of wine. Unlike the clustered distribution of the Premier Grand Cru Classé properties along the "cotes" and limestone plateau, these growths are almost evenly divided among the three most-important soil types. No fewer than twenty-five are located on "côtes" sites, eighteen are located on the limestone plateau, and the remainder are scattered on the "graves" plateau to the north and west of the town of St.-Emilion.

   Ch. l'Angelus* is a 28-hectare property downslope from both Beauséjour estates that has not, until recently, produced the quality wine possible from its superb exposure and soils.* At its best, the wine is supple, fine-grained, with a long, penetrating bouquet. Yet the wine is inconsistent and can be overly rustic and often coarse. Output regularly exceeds 13,000 cases. *Ch. l'Arrosée,* a 16-hectare property superbly situated on the "côtes," is currently making wine equal to the top-ranked growths—big, rich, powerful yet supple, well-flavored, and scented. This highly underrated wine offers outstanding value and should be part of every serious cellar. *Ch. Baleau** is a 15-hectare property united with *Ch. Grandes-Murailles,* both of which have been demoted to Grand Cru status. *Ch. Balestard-la-Tonnelle**, one of the best and most underrated properties, dates to the 15th century. This 11-hectare estate makes 5,000 cases of full-bodied, dark, flavorful, and altogether first-class wine, high in extract and consistently above average. *Ch. Bellevue,* located along the lower margins of the western "côtes," is an obscure 9-hectare property that dates to the 18th century. Part of a small stable of properties, it produces 3,000 cases of full-bodied, average-quality wine. *Ch. Bergat* is an obscure 3-hectare property that makes 1,500 cases of above-average but often dull wine. *Ch. Berliquet,* a 9-hectare "côtes" property lying in the center of a cluster of prestigious chateaux, produces 4,000 cases of excellent, full-flavored, and scented wine. *Ch. Cadet-Bon,* a small, obscure 3-hectare property located on the limestone plateau, produces 2,000 cases of good, sound, fruity, long-lasting wine that often offers good value. *Ch. Cadet-Piola**, located on the limestone plateau just north of St.-Emilion, consists of 7 hectares that produce more than 3,000 cases of wine. Rarely disappointing, this little-known estate consistently makes complex, con-

*The 27 properties listed with an asterisk belong to the Association de Propriétaires de Grands Crus Classés de St.-Emilion, a syndicat whose objective is to defend the integrity of the St.-Emilion name with effective advertising and to regulate quality by restricting the yield to 37 hectoliters per hectare. These properties collectively account for half the hectarage of all Grand Cru Classé growths and 32 percent of total production.

centrated, big wines that often approach the quality levels of Premier Grand Cru and thus offer outstanding value. *Ch. Canon-la-Gaffeliere** is a 20-hectare property, located along the lower slopes of the southern "côtes." The wine, rarely more than 10,000 cases, is good but often dull, and is not as distinctive as other neighboring properties.

*Ch. Cap-de-Mourlin**, which consists of two recently reunited, identical properties of 18 hectares, makes 7,500 cases of close-knit, chewy, flavorful wine. *Ch. la Carte,* lying immediately west of the northern section of the town of St.-Emilion, was incorporated with *Ch. Beauséjour-Bécot* and is no longer being bottled under its own label. *Ch. Chapelle-Madeleine* is a small plot of less than 1 hectare now incorporated with *Ch. Ausone. Ch. le Chatelet,* a small 5-hectare property, produces fewer than 2,500 cases of full-bodied, dark, fruity wine with a good reputation. *Ch. Chauvin,* adjoining *Ch. Ripeau,* is a 13-hectare property located on gravel soil. The wines are inconsistent and often dull, although in above-average vintages they can be full-bodied, solid, and long-lived. *Ch. la Clotte* is an 11-hectare "côtes" property that produces 2,000 cases of Merlot-dominated wine known for its soft, fruity, supple character. It often rivals the better growths and can offer good value. *Ch. la Clusiere** is a 3-hectare property located next to its owner, *Ch. Pavie.* It produces 1,500 cases of light, early maturing wine that has been recently improved. *Ch. Corbin,* a 15-hectare property located in the center of the northern sand/clay region, produces more than 7,000 cases of wine. Like all Corbin properties, the wine is tannin-rich and overpowers the fruit of the wine until it softens over a prolonged period of bottle-aging. An outstanding wine, this and all other Corbin wine is recommended for the serious cellar. *Ch. Corbin-Michotte* is a 7-hectare property making more than 3,000 cases of consistently good, sound, well-structured wine that requires extensive cellaring. *Ch. la Couspaude* is a little-known 7-hectare vineyard that makes 4,000 cases of firm, often rustic wine. In 1985 it was demoted to Grand Cru status.

Ch. Coutet is a little-known 17-hectare "côtes" property that makes more than 6,000 cases of full-bodied, firm, dark, chewy, but inconsistent wine. In 1985, it was also demoted to Grand Cru status. *Ch. Couvent-des-Jacobins* is a postage-stamp-sized property making fewer than 1,000 cases of highly variable wine. *Croque-Michotte**, a 14-hectare property, is superbly located in the gravelly plateau portion of the appellation. The wines are outstanding—full-bodied, dark, well-structured, intensely flavored, capable of extensive cellaring—and offer excellent value. Output exceeds 6,000 cases. *Ch. Curé-Bon* is a 5-hectare, 16th-century property located on the western fringes of the limestone plateau of St.-Emilion. The vineyards, located on a steep slope, produce outstanding dark, well-flavored, and scented wine that has a wide following. *Ch. Dassault**, 28-hectare property facing St-George, produces 11,000 cases of good, sound, flavorful wine. *Ch. la Dominique**, a 17-hectare property located in the northern gravel plateau next to *Ch. Cheval Blanc,* is currently a very popular wine in the United States and the United Kingdom. It is known for eminently fruity, supple, and early maturing features; much improved over the past twenty years, it is very reliable and offers excellent value. *Ch. Faurie-de-Souchard**, an 11-hectare, "côtes" property owned by *Ch. Cadet-Piola,* makes rather hard, single-dimensional, and unyielding wine when young. Production is approximately 4,500 cases, offering value only in good vintages. *Ch. Fonplegade** is a superb 18-hectare property, reputedly a Roman site, located upslope from *Ch. l'Arrosée.* It is owned by Armand Mouiex and forms the center of a large stable of above-average estates in St.-Emilion and Pomerol. The wine is full-bodied, well scented and flavored and, because it is very reliable, offers excellent value. Output exceeds 8,000 cases. *Ch. Fonroque**, a 19-hectare estate located on the limestone plateau, produces more than 11,000 cases of dark, robust, well-structured wine in good vintages. *Ch. Franc-Mayne* is an obscure 6-hectare property located on the northern fringes of the limestone plateau next to the larger and more important *Ch. Grand-Mayne.* The wine is full-bodied and well flavored, with a lingering finish. Output approaches 3,000 cases.

Ch. Grand-Barrail-Lamarzelle-Figeac, a large 40-hectare "graves" property located in the northwest section of the producing district, produces more than 20,000 cases. Although well regarded in the area, the wine appears to be brawny, and is often unbalanced. Recent changes indicate that wine quality has improved. *Ch. Grand-Corbin-Despagne* is a 23-hectare property in the center of the Corbin cluster in the extreme northern section of the "graves" area. It is a superb estate, making full-bodied, generous, mouth-filling, highly concentrated wine that is consistently well made, and offers outstanding value. It is a wine for the serious collector and requires fifteen years of bottle-aging for complete maturation. Output exceeds 12,000 cases. *Ch. Grand-Corbin* (Giraud) is a 15-hectare property that makes more than 6,000 cases. Unlike other Corbins, the Giraud estate contains more Cabernet Sauvignon and produces huge, muscular, concentrated, full-bodied and exceptionally dark wines that require at least fifteen years to mature fully. Impeccably made, the wine offers outstanding value for the patient collector.

Ch. Grandes-Murailles* is a 20-hectare "côte" property that makes 11,000 cases of fruity but thin, inconsistent wine. As of 1985, the property has been demoted to Grand Cru status. *Ch. Grand-Mayne,* a 16-hectare property on the western extension of the "côtes," produces 10,000 cases of soft, delicate, early maturing wine. *Ch. Grand-Pontet,* a 15-hectare "côtes" property, was once owned by Barton and Gustier. Since 1980, when the property changed ownership, the quality has improved noticeably from a dull and brawny-type character to an easier, fruity, and more supple style. Output exceeds 5,000 cases. *Ch. Gaudet-St.-Julien** is a small 6-hectare propety that dates back to the second half of the 18th century. Lying on the northern outskirts of St.-Emilion, the property is known for full-bodied, well-structured wine that exhibits a good dose of elegance, finesse, and flavor. Output is about 2,500 cases. *Ch. Haut-Corbin,* with less than 5 hectares, is the smallest of the Corbin estates. Output consists of fewer than 2,600 cases of full-bodied, firm, extremely long-lived wine, presenting outstanding value. *Ch. Haut-Sarpe*,* an 11-hectare property lying mainly within St.-Christophe, produces approximately 5,500 cases. Once weak and inconsistent, the improved wine is now fuller, more generous, and concentrated. *Clos des Jacobins* is a 9-hectare property on the northern edge of the limestone plateau. It produces 6,000 cases of smooth, dark, medium-bodied wine that is impeccably made, firm, well structured and, like all Cordier properties, always consistent.

Ch. Jean-Faure is a 20-hectare property exquisitely located in the western gravel/clay region. A highly regarded property known for full-bodied, well-structured wines that suffer from inconsistency, its output is approximately 8,000 cases. As of 1985 the property was demoted to Grand Cru status. *Ch. Laniote* is an obscure 5-hectare property that makes 2,500 cases of average-quality wine. *Ch. Larmande*,* dating to the 16th century, is an 18-hectare property known for its meticulous care in the making of complex, well-flavored and scented wine that ages well. Output exceeds 8,000 cases. *Ch. Larcis-Ducasse*,* a 10-hectare "côtes" property adjoining *Ch. Pavie,* is located in the neighboring parish of St.-Laurent. A good, well-made, but somewhat austere wine, it is dark, well-scented, yet inconsistent. In good vintages it offers exceptional value despite the fact that the property is not producing wine equal to its potential. *Ch. Laroze,* a 25-hectare property lying on sand and clay soils, produces 11,500 cases of wine known for balance and scent. *Clos la Madeleine,* a tiny 2-hectare property lying on the limestone plateau, makes fewer than 1,000 cases of wine are exported only to Belgium. *Ch. Lamarzelle,* a 15-hectare property, produces 3,000 cases of good, sound, but often dull wine. *Ch. Matras* lies along the foot of the western "côtes." This old 17-hectare estate has recently been expanded and now produces more than 5,000 cases of average but "grassy"-tasting wine. The property is well regarded in the area, and its wine is rather expensive. *Ch. Mauvesin,* a small 4-hectare property lying along the northeast edges of the limestone plateau, produces 2,000 cases of above-average, well-flavored, and scented wine. *Ch. Moulin-du-Cadet* is a little-known property of 5 hectares with an output of 2,000 cases. The wine is expertly made, delicate, fruity, supple, and consistently good.

Clos de l'Oratoire,* is an 8-hectare "côtes" property that makes 3,000 cases of outstanding, dark, supple, and well-flavored wine. *Ch. Pavie-Decesse*,* a superbly situated 8-hectare "côtes" property, is owned by *Ch. Pavie.* Although lighter and fruiter than most neighboring properties, the wine can easily captivate the wine lover. Regularly offering good value, output is approximately 4,000 cases. *Ch. Pavie-Macquin* is a 9-hectare "côtes" property that makes 4,000 cases of light, fruity, eminently drinkable wine. *Ch. Pavillon-Cadet,* a small, obscure property of less than 2 hectares, makes 1,000 cases of wine that is sold principally to private clients. *Ch. Petit-Faurie-de-Soutard**, dating to the 19th century, is an 8-hectare "côtes" property that makes 3,400 cases well-flavored and scented wine. Locally said to be "thick," it requires at least ten years to mature fully, is very scarce, and well worth the effort to locate. *Ch. le Prieuré,* an obscure 6-hectare property lying along the eastern edges of the town of St.-Emilion, manages to maintain a loyal following. Its output consists of 2,000 cases of well-made, impressive, long-lived wine that offers good value. *Ch. Ripeau* is a 20-hectare property located just south of the cluster of Corbin estates. Twenty years ago it was considered superior to *Ch. la Dominique,* its immediate neighbor to the west, but no more. The wine, now made lighter, suffers from inconsistency; the property, however, has a fantastic capacity for the production of superb, well-balanced, complex wine, with an output of approximately 8,000 cases. *Clos St.-Martin**, a 4-hectare vineyard located on a good, elevated site, is now united with *Ch. Grandes-Murailles. Ch. St.-Georges-Côte-Pavie,* a small, obscure 6-hectare "côtes" property, makes 2,500 cases of mild, supple, early maturing, but often dull wine. *Ch. Sansonnet,* an 8-hectare property, produces fewer than 3,000 cases of average-quality but undistinguished wine.

    Ch. la Serre*, a 7-hectare property lying immediately to the east of St.-Emilion, is an underrated and little-known property producing nearly 4,000 cases of fruity, well-balanced, flavorful, and early maturing wine. *Ch. Soutard,* a large 24-hectare property lying on well-drained chalky soil, produces more than 9,000 cases of outstanding wine. Having excellent color, a fine, delicate bouquet, and a long, lingering finish, it is one of the most popular in the appellation. *Ch. Tertre-Dugay,* a 15-hectare property sitting on a promontory, produces approximately 7,000 cases. An old property recently acquired by *Ch. la Gaffelière,* it is again producing first-class wine. *Ch. la Tour-du-Pin-Figeac** (Giraud), located west of *Che. Cheval Blanc* on the Pomerol border, is the largest portion of a vineyard divided long ago. The wine can be excellent, but it suffers from inconsistency and a bitter finish. *Ch. la Tour-du-Pin-Figeac** (Mouiex), with 5 hectares, produces 2,100 cases of firm, austere, tannin-rich, classic wine. The wine, much the better of the two properties, offers excellent value. *Ch. Trimoulet* is an 18-hectare property facing the Barbanne River in the extreme northeastern portion of the appellation. The wine is not only concentrated but is perfectly balanced and consistently good. Very distinctive due to its austere flavor, its tannin-rich and well-structured character requires long cellaring to soften. Usually offering outstanding value, the output is approximately 6,000 cases. *Ch. Trois-Moulins* is an obscure property of approximately 4 hectares now incorporated with *Ch. Beauséjour-Bécot. Ch. Troplong Mondot**, a 29-hectare estate located on the highest portion of the limestone plateau southeast of St.-Emilion, produces 13,000 cases of wine known for its suppleness, fruit, and balance. *Ch. Villemaurine,* an 8-hectare property on the northeast edge of St.-Emilion, makes 3,000 cases of astringent and "grassy"-flavored wine—but one that ages surprisingly well. *Ch. Yvon-Figeac,* a 21-hectare property located on flat ground in the west-central portion of the appellation, produces 10,000 cases of good, well-structured wine. *Ch. la Tour-Figeac**, a 40-hectare "graves" property that was once part of *Ch. Figeac,* produces nearly 7,000 cases of excellent wine—full-bodied, dark, well structured, offering superb value. One of the sturdiest wines of the appellation, it should not be missed.

Grand Cru and Other Important Properties

In addition to the Premier and Grand Cru Classé properties, there are more than 500 additional properties, three-quarters of which frequently qualify for Grand Cru status. It must be remembered that while all Premier and Grand Cru Classé growths must be located within the confines of the commune of St.-Emilion (there are two exceptions), Grand Cru growths need not. They are distributed by commune in the following manner: St.-Emilion 52, St.-Sulpice 95, St.-Christophe 65, St.-Etienne 65, St.-Laurent 36, St. Pey 34, Vignonet 30, and St.-Hippolyte 22. Occupying terrain that is less than ideal, the properties produce wine that is similar in style, but not as good as Premier and Grand Cru Classé in terms of concentration, depth of flavor, and fragrance. The wines are well made but slightly lower in alcohol, and the average yield is at least 20

Plate 9.4   Ch. Troplong-Mondot

percent higher. Not terribly popular in the United States, they are more common in the United Kingdom, the Low Countries, West Germany, and Scandinavia. Within France, they answer the need for less expensive Bordeaux for medium-grade restaurants and hotels. All but the very best (but not necessarily the largest growths) will not barrel-age prior to bottling. Because the number of growths awarded the rank of Grand Cru varies annually, a separate list is not given, but the principal properties by commune are listed below.

Within the commune of St.-Emilion, the majority of the third- and fourth-tier properties are located in the central, sandy region of the appellation and southeast of the town of St.-Emilion. Since 1973, in addition to the properties included within the confines of the St.-Emilion communal appellation, the wines of two small areas—Sables and Libourne—were also included. The principal properties follow: *Ch. le Couvent,* located in the eastern margins of the town of St.-Emilion, is a tiny property of less than 2 hectares that makes excellent wine worthy of higher rank. *Ch. Pindefleurs* is a 10-hectare "côtes" property that makes 3,000 cases of light, early maturing, well-flavored wine. The tiny, 4-hectare property of *Ch. le Tertre-Roteboeuf* makes fewer than 2,000 cases of surprisingly full-bodied, powerful, well-flavored wine offering excellent value. *Ch. Cadet-Pontet* is an 8-hectare "côtes" property that makes 1,800 cases of full-bodied, tannin-rich wine. *Ch. Cormeil-Figeac,* a large 20-hectare property, makes 4,000 cases of highly distinctive wine. It is an ecological-minded estate that does little to tamper with the vine and its wine. As a result, the wine is full, well-structured, concentrated, high in extract, and very flavorful. *Ch. Haut-Pontet* is a 5-hectare property that makes 2,200 cases of above-average, full-bodied wine that offers excellent value. *Ch. la Fleur,* a 9-hectare property, makes 3,500 cases of superb, flavorful wine that consistently offers good value. *Ch. Bonnet* is a 23-hectare property making 11,000 cases of wine known for fruity flavor and a lingering finish. *Ch. la Commanderie,* one of the best of the Grand Crus, is a 4-hectare property making 1,300 cases of full-bodied, rich, long-keeping wine. *Ch. Cardinal Villemaurine* is a large 30-hectare property making 4,000 cases of full-bodied, fruity, tannin-rich wine intended for long keeping. A recently expanded and rehabilitated property, *Ch. Rocher-Bellevue-Figeac* is currently making excellent medium-bodied, fruity and supple wine that offers outstanding value.

Ch. la Grâce-Dieu-les-Menuts, a 13-hectare property, produces 6,300 cases of superb, well-made, full Médoc-type wine, tannin-rich, astringent, and old fashioned, requiring time to mature. *Ch. Varteau-Matras,* a 15-hectare property, makes 6,000 cases of very fragrant and distinctive wine. *Ch. la Grave Figeac* is a small, reliable 5-hectare "graves" property making above-average, full-bodied, meaty wine. *Ch. Franc-Pourret* is a "côtes" property making 3,000 cases of well-knit, solid, masculine wine that ages well. *Ch. Petit-Figeac,* a minor 1.5-hectare property located in the "graves" section, makes fewer than 600 cases of full-bodied, fragrant wine strongly influenced by a high percentage of Cabernet Sauvignon. *Ch. Magnan-la-Gaffelière* is an 8-hectare property making 3,000 cases of outstanding wine—rich, concentrated, high in extract, and well flavored. *Clos des Menuts,* a 22-hectare property, produces 11,000 cases of supple, light-colored, and early maturing wine. *Ch. Montlabert,* a 15-hectare property located to the west of St.-Emilion, produces 6,000 cases of supple, early maturing wine. *Ch. Patris,* an 8-hectare "côtes" property, produces 3,500 cases of full-bodied, assertive wine that ages well and offers excellent value. Other important properties include: *Clos St.-Julien, Ch. la Rose Trimoulet, Dne. de la Gaffelière, Ch. Carteau-Côte-Faugay, Ch. Haut-Mazerat, Ch. Truquet, Ch. Croix-de-Figeac, Ch. Peyrelongue, Ch. Peyreau, Ch. Grand-Fortin, Ch. Grand Lartigue, Ch. Grand Corbin-Manuel,* and *Ch. Martinet.*

The good-sized village of St.-Sulpice-de-Faleyrens is located southwest of St.-Emilion on the edge of the Dordogne floodplain. With more than 850 hectares of vineland, it is second only to St.-Emilion in wine production. While more than three-quarters of production is not worthy of communal designation, a number of properties have a national reputation. Among the many growths, the following are considered above average to excellent in the production of quality wine. *Ch. Monbousquet,* an elegant 40-hectare property, makes 15,000 cases of wine that is consistently well made, supple, with a long finish, that offers excellent value. It is the leading estate in the area and the standard for the commune. *Ch. le Castelot,* a 6-hectare property, makes 2,000 cases of expertly made, full-bodied wine that offers outstanding value. *Ch. Bigaroux,* the largest of the four properties with a similar name, makes 6,300 cases of above-average, meaty, well-flavored wine that offers considerable value. *Ch. Grand Bigaroux,* with 6 hectares and an output of 1,500 cases, makes rustic, well-flavored wine. *Ch. Franc-Bigaroux* is a 9-hectare property making 3,900 cases of light-bodied yet flavorful wine. *Ch. Petit-Bigaroux,* the fourth and smallest of the Bigaroux properties, makes fewer than 2,000 cases of dark, plummy, well-flavored wine. *Ch. de Lescours* is a large, 35-hectare property making more than 15,000 cases of wine for the mass overseas market.

Ch. la Chapelle-Lescours is an 8-hectare property making 3,000 cases of surprisingly smooth, well-structured red and 500 cases of fragrant and fruity white wine. *Ch. Moulin-de-Pierrefitte* is a 7-hectare property making 2,000 cases of full-bodied, flavorful, well-structured wine offering good value. *Ch. Jacqueminot,* a tiny, little-known property of less than 2 hectares, is currently making outstanding, well-structured wines that offer excellent value. *Ch. Flouquet* is a 20-hectare property producing fragrant and well-colored wine. *Ch. Gravet-Renaissance* is a 14-hectare property producing more than 5,500 cases of full-bodied, well-flavored wine. *Ch. Palais-Cardinal-la-Fuie* is a 15-hectare "côtes" property produc-

Plate 9.5   Ch. Monbousquet, St.-Sulpice

ing 6,000 cases of good, sound, appellation-quality wine. *Ch. Faleyrens* is a 6-hectare property producing 3,000 cases of well-structured, tannin-rich wine with a capacity to age. Other properties include *Ch. Croix-Bertinat, Ch. Grand-Pey-Lescours, Ch. Gravet, Ch. Plaisance,* and *Ch. la Sablonerie.*

Containing 614 hectares of vineland and about 95 growers, the village of St.-Christophe-des-Bardes, located east of St.-Emilion, is one of two villages surrounding St.-Emilion with a Grand Cru Classé growth—*Ch. Haut-Sarpe.* Of the 63 growers, the following have established reputations. *Ch. Fombrauge,* a large 75-hectare property located east of St.-Christophe, produces 22,000 cases of well-made wine intended for the mass market. *Ch. Laroque,* the second-largest property, makes a similar amount of wine and is well represented in foreign markets. *Ch. Tour St.-Christophe* is a 20-hectare property producing 7,000 cases of full-flavored, tannin-rich wine that often approaches Grand Cru Classé quality. *Ch. Coudert-Pelletan* is a 6-hectare property that makes 3,000 cases of full-bodied, concentrated, high-extract wine that repays keeping. *Ch. Barde-Haut,* a well-situated property of 16 hectares, produces 8,300 cases of robust, tannin-rich, mouth-filling wine. *Ch. Gaubert* is a 10-hectare property producing 4,200 cases of above-average appellation-quality wine. Other properties include: *Ch. Laplagnotte-Bellevue, Ch. Vieux-Sarpe, Ch. du Cauze, Ch. Lapelletrie, Ch. Haut-Lallade, Ch. Puyblanquet-Carille, Ch. Lavallade, Ch. Tauzinat, Ch. St.-Christophe,* and *Ch. Milon.*

The small hamlet of St.-Etienne is located in the eastern section of the St.-Emilion vineyard and consists of two types of properties: the "côtes" sites that produce the lowest yields and the best wine, and the flatter, less gravelly, richer sites making very high yields and "grassy-flavored" wine. Historically known as St.-Estèphe de St.-Emilion, the hamlet contains 509 hectares of vineland and more than sixty growths, of which the following are important: *Ch. Gaillard-de-la-Gorce, Ch. du Calvaire, Ch. Puy-Blanquet, Ch. de Pressac, Ch. Tour-de-Pressac, Ch. Tour-Puyblanquet, Ch. du Vieux-Guinot, Ch. Mon-Bel-Air, Ch. Côtes Bernateau,* and *Ch. Fleur Cardinale.*

The village of St.-Laurent-des-Combes, located just 2 kilometers from St.-Emilion, is well situated on the edge of the limestone plateau. It contains one Grand Cru Classé *(Ch. Larcis-Ducasse),* 283 hectares of vineland, and thirty-six growths, of which seven have the potential of producing wine of Grand Cru Classé quality. In general, the quality of wine produced from this village is quite high and includes the following properties: *Ch. Bellefont-Belcier,* a 20-hectare "côtes" property, makes 6,500 cases of excellent, full-bodied, well-structured, firm wine capable of extended cellaring. *Belleton-Belcier-Guiller* is a much smaller property making less than 3,000 cases of similar quality wine. *Ch. Tour-Baladoz,* an 11-hectare property, makes 2,500 cases of superb wine from low-yielding vines that offer outstanding value. *Ch. le Tertre* is a small 5-hectare property making approximately 2,000 cases of exceptional wine from very low yields. *Ch. Pipeau* is a superb, 35-hectare property consistently producing above-average, full-bodied, well-structured, and scented wine offering excellent value. *Ch. Rozier,* an 18-hectare property located at the foot of the limestone plateau, produces 5,000 cases of above-average, stylish wine. *Ch. la Barde* is a 5-hectare property making 2,000 cases from low-yielding vines. The full, old-fashioned wine has plenty of staying power without excessive tannin and astringency. Other properties include *Ch. la Mondotte, Ch. Beard-la-Chapelle, Ch. Beard, Ch. la Bouygue,* and *Ch. de la Barde.*

At the intersection of three roads leading to Bergerac, Libourne, and Bordeaux lies the small village of St.-Pey with 384 hectares of vineland and nearly three dozen growers, eight of which are important: *Ch. de St.-Pey* (Musset), *Ch. de St.-Pey* (Blanche Aînée), *Ch. Fourney, Ch. St.-Hubert, Ch. la Pointe-Bouquey, Ch. St.-Lô, Ch. Bonnet,* and *Ch. la Croix-Fourney.*

The port village of Vignonet is located on the Dordogne in the extreme southern portion of the vine-producing district of greater St.-Emilion. It is a large vineyard of 415 hectares (mostly *palus*) producing coarse, unappealing wines. Nevertheless, out of approximately thirty growers, nearly half are located on higher, better-drained, former river terraces and have attained Grand Cru status. The following eight growths have established reputations: *Ch. Haut-Brisson, Ch. Moulin-Bellegrave, Ch. du Paradis, Ch. Hautes-Graves-d'Arthus, Ch. Bellegrave, Ch. Teyssier, Ch. du Val d'Or,* and *Ch. Destieu.*

The small village of St.-Hippolyte, lying at the foot of the limestone plateau, contains approximately 285 hectares of vineland and twenty-two growths, nearly all of which are of Grand Cru quality. In general, the yield is high with the best properties oriented on or near the "cotes." The following enjoy well-established reputations: *Ch. Destieux* (an excellent 8-hectare property making 4,000 cases of big, tannin-rich wine); *Ch. de Ferrand* (owned by Marcel Bich, a large, immaculate 28-hectare estate that makes 12,000 cases of dark, concentrated wine); *Ch. Lasseque* (a large 23-hectare property with an excellent exposure, making 10,000 cases of dark, full-bodied, well-structured, but often dull wine); *Ch. Haut-Plantey; Ch. Gaillard, Dne. de la Vieille-Eglise, Ch. Tour-du-Sème, Ch. Bouquey, Ch. Pailhas, Ch. Capet, Ch. Maurens, Ch. Monlot-Capet, Ch. Pipeau-Ménichot,* and *Ch. la Melissière.*

St.-Emilion Satellites: Lussac, Montagne, Parsac, Puisseguin, and St.-Georges

A very productive area, the region north and east of St.-Emilion consists of the communes of Lussac, Montagne, Parsac, St.-Georges, and Puisseguin, all of which, since 1936, have earned the right to hyphenate their name to St.-Emilion. Collectively, they are known as the St.-Emilion satellites; as of 1973, St.-Georges and Parsac have become part of Montagne.

The entire area, with more than 3,000 hectares of vineland, is growing at a rate of more than 20 hectares per year. The wine is overwhelmingly red, with only minor amounts of rosé and white being made; the former, from a maximum yield of 42 hectoliters to the hectare, contains at least 11 percent alcohol. The wines, in general, are well made but suffer from a lack of recognition. They are usually the product of overcropping, are hastily made, and receive scant barrel-aging prior to bottling. The very best rank with the top-of-the-line Grand Cru wines of St.-Emilion, but most of them are humble table wines with little pretense to greatness. While a large number offer excellent value within the producing region, most (with a few rare exceptions) are unable to compete with comparable wines from neighboring appellations, particularly Fronsac.

The satellite commune of Montagne, located 4 kilometers due north of St.-Emilion, contains more than 1,300 hectares of vineland and a number of good to excellent properties, some with formidable histories. The best growths are almost always on hilly terrain along the southern border overlooking the Barbanne River. Soils, composed of limestone and gravel, are well drained and associated with a range of hills. The large village of Montagne, with 2,000 residents and 1,300 hectares of vineland, is the largest of the satellite towns and nearly three times the size of Pomerol. Of the more than 300 growers, most are part-time farmers, with only two dozen growths generating a national or international reputation.

Overall wine quality is surprisingly high. While the hilltop vineyards produce very robust wine, full-bodied and well flavored, those from the lower slopes make more delicate and supple wine. The best wine from the commune of St.-Georges is virtually indistinguishable from Grand Cru (or better) St.-Emilion–quality wine. La Cave Coopérative de Montagne-St.-Emilion, the largest producer, vinifies about 12,000 hectoliters of wine annually under the "La Tour–Mont d'Or" label. Among the many private producers, the following are considered above average: *Ch. Roudier,* a 42-hectare property overlooking the Barbanne, produces 14,000 cases of outstanding wine equal to Grand Cru Classé quality. It is dark, full-bodied, meaty, concentrated, and capable of extended cellaring, offering excellent value. *Ch. Maison-Blanche* is a 28-hectare, well-managed property that was once part of the large feudal Corbin estates in the region. Today the vineyard produces 12,400 cases of expertly made wine that offers good value. The wine is dark in color, full-bodied, firm, and requires long cellaring. *Ch. des Tours* is one of the most beautiful 14th-century fortresses to be found anywhere in the Gironde. The well-managed and mechanized property of 100 hectares makes 28,000 cases of above-average, but early maturing wine that is widely exported. *Ch. Calon* (Boidron), a 26-hectare property located north of Montagne, makes 11,500 cases of dark, fleshy, concentrated wine, offering outstanding value. *Ch. Montaiguillon,* a 42-hectare property located on the St.-Emilion border, makes more than 13,000 cases of above-average wine. *Dne. du Roudier,* a superb 10-hectare property located in the southern portion of the producing district, makes 4,500 cases of consistently good, sound wine. *Ch. Coucy,* an old 18-hectare property located south of Montagne, makes 8,000 cases of well-structured, yet supple and fruity wine. Other properties include *Ch. Beauséjour, Ch. Jura-Plaisance, Ch. la Bastienne, Ch. Petit-Clos-du-Roy, Ch. les Tuileries-de-Bayard, Ch. des Moines, Ch. la Croix-Mouchet, Ch. Plaisance* (Larribiere), *Ch. Rocker-Corbin, Ch. la Papeterie, Ch. Haute-Faucherie, Ch. Corbin, Ch. de la Vieille-Montagne, Ch. Tour-Calon, Vieux-Château-Bayard, Ch. Bayard, Ch. Negrit,* and *Ch. Bellevue.*

The most important growths in the small hamlet of St.-Georges include: *Ch. St.-Georges,* a large 64-hectare property located on a former Roman villa on top of a ridge overlooking St.-Emilion, contains a magnificent chateau built in 1774 by Victor Louis. Output, which regularly exceeds 24,000 cases, is widely exported, modestly priced, and offers excellent value. *Ch. St.-André-Corbin* is a 17-hectare property located to the west of Montagne that produces 8,000 cases of well-made, full-bodied, rustic wine that is very reliable in off vintages. Offering outstanding value, it is one of the best in the area. Other properties include *Ch. Tour-du-pas-St.-Georges, Ch. Calon, Ch. Cap d'Or, Ch. Belair-St.-Georges, Ch. Macquin-St.-Georges,* and *Ch. Guillon.*

The small 7,000-hectoliter Parsac subregion contains nearly three dozen growers but only four properties with a good and reliable reputation. *Ch. de Musset* is a small property of 8 hectares located on a steep hill that is widely considered the leader in the production of quality wine in the region. The wines are dark, well structured, flavorful, and capable of extended bottle aging. *Ch. Tour-Musset,* a 25-hectare property well situated on a high ridge, makes 11,000 cases of excellent, meticulously made wine that offers good value. Equally good is *Ch. du Puy,* a small 8-hectare property that makes 3,000 cases of well-structured and flavored wine. *Ch. de Melezin* is a 34-hectare property producing 13,500 cases of light-bodied, early maturing wine.

Lussac is located in the extreme northeastern portion of the St.-Emilion viticultural region. It contains more than 1,100 hectares of vineland and 177 growers, twenty of whom are quite large and important. More than half of all growers are members of the local cooperative, and close to 50 percent are part-time farmers. The wines are robust, full-bodied, dark, and above average in quality. The principal properties: *Ch. du Lyonnat,* with 74-hectares and an output of 25,000 cases, is the largest estate in the commune. The vineyard, well sited on limestone soil, produces well-structured, wood-aged wine that often approaches Grand Cru Classé–quality levels. *Ch. de Lussac* is a meticulous 35-hectare property located on the northern approaches of the village of Lussac. One of the few making a Cabernet Sauvignon–dominated wine, it produces 7,000 cases of good, solid, well-flavored wine that enjoys a fine reputation. *Ch. Lucas* is a 16th-century property of 33 hectares that makes polished, refined wine for the mass market. Other properties include *Ch. Bel-Air, Ch. Tour-de-Segur, Ch. de Bellevue, Ch. Barbe-Blanche, Ch. Tour-de-Grenet, Ch. Petit-Refuge, Ch. Haut-Piquat, Ch. Haut-Larose, Ch. Croix-de-Rambeau, Clos Lyonnat, Ch. du Courlat, Ch. Croix-Blanchon, Ch. la Grenière,* and *Ch. Milon.*

The village of Puisseguin, the easternmost of the satellite communes, derives its name from the French-Celtic names for "hill with a strong wine." It contains 659 hectares of vineland and about fifty-five growers, of which twelve enjoy a good reputation. Annual production exceeds 25,000 hectoliters. With an annual output of 30,000 hectoliters, the local cooperative is the largest producer. In addition to Puisseguin sold under the "Roc-de-Puisseguin" label, more than half of total output is AOC Lussac and Bordeaux Supérieur. Among private producers, the following are considered the most important: *Ch. des Laurets,* a magnificent 150-hectare property, produces 20,000 cases of dark, concentrated, full-flavored, yet delicate wine. *Ch. Bel-Air,* is an 11-hectare property making 5,000 cases of above-average, meaty wine that improves with bottle-aging. *Ch. Teillac* is a well-regarded, reliable 18-hectare property making 9,000 cases of good, but light-bodied, supple wine. *Ch. de Roques* is an old 16th-century vineyard of 15 hectares that makes good, solid, well-knit wine that ages well. *Ch. Soleil,* a recently refurbished 13-hectare property, makes 5,000 cases of well-structured, tannin-rich wine that ages well. Other properties include *Ch. Guibeau, Ch. Teyssier, Ch. du Moulin, Ch. Puisseguin, Ch. la Croix-de-Justice, Ch. Gontet, Ch. du Mayne,*

Ch. Roc du Boissac, Ch. Puy-de-Boissac, Ch. Durand-Laplagne, and *Ch. Moulin-des-Laurets.*

COTES DE CASTILLON

The little-known Côtes de Castillon wine region is a compact, intensively cultivated area located between St.-Emilion (of which it is an extension) on the west and the Bergerac region on the east. Although viticulture dates back to Roman times, its modern winemaking history, as reflected by the numerous castles and fortifications found in the area, begins with the Plantagenet occupation. Its principal city—Castillon la Bataille—is named after the historic battle fought at the site, which ended the Hundred Years' War in 1453.

The Côtes de Castillon is rich agricultural country; the land is not only gently undulating, but very green, with scattered woodlands peppered throughout. Its 2,500 hectares of vineland, distributed among eight communes (Monbadon, St.-Philippe D'Aiguille, Les Salles de Castillon, Gardégan, St.-Gènes de Castillon, St.-Colombe, Bèlves de Castillon, and St.-Magne de Castillon), produce more than 120,000 hectoliters of wine annually. Few holdings are large: most of the four hundred or so growers own between 2 and 5 hectares, with only a handful owning more than 25. Approximately 60 percent of all growers belong to the only cooperative in the area (located in Gardégan), which makes slightly more than 25 percent of the region's total output.

With only minor exceptions, the entire area is an extension of the St.-Emilion plateau with rich clay-loam soils (although the Dordogne River margins contain richer alluvial material unsuitable for viticulture). The best sites are the rises of the plateau, all of which are underlain by hard limestone. Unlike surrounding areas, the Côtes de Castillon is more subject to killing frosts, with at least nine major outbreaks during the past thirty years.

The wines of the Côtes de Castillon, nearly all red, are very similar in terms of grape varieties and style to those adjoining St.-Emilion. Most growers will plant a vineyard with 60 to 70 percent Merlot, 10 to 25 percent Cabernet Franc, and the remainder with Malbec and Petit Verdot, with only scattered plantings of Cabernet Sauvignon. The wines are coarse and lack suppleness and delicacy when compared with the finer properties of St.-Emilion. The better estates, however, having taken advantage of the latest vineyard techniques and vinification technology, are now producing wines that are virtually indistinguishable from those made in the more-celebrated appellation to the west. On average, the wines are very reliable and fruity, with enough extract and tannin to enable them to age with considerable improvement beyond their tenth birthday. It is estimated that approximately 20 percent are made in a *vin de garde* style, and those wines deserve to be better known and appreciated. Nevertheless, the success of this appellation since 1945 is evident by the fact that

production has increased fivefold over the past thirty years. Local aficionados indicate that the current production figure could easily double within
the next twenty years.

The wines were sold as "St.-Emilionais" or "Libournais" until 1928,
and during the period 1929–54 as "Bordeaux" or "Bordeaux Supérieur."
When appellation status was awarded in 1955, the official appellations
became "Bordeaux-Côtes de Castillon" or "Bordeaux Supérieur–Côtes de
Castillon," the latter considered the better of the two. The requirements
necessary to meet both designations are that yields be limited to 40
hectoliters to the hectare, minimum alcohol be 11 percent, and the
minimum must density be 187 grams to the liter. If the full requirements
of the appellation are not met, the official designation is "Bordeaux–Côtes
de Castillon," a designation rarely used, as nearly all of production is
marketed under the higher appellation of "Bordeaux Supérieur–Côtes de
Castillon."

Lying northwest of Castillon-la-Bataille, St.-Magne is easily the largest
commune in the appellation, with 758 hectares of vineland and sixty-six
growers cultivating more than 5 hectares. The following properties enjoy
a good reputation, of which the first seven are considered the finest: *Ch.
Moulin-Rouge, Ch. des Demoiselles, Ch. Blanzac, Ch. la Terrasse, Ch. Beynat,
Ch. Fontbaude, Ch. Maizières-Aubert, Ch. du Bois, Ch. Haut-Tuquet, Ch.
Rocher-Bellevue, Ch. Puylazat, Ch. Lebesse, Ch. Germant, Ch. les Fosses de la
Treille, Ch. la Forêt, Ch. de Laussac, Ch. les Murailes, Ch. Hoyt, Ch. Clos
Maisières,* and *Ch. Beauséjour.* Lying north of St.-Magne, the hamlet of
St.-Colombe contains 150 hectares of vineland and five important
growths: *Ch. du Palanquey, Ch. Haut-Peyroutet, Ch. Poupille, Ch. Faugeres,*
and *Ch. Briand.* Located north of Castillon-la-Bataille, the hamlet of
Belves-de-Castillon, with 239 hectares of vineland, is considered ideal for
the production of full-bodied, dark, highly concentrated *vin de garde*–type
wines. Of the twenty major properties, the following enjoy good reputations: *Ch. de Prade, Ch. Lartigue, Ch. Puy Arnaud, Ch. Tarreyo,* and *Ch.
Castegens.*

The small hamlet of St.-Gènes, located on the St.-Emilion border,
includes 230 hectares of vineland and four important growths: *Ch. la
Croix Bigorre, Ch. Parent-Beauséjour, Ch. Lestang,* and *Ch. Tour-Bigore.* The
small village of St.-Philippe d'Aiguille contains 227 hectares of vineland
and six important growths: *Ch. Grand-Tuillac, Ch. d'Aiguilhe, Ch. Vernon,
Ch. Roquevieille, Ch. Lamartine,* and *Ch. de Saint-Philippe.* Located in the
northernmost portion of the district, the little-known village of Monbadon contains 205 hectares of vineland and five major growths: *Ch.
Fongaban, Ch. Monbadon, Ch. Lagrange-Monbadon, Ch. Tour de Courrech,*
and *Ch. Cantegrive.* The small hamlet of Gardégan, located in the eastern
portion of the district, contains 229 hectares of vineyards, an important
cooperative, and three important growths: *Ch. de Pitray, Ch. de la
Pierrière,* and *Ch. la Gasparde.* Castillon-la-Bataille, the largest city in the

appellation, contains about 180 hectares of vineland and fourteen major growths, of which *Ch. Blanzac,* and *Ch. Tour d'Honorable* are the most important.

COTES DE FRANCS

Located immediately to the north of the more-important Côtes de Castillon vineyard, the small but old Côtes de Francs wine-producing region dates from the 11th century. The appellation of "Bordeaux–Côtes de Francs," created in 1976, includes nearly 600 hectares of vineland, of which one-fifth is planted in white grapes.

The physical geography of the region is similar to that of Castillon, except that the soils contain more clay and less alluvium and limestone, and frost is more common. Four villages—Tayac, St.-Cibard, Francs, and Les Salles—account for the entire output of wine, the last two being responsible for nearly two-thirds of the total. Of the approximately seventy-three growers, half are part-time farmers, and the one cooperative in Francs is responsible for 80 percent of total output. Average annual production increased from less than 1,500 hectoliters in the early 1950s to nearly 10,000 hectoliters by 1982, with expectations that output will exceed 25,000 by 1995.

The wines, although coarse on the palate, are well colored and have a distinct *terroir* flavor. Red wines, made from Cabernet Sauvignon, Cabernet Franc, Malbec, and Merlot, are limited to a yield of 40 hectoliters to the hectare and have a minimum alcoholic content of 11 percent. They are marketed under the "Bordeaux–Côtes de Francs" banner or as "Bordeaux Supérieur–Côtes de Francs," the latter considered slightly better. White wines, made from Sémillon, Sauvignon Blanc, and Muscadelle, are marketed under the same appellation names and under "Bordeaux Supérieur-Côtes de Francs Liquoreux," the latter considered finest because of a higher must density and a half-degree more alcohol.

Les Salles, the largest hamlet with twenty-two growers, is also the largest vineyard with 214 hectares. It adjoins Castillon and produces mainly red wine. The principal growths are *Ch. Puy-Landry, Ch. Strabourg, Ch. de Belcier, Ch. de Clotte, Ch. Mauperier, Moulin-de-Clotte,* and *Ch. Chêne-Vert.* The small hamlet of Francs is known for the only cooperative in the region. It has 137 hectares of vineland and the following four growths: *Ch. les Mayneries, Ch. de Francs-de-Bucherie, Ch. Godard,* and *Ch. de Francs-la-Comtesse.* Adjoining Francs to the south, the red wine hamlet of St.-Cibard enjoys the best reputation of the four in the production of full-bodied, dark, yet supple wines. Among the many properties, the following are considered reliable: *Ch. Puyfromage, Vieux-Château du Colombier, Ch. de Pimpine, Ch. Lavergasse,* and *Dne. de Negrie.* The smallest settlement in the appellation, the commune of Tayac, cultivates nearly 130 hectares, of which half are planted in white grapes. The largest properties are *Dne. de Nardou, Ch. Tayac,* and *Ch. Lalande.*

10

The Wines of the Medoc

POMEROL produces the most-expensive red wine in the Gironde, *Ch. Petrus*; Sauternes, the most-expensive sweet wine, *Ch. d'Yquem*; and Graves, the most-expensive dry white wine, *Ch. Haut-Brion*. Nevertheless, the Médoc, an area north of the city of Bordeaux, has captivated and sustained the Gironde's reputation for quality red wine throughout the world. In this region are the largest negociant houses and the most-magnificent wine estates in the Gironde. The Médoc is known for eight important appellations, whose size in hectarage and average

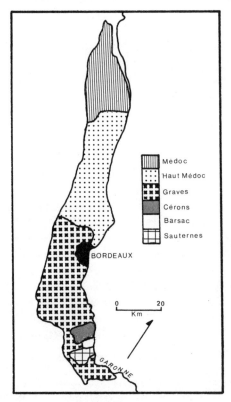

Figure 10.1   AOC Wine Appellations along the South Bank of the Gironde and Garonne

annual production are indicated in Table 10.1. (See Fig. 10.3 for their location in the Gironde.) The combined hectarage of approximately 10,000 hectares represents 11 percent of the total vineland of the Gironde, but only 7 percent of its production. With about 500 major properties, it is the most-important wine region in the Gironde department. Of the total, approximately half are considered world-class producing units and command very high prices in the international marketplace.

The Médoc (derived from the Latin *in medio aquae*, "in the middle of the waters") consists of a narrow strip of land (80 kilometers long by 5 wide) occupying the eastern section of a peninsula north of Bordeaux. To the west lies the largest pine forest in France—the Landes—with numerous sand spits, *étangs* (lagoons), and beaches. To the east is the Gironde estuary, and to the south, the Médoc is bounded by the Jalle de Blanquefort. It is rather flat in the south but becomes progressively hillier in St.-Estèphe and beyond. The entire area is drained by small, shallow streams ("jalles"). The Landes offers a small measure of protection from the prevailing westerlies, but in general the area is wet, relatively humid, and verdant; and with only minor exceptions, arable land is devoted exclusively to viticulture. Although vine growing is now responsible for more than 90 percent of the agricultural product of the peninsula, historically the Médoc was an area of extensive grazing, with sheep and horse husbandry particularly popular. The countryside evokes a sense of equanimity and a feeling of permanence. While it lacks the elegance and aristocratic ambiance of the middle Loire or the charm and friendliness of Alsace, the Médoc has not experienced ruinous military and social conflict for centuries. Its fortunes for the past two centuries were dictated by solid, reliable, sober commercial interests. The entire region is studded with small hamlets and villages and approximately 100 large country mansions.

Viticulture in the Médoc arrived rather late, compared to other producing districts within the Gironde. It dates back only to the later medieval period with the arrival of religious orders in the 13th century, particularly the Benedictines, who founded the present *Ch. Prieuré-Lichine*

Table 10.1 Médoc Region AOC Wine Production, 1980

Appellation	Hectoliters	Percent of total	Appellation	Hectoliters	Percent of total
Médoc	95,106	27.3	Pauillac	32,733	9.4
Haut-Médoc	94,323	27.1	St.-Julien	23,580	6.8
St.-Estèphe	40,904	11.8	Listrac	15,298	4.4
Margaux	34,512	10.0	Moulis	11,332	3.2
			Total	347,788	100.0

Source: French Ministry of Agriculture.

and *Ch. Pouget.* Although their influence in the history of winemaking was considerable, few of the more than a dozen commanderies, priories, and abbeys remain today. Drainage of the eastern Médoc marshlands under the first Bourbons in the 17th century accelerated the formation of large estates. Lowland areas were turned into meadow, middle slopes into wheatfields, and the highest gravel elevations into vineland. By the second half of the 17th century, the old feudal gentry had been replaced by the merchants of Bordeaux, who planted vines in the finest locations and established a pattern of land use that has remained firmly in place for more than 200 years.

The Wines

Approximately 98 percent of all Médocain wine is red, known for its distinctive bouquet, finesse, and marvelous flavor. In addition to its beautiful color and moderate alcohol content, the wine is not "heady" and will improve enormously when bottle-aged. In above-average to excellent vintage years, the wine represents the culmination of perfection. Perhaps the easiest way to describe the wine is to say that it is *un vin de plaisir* ("a wine that is pleasing") and one that rarely disappoints. Indeed, the vignerons' capacity for the production of superb wine reaches Olympian heights in the Médoc, and as a result the wine has become the standard to which all red, especially Cabernet Sauvignon wine, is compared.

Overall wine quality has improved over the past twenty years because of better vinification, mechanical harvesting, better hygiene, and consistent and judicious use of vineyard sprays—all of which have led to a more-reliable product. Prior to 1960, the Médoc was able to produce an above-average vintage only once in four years, but now poor vintages, like 1965 and 1968, have become the exception. As in all French viticultural regions, "traditional" winemaking techniques have succumbed to the latest technology and changing consumer taste. The Médoc of old, meant to outlast the generation that made it, was based on a large percentage of *vin de presse,* a lengthy wood fermentation, and excessive barrel-aging. The new techniques, in contrast, filter or centrifuge out the grape skins and seeds early in the fermentation process, producing wine that is less tannic, charming in its youth, but unable to age like the wine of old. The new style is not inferior to the old, nor does it produce second-rate wine—it is just different, and when compared to the *méthode ancienne,* is less concentrated and mouth-filling. This *vin de coule* (wine of the "first pressing") is more supple and certainly more *gouleyant* (fresh, light, and quaffable). It emphasizes "softer" tannins, is less acidic and less astringent, and is very appealing to the modern consumer who lacks the inclination and space to lay down classic Médoc for twenty years.

Emile Peynaud, a university professor, sought-after viticultural and enological consultant, author of more than 400 professional articles and more than twenty books, is the prime promoter of the "new style" of Bordeaux wine. In his home base of Bordeaux, he has revolutionized the style of traditional Bordeaux from a more austere, tannin-rich, Cabernet Sauvignon–dominated and long-lived wine to one that conforms to the contemporary tastes. The grapes are harvested as ripe as possible, there is a limitation on the amount of *vin de presse,* a careful selection of grape berries, maximum color extraction, and a stricter separation of superior cuvées from those considered less good to carry the primary label. This "Peynaud-style" wine is characterized by more Merlot and reduced astringency and bitterness. The style is very popular and growing in importance: even tradition-minded *Ch. Montrose* has succumbed to the temptation. Acting as consultant, Peynaud has improved the wines of all the following major growths: *Batailley, Malescot-St.-Exupéry, Margaux, Haut-Batailley, Beychevelle, Rauzan-Gassies, Pavie, d'Yquem, Prieuré-Lichine, Pape-Clément, Lagrange, Malartic-Lagravière, la Mission Haut-Brion, la Lagune, Haut-Bailly, Ducru-Beaucaillou,* and *Boyd-Cantenac.*

Minor amounts of undistinguished dry white wine is made from Sauvignon Blanc and Sémillon by a small number of vignerons. The white wine, with a reputation for consistency and balance, that fetches high prices is *Ch. Margaux.* All white and the minuscule amounts of rosé, according to appellation regulations, must be marketed as Bordeaux or Bordeaux Supérieur.

The Médoc Cooperatives

The first of the thirteen Médoc cooperatives was established in 1933 at the depth of the depression. Today there are approximately 1,300 members cultivating 2,400 hectares, producing more than 125,000 hectoliters, or one-third of the entire Médocain output. They play a pivotal role in the viticultural life of the region by being leaders in the introduction of the latest technical innovations, by providing all manner of assistance to the smaller growers, and by making good wine at a much lower cost than do medium-sized properties. They produce approximately 40 percent of total in the Médoc appellation, 15 percent in the Haut-Médoc, 30 percent in Listrac and St.-Estèphe, and 15 percent in Pauillac. Bulk sales, mostly to negociants, represent two-thirds of total sales, but the amount of wine sold in bottle continues to increase at the cooperative site.

The Classification of 1855

The directors of the 1855 Exposition Universelle in Paris requested that the Bordeaux Chamber of Commerce present, on exhibition, the finest wines from the Gironde. A committee of wine brokers created a list of sixty-two properties, based on the then-current and historic prices. They were divided into five groups collectively called "Grand Crus" ("great growths"; the official name is "Classification des Grandes Crus Rouges de Bordeaux"), all of which were from the Médoc except *Ch. Haut-Brion,* which is located in Graves.* This ranking, the most famous in France, persists to this day, although many questions have been raised through the years that undermine its contemporary veracity. Since 1855 there have been many attempts and counterproposals to alter the listing, but the "classification" has remained fixed in concrete, with only one exception: the 1973 elevation by national decree of *Ch. Mouton-Rothschild* from second- to first-growth (Table 10.2).

The sixty-one Grands Crus Classés, containing less than 2 percent of total vineland and 1 percent of total wine output in Gironde, account for 5 percent of the total value of wine production and nearly 100 percent of the publicity. Compared with all other Médocain properties, the Grand Cru Classé estates are much larger in size, maintain the largest storage facilities, hire the most-proficient winemakers, and spend the largest sums on public relations. Nearly all have stately country mansions, and some have extraordinary libraries and museums. Compared with other Médocain appellations, the Grand Cru Classé properties collectively (but not singularly) maintain the lowest grape yields, oldest vines, and longest fermentation and aging in wood. Significant variations do exist within the group, but the very best properties, produce world-class wines with few equals. Their wines have been imprinted by history and are likely to remain at the pinnacle of the red wine peerage. What makes them unique in the wine hierarchy of French codification is the fact that their higher prices reflect superior quality, which in turn is based on the concept of *terroir,* or the nonpareil character of soil and microclimate.

Over the years, the following issues questioning the legitimacy of the 1855 classification have arisen:

1. The issue of *terroir.* Grand Cru properties are invariably sited on the highest elevations, on eastern exposures along the Gironde, on the edges of jalles, on gravelly soil, and on a subsoil containing *alios,* an iron-bearing clay. Elevation in the Médoc is a function of gravel *croupes:* the highest and those with the steepest slopes incline toward the Gironde and are mainly confined to the communes of St.-Estèphe, Pauillac, St.-Julien, and Margaux. It is important to note that while all the Grand Cru properties are located on gravel *croupes* whose elevation exceeds 10 meters, no fewer than forty, or 65 percent of the total, are located on *croupes* that overlook the Gironde, and that only twenty-four, or 39 percent, border on jalles. Highly significant is the fact that the all important *alios* subsoil is highly irregular, with only a very small portion of the producing region benefiting from its existence. The proponents for a revision of the 1855 classification maintain that in 1855, only a small portion of the Médoc

---

*The sweet wines of Sauternes-Barsac were also classified.

was actually planted in vines, and that not all of the *classic terroir* sites were utilized for vinegrowing. (For topographic cross-sections, see Fig. 10.2.)

2. The 1855 classification is outdated. The proponents of the status quo assert that soil and microclimate are the most important elements in the determination of wine quality. It is estimated that in 1855 the combined planted hectarage of the sixty-two Grand Cru sites was less than 750 hectares, producing less than 15,000 hectoliters of wine. Today, planted hectarage has more than doubled, and production has increased more than fivefold. Empirical evidence has shown that not one Grand Cru property has maintained its original vineyard boundaries. Can all newly planted vineland be of the same quality? None of this newly planted land was "classified" in 1855. For example, one of the leading revisionists of the 1855 classification, Mr. Alexis Lichine, increased his property from 10 hectares in 1952 to more than 58 in 1979. Moreover, classified properties regularly lease land to each other, trade individual sections, and sell land to each other on a routine basis. In addition, nearly all Grand Cru properties are fragmented—some, like *Ch. Lascombes,* in as many as fifty small fields. *Ch. Desmirail,* which had ceased to exist for more than forty years, has been recently resurrected and does not wholly reflect its 1855 "terroir." Even more preposterous, *Ch. Duhart-Milon* has changed its location by a significant distance. It is also interesting to note that each property owner divides his vineland into specific, irregular sized plots, each having specific soil and drainage characteristics that produce wine of differing quality. The wine of each plot often becomes a special cuvée, which may or may not be "homogenized" with others when it is time to be bottled.

3. The 1855 classification is not an accurate portrait of quality. After the dispensation of trading privileges to local merchants by the Plantagenet kings, the merchants created a trading monopoly in the transportation of wine originating in the Gironde and in the interior "high country." Over the centuries, they not only monopolized a good deal of the export trade, but they grew into a small and powerful class of merchants/growers. It was the latters' influence that excluded the less well known "red and dry white wines" of the Gironde from the 1855 classification. In a cavalier fashion, the 1855 committee excluded all Graves (except *Ch. Haut-Brion*), Sauternes, Barsac, Pomerol, and St.-Emilion properties, among others.

4. Grand Cru properties do not always produce the best wine. Grand Cru property owners maintain that high prices are related to quality, and that, with few exceptions, these wines are still the finest in the Gironde. Reality, however, paints a different picture: the 1855 classification no longer reflects current quality, and the ranking in each category is no longer a guarantee of quality. The classification is fixed and, in effect, acts as an official trademark for those fortunate enough to be included. As

Table 10.2   1855 Bordeaux Classification

First Growths (Premiers Crus)

	Commune
Ch. Lafite	Pauillac
Ch. Latour	Pauillac
Ch. Margaux	Margaux
Ch. Haut-Brion	Pessac. Graves
Ch. Mouton-Rothschild[a]	Pauillac

Second Growths (Deuxièmes Crus)

Ch. Rausan-Ségla[c]	Margaux
Ch. Rauzan-Gassies[c]	Margaux
Ch. Léoville-Las-Cases	St.-Julien
Ch. Léoville-Poyferré	St.-Julien
Ch. Léoville-Barton	St.-Julien
Ch. Durfort-Vivens	Margaux
Ch. Lascombes	Margaux
Ch. Gruaud-Larose[b]	St.-Julien
Ch. Brane-Cantenac	Cantenac-Margaux
Ch. Pichon-Longueville (Pichon Baron)[c]	Pauillac
Ch. Pichon-Longueville (Pichon Lalande)[c]	Pauillac
Ch. Ducru-Beaucaillou	St.-Julien
Ch. Cos-d'Estournel	St.-Estèphe
Ch. Montrose	St.-Estèphe

Third Growths (Troisièmes Crus)

Ch. Giscours	Labarde-Margaux
Ch. Kirwan	Cantenac-Margaux
Ch. d'Issan	Cantenac-Margaux
Ch. Lagrange	St.-Julien
Ch. Langoa	St.-Julien
Ch. Malescot-Saint-Exupéry	Margaux
Ch. Cantenac-Brown[c]	Cantenac-Margaux
Ch. Palmer	Cantenac-Margaux
Ch. La Lagune	Ludon
Ch. Desmirail	Margaux
Ch. Calon-Segur	St.-Estèphe
Ch. Ferriere	Margaux
Ch. Marquis-d'Alesme-Becker	Margaux
Ch. Boyd-Cantenac[c]	Margaux
Ch. Dubignon[d]	Margaux

Table 10.2 *Continued*

Fourth Growths (*Quatrièmes Crus*)

Ch. Prieuré-Lichine[e]	Cantenac-Margaux
Ch. St.-Pierre	St.-Julien
Ch. Branaire-Ducru[f]	St.-Julien
Ch. Talbot	St.-Julien
Ch. Duhart-Milon-Rothschild	Pauillac
Ch. Pouget[c]	Cantenac-Margaux
Ch. La Tour-Carnet	St.-Laurent
Ch. Lafon-Rochet	St.-Estèphe
Ch. Beychevelle	St.-Julien
Ch. Marquis-de-Terme	Margaux

Fifth Growths (*Cinquièmes Crus*)

Ch. Pontet-Canet	Pauillac
Ch. Batailley[c]	Pauillac
Ch. Grand-Puy-Lacoste	Pauillac
Ch. Grand-Puy-Ducasse[g]	Pauillac
Ch. Haut-Batailley[c]	Pauillac
Ch. Lynch-Bages	Pauillac
Ch. Lynch-Moussas	Pauillac
Ch. Dauzac	Labarde-Margaux
Ch. Mouton-Baron-Philippe[h]	Pauillac
Ch. du Tertre	Arsac-Margaux
Ch. Haut-Bages-Liberal	Pauillac
Ch. Pédesclaux	Pauillac
Ch. Belgrave[i]	St.-Laurent
Ch. Camensac	St.-Laurent
Ch. Cos Labory	St.-Estèphe
Ch. Clerc-Milon[j]	Pauillac
Ch. Croizet-Bages	Pauillac
Ch. Cantemerle	Macau

[a]Elevated to first growth in 1973.
[b]Originally two vineyards: Gruaud-Larose-Sarget and Gruaud-Larose-Bethman. They were combined in 1934.
[c]Originally one property.
[d]No longer in existence.
[e]Originally Chateau Le Prieuré.
[f]Originally Chateau Duluc.
[g]Originally known as Chateau Artigues-Arnaud.
[h]Originally known as Chateau D'Armailhacq.
[i]Originally known as Chateau Coutenceau.
[j]Originally known as Chateau Clerc-Milon-Mondot.

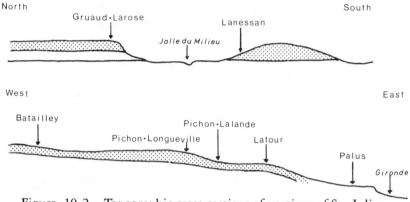

Figure 10.2   Topographic cross-sections of portions of St.-Julien
and Pauillac

(The heavy pebbled soils in the four principal communes of the Médoc contain a
narrow belt of Gunzian gravel, which is a varying mixture of quartz-dominated
stone, gravel, and coarse sand. The subsoil consists of varying quantities of hard
and soft limestone and oligocene clay mixed with iron oxide, aluminum oxide
and potash. All of the finest sites are located on well drained gravel banks called
croupes.)

proof, the opposition maintains that *Ch. Petrus,* over the past twenty
years, has received prices higher than other Gironde growths. The price
hiatus between first, second, third, fourth, and fifth growths is also
inexplicable. *Ch. la Lagune* regularly outperforms a number of second
growths, yet its prices rarely reflect its consistently higher quality.
Conversely, the price of *Ch. Lafite-Rothschild* and *Ch. Margaux* continued
to rise in the 1960s and 1970s when the wine quality was substantially
below their exalted rank.

5. The 1855 classification nomenclature gives the often-false accolade
that a first growth is dramatically superior to a fifth growth. The
numbering system between categories adversely affects those at the
bottom; a fifth growth is not a lesser wine by a factor of five in relation to a
first growth, but consumers apparently think so.

6. Grand Cru properties do not always offer the best value, as blind
tastings repeatedly prove. High prices reflect scarcity, the price of
production, and snob appeal, and the latter usually offers the most
accurate portrayal of the current pricing structure. In the final analysis,
the wine consumer is advised to purchase only good bottles, not absurd
130-year-old "official" rankings.

7. What did the 1855 classification classify? Did the brokers classify
potential or then-current wine quality, prevailing fashion, prices, or the
ability of an aggressive vigneron to provide ample samples to the rating
committee?

8. The 1855 committee not only lacked fairness but failed to take into account special circumstances. *Ch. Lanessan,* whose owner was too busy to provide samples to the committee, was not classified, although its price structure fell within the guidelines of the other properties that were included. *Ch. Citran* and *Ch. la Mission Haut-Brion* also exhibited high prices, but although they were included in an unofficial list of important properties, were excluded in the 1855 classification. *Ch. Cantemerle,* historically sold in Belgium and Holland, had no established price history but was summarily included. It is also important to note that many a property that did not offer samples, did not wish to participate, or sold its wines privately was excluded from the 1855 classification.

9. The 1855 classification failed to institute procedures to update the rankings. For a large number of reasons, the winemaking fortunes of winemaking estates have exhibited severe up and down phases throughout their history. It is unreasonable to think that sixty-one properties can be consistent in their winemaking abilities. Over the past twenty years, *Ch. Brane-Cantenac, Ch. Kirwan, Ch. Belgrave,* and *Ch. Dauzac,* among others, have been notorious in their inability to produce reliable wine. On the other hand, *Ch. la Lagune, Ch. Latour, Ch. Ducru-Beaucaillou, Ch. Gruaud-Larose* and others have exhibited exemplary performances.

The 1977 Cru Bourgeois Classification

Because the 1855 classification left more than 99 percent of all properties unclassified, most of them were overshadowed by the notoriety of the Grand Crus Classés and languished for years in semi-obscurity. They were referred to as Crus Bourgeois if they were sizable, and smaller part-time growths were called Cru Artisan or Cru Paysan. Since the properties lacked the power and financial resources to expand hectarage, ferment, age, and bottle wine, the wines suffered from poor image and inconsistency. Except for the largest properties, the overwhelming majority were bound to one or more negociants for assistance in the disposition of their grapes or wine. In the 1920s, a syndicate of Crus Bourgeois and Bourgeois Supérieurs was formed to promote their number and name. In 1932, the Bourgeois properties were evaluated by a semiofficial group of wine brokers for the purposes of classification and rank. By 1936, approximately 443 properties were classified in three broad groups: 6 Bourgeois Supérieurs Exceptionnels; 100 Crus Bourgeois Supérieurs; and 250 Crus Bourgeois. An additional 87 Crus Bourgeois were identified but not officially ranked. During the depression years, more than half of these properties were abandoned or sold to larger estates. By 1940, their number was reduced to fewer than 140 viable economic viticultural enterprises.

In 1962, the syndicate was revived with 94 members out of a total of 110, and after four years of intensive maneuvering, the syndicate classified

Table 10.3 1977 Bordeaux Bourgeois Growth Classification

Grand Bourgeois Exceptionnel

	Commune		Commune
Ch. d'Agassac	Ludon	Ch. Fourcas-Dupré	Listrac
Ch. Andron-Blanquet	St.-Estèphe	Ch. Fourcas-Hosten	Listrac
Ch. Beau-Site	St.-Estèphe	Ch. du Glana	St.-Julien
Ch. Capbern-Gasqueton	St.-Estèphe	Ch. Haut-Marbuzet	St.-Estèphe
Ch. Caronne-Ste.-Gemme	St.-Laurent	Ch. de Marbuzet	St.-Estèphe
Ch. Chasse-Spleen	Moulis	Ch. Meyney	St.-Estèphe
Ch. Cissac	Cissac	Ch. Phelan-Ségur	St.-Estèphe
Ch. Citran	Avensan	Ch. Poujeaux	Moulis
Ch. le Crock	St.-Estèphe	Ch. Tronquoy-Lalande	St.-Estèphe
Ch. Dutruch-Grand-Poujeaux	Moulis		

Grand Bourgeois

	Commune		Commune
Ch. Beaumont	Cussac	Ch. de Malleret	Le Pian
Ch. Bel-Orme-Tronquoy-de-Lalande	St.-Seurin-de-Cadourne	Ch. Martinens	Margaux
Ch. Brillette	Moulis	Ch. Morin	St.-Estèphe
Ch. la Cardonne	Blaignan	Ch. Moulin-à-Vent	Moulis
Ch. Colombier-Monpelou	Pauillac	Ch. le Meynieu	Vertheuil
Ch. Coufran	St.-Seurin-de-Cadourne	Ch. des Ormes-de-Pez	St.-Estèphe
Ch. Coutelin-Merville	St.-Estèphe	Ch. les Ormes-Sorbet	Couquèques
Ch. Duplessis-Hauchecorne	Moulis	Ch. Patache-d'Aux	Bégadan
Ch. la Fleur-Milon	Pauillac	Ch. Paveil-de-Luze	Soussans
Ch. Fontesteau	St.-Sauveur	Ch. Peyrabon	St.-Sauveur
Ch. Greysac	Bégadan	Ch. Pontoise-Cabarrus	St.-Seurin-de-Cadourne
Ch. Hantellan	Cissac	Ch. Potensac	Potensac
Ch. Lafon	Listrac	Ch. Reysson	Vertheuil
Ch. de Lamarque	Lamarque	Ch. Ségur	Parempuyre
Ch. Lamothé-Cissac	Cissac	Ch. Sigognac	St.-Yzans-de-Médoc
Ch. Larose-Trintaudon	St.-Laurent	Ch. Sociando-Mallet	St.-Seurin-de-Cadourne
Ch. Laujac	Bégadan	Ch. du Taillan	Le Taillan
Ch. Liversan	St.-Sauveur	Ch. la Tour-de-By	Bégadan
Ch. Loudenne	St.-Yzans-de-Médoc	Ch. la Tour-du-Haut-Moulin	Cussac
Ch. Mac-Carthy	St.-Estèphe	Ch. Verdignan	St.-Seurin-de-Cadourne

the entire group with the following designations: 19 Grand Bourgeois Exceptionnel, 44 Grand Bourgeois, and 38 Bourgeois. But because the above classification was deemed unofficial, too restrictive in number, and the product of a "private" endeavor, the new classification was not recognized by the INAO and could not be mentioned on the label. Their persistence was finally rewarded, because in 1977 the syndicat revised the ranking, which, with the blessing of the INAO, was legitimized. The final listing included 122 properties in the following groups: 19 Grand Bourgeois Exceptionnels, 40 Grands Bourgeois, and 63 Bourgeois. The ranking presented in Table 10.3 is neither complete nor free of criticism. A number of properties, most notably *d'Angludet, Bel-Air-Marquis-d'Aligre, Villegeorge, Siran, Gloria,* and *Lanessan,* refused to join, hoping for higher classified status at some future time.

While the Bourgeois properties do not meet the standards of the Grand Crus Classés, their ranking is based on a number of important considerations. For the rank of Bourgeois, the property must be at least 7 hectares and have at least one cuvier (fermenting facility) and chai (aging facility), with barrel-aging optional. For the rank of Grand Bourgeois, the property must be at least 7 hectares in size, the cuvier and chai must be at a higher-quality level and more modern, and barrel-aging be obligatory. For the rank of Grand Bourgeois Exceptionnel, the property can be located only in the communes stretching from Ludon in the south to St.-Estéphe in the north and be at least 7 hectares in size, must contain a modern chai and cuvier, and must practice both barrel-aging and estate-bottling.

Since the initial adoption with the 1978 vintage, the Syndicat has met with considerable success. A number of additional growths have applied for admission but cannot enter until 1987. While prices for Grand Cru Classé wine continue to escalate, the Bourgeois growths have a considerable future, since the wines are much improved and sell well, particularly in Holland, Belgium, and West Germany. A number of properties are equal to classified quality and are so indicated in the property descriptions that follow.

As of 1986, classified Bourgeois properties produce more than 35 percent of all wine in the Médoc: more than 40 percent in the Médoc appellation, 60 percent in the Haut-Médoc appellation, and at least 65 percent in the communes of Listrac and Moulis. Because of limited available land, their production as percent of total is less than 20 percent in Margaux, St.-Julien, and Pauillac. For the Médoc as a whole, Crus Bourgeois properties encompass approximately 2,000 hectares (see Figure 10.3).

St.-Estèphe

Of the six quality communes in the Médoc, St.-Estèphe, with more than 1,200 hectares, is the most important in the production of wine but the

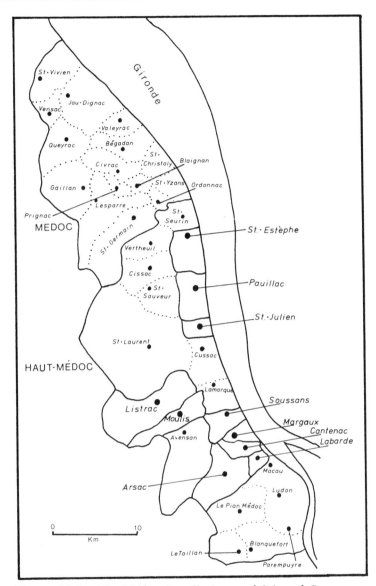

Figure 10.3   The Médoc Appellations and Selected Communes

least consequential in the concentration of upper-tier classified growths. It contains no first growths, two second growths, and only one each in the third, fourth, and fifth rankings, or 8 percent of the total. In addition, St.-Estèphe contains nine Grand Bourgeois Exceptionnel, four Grand Bourgeois, and two Bourgeois properties, or approximately 12 percent of all Bourgeois growths.

The commune differs from Pauillac, St.-Julien, Margaux, Moulis, and

Listrac in a number of ways. The soil, less well drained, contains more clay and sand but less gravel and hardly any iron-bearing subsoil. Furthermore, the historical tradition of planting Cabernet Sauvignon to the near exclusion of Merlot produced wines that were green, hard, tannin-rich, with a muted bouquet, and a predilection for longevity. In the final analysis, all of the above, plus excess atmospheric humidity and considerable fog and wind, create an environment for the production of wine marred by excess acidity and coarseness.

Responding to market conditions and the forces for modernization, the growers of St.-Estèphe have, over the past twenty years, enlarged their producing fields (see Fig. 10.4) to take advantage of increased efficiencies, improved vinification techniques, and increased the percentage of Merlot in the final blend. As a result, the wines of today are more supple, aromatic, and fleshy—sharp departures from the thin, acidic, astringent wines that once lacked suppleness and gave the impression of excessive dryness on the palate.

The best sites either overlook the Gironde, lie on the edge of a south-facing croupe, or are sited inland on high ground. *Ch. Calon-Ségur, Ch. Phélan-Ségur, Ch. Meyney,* and *Ch. Montrose* are good examples of the first category; *Ch. Cos d'Estournel, Ch. Cos Labory,* and *Ch. Lafon-Rochet,* of the second; and *Ch. de Pez, Ch. Pomys, Ch. Tronquoy-Lalande,* and *Ch. Houissant,* of the last category. Southwest of the small, irregular village of St.-Estèphe is the only cooperative, a good-sized facility controlling more

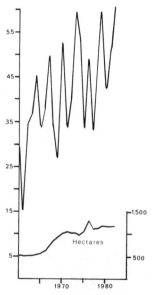

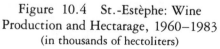

Figure 10.4   St.-Estèphe: Wine Production and Hectarage, 1960–1983
(in thousands of hectoliters)

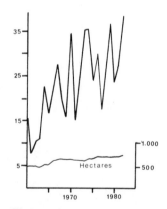

Figure 10.5   St.-Julien: Wine Production and Hectarage, 1960–1983
(in thousands of hectoliters)

than 350 hectares of vines and producing more than 170,000 cases of well-made, average to above-average wines. It markets its best wine under the "Marquis de St.-Estèphe" label. The principal Pauillac growths follow.

Ch. Cos d'Estournel is a 60-hectare property located on a superb hill with well-drained soils across the Jalle de Breuil from Lafite. It is the most prestigious name in the commune and has, over the past fifteen years, consistently outperformed *Ch. Montrose,* its arch-rival. In exceptional years, this is a big, powerful wine, well scented, and one of the few vineyards (*Ch. de Pez* is another) that retains a little fruit as it ages. The trend over the past fifteen years has been to reduce the proportion of Cabernet Sauvignon and Cabernet Franc and to increase Merlot, thus producing softer, fruitier wine. Production now regularly exceeds 22,000 cases. "Maitre d'Estournel" is a popular branded, generic Bordeaux and should not be confused with the actual property. *Ch. Montrose* is a meticulously managed property of 67 hectares, superbly situated on a rise overlooking the Gironde. It is a very traditional estate whose wines are extremely long-lived, generous, and full-bodied, but not as dark or fruity as *Ch. Cos D'Estournel.* Due to the presence of clay and the predominance of Cabernet Sauvignon, the wines are hard, green, tannin-rich, and as a result do not score favorably in comparative tastings with other growths whose encépagement contains a larger proportion of Merlot. When allowed to mature fully, its astringent youth and austere, dry taste transform into a superb multifaceted "classic" Médoc that is absolutely stunning. It is underrated, so for those with patience and an appreciation

Plate 10.1 Ch. Cos d'Estournel, St.-Estèphe

for "traditional" Médoc, this wine offers outstanding value and should be part of any serious cellar. *Ch. Calon-Ségur,* with all its inherent advantages of history, large size, and excellent location, should be making far better wine than it actually does. A high percentage of Cabernet Franc sets it apart from *Ch. Cos D'Estournel* and *Ch. Montrose,* but its main flaws are dullness and inconsistency. Recently, however, the wine has become more supple and foreword, and overall quality has improved. The property is more than 50 hectares and produces 20,000 cases. *Ch. Lafon-Rochet* is a recently rehabilitated 40-hectare property that has been producing average to above-average wine for its class. Made in a modern, early maturing style, the wine is expected to become fuller and bigger with time. Its output is 15,000 cases. *Ch. Cos-Labory,* located next to *Ch. Cos d'Estournel,* with 15 hectares and an annual output of 6,000 cases, is the smallest of the classed growths. The recently improved wine is underrated and offers superb value and excellent aging potential.

Among the nonclassified growths, the following two properties enjoy superlative reputations and offer outstanding value *Ch. de Pez* is a leading estate that consistently makes superb third-growth-quality wine. It is an old 22-hectare property known for full-bodied, sturdy, flavorful, well-balanced wine that ages to perfection. Although a high Cabernet Sauvignon percentage is used, the wines remain supple because *vin de presse* is not allowed. Output is more than 10,500 cases. *Ch. Meyney* is a superb 50-hectare property currently producing more than 24,000 cases of consistently good, soft, stylish, flavorful wine. It is made much lighter than *Ch. de Pez,* but like all Cordier properties is impeccable in every sense.

Other nonclassified properties include *Ch. Andron-Blanquet,* an outstanding property of 15 hectares whose 7,000 cases of expertly made wine are made at *Ch. Cos Labory.* This small, obscure property makes fragrant, fruity, soft, early maturing wine that offers good value but is hard to find. *Ch. Beau-Site* is, with more than 15 hectares, a property with considerable potential. It is a well-run Casteja estate that makes surprisingly good wine in above-average vintages. Well sited next to *Ch. Calon-Ségur,* it is one of the better "lesser" Bourgeois wines, offering good value. The wine is substantial on the palate, fruity, and often complex. Output exceeds 7,000 cases. *Ch. Capbern* is a 30-hectare property that makes average to above-average flavorful wine that is a cut above most other Bourgeois growths and thus offers good value. The property is known by several other names, and output exceeds 11,000 cases. *Ch. le Crock,* lying on the western edge of a group of "Marbuzet" growths south of *Ch. Montrose,* produces more than 14,000 cases of average, acidic, solidly structured wine that requires time for full maturation. The 31-hectare property enjoys a wide following, particularly in the restaurant trade. *Ch. Haut-Marbuzet,* less than thirty-five years old, is a well-run, 36-hectare estate that is the largest of all Marbuzet properties. It is currently enjoying a good reputation for outstanding, full-bodied, multidimensional wine, and output is approximately 18,000 cases. *Ch. Phélan-Ségur* is an early maturing, popular wine with a wide following. At its best it is dark and heavily scented, but it can be harsh, thin, and overly acidic in poor years. The 50-hectare, 20,000-case property also includes two smaller fields, each carrying their own label.

Ch. de Marbuzet is a 7-hectare property whose wine is made in association with *Ch. Cos d'Estournel,* and is considered the second label. *Ch. les Ormes-de-Pez* is a first-class 30-hectare property owned by *Ch. Lynch-Bages.* The wine, impeccably made with plenty of staying power, is flavorful and usually offers good value. *Ch. Tronquoy-Lalande* is a 20-hectare property producing more than 7,000 cases of full-bodied, dark, distinctive wine offering excellent value. *Ch. Pomys,* a small 5-hectare property well situated in the south-central portion of the producing district, makes distinctive, full-bodied, dark, robust wine with the capacity to age. Production of less than 3,000 cases; offers good value. *Ch. St.-Estèphe* is a well-managed 12-hectare property producing 6,000 cases of average but very agreeable wine that offers good value.

Ch. Mac-Carthy, an obscure 6-hectare growth adjoining the Marbuzet cluster, makes good, sound, supple and often substantial wine. Output rarely exceeds 2,800 cases, and it is very difficult to find. *Ch. Coutelin-Merville* is a 16-hectare growth that made 5,000 cases of average, undistinguished wine until recent vineyard expansion and improvements raised overall quality. *Ch. Morin* is a respectable 9-hectare growth that makes 4,000 cases of dark, meaty, chewy wine offering good value. *Ch. Chambert* and *Ch. Mac-Carthy-Moula* are part of *Ch. Haut-Marbuzet* and are considered second labels. *Ch. Houissant,* a 22-hectare property with an enviable site, is currently making 1,200 cases of early maturing, smooth, fruity, but otherwise undistinguished wine. *Ch. La Tour-de-Marbuzet,* a medium-sized property located on the eastern edge of the Marbuzet cluster, produces more than 4,000 cases of solid, brawny, full-bodied and chewy wine that offers considerable value. Other growths include *Ch. le Boscq* (12 hectares, 6,000 cases), *Ch. la Commanderie* (14 hectares, 5,500 cases), *Ch. Domeyne* (1,200 cases); *Ch. Laffitte-Carcasset-Padirac* (22 hectares, 11,000 cases); *Ch. la Haye* (3,000 cases); *Ch. Beauséjour* (17 hectares, 5,000 cases); and *Ch. la Tour-des-Termes* (20 hectares, 7,000 cases).

Pauillac

Although Pauillac, with 6,000 people, is the largest village in the Médoc north of Bordeaux, it is dull, unpretentious, and without a reasonable hotel or passable restaurant—features that do not reflect the international repute of its prestigious wines. Containing 950 hectares of vineland, it produces more than 40,000 hectoliters of above-average to outstanding wine. Eighteen of the sixty-one Grand Cru Classé properties are located here: three first growths, two second, no third, one fourth, and no fewer than twelve fifth growths—more than any other commune. In addition, it has two Grand Bourgeois, five Bourgeois, and a cooperative with a good reputation—*Cave Coopérative La Rose Pauillac*. This is a well-managed firm that produces more than 50,000 cases of average to above-average wine marketed under the "Ch. La Rose" label.

The best vineyards, as in the other three famous communes of the Médoc, are located on well-drained gravel *croupes* that face the Gironde. In Pauillac there are two such gravel banks: the northern portion consisting of the two *Rothschild* properties, *Ch. Pontet-Canet,* and others, is separated by the Chenal du Gaer from the much-larger *croupe* that includes *Ch. Latour,* the two *Longuevilles,* four *Bages,* and two *Puys,* among others. A third and less-distinguished wine-producing area is found in the more heavily forested central and western portion centered around the hamlet of St.-Sauveur. The superior coastal producing section owes its attributes not only to the presence of gravel in the soil, but to an excellent aspect and a bed of *alios,* whose thickness varies widely throughout the region.

The wines of Pauillac, due to their heavy concentration of Cabernet Sauvignon, are known for their full, tannin-rich, robust character, and often require fifteen to twenty years of bottle-aging before they lose their astringency and harshness. Big, masculine, dark, and well-structured, they lack the suppleness, fragrance, and early maturing features of the smoother, early maturing, softer wines of St.-Julien and Margaux. Over the past twenty years hectarage has increased by 200, and it is approaching the uppper limits of the commune's potentially exploitable vineland. As with other Médoc communes, wine production has more than doubled for the same period—a cause for serious concern since overcropping does nothing to improve wine quality. The principal properties follow.

Ch. Latour is a 60-hectare property producing more than 23,000 cases of wine annually. It is located in the southern portion of Pauillac, separated only by a tiny jalle from St.-Julien. The soil is a collection of thick gravel mixed with rather large stones, and the encépagement emphasizes the character of the Cabernet Sauvignon grape. The superbly made wine is tannin-rich, full-bodied, highly concentrated, and intended for long keeping. Although it is marginally less perfect today than *Ch. Marqaux* in quality, it has been, over the past fifty years, the most consistent of all first growths in the production of first-class wine. The best wine comes from old vines on a plot called "l'Enclos de Latour." Two other fields, "le Pineda" and "Petit Batailley," produce grapes for "Les Forts de Latour" (the second label), the latter often consuming up to 20 percent of all output. For those who can afford this truly luxurious wine, it is a must for the complete cellar. *Ch. Mouton Rothschild,* one of the most-interesting properties, was founded by Baron de Pons, a descendant of the Duke of Gloucester, in 1430. It is a large 72-hectare property

Plate 10.2   Ch. Latour and the Gironde, Pauillac

whose colorful, publicity-prone owner is now making full-bodied, generous, well-flavored, and long-lived wine. The unique museum, aristocratic
ambiance, engaging labels, and the fact that it was the only property to
elevate its status in the archaic 1855 classification make this a very
captivating estate. The "Mouton Cadet" label is generic Bordeaux and
should not be confused with this fine growth. *Ch. Lafite*, probably the
most-famous wine property in France, is a 90-hectare estate located in the
northern portion of Pauillac. Its name is derived from the medieval
French word for "hill," the source of its best wine (a 12-hectare portion
that is not only elevated and well drained, but whose grapes mature two
weeks earlier than neighboring fields). The wine at its best is a sublime
version of liquid velvet, smooth, overrated, and highly variable.

   Ch. Pichon-Longueville-Comtesse-de-Lalande is a superb growth of 55
hectares widely recognized as the better of the two Longuevilles. Due to
cépage differences, Baron is darker, more concentrated, and traditionally
takes longer to mature than the softer, classy, supple wine of Lalande that
is often described as sublime. Improvement over the past fifteen years has
been steady, resulting in high consistency matched by equally high
asking prices. Its output, in excess of 25,000 cases, offers excellent value
since it regularly outperforms some of the first growths. *Ch. Pichon-
Longueville-Baron* is a 50-hectare estate whose above-average winemaking
capabilities are marred by inconsistency. When good, the wine is known
for its fragrance, color, and flavor, and although the percent of Cabernet
Sauvignon has recently been reduced to soften the wine, it still requires at
least fifteen years to mature fully. Output is 14,000 cases. *Ch. Lynch-*

Bages, a fifth-growth property located south of the town of Pauillac, maintains a good reputation and a wide following for full-bodied, firm, robust wine that requires long cellaring. The wine is consistently good and rarely disappoints. It once offered excellent value, but recent price escalations have reduced its inherent advantage. While a good portion of the producing vineyard sits on a gravel bank that is deeper than 3 meters, the recent incorporation of hectarage considered less good may dilute quality. *Ch. Grand-Puy-Lacoste* is a 45-hectare fifth-growth estate producing 14,000 cases of wine whose quality is the equal of nearly all second growths. A middle-of-the-road property twenty years ago, this recently improved growth, whose producing hectarage has recently expanded, now makes consistently solid, well-structured wine with excellent color, balance, multiple layers of fruit and flavor, and a long, lingering finish. *Ch. Batailley,* named after the site of a famous battle, is a well-managed 50-hectare property that consistently makes excellent wine offering outstanding value. The wine is solid, tannin-rich, well structured, strapping, and made for the long haul. The vineyard, located to the west of the Longueville's, consists of one field—a very unusual occurrence— whose output is 22,000 cases. *Ch. Pédesclaux* is a little-known 17-hectare property that makes 8,000 cases of solid, tannin-rich, old-fashioned wine with an excellent aging potential. The underrated wine, dominated by Cabernet Sauvignon, is big, dark, and the product of traditional practices—features that set it apart from the supple, fruity wines currently in fashion. This truly "classic" wine is modestly priced and offers excellent

Plate 10.3   Ch. Batailley, Pauillac

value. *Ch. Pontet-Canet* is a large 90-hectare property well situated on a knoll overlooking the port of Pauillac. Previously owned by the Cruse family, the estate is now part of a small but excellent stable of properties owned by Guy Tesseron, who has done much to improve vineyard practices and winemaking techniques. This historic property located next to Mouton is currently making more than 40,000 cases of stylish, early maturing wine; it is a property to watch.

Ch. Duhart-Milon-Rothschild, located north of Mouton and southwest of Lafite, is a little-known fourth growth with average pedigree. Its 41 hectares produce 15,000 cases of less-concentrated and refined wine short of its classified status. *Ch. Haut-Bages-Libéral,* located to the west of route D2, is a 22-hectare property producing 11,000 cases of consistently full-bodied, concentrated, and supple wine that is solid and well made, with a good "middle" and a pronounced nose. Like *Ch. Pédesclaux,* this property is little known and rarely appreciated, but offers good value. *Ch. Croizet-Bages* is an underrated fifth-growth property currently making above-average wine known for its balance. The wine, due to a high percentage of Cabernet Franc, is distinctive, firm, yet refined and absolutely marvelous even in off vintages. This 25-hectare property regularly produces more than 10,500 hard-to-find cases. *Ch. Haut-Batailley,* an underrated 20-hectare property, makes soft, highly polished, and refined wine offering good value. *Ch. Grand-Puy-Ducasse* is a 35-hectare estate recently improved by the owners of *Ch. Chasse-Spleen.* Although the fields are scattered a considerable distance from the chai, the wines are expertly made and offer excellent value. Output exceeds 13,500 cases. *Ch. Mouton-Baronne-Philippe,* once known as *Ch. Mouton d'Armailhacq,* is a 50-hectare estate that makes sound, early maturing, but otherwise undistinguished wine. Output is 20,000 cases. *Ch. Clerc-Milon* is another property belonging to the energetic Baron Philippe de Rothschild. This 30-hectare estate, historically known as *Ch. Clerc-Milon-Mondon,* makes 8,500 cases of highly variable, hard, acidic wine. *Ch. Lynch-Moussas* is a little-known property located in a forest clearing in the southwestern portion of Pauillac. Since 1975 it has made consistently good, medium-bodied, fruity, supple wine. Output exceeds 11,000 cases. *Ch. Fonbadet,* a 15-hectare vineyard, produces 7,000 cases of big, vigorous, well-balanced, and flavored wine capable of extended cellaring, offering excellent value. The property is well situated on high, well-drained ground near the Gironde. *Ch. Haut-Bages-Avérous,* a popular 6-hectare property owned by *Lynch Bages,* makes above-average wine.

Other, less well known and distinguished properties include: *Ch. Colombier-Monpelou,* a small, little-known property of 14 hectares, owned by *Ch. Pédesclaux.* The well made and consistently good wine rarely disappoints, and it maintains a loyal following. Output exceeds 5,000 cases. *Ch. Pibran* is a little-known property of 20 hectares that enjoys a good local reputation for sound, well-made, and consistently well-flavored wine. The property, with an excellent aspect overlooking the Chenal de Gaer, has the possibility of tripling production. *Ch. Plantey,* carved out of two other properties, is a rather large 30-hectare vineyard that produces more than 12,000 cases of good, supple, early maturing wine that is mainly exported to Holland. *Ch. Haut-Bages-Monpelou,* a 15-hectare property carved out of a number of neighboring vineyards, produces wine that is robust, rustic, inconsistent, but substantial in good vintages. This recently improved property makes more than 5,000 cases. *Ch. la Fleur-Milon* is an 11-hectare property whose 4,300 cases are casually made and inconsistent. *Ch. Bellegrave* is an obscure 4-hectare property producing 1,000 cases of surprisingly good, firm, well-structured wine. *Ch. la Tour-Pibran* is a small 8-hectare property that makes 3,000 cases of hard-to-find, light-bodied, early maturing wine.

St.-Julien

A small, unpretentious village of 1,100 people, St.-Julien is located in the center of the quality-producing Médoc region. Surrounded by the Cussac canal in the south, St.-Laurent in the west, and Pauillac in the north, its production averages 30,000 hectoliters from approximately 750 producing hectares. It contains eleven of the sixty-one classified growths, and while it contains no first or fifth growths, it does have five seconds, two thirds, and four fourths. The commune also contains one Grand Bourgeois Exceptionnel and one Bourgeois property. Despite its fame as a fine wine commune, St.-Julien is the smallest of the "big four" Médoc communes and is only marginally larger than Listrac and Moulis.

The distinctiveness of the region lies in the presence of two *croupes* located in a north-south line beginning with *Ch. Talbot* and continuing south to *Ch. Gruaud-Larose.* The best sites, overlooking the Gironde from higher ground, have more gravel and are better drained than the growths that lie on flatter land in the western-facing portion of the district. The wines from the eastern portion are finer, more aromatic, and more delicate than the interior growth sites that produce wine with more body, a darker color, and appear to be more fleshy on the palate. The thirteen major growths are all large, and their wines are considered the most consistent of the six Médoc communes.

The recent history of wine production is presented in Figure 10.5. While it exhibits a doubling of output since 1960, hectarage has increased by half as much (from 500 to 750 hectares), a condition suggesting dilution of extract. As prices remain firm or continue to rise, there will be strong economic pressures to bring into production as many as 200 hectares of additional, but marginal land. Of the nearly three dozen growths in the commune, twenty-four are considered important. *Ch. Ducru Beaucaillou,* with 210 hectares, is widely recognized as the leading property in the commune. Seven vineyard fields with 45 hectares produce 22,000 cases. The wine is full-bodied, well scented and flavored, silky on the palate, consistent to a fault and, until recently, moderately priced, offering excellent value. The owner, Jean Borie, also owns several other properties. *Ch. Gruaud-Larose* is a property with impeccable credentials producing more than 40,000 cases of excellent wine from 81 hectares of vineland. Expertly and consistently well made, the wine is fragrant, and because the final blend contains only a small amount of *vin de presse,* it is particularly supple and ready after five years. As the wine is consistently above average even in average to below-average vintages, prices are remarkably low in comparison to quality. The estate is the flagship of a stable of excellent properties located on both sides of the Gironde and Entre-Deux-Mers. *Ch. Branaire-Ducru* is currently making first-class wine with immense depth of flavor and bouquet rivaling first growths. The 48-hectare estate produces 19,000 cases of absolutely outstanding wine; because it is underrated and little known, it offers excellent value and is a must for any serious cellar. *Ch. Léoville-las-Cases* is the largest and most-celebrated of the three Léoville vineyards. It consists of 135 hectares (80 planted in vines, divided into three large fields), and makes more than 28,000 cases of wine whose quality is only slightly better than *Ch. Léoville-Barton. Ch. Léoville-Barton* is the smallest of the three Léovilles, with an annual output of just 15,000 cases from 40 hectares of vineland. The wine is superb, classic, always full-bodied and robust, requiring time to fully mature (Cabernet Sauvignon and Petit Verdot percentages are higher than normal). This traditional property makes well-structured wine offering remarkable value, also a must for the serious cellar.

Ch. Léoville-Poyferré is usually considered the lightest, fruitiest, most-supple and unreliable of the three Léovilles. This unfair description may have been true twenty years ago, but the property has recently been improved, and the wine currently offers excellent value. Production exceeds 19,500 cases annually from 58 hectares. The wine (due to increased percentages of Merlot and the elimination of Petit Verdot) is much more supple and early maturing than its two sister properties. *Ch. Beychevelle,* one of the oldest and most-popular properties in the commune, has recently lost a good deal of its panache. Until recently, the wine was robust, full-bodied, dark in color, and required at least ten years to mature fully. Today the 72-hectare property produces more than 30,000 cases of light, fruity, supple, and early maturing wine. *Ch. Langoa-Barton,* a 70-hectare property located in the center of the more prestigious portion of the commune, is one of the most underrated properties in the Médoc. Very harsh during its first five years, the wine (9,200 cases) requires plenty of patience to fully mature into a firm, well-flavored and scented libation. It is consistently well made and offers outstanding value. Very similar to *Ch. Léoville-Barton,* it is slightly fruitier and more supple. *Ch. Lagrange* is a beautiful 56-hectare property that has recently been acquired by Suntori International, a large Japanese spirits company that also has interest in the Firestone vineyard in California. The estate has a mixed reputation: at its best, the property produces wine that is dark, chewy, full of fruit and balance; at its worst, the wine is thin and unappealing. Over the past ten years it has produced several excellent vintages and usually offers good value. Output exceeds 20,000 cases. *Ch. Talbot* is the largest producer in St.-Julien, with an output of 50,000 cases. The property, owned by Cordier, is well managed, impeccably clean, and known for consistency. Although less refined than the wine of *Ch. Gruaud-Larose*, it is above average in quality and moderately priced. The estate also produces a rare "Caillou Blanc," made principally from Sauvignon Blanc and Sémillon, that is fruity and interesting, but otherwise undistinguished. *Ch. St.-Pierre-Sevaistre* (also called St.-Pierre) is an obscure fourth growth, historically known for inconsistent, light-bodied, bland wine. The recently improved wine is now made darker in color, fruitier, and more supple. Production is approximately 9,000 cases from the 30-hectare property. *Ch. Gloria*, a well-known, non-classified 50-hectare property, produces more than 21,500 cases. Despite the energetic efforts of its owner, Henri Martin, the wine, though solid and consistent, is overrated. *Ch. Terrey-Gros-Cailloux,* a 20-hectare property, produces more than 8,000 cases of full-bodied, concentrated, well-flavored wine that offers exceptional value. *Ch. du Glana* is a much-improved Grand Bourgeois Exceptionnel, 44-hectare property that makes 20,000 cases of fruity, supple, early matur-ing wine. *Ch. Lalande-Borie,* a good, but overpriced Eugène Borie property, makes 7,500 cases. *Ch. de la Bridane,* a good, reliable 13-hectare Bourgeois growth, makes 7,000 cases of rather robust, rustic wine. *Ch. Teynac* is a 20 hectare, recently refurbished property.

Margaux

The village of Margaux, located on the first major gravel *croupe* north of Bordeaux, lends its name to one of the most-famous wine communes in France. While Margaux proper contains 400 hectares of vineland, the entire communal appellation has 1,183 hectares and includes the four satellite hamlets of Cantenac (404 hectares), Soussans (157 hectares), Labarde (130 hectares), and Arsac (95 hectares). With twenty-one classi-fied properties, Margaux has a disproportionate share of estates ranked in the 1855 classification: one first growth, five second growths, ten third growths, three fourth growths, and two fifth growths.

The soil of Margaux, containing an abnormal amount of alluvial pebble, gravel, and sand, rests on a subsoil of gravel and clay with isolated concentrations of iron oxide. In general, the best sites are found to the east and south of the village of Margaux where the thickest beds of gravel in the entire Médoc are found. On these soils the grapes produce the finest wine in the appellation.

The growth of hectarage and production, follow the pattern of growth typical of all communal appellations over the past thirty years. It is interesting to note that while hectarage increased by 42 percent since pre-1960 levels, the wine production has increased by nearly 68 percent, a good indication that yields have risen to dangerous levels. Of the four premier communal appellations, Margaux is the most vulnerable to adverse publicity concerning the quality of wine produced. For a long time, the wines of Margaux sold themselves, and growers became complacent. Fields became dangerously fragmented, yields rose, and the quality of the wine, when compared to rapid improvements in the Haut-Médoc, Médoc, St.-Emilion, and Pomerol appellations, began to decline. As a result, a number of properties, notably *Ch. Brane-Cantenac, Ch. Rausan-Ségla, Ch. Rauzan-Gassies, Ch. Ferrière, Ch. Dauzac,* and *Ch. Durfort-Vivens,* were producing wine of less than Bourgeois quality, let alone classified growth status.

Because of the unprecedented stability in the Bordeaux wine market, new plantings within the Margaux appellation have increased at a rate of about 10 hectares a year. Since the amount of prime real estate is already near the saturation level in the village of Margaux, Cantenac, and Labarde, additional vine hectarage can be added only in the more marginal areas of Soussans and Arsac.

Ch. Margaux since 1978, without question has made extraordinary wine—the finest among first growths. The 250-hectare, immaculately managed and cared-for estate produces 24,500 cases of red and fewer than 4,000 cases of "Pavillon Blanc du Ch. Margaux," a stylish and expensive dry white wine. The latter is a rare wine that is barrel-fermented, wood-aged for six months, and bottle-aged for one year prior to release. The second wine—"Pavillon Rouge," accounting for 15 to 30 percent of the annual harvest, is made from younger vines and grapes growing on less-desirable land. The finest wine bottled under the chateau's famous label is nothing short of spectacular—rich, perfectly balanced, with multiple layers of flavor and bouquet, and absolutely outstanding in every way. It is made from grapes grown in two vine fields known as "Puch Sem Peyre" and "Cap de Haut," both of which are composed of pure gravel. Winemaking at *Ch. Margaux* dates at least from the 13th century when the estate was known as the *Ch. de la Mothe Margaux.* Archives at the château indicate that between 1300 and 1380 it possibly belonged to the king of England. The modern period in its history begins with Count Du Barry, brother-in-law to the countess who was Louis XV's favorite. The count became the lord of Margaux in 1770 and kept the property until 1793, when it was sold to the Marquis Douat de la Colonilla, who demolished the old castle and filled in the moat and watercourses. He enlarged the estate and built a new mansion in Palladian style, with Doric columns, the graceful, elegant building that stands today. The marquis died in 1816, and in 1835 his children sold the property to the progressive, brilliant Alexandre Aguado, Marquis de la Marismas. He was among the first of a long list of bankers who established a presence in the Médoc in the mid-19th century. In addition to producing excellent wine, the marquis was the patron of the composer Rossini. After his death, the estate changed ownership many times until 1925, when it was acquired by Bernard and Pierre Ginestet. It remained in the Ginestet family until André Mentzenopoulos purchased it in 1977.

Ch. Rausan-Ségla is a 42-hectare property composed of four large fields, all located immediately south of the village of Margaux. Historically, the wine was made with a good deal of *vin de presse,* and hence took time to mature fully. After a series of mediocre vintages in the 1970s, the wine is again exhibiting individuality and character. Output is approximately 15,000 cases. *Ch. Rauzan-Gassies* is a highly overrated, second-growth property that produced a dreadful number of less-than-classed-growth vintages in the 1960s and 1970s. The wine lacked depth, flavor, and consistency, and offered little value. The 25-hectare property, which is fragmented into nine irregular fields, west, south, and east of Margaux, changed ownership in 1978; while the wine improved markedly, it is still not up to second-growth standards. Output is approximately 10,000 cases.

Ch. Lascombes, an 87-hectare property, is fragmented into more than twenty small fields, mainly to the south of Margaux. The wine is fruity, supple, early maturing, but undistinguished and certainly not up to second-growth standards. Ownership has recently changed hands, and major innovations are taking place, one of which is the introduction of a regional white and red blend called "Chevalier Lascombes," similar to "Mouton Cadet." Output is an impressive 40,000 cases. *Ch. Durfort-Vivens* is a 35-hectare property fragmented into five principal fields, most of which are located on deep gravel south of Margaux. For a considerable period, this estate produced wine that was not up to second-growth standards—inconsistent, coarse, thin, lacking in suppleness and finesse. There are indications, however, that improvement is taking place, which should be reflected in the wine. Output is approximately 7,000 cases. *Ch. Malescot-St. Exupéry,* a 32-hectare property, produces what can only be described as a classic Médoc—a wine that is full-bodied and rather austere and requires fifteen to twenty years to mature fully. The wine is fermented at high temperatures, with a high percentage of *vin de presse.* The vineyard is a near-perfect blend of grapes that slopes down to the Gironde; the soil contains up to 3 meters of gravel over a bed of iron-bearing clay. It is an underrated wine that offers excellent value; output is about 13,000 cases. *Ch. Marquis d'Alesme-Becker* is a 9-hectare property making 3,800 cases. The vineyard, recently separated from the management of *Ch. Malescot-St.*

Exupéry, is being replanted and renovated. At its best the wine has a pronounced depth of flavor and a long, lingering finish.

Ch. Ferrière is a small 4-hectare property making fewer than 1,800 cases of supple, fruity, but almost always overpriced wine. The wine and winemaking have long been associated with *Ch. Lascombes. Ch. Desmirail,* an 18-hectare property, makes fewer than 4,000 cases. During the depression of the 1930s, the property was subdivided among the various neighboring growths, *Ch. Palmer* acquiring a large portion. It was reunited in 1980 by Lucien Lurton, owner of *Ch. Brane-Cantenac.* Production will, no doubt, increase to maximum limits shortly. *Ch. Marquis-de-Terme* is a recently restored 30-hectare property that has been making wine equivalent to second-growth standards. The historic, light, fruity, and early maturing wine is now made in a more concentrated chewy, mouth-filling style. Offering excellent value, output is approximately 14,500 cases.

Among nonclassified growths, six have established reputations: *Ch. la Gurgue* is an obscure 12-hectare property that historically produced light, supple wine with little character. Purchased and refurbished by Mestre-zat-Preller in 1978, it is currently making full-bodied, chewy, flavorful wine that offers excellent value. A label to look for, its output is 5,000 cases. *Ch. Labégorce,* a 30-hectare property located in the extreme northern portion of the Margaux district, produces 14,000 cases of full-bodied, robust, somewhat rustic wine not typical of its neighbors. Over the past ten years, the wine has become more delicate with predictions of even better things to come. *Ch. Canuet* is a little known 10-hectare property making 4,200 cases of light, thin, often unstructured wine. *Ch. l'Abbé-Gorsse-de-Gorsse,* a 10-hectare property located next to *Ch. Labégorce,* makes 4,700 cases of good, average-quality, but unspectacular wine. Recently renovated and replanted, improvement in quality is highly probable. *Ch. Charmant* is a little-known 6-hectare property making 2,000 cases of typical appelation-quality wine. *Dne. de l'Ille-Margaux,* not technically part of the appellation, is located on a small island in the Gironde opposite Margaux. It produces 1,500 cases.

Cantenac

The village of Cantenac (1,000 people), with 404 hectares of vineland and eight classed growths, is second in importance to Margaux. The principal properties are as follows: *Ch. Palmer* is a 35-hectare property making 11,000 cases of wine known for its softness, small amounts of *vin de presse,* comparatively early maturing features, and high Merlot content. At its best, the wine is luscious, very fruity, well balanced and superior to any other in Cantenac. Unfortunately it is marred by inconsistency and thus offers little value. *Ch. Boyd-Cantenac,* an 18-hectare property, makes old-fashioned, full-bodied, rich, silky wine, which offers extraordinary value, due to its underrated status. Although a third growth, it consistently outperforms *Ch. Brane-Cantenac* and a number of additional growths. Output is 6,500 cases; it is a must for the serious cellar. *Ch. Cantenac-Brown* is an underrated 30-hectare estate making 15,000 cases of austere, old-fashioned, but full-bodied, well-scented wine capable of extended cellaring. Scorned by critics because it is not made in a modern "Peynaud" method, the wine offers excellent value, especially in good vintages. *Ch. Brane-Cantenac,* an old 85-hectare property divided into four large fields, produces more than 28,000 cases. Despite its admirable location on deep gravel, the wine of this estate has long been overrated, overpriced, and disappointing on a regular basis; it is thin, somewhat coarse, early maturing, unbalanced, and certainly not up to classed-growth standards. It is the flagship for a large stable of properties. *Ch. Prieuré-Lichine* is a fragmented 58-hectare property that makes more than 25,000 cases of surprisingly supple, fruity, fine-textured wine. In good vintages it offers excellent value. *Ch. Pouget,* an 8-hectare property associated with *Ch. Boyd-Cantenac,* once belonged to a Benedictine order. Vinified in conjunction with Boyd-Cantenac, the wine is always above average in quality, and often complex, supple, and well balanced. Highly underrated, this traditionally made wine is consistent and offers excellent value. Output is approximately 3,500 cases. *Ch. d'Issan* is a 35-hectare property whose wine has recently improved after a generation of rather inconsistent vintages. The wine, the product of a small amount of *vin de presse* and a brief maceration, is light in color, medium-bodied, early maturing, with a sweetish scent, and not necessarily up to third-growth standards. The property, with an impressive moated chateau, produces more than 11,000 cases. *Ch. Kirwan,* a 30-hectare property, is divided into seven fields located east of *Ch. Brane-Cantenac* and adjoining *Ch. Pouget.* The soil in some fields is poorly drained, and the wine, historically, was somewhat coarse and needed time to mature. The inconsistency and dullness of the wine has now largely disappeared, and as a result the wine offers excellent value.

The most important of the handful of nonclassified properties is *Ch. d'Angludet,* a 30-hectare property that was in disrepair until purchased by Peter Sichel in 1961. The 12th-century estate, lying on the slope of a minor stream, produces 9,000 cases of average, rustic, yet full-bodied, brawny-type wine that usually offers good value. *Ch. Martinens,* a little-known but sizable property of 60 hectares, produces more than 8,000 cases of good, sound, attractive wine. It is located on a slight slope in the western portion of the producing region. *Ch. Montbrun,* an obscure 8-hectare property that was once a part of *Ch. Palmer,* makes 2,800 cases of average-quality wine. *Ch. Pontac-Lynch* is an obscure, well-sited 5-hectare property located next to *Ch. Montbrun.* It is difficult to locate, and output is 2,000 cases.

Labarde

The gravel *croupe* of Labarde, sandwiched between a low-lying marshy meadow and Macau, is located 1 kilometer southeast of Margaux. It contains 130 hectares of semiprecious vineland, two Grands Crus, and a superb Bourgeois growth. *Ch. Giscours* is a 75-hectare property with more compact and homogeneous fields than most other estates in the area. The wine, made from a high percentage of *vin de presse,* is lean, bold, full on the palate, and not typical of its neighbors. Often an excellent value, it is marred only by dullness, inconsistency, and a lack of patience. Output is approximately 24,000 cases. *Ch. Dauzac,* a large property located along the eastern edge of Labarde near the Gironde, produces more than 20,000 cases. After a long period of neglect, the estate has been improved and the wine is now much fuller, fruitier, and supple. Among nonclassified properties, *Ch. Siran,* a 25-hectare property along the Gironde, produces 12,000 cases of excellent wine. Rarely seen in the United States but very popular in the United Kingdom, the wine is rather austere, but pleasant, full-bodied, and highly reliable.

Soussans

The small village of Soussans (965 people), with approximately 157 hectares of vineland, sits east of Avensan on the northern extension of the large Margaux gravel *croupe.* The wine here is firmer, fuller, and less delicate than that of Margaux. While there are no classified growths, several nonclassified properties deserve mention. *Ch. Labégorce-Zédé,* the leading growth in the village, is a 42-hectare property. Under Belgian ownership, it produces 8,000 cases of full-bodied, well-flavored, mouth-filling wine that is quite consistent, has an excellent potential, and offers good value. *Ch. la Tour-de-Mons* is a quaint 110-hectare property that makes 12,000 cases of sound, medium-weight, traditionally produced wine offering good value. Although lighter in style than most neighboring properties, it is more refined, and its elegant structure is of classed quality. *Ch. Tayac,* a 34-hectare property, is located on the edge of a north-facing ridge south of Arcins, on the south bank of the Estey de Tayac. Despite its rather large output of more than 16,000 cases, the full-bodied, well-structured wine offers good value. *Ch. Paveil-de-Luze* is an old, but recently improved, 23-hectare property located between *Ch. Citran* and *Ch. Tayac.* It produces 6,000 cases of well-made but light, early maturing wine that is a reliable restaurant wine. *Ch. Bel-Air-Marquis-d'Aligre* is an 18-hectare property that makes more than 4,000 cases of traditionally made, full-bodied, fat, concentrated wine atypical of its immediate neighbors. *Ch. Marsac-Séguineau* is a 10-hectare property recently acquired by Mestrezat-Preller. The wine, historically of average and undistinguished quality, has improved and will continue to do so. *Ch. Haut-Breton-Larigaudière* is a 4-hectare vineyard that makes fewer than 2,000 cases of average-quality wine.

Arsac

Located due south of Margaux, the village of Arsac (1,600 people) represents the most-westward extension of gravel within the five Margaux parishes. It contains 95 hectares of vineland and one fifth-growth property. *Ch. du Tertre* is a 47-hectare vineyard that, unlike most other vineyards in Margaux, is divided into two large fields, both located on gravel surrounded by forest. A "traditionally made" Cabernet wine, it is full on the palate and well scented. Dramatically improved since it was acquired by *Ch. Calon-Ségur,* its future appears quite bright. Of the more than ten nonclassified properties, two enjoy well-established reputations: *Ch. Monbrison* and *Ch. Pontet-Chappaz.* The former is a 15-hectare property little known in the United States, because a portion of the vineyard was part of *Ch. Desmirail.* Making 6,000 cases of surprisingly good wine—full on the palate, dark in color, fruity, and well balanced— it is marred only by inconsistency. It is expected that in 1987 it will be elevated to the rank of Grands Bourgeois Exceptionnel. *Ch. Pontet-Chappaz* is a 6-hectare property that makes about 3,000 cases of soft, agreeable, supple wine. The property is owned by an aggressive grower who is steadily improving its quality.

Listrac

The village of Listrac (1,300 residents) lies northwest of Margaux on one of the largest and highest gravel banks in the Médoc. The entire commune is composed of three *croupes* that are at least 30 meters high, with individual spots being an additional 8 meters in elevation—an unusual feature in an otherwise flat area. Approximately two dozen properties produce more than 30,000 hectoliters of red wine from 585 hectares of vineland, the latter figure representing about 10 percent of all land in the commune. Lying next and to the west of Moulis, Listrac is almost totally surrounded by forest.

Vine hectarage, severely reduced in size after the *phylloxera* epidemic, stood at 1,350 hectares in 1910 and fell to fewer than 200 in 1945. Since 1960, however, the gradual and persistent improvement in the economic climate has enabled the consolidation of small holdings into larger units of production, and hectarage has more than doubled. Although over-looked in the 1855 classification, Listrac today contains two Grand Bourgeois Exceptionnel, one Grand Bourgeois, and five Bourgeois proper-ties.

Made from the usual mixture of red Médocain grapes, the wines, although less fine and delicate than those of Margaux, Pauillac, and St.-Julien, are nevertheless full-bodied, well colored, flavorful, and surprisingly long-lived. The growths, located on higher ground with more gravel and less sand, use Petit Verdot to produce excellent, highly underrated wines that currently offer exceptional value and belong in every serious cellar. The cooperative of Listrac, accounting for approximately half the commune's total output, sells its bottled wine under the name of "Grand Listrac," a good, well-made wine that is moderately priced. The principal growths are as follows.

Ch. Fourcas-Hosten, a large, recently rehabilitated 45-hectare property, produces more than 19,000 cases. Because the wine does not receive exhaustive wood-aging, it is very supple, fruity, round, smooth, and can age for more than ten years. The well-made wine, consistent and very popular, offers excellent value and should be part of any serious cellar. *Ch. Fourcas-Dupré,* a 40-hectare property located on excellent gravel soil in the northern limits of Listrac, produces approximately 19,000 cases. Although the wine is rather dull, quality has recently improved. *Ch. Fonréaud,* a well-situated 90-hectare estate on the southernmost hill in the producing commune, has recently been improved and now makes well-structured wine that is above average in quality in good vintages. Production exceeds 21,000 cases. *Ch. Lestage* is a 120-hectare property (54 planted in vines) that consistently makes more than 22,000 cases of solid, well-structured, yet supple, fruity, full-bodied wines that are capable of aging past their tenth birthday. Located on gravel soil, the

Plate 10.4   Ch. Fourcas-Dupré, Listrac

property makes highly underrated wine that often provides outstanding value. *Ch. Lafon,* a much-improved wine since 1975, is well made, solid, early maturing, with a good dose of complexity. The 14-hectare property, jointly managed with *Ch. la Bécade,* makes more than 5,000 cases offering good value. *Ch. Clarke,* with 140 hectares and an output of 41,000 cases, is the largest producer as well as one of the newest in Listrac. Owned by Baron Edmond de Rothschild since 1973, the wine has steadily improved, but remains overpriced.

Ch. Cap-Léon-Veyrin is a small, obscure property of 25 hectares (8 in vines) currently making surprisingly good, fleshy wine that is soft, supple, well flavored and scented. Production exceeds 3,000 cases. *Ch. la Bécade* is a good, sound, above-average wine that consistently offers good value. Production exceeds 12,000 cases, half of which is distributed by a large shipper under various labels. *Ch. Lalande* is a large 200-hectare estate (14 under vines) that consistently makes unusual and distinctive wine due to a high percentage of Merlot and Petit Verdot. The vineyard is meticulously tended, and the wines, full-bodied, flavorful, and well scented, offer excellent value. Production exceeds 5,000 cases. *Ch. Sémeillan* is a medium-sized property of 4,000 cases, known for light-bodied, supple, and fruity wine that is hard to find. *Ch. Saransot-Dupré* is an obscure 12-hectare estate making more than 5,000 cases of acidic, often hard, unstructured wine that offers little value. *Ch. Peyredon-la-Gravette* is a 6-hectare property that makes fewer than 2,000 cases of soft, appealing, supple wine. Consistently well made, it offers excellent value. *Ch. Moulin-de-Laborde,* a 10-hectare property, makes more than 5,000 cases of average, well-balanced, but often dull wine. Other properties include *Ch. Ducluzeau* (4 hectares, 2,000 cases), *Ch. Bellegrave* (15 hectares, 5,000 cases), *Ch. Fourcas-Loubaney* (5 hectares, 2,000 cases), and *Ch. Pierre-Bibian* (15 hectares, 7,000 cases), and *Ch. Moulin-de-Laborde.*

Moulis

Lying to the east of Listrac on the margins of the Jalle de Tiqueforte, the small village of Moulis (population 1,000) separates the central Médoc from Margaux. It is lower in altitude (the entire commune is less than 25 meters), flatter, and sandier than Listrac. Although there are pockets of pure gravel, clay, and limestone, which produce average to above-average libations, emotions run deep as to which commune produces the better wine. The best vineyards *(Ch. Chasse-Spleen, Ch. Maucaillou,* and the *Poujeaux)* lie northeast of Moulis on a gravel *croupe* with an easterly orientation, and only *Ch. Brillette* faces south overlooking the Jalle de Tiqueforte and the vineyards of Avensan. The commune contains three Grand Bourgeois Exceptionnel, three Grand Bourgeois, and three Bourgeois properties.

The elongated boundaries of Moulis contain 400 hectares of vineland (representing nearly 20 percent of the commune's total hectarage), which produce more than 18,000 hectoliters of wine annually. Of the three dozen growths, more than fifteen have generated substantial national and international reputations. The wines, due to a high percentage of Cabernet Sauvignon, are dark in color, somewhat rustic, and not as refined and supple as those of Margaux or even Listrac. Yet they are concentrated in flavor, well made, sound, distinctive, and capable of extended cellar improvement. Because Moulis was overlooked in the 1855 classification, the wines (like those of Listrac) have long been neglected; as a consequence, prices are comparatively low and value significantly high. The major properties are:

Ch. Chasse-Spleen is a superbly managed property sited on high ground containing gravel. The 55-hectare property produces more than 23,000 cases of above-average (classed-growth quality) wine that is expertly made, consistently good, well flavored, and with a good finish. The property is the flagship of a large stable of properties owned by the Mestrezat-Preller group. *Ch. Poujeaux,* also known as "Poujeaux Theil," is one of the oldest properties in the commune, dating to the 16th century. Although a sizable property of 40 hectares with an output of 17,000 cases, it remains little known and hard to find. The property is well sited on gravelly, well-drained soil, and the wine, very popular during the interwar years, is made from a high percentage of Petit Verdot. It is well made, tannin-rich, substantial on the palate, ages well, and offers outstanding value. *Ch. Dutruch-Grand-Poujeaux,* unlike its neighbors, is a lighter and more delicate wine whose quality is not up to historic levels. Although uninspiring in average vintages, it produces outstanding, dark-colored, complex, well-structured wine in excellent years. The 25-hectare property produces nearly 13,000 cases. *Ch. Brillette,* located on a *croupe,* has recently been replanted and much improved. Consistent in quality and moderately priced, it offers excellent value. The above-average wine is solid, full-bodied yet supple, and well flavored. The 70-hectare estate has 30 hectares planted in vines that produce more than 12,000 cases. *Ch. Duplessis-Hauchecorne,* with 44 hectares, is one of the largest and most-consistent quality growths. It is known for solid, well-made, uncomplicated wine, offering good value. Production exceeds 14,000 cases. *Ch. Moulin-à-Vent* is a recently improved property well situated on high ground that makes dark-colored, richly flavored and scented wine. Historically, the wine was hard and unyielding, but as the percentage of Cabernet Sauvignon declined and Merlot increased, the wine has become more supple and offers outstanding value. Output is 10,000 cases. *Ch. Duplessis-Fabre,* a small but expanding growth that makes 4,900 cases of above-average, soft, supple wine, offers excellent value. *Ch. la Closerie* is a medium-sized growth of 5,000 cases of average, well-made, but often dull wine, requiring time to mature fully.

Ch. Maucaillou is an excellent, impeccably managed 50-hectare property well sited on gravelly soil. The wine—supple, low in tannin, always well made and early maturing—is not as robust or as rustic as other Moulis properties. Output often exceeds 23,000 cases. *Ch. Gressier-Grand-Poujeaux* is an 18-hectare property whose wine, made by traditional methods, is full-bodied, flavorful, tannin-rich, well scented, but inconsistent. One of the oldest properties in the commune, it has the ability to produce full-bodied, complex, multilayered wine in exceptional vintages. Output approaches 9,000 cases. *Ch. Branas* is a well-regarded estate that produces above-average, meticulously made, fruity and supple wine that offers excellent value. Production approaches 2,000 cases. *Ch. Moulis* is a medium-sized property whose wine is rarely seen on retail shelves, because most of its 5,000-case output is sold at the property or by mail. *Ch. Mauvesin,* with 62 hectares and an output of 30,000 cases, is one of the largest properties in Moulis. Although palatable, soft, and supple, the wine is undistinguished. *Ch. Anthonic* is an 18-hectare property making 5,000 cases of soft, early maturing wine. *Ch. Bel-Air-Lagrave,* lying next to *Ch. Poujeaux,* is an excellent 12-hectare property located on well-drained soil. The wine is full-bodied, tannin-rich, often dull, and requires patience to mature fully. Never living up to expectations, the wine should be purchased only in good vintages. Output is more than 5,000 cases. Other properties include *Ch. Pomeys* (4,000 cases), *Ch. Tour-Granins* (4,000 cases), *Ch. Ruat, Ch. Biston-Brillette, Ch. la Mouline,* and *Ch. Bouqueyran.*

The Haut-Médoc

The Haut-Médoc, with 2,797 hectares of vineland, is the second-largest appellation in the Médoc. Although the area encompasses sixteen communes, eleven contain more than 100 hectares, and two, St.-Seurin-de-Cadourne and St.-Laurent-et-Benon, account for nearly one-third of the planted area. The appellation includes a collection of better commune sites not included within the more prestigious 1855 classification. The appellation surrounds the six communal appellations and stretches from Blanquefort in the south to St.-Seurin, just north of St.-Estèphe.

Although this appellation has been in existence since 1936, it remained obscure until the post–1945 wine boom, when its hectarage and production more than doubled (see Table 10.4 and Figure 10.6). Within appellation boundaries are found five Grand Cru Classé, five Grand Bourgeois Exceptionnel, and eighteen Grand Bourgeois growths. More than forty additional properties produce above-average to excellent wine offering outstanding value. The principal communes and their vineyards follow, listed from north to south.

St.-Seurin is the northernmost village within the Haut-Médoc appellation, and with 459 hectares of vineland, it contains one sixth of the appellation's total hectarage. It is a small village located just north of St.-

Table 10.4   Sale of Haut-Médoc, 1982

Sale	Hectoliters	Percent	Sale	Hectoliters	Percent
Holland	4,518	12.5	Denmark	3,320	9.2
Belgium	9,417	26.1	Other	3,691	10.2
United States	4,642	12.9	Total exports	36,039	100.0
West Germany	3,701	10.3			
United Kingdom	3,088	8.6	France	47,709	57.0
Switzerland	3,662	10.2	Total sales	83,748	100.0

Source: Conseil Interprofessionnel du Vin de Bordeaux.

Estèphe on a *croupe* overlooking the Gironde, and it contains seven above-average growths and a small, but good cooperative. The latter, founded in 1935, has seventy members, controls 148 hectares, and produces 8,000 hectoliters of wine annually. Made with equal amounts of Cabernet Sauvignon and Merlot with small infusions of Cabernet Franc, the wine appears under the brand name of "La Paroisse." Twenty percent is bottled, while the rest is sold in bulk to negociants. The principal properties are:

Ch. Sociando-Mallet, little known in the United States, is a 17th-century 30-hectare property purchased by Jean Gautreau in 1969. Completely renovated and replanted, it now makes excellent to outstanding wine. Unlike most properties in the region that make early maturing wines, the wine of *Ch. Sociando-Mallet* is loaded with tannin and requires extended cellaring for full maturation. It is consistently good, dark in color, full-bodied, complex in flavor and scent, and equal to most third growths. Needless to say, it offers outstanding value and should be part of every serious cellar. It is the finest estate in the commune, and its output is 13,000 cases. *Ch. Coufran* is a large 160-hectare property making

Figure 10.6   Haut-Médoc: Wine Production and Hectarage, 1949–1984

Figure 10.7   Médoc: Wine Production and Hectarage, 1949–1984

(in thousands of hectoliters and hectares)

45,000 cases of very soft, inviting, and unimpeachably satisfying wine due to a high Merlot content and flawless vinification practices. The wine, lavish in ripe fruit flavors, rarely disappoints. *Ch. Verdignan,* a 46-hectare property, makes more than 22,000 cases of dark-colored, full-bodied, stylish wine with a good measure of complexity. It is a newly expanded estate with the latest physical facilities. *Ch. Bel-Orme-Tronquoy-de-Lalande* is a 26-hectare property that had, until recently, a dull, inconsistent reputation. The wine now is assertive and full-bodied, requiring time to mature. Output is 12,000 cases. *Ch. Pontoise-Cabarrus-Brochon* is a 22-hectare property, little known and rarely seen in the United States. Output is 8,600 cases. *Ch. Soudars,* a 14-hectare property, produces 7,000 cases of expertly made, supple, fruity, early maturing wine. *Ch. Grand-Moulin* is a 15-hectare property making full-bodied, rustic, tannin-rich wine requiring patience. The property was little known until it changed hands in 1958. Also known as *Ch. Lamothe,* its output is 6,800 cases. *Ch. Bardis* is a small 16th-century farmstead with an interesting history that produces traditional Bordeaux—full-bodied, well structured and chewy. *Ch Charmail* is a 24-hectare property making wine for mass appeal. Its 9,800 cases are widely exported. Other properties include *Ch. St-Paul* (20 hectares, 11,000 cases), *Ch. Bonneau-Livran* (5 hectares, 3,000 cases), *Ch. Lestage-Simon* (12 hectares, 6,500 cases), *Ch. Sénilhac* (11 hectares, 5,000 cases), *Ch. Pabeau* (10 hectares, 4,000 cases), and *Ch. Doyac* (16 hectares, 4,000 cases).

The village of Vertheuil, lying to the north of Cissac, contains 241 hectares of vineland, seven good growths, and one cooperative. Founded in 1935, this cooperative has eighty members, controls 114 hectares, and produces 6,000 hectoliters of wine annually. The wine is made from equal amounts of Merlot and Cabernet Sauvignon, and its brand name is "Ch. Chatellenie." The principal growths: *Ch. Victoria,* recently expanded and renovated, is currently producing 6,500 cases of outstanding wine offering excellent value. *Ch. le Bourdieu* is a 30-hectare property making 14,500 cases of full-bodied, tannin-rich, distinctive wine. It consistently makes wine of classified quality. *Ch. le Reysson,* a large 200-hectare property, has recently been purchased by the Mestrezat group and is completely renovated and enlarged. Output exceeds 24,000 cases and is expected to grow. *Ch. Meynieu* is a 12-hectare property making 5,000 cases of full-bodied, well-structured, old-fashioned, tannin-rich wine. It consistently makes wine of classified quality. *Ch. Picorneau* is a medium-sized property making 4,600 cases of average-quality wine.

The large village of Cissac lies on a gravel *croupe* north of the Chenal du Lazaret and west of the southern margins of St.-Estèphe. It contains 282 hectares of vineland, one cooperative, and a number of growths with a national and international reputation. Founded in 1935, the cooperative of Cissac, the smallest in the entire Médoc, contains just thirty-five members, controls fewer than 50 hectares, and produces 2,000 hectoliters annually. The wine, made from 55 percent Cabernet Sauvignon and 45 percent Merlot, is bottled under the brand name of "Bouquet de Cissus." The principal growths are as follows:

Ch. Cissac is a 70-hectare property, much improved in the past ten years, making full-bodied, well-structured wine that ages well. It is considered by many to be the leading estate in the commune, but its inconsistency keeps it from among the top Haut-Médoc properties. Output is 10,000 cases, and the second label is *Ch. de Martiny. Ch. du Breuil* is a little-known 23-hectare property making 11,000 cases of excellent, robust *vin de garde* wine that rarely disappoints. Its quality is more consistent than *Ch. Cissac,* and for that reason alone, a number of local aficionados give the nod to this estate. It is hard to find, but well worth the effort as it offers good value. *Ch. Tour-du-Mirail* is a 45-hectare property making 8,000 cases of soft, well-rounded, hard-to-find wine. *Ch. Hanteillan,* a 75-hectare, recently rehabilitated and expanded property, makes more than 24,000 cases of first-class, supple, early maturing wine. The second wine is called *Ch. la Tour du Vatican. Ch. la Tour-St.-Joseph* is a 19-hectare property making 10,000 cases of above-average, full-bodied, robust wine, capable of extended aging. *Ch. Vieux-Braneyre,* a 10-hectare property, makes 4,000 cases of well-made, full-bodied, tannin-rich, and stylish wine that offers considerable value. *Ch. Puy-Castéra* is a 35-hectare, recently planted property well situated on a knoll. Although the property has considerable potential, high yields reduce concentration, and quality therefore falls short of the leaders in the commune. The second label is *Ch. Holden;* the output exceeds 13,000 cases. *Ch. Haut-Logat,* a 24-hectare property, makes 6,000 cases of wine that is average at best. *Ch. Lamothe-Cissac* is a 30-hectare property making 15,000 cases of above-average wine. It is a well-maintained estate, and a leading growth whose quality has recently improved.

The village of St.-Sauveur is located on a crossroads due west of Pauillac. The vineyards, located on two *croupes* separated by a small stream, collectively contain 258 hectares and a number of important growths. *Ch. Ramage-la-Bâtisse* is a 40-hectare east-facing property that produces 20,000 cases of well-made, tannin-rich wine offering outstanding value. *Ch. Peyrabon,* a 70-hectare property located on the east-facing side of a knoll, makes more than 22,000 cases of hard-to-find, dark-colored, mouth-filling wine that offers good value. *Ch. Liversan,* a 47-hectare property, has historically made good but uninspiring wine. The property was recently purchased by a large Champagne firm, and the estate has been completely altered for the better. *Ch. Fontesteau,* an 80-hectare property that dates back to the 13th century, produces 4,500 cases of rather dull, often tannin-rich wine requiring time to mature. The style has recently been changed to a lighter, more supple and early maturing type. It is very difficult to locate as most of it is sold at the property. Other properties include *Ch. Haut-Madrac, Ch. Lieujan,* and *Ch. Hourtin-Ducasse.*

The 395 hectares of vineland of St.-Laurent are located west of St.-Julien on comparatively lower elevations than the more-famous growths that overlook the Gironde. Except for the important properties of *Ch. la Tour-Carnet, Ch. de Camensac, Ch. Belgrave, Ch. Caronne-Ste.-Gemme,* and *Ch. Larose-Trintaudon,* which are located on higher ground along the eastern edges of the producing district, all other growths are sited on flatter, less gravelly, and imperfectly drained soil. St.-Laurent is an important Haut-Médoc village because it contains three classed growths and is the largest producer in the appellation. The principal growths follow.

Ch. la Tour-Carnet is a 32-hectare fourth-growth property making more than 16,000 cases of early maturing wine. Although little known in the United States, the wine, overrated and the product of severe overcropping, is a hollow, light-bodied, and flavorless libation not worthy of classified status. *Ch. de Camensac,* a 60-hectare fifth-growth property, makes about 30,000 cases of fresh-flavored wine with an agreeable bouquet and considerable staying power. It is located west of *Ch. Lagrange* on the hilliest *croupe* in the area overlooking the Jalle du Nord. Quality has recently improved, and it now offers considerable value, especially in good years. *Ch. Belgrave* is an 80-hectare fifth growth that was once owned by Maison Dourthe. It was a neglected property and produced wine below classified standards—thin, light, and early maturing. Since its takeover by a syndicate, a number of physical innovations have taken place, and more progressive winemaking philosophies have been implemented. As a result, the wine has improved greatly and bears watching. Output is about 25,000 cases. *Ch. Larose-Trintaudon,* with 185 hectares and an annual output of more than 84,000 cases, is the largest property in the entire Médoc. It is located north of *Ch. Belgrave* and adjoins *Ch. Peymartin* in St.-Julien. Quality has been maintained consistently over the past ten years, despite its large volume of production. The wine is fruity, well scented, medium-bodied, matures within five years, and definitely is not exaggerated by tannin and acid. It is owned by the Spanish Forner family, who also acquired *Ch. Camensac,* the latter being the heavier, more masculine, and longer-lasting wine. *Ch. Caronne-Ste.-Gemme* is a 154-hectare property making more than 23,000 cases. Tannin-rich, hard, and rather austere, the wine is now made much lighter and is very popular in Holland and Belgium. *Ch. de Labat* is the second label. *Ch. Balac,* a 15-hectare property, makes more than 7,000 cases of technically sound but uninspiring wine—light, fruity, early maturing, but often dull. Recent vintages, however, have been greatly improved; the property is now owned by the Touchais family of Anjou. *Ch. Barateau* is an obscure little property making 4,500 cases of standard appellation-quality wine at best.

Between the hamlets of Beychevelle and Soussans lie the three wine-producing villages of Cussac, Lamarque, and Arcins—all on a series of small *croupes* in a surrounding area commonly referred to as the Central Médoc. The largest of the three, both in population and wine production, is Cussac, a village of 850 people, 247 hectares, a small number of good growths, and one small cooperative. The latter, founded in 1966, has but twenty-five members, controls 59 hectares, and makes 3,500 hectoliters of wine annually. Approximately 60 percent of the *encépagement* is Cabernet Sauvignon, 35 percent Merlot, and the remainder Cabernet Franc. Despite its small size, the quality is quite impressive; 20 percent of production is bottled under the brand name of "Chevaliers du Roi Soleil." The principal growths are:

Ch. Lanessan is a huge 264-hectare property located in the extreme northern portion of the parish boundary overlooking the Chenal du Milieu and *Ch. Gruaud-Larose.* The premier growth in the entire Central Médoc, it consistently makes wine of classed quality. The wine is well made, intensely scented, full-bodied, and very hard when young, thus requiring patience to mature fully. This grossly underrated property, owned by *Ch. Pichon-Longueville-Baron,* has a fantastic potential for future growth and offers outstanding value. Output exceeds 14,500 cases. *Ch. la Chesnaye* is the 115-hectare, rapidly expanding sister property of *Ch. Lanessan.* The wine is soft, supple, fruity, and early maturing. Output is 10,000 cases. *Ch. Beaumont,* a recently rejuvenated property of 40 hectares, makes 20,000 cases of well-made and consistently good wine that rarely disappoints. Expectations are that within the next ten years,

Plate 10.5   The cellars of Ch. Lanessan

there will be 100 hectares producing nearly 50,000 cases. The property is located due west of Cussac near the Moulis-Listrac border. *Ch. Tour-du-Haut-Moulin* is a 30-hectare property making 10,000 cases of robust, concentrated, full-bodied wine that ages well, rarely disappoints, and offers good value. *Ch. du Moulin-Rouge* is a 10-hectare property that straddles route D2 along the northern fringes of the producing district. The wine of this well-managed, 4,400-case property is little known, always reliable, distinctive, and offers excellent value. *Ch. Lamothe-de-Bergeron,* a beautiful property of 50 hectares that faces the Gironde, makes 21,000 cases of solid, robust wine that ages well. This historic property is now owned by *Ch. Grand Puy-Ducasse.* Other growths include *Ch. du Rétout, Ch. Fort-de-Vauban, Ch. du Raux, Ch. Aney,* and *Ch. Bernones.*

The village of Lamarque is located on flat land that is less than 10 meters above sea level, in contrast to Listrac, 4 kilometers to the southwest, which is 40 kilometers high. Even the gravel *croupes* of St.-Julien in the north and Margaux toward the south are higher. More significant, the soil is a mixture of sand and *palus* resting on a subsoil of gravel and clay, with the latter dominating in a few places. As a result, there are few vineyards of consequence except for *Ch. Lamarque, Ch. Malescasse,* and *Ch. du Cartillon. Ch. Lamarque,* a 47-hectare property located on sloping ground along the south bank of the Jalle du Cartillon, makes more than 28,000 cases of light-bodied, soft, and supple wine. It is one of the oldest properties in the Médoc, and the castle dates back to the 11th century. *Ch. Malescasse* is a 35-hectare property that makes 13,000 cases annually. It has been recently renovated and is a property to watch. The wine is soft, fruity, and steadily improving. *Ch. du Cartillon* is a large 100-hectare property located west of the village of Lamarque. Although well sited on gravel soil, the wine remains common and undistinguished. The output is 10,500 cases.

Except for an east-west ridge of higher ground containing gravel, Arcins lies on the northern edge of the Estey de Tayac, an area known for rich *palus* soils and, hence, inferior vineyard land. Arcins contains 175 hectares of vineland and five growths of significance, all of which lie on gravel *croupes. Ch. d'Arcins* is an 80-hectare property owned by the large negociant firm of Castel. With an output of 38,000 cases, it is the leading estate by a wide margin. The wine, made for the mass market with no pretenses of extraordinary distinction, is well made, light in body, and intended for early consumption. *Ch. Barreyres* makes 32,000 cases of similar-quality wine. *Ch. Arnauld,* a little known 25-hectare property owned by Jean Theil of *Ch. Poujeaux,* makes 4,400 cases of distinctive, highly flavorful, and well-scented wine. It is the leading quality producer in the hamlet and a property to look for. *Ch. Tour-du-Roc* is a litle known 11-hectare property making more than 4,000 cases of solid, firm, fruity, and flavorful wine, offering excellent value. It is slated for elevation into the Grand Bourgeois Exceptionnel rank in 1987.

The village of Avensan (1,500 people), lying along the south bank of the Jalle of Tiquiforte immediately west of Soussans, contains 137 hectares of vineland and is known for four major growths. *Ch. Citran,* dating from the 13th century, is a large 400-hectare property making 48,000 cases. The wine, until ten years ago, was well made, classy, stylish, often refined with great depth of flavor and bouquet, offering exceptional value. Recently it has been less consistent, but this condition will soon change as the new owners improve quality. *Ch. Villegeorge* is a 15-hectare property making 5,100 cases of well-made, round, smooth, but overpriced wine that is not always reliable. *Ch. Bonneau* and *Ch. Tour-Carelot* are two less well known properties.

The village of Macau (2,000 people) lying immediately to the south of Labarde, contains 126 hectares of vineland and one superb classified growth. *Ch. Cantemerle* is an old, historic property producing 10,000 cases of wine annually. Expertly improved by the Cordier firm, this estate, after decades of mismanagement, is again producing outstanding wine offering excellent value. The wine, highly underrated and equivalent to second-growth status, is dark in color and tannin-rich, requiring ten years to ripen fully. Output is certain to increase, it is a wine to look for. *Ch. Maucamps* is a 61-hectare property producing 4,400 cases of good, solid, full-bodied wine, offering substantial value. *Ch. Maucamps-Courtois* is a 60-hectare property currently being replanted after decades of neglect.

The village of Ludon (2,000 people), like all other wine-producing towns near the Gironde, contains *palus* soils in the east and gravel farther inland. The latter, found mainly in two locations, produces some of the finest wine in the Haut-Médoc appellation. *Ch. la Lagune* is a 55-hectare property that rivals the finest second growths. A meticulous, highly mechanized estate owned by the Ayala Champagne house, it is currently making absolutely marvelous wine—elegant, silky, refined, luscious, fruity, well balanced, and never astringent. Not only is it above average in quality, but it is consistent, thus offering extraordinary value to the dedicated consumer. Output is 24,000 cases. *Ch. d'Agassac* is an historical 100-hectare property dating from the 13th century. Now owned by *Ch. Calon-Ségur,* it is about to embark on a carefully thought out expansion program. This classy, low-key estate makes concentrated, dark wine that ages well and deserves a higher classification. *Ch. d'Arche* is a small, underrated 7-hectare property making 2,100 cases of rather hard to find, dark, fleshy, and consistently above-average wine offering excellent value.

The remaining five villages in the Haut-Médoc appellation—Castelnau, Le Pian, Parempuyre, Blanquefort, and Le Taillan—collectively contain about 200 hectares of vineland and fewer than twenty properties, of which nine are important. *Ch. de Malleret* is a 150-hectare property making 8,300 cases of soft, fruity, early maturing wine. *Ch. Dillon,* a 32-hectare property owned by the Agricultural College of Bordeaux, makes

13,000 cases of average, soft, fruity wine. *Ch. Sénéjac,* a 165-hectare property, makes 7,000 cases of above-average-quality wine. *Ch. Ségur* is a large 100-hectare property that makes 12,500 cases of average, but often coarse wine. *Ch. Pichon,* in the process of reconstruction, is currently making fewer than 2,000 cases of above-average-quality wine. Other properties include *Ch. Ségur-Fillon, Ch. St.-Ahon. Ch. Grand-Clapeau-Olivier.* and *Ch. Cambon.*

The Médoc

North of St.-Estèphe, in what historically was called the "Bas Médoc," lies an area of sixteen parishes and five cooperatives that produce more than 150,000 hectoliters of wine annually from 3,000 hectares of vineland. Over the past twenty years, this region has become the center of feverish land speculation and the establishment or enlargement of large properties, producing a substantial volume of good, sound, fruity, fragrant, and moderately priced wines (see Fig. 10.7, p. 181).

In contrast to the prestigious communes farther south, the topography of the Médoc is more irregular, the amount of gravel in the topsoil is less, and the amount of clay and sand increases markedly. The climate, which is more humid and cloudier, combines to produce a more acidic soil, hence the wines' lack of finesse, balance, and inability to age like the superior growths to the south. Whatever the physical environmental shortcomings, high land prices and ever-increasing wine prices have generated significant interest in the area and, as a result, vine hectarage since 1965 has increased from 2,174 to 3,079. The appellation contains nine Grand Bourgeois and twenty Bourgeois properties. Approximately 45 percent of the hectarage and wine production is controlled by cooperatives. The sixteen settlements of the appellation Médoc, along with their approximate vine hectarage and principal growths, are listed below:

Representing the northernmost limits, the three villages of St.-Vivien, Jau-Dignac, and Vensac, with 133 hectares, are the least-important in the appellation. Northernmost in location and the largest in population, St.-Vivien contains only 18 hectares of vineland and four growers, none of whom have generated a good reputation. Jau-Dignac is two hamlets with a combined population of 800 people, 57 hectares of vineland, seven growers, and the site of a good growth, *Ch. Sestignan.* This 9-hectare vineyard, making more than 3,500 cases of good, solid, well-flavored and scented wine, is one of the few properties in the Médoc appellation that still maintains a high percentage of Cabernet Sauvignon vines. Southernmost of the three, Vensac, a village of 600 people, is located on route D1 in the westernmost portion of the appellation. It cultivates 58 hectares of vineland and has ten growers, seven of whom produce fewer than 600 cases of wine annually.

Situated on a knoll, the village of Valeyrac contains 209 hectares of vineland and fifteen growers, of which four have established reputations. *Ch. Roguegrave-Haut-Valeyrac* (36 hectares, 15,500 cases of good, well-scented and balanced wine), *Ch. Bellevue* (13 hectares, 6,400 cases), *Ch. Bellerive-Clos-Valeyrac* (10 hectares, 4,500 cases), and *Ch. Bellegrave* (11 hectares, 3,000 cases).

In the center of the Médoc appellation, Queyrac is a large village of 1,000 people that contains 164 hectares of vineland, one small cooperative, and eleven growers, one of whom has established a good reputation. The Cooperative Cellar of Queyrac, the northernmost in the Médoc, contains 165 members, cultivates 135 hectares of vineland, and makes more than 5,500 hectoliters of wine annually. Fermentation capacity exceeds 25,000 hectoliters, and the wine, which is made from equal amounts of Cabernet Sauvignon and Merlot with minute amounts of Petit Verdot, is mainly sold in bulk to negociants. The cooperative's brand label is "Cave St.-Roch." *Ch. Carcanieux,* a 25-hectare property located on well-drained, gravelly soil, produces more than 10,000 cases of good, solid, rustic wine that offers good value.

The medium-sized village of Bégadan, located on one of the highest elevations in the Médoc appellation, contains 584 hectares of vineland, four Grand Bourgeois properties, and the largest cooperative. The latter produces 28,000 hectoliters, has 178 members, and controls 600 hectares. Not only is it the biggest, but it bottles more than 50 percent of production and has a fermenting capacity of more than 60,000 hectoliters. The encépagement is roughly 45 percent Cabernet Sauvignon, 40 percent Merlot, and 15 percent Cabernet Franc. The cooperative brand name, "Cave St.-Jean," an above-average libation full of fruit, is designed for early consumption. Of the nearly twenty major properties, the following have generated significant interest: *Ch. la Tour-de-By,* a 60-hectare Grand Bourgeois property located on a gravel *croupe,* produces superb wine equivalent to classified-growth standards. Although lighter than *Ch. de Pez,* it is round, delicate, and altogether a first-class wine. Expertly made, supple, and consistently good, it offers excellent value; output exceeds 26,000 cases. *Ch. Patache-d'Aux* is a 46-hectare property that makes more than 21,000 cases of good, solid, full-flavored, meaty wine. Rarely encountered in the United States, it offers good value. *Ch. Greysac,* a 65-hectare property, produces more than 27,000 cases of fruity, early maturing wine very popular in the United States. In good years it offers good value; otherwise a definite grassy taste and flavor detract from its usual fat, full flavor. *Ch. Laujac,* at one time the largest property in the village, today contains less than 75 hectares, less than one-tenth its former size. The wine, average at best, is highly inconsistent, hard, acidic, and rarely supple. Output exceeds 13,500 cases. Other properties include *Ch. la Clare, Ch. du Monthil, Ch. Plagnac, Ch. de By, Ch. Vieux-*

Robin, Vieux-Château-Landon, Ch. la Gorre, Ch. la Croix-Landon, Ch. le Tréhon, Ch. Laborde, and *Ch. Grand-Combes.*

The hamlet of St. Christoly, sited on a rise overlooking the Gironde, contains 275 hectares of vineland and nearly two dozen properties, five of which enjoy a good reputation; *Ch. la Tour-St. Bonnet* (54 hectares, 19,000 cases); *Ch. la Tour-Blanche* (30 hectares, 12,000 cases); *Ch. St.-Christoly* (15 hectares, 7,000 cases); and *Ch. le Boscq.* The small hamlet of Couquèques, located next to St.-Christoly, contains but 95 hectares of vineland and is known for one important growth—*Ch. les Ormes-Sorbet,* a 20-hectare, 16th-century property producing 10,000 cases of excellent, concentrated wine from comparatively low yields. The hamlet of Civrac, located in the center of the appellation, contains 105 hectares of vineland and two properties with a reputation—*Ch. Panigon* and *Ch. Bournac.*

Prignac sits in the middle of the largest cluster of wine-making parishes in the appellation. With only 89 hectares of vineland, it has a good cooperative and two above-average growths: *La Société Coopérative Intercommunale de Vinification de Prignac-en-Médoc, Ch. Tour-Prignac,* and *Ch. Hourbanon.* The good-sized village of Gaillan, one of three parishes located along D1, contains 146 hectares of vineland, one average growth *(Ch. Font-Bonnet)* and the headquarters of *Groupement Caves Coopératives Uni-Médoc,* the marketing union of the cooperatives of Bégadan, Ordonnac, Queyrac, and Prignac. Blaignan, a small hamlet located on a slight rise 3 kilometers inland from the Gironde, contains 230 hectares of vineland and several important growths. *Ch. la Cardonne,* easily the largest in the hamlet, is a comparatively new 100-hectare property established and owned by *Domaine Lafite Rothschild.* This highly efficient enterprise produces more than 36,000 cases of average-quality but rather expensive, fruity, and early maturing wines. *Ch. Blaignan,* the second-largest property with an output of 24,000 cases makes surprisingly full-bodied, flavorful wines that offer good value. *Ch. la France, Ch. Pontet, Ch. des Tourelles,* and *Ch. la Gorce* are four additional growths with a regional reputation.

The hamlets of St.-Yzans, Ordonnac, and St.-Germain are located in the extreme southern section of the appellation, bordering the Haut-Médoc and St. Estèphe appellations. Collectively, they have more than 25 percent of all vineland in the Médoc appellation and a number of important properties: *Ch. Loudenne* is a large 200-hectare Gilbey property with an old and colorful history. For over 100 years it was the center of large negociant and shipping activities, and at one time was responsible for more than 5 percent of all wine shipped to the United Kingdom. The vineyard declined and remained in need of repairs during the 1914–50 period. Today yields are high, and the wine, although not better than average, is light and fruity and remains very popular in the United Kingdom; *Ch. Sigognac* (48 hectares, 21,000 cases); *Ch. des. Boustéras* (18 hectares, 6,000 cases); *Ch. Mazails* (17 hectares, 5,000 cases); and *Ch. Bois-de-Roc* (20 hectares, 9,000 cases).

The large village of Lesparre, with 4,000 inhabitants and 249 hectares, is known for one small, good cooperative and three properties: *Ch. Vernous, Ch. d'Escot,* and *Ch. Preuillac.* Located near the Haut-Médoc-St. Estèphe border, St.-Germain, with 327 hectares, is the second-most-important wine village in the Médoc appellation. It is known for four growths: *Ch. du Castéra* (165 hectares, 21,000 cases); *Ch. Livran* (117 hectares, 19,000 cases); *Ch. Hautrive* (57 hectares, 31,000 cases); and *Ch. Brie-Caillou* (15 hectares, 7,000 cases). Representing the southernmost vine-growing parish in the Médoc appellation, the small hamlet of Ordonnac contains 192 hectares of vineland, one important growth, and an above-average-quality cooperative. *Ch. Potensac,* with an output of 17,000 cases, is the largest estate, and known for light-bodied, fruity, early maturing wines.

11

THE WINES OF GRAVES

THE Graves appellation is an irregularly shaped district that begins south of Bordeaux and totally surrounds the sweet white wine regions of Cérons, Barsac, and Sauternes (see Fig. 11.1). Bounded by the Garonne on the east and framed by thick forest along its western margins, Graves stretches for 48 kilometers in length and up to 24 kilometers in width. The entire district encompasses about forty villages and produces 100,000 hectoliters of red wine and 65,000 hectoliters of white.

Hectarage declined from more than 10,000 in 1975 to only 3,000 hectares in 1985. A number of large properties have ceased cultivating vines, and until the recent resurgence in dry white wine and in well-flavored but comparatively early maturing red wine, the Graves appella-

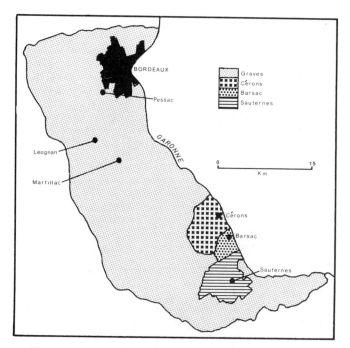

Figure 11.1   AOC Appellations South of Bordeaux

tion was one of the most depressed viticultural districts in the Gironde. Of the forty-three communes within the Graves appellation, thirty-two produce wine (Table 11.1). The most important in terms of total output and hectarage are Portets, Léognan, St.-Pierre-de-Mons, Langon, Martillac, Landiras, and Budos. These seven communes collectively account for nearly 60 percent of the appellation's total hectarage. The remainder contain fewer than 150 hectares each, and some of the most-celebrated, such as Mérignac, Talence, and Pessac, contain fewer than 70 hectares. In addition to the above, the neighboring appellation of Cérons contains a minimum of 600 hectares whose wines are entitled to the appellation name of Graves and Graves Supérieures. It is interesting to note that Graves is the only quality wine region in the Gironde that produces classified red and white wine, the former contributing more than 55 percent of total output.

Graves is a region whose reputation captivated historians and literary personalities for centuries. Its history is filled with the exploits of the Black Prince, Montesquieu, and Cardinal de la Mothe, who became Pope Clement V in 1305. Historically an area of large medieval estates, it boasts many moated fortresses, such as *Ch. d'Olivier, Ch. de la Brède,* and *Ch. Roquetaillade.* Religious orders have also been active: *Ch. Carbonnieux* was founded by Benedictines, *Ch. la Louvière* by Carthusians, and *Ch. la*

Table 11.1 The Winemaking Communes of Graves
(arranged from north to south)

	Hectares		Hectares
Mérignac	15	Arbanats	96
Talence	25	St.-Selve	51
Pessac	70	Virelade	96
Gradignan	4	St.-Morillon	74
Villenave-d'Ornon	50	St.-Michel-de-Rieufret	6
Canéjan	7	Landiras	195
Cadaujac	64	Pujols-sur-Ciron	107
Léognan	338	Toulenne	54
Isle-Saint-Georges	71	Langon	220
St.-Médard-d'Eyrans	39	St.-Pardon-de-Conques	38
Martillac	200	St.-Pierre-de-Mons	294
Ayguemorte-les-Graves	21	Guillos	34
Beautiran	91	Bodos	150
Castres	105	Léogeats	5
Portets	488	Roaillan	42
La Brède	105	Mazères	127
		Total hectares	3,282

Note: An additional 600 hectares of vineland in neighboring Cérons have the right to market wine under the Graves and Graves Supérieur designations.

Mission-Haut-Brion, Clos de l'Abbaye de la Rame, and *l'Hermitage* by the Vincentians.

Today the Graves region has a comparatively small number of large estates with imposing châteaux in the Médocain manner. Less than 10 percent of the 3,300 hectares constitutes classified-growth land, a sharp departure from the Médoc and St.-Emilion, whose percentage is more than one-third and two-thirds, respectively, of total hectarage. The remainder is a vast sea of small growers, half of whom are part-time farmers. About 20 percent of the total land area is composed of properties whose hectarage varies between 7 and 15 hectares. Despite the relatively small size of the producing units, the appellation, unlike Entre-Deux-Mers, the Médoc, and the north bank of the Gironde and Dordogne, lacks cooperative development.

There are two types of vineyards: large properties (both classed and unclassed) that make and bottle their wine, and an army of small growers who sell their wine to negociants. Petit chateaux exist, but until recently they were minor and unimportant in the national and international markets. In the former category are sixteen classified growths, and in the latter, sixty additional, unclassified properties good enough to receive individual treatment in the pages that follow.

The location of vineyards is not randomly distributed over this large area, but is gathered along the numerous and widely scattered gravel banks, each vineyard separated and bounded by pine and deciduous forest, pasture, or market-gardening farms. The name "Graves" is derived from the alluvial and glacial gravel deposited thousands of years ago, mixed with clay, sand, and limestone fragments. Gravel can vary from several millimeters to five meters or more in depth, but when mixed with clay and limestone it becomes the most widely sought soil in the appellation. Soil that is pure gravel produces bright, well-flavored and scented wines that are very agreeable. Vines growing on a mixture of gravel and clay, however, produce strong, big, darker-colored libations that are full-bodied, long-lasting, and characterized by the peculiar flavor of *terroir.* The best Graves is made from a mixture of both, particularly in the communes of Pessac, Talence, Gradignan, Léognan, Villenave, Martillac, and Cadaujac—all located in the northern portion of the producing district. South of Martillac, the number of gravel banks decrease and the soil becomes sandier and heavier in clay. White wine production is generally associated with those areas containing the smallest amount of gravel and the highest concentration of limestone.

Despite the fact that soils are considered and often casually described as "gravelly," there is considerable variability in their composition, hence the preference for individual growth identification as opposed to communal labeling. In general, we can say that gravel is everywhere although not in the same intensity, and the amount is often mitigated by poor drainage due to the presence of low-lying areas. Not only is the deepest gravel found in the northern areas of the appellation, but the special character of the wine from this region is dependent upon the amount of *alios* in the clayey subsoil and/or conglomerate pebbles called *arène*. When the *arène* and *alios* constituents are sizable, the color of red Graves is a brilliant scarlet and the bouquet rather profound.

The entire region is bowl-shaped, thus facilitating the flow of air toward the Garonne, but because of the thick forest cover in the west, cold air frequently becomes trapped, promoting the formation of numerous frost pockets—the prime environmental hazard in the appellation.

The Red and White Wines of Graves

Red wine marketed only as "Graves" must be the product of Cabernet Sauvignon, Merlot, Cabernet Franc, Malbec, and Petit Verdot. Minimum alcohol content is 10 percent, and the yield is limited to 40 hectoliters to the hectare. It is often compared to Médoc because it has excellent color, is full-bodied, well flavored and scented, ages well, and is made from the same grape varieties. But while the Cabernet dominates in both areas, Graves contains a bit more Cabernet Franc and Malbec; Merlot, in recent years, appears to be making serious inroads at the expense of all. A more-fundamental departure lies in the peculiar *terroir* flavor and a less-sweet, yet pronounced finish—features that in no way diminish nor detract from its surprisingly high-quality standards. Red Graves is not only spicy and austere on the palate, but rich and luscious in flavor, and while it does not attain the distinctiveness or elegance of fine Médoc, its earthy and full flavor is eminently satisfying.

Because tradition is flexible in Graves, the wine defies easy generalization as to a typical style or character. The encépagement varies enormously from Cabernet Sauvignon–dominated wine to 100 percent Merlot; a long and short vinification can be at high or comparatively low temperatures; and the time of cellar-aging can vary from three months in stainless steel to two years in new oak. In recent years, one aspect of Graves winemaking has become certain—red Graves is becoming lighter in color and lower in tannin, and is generally ready to drink far sooner than formerly—features that seem very popular with consumers.

Production of red Graves has increased fivefold during the past thirty years, prompting many local experts to predict that by the end of this century annual production will exceed 250,000 hectoliters—a not unreasonable figure given the region's pre-*phylloxera* history (see Fig. 11.2). A good deal of the expanded hectarage in red grapes has occurred south of Martillac in what was once white wine country and is a clear reflection of optimism in the future of the appellation.

Exports, which are increasing rapidly (currently one-third of total sales), exceed all Médocain communal appellations and are second (as a quality wine region) only to those of St.-Emilion (see Table 11.2). A

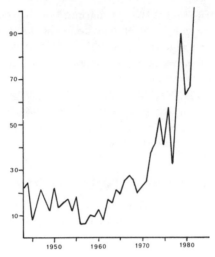

Figure 11.2   Graves: Wine Production of Graves Rouges, 1944–1983
(in thousands of hectoliters)

recent development, this trend is expected to continue in the near future. Historically, red Graves failed to captivate the overseas market in the manner of the more-famous growths north of Bordeaux, and although far better known than Pomerol and St.-Emilion prior to 1950, they took a secondary position to Médoc in export markets. Exports during the interwar years, as well as the post–1945 period, amounted to fewer than 5,000 hectoliters. While foreign demand exhibited consistent growth in the 1960s, it was unspectacular in absolute amounts, with fewer than 6,000 hectoliters exported in 1963; by 1970, the figure had risen to a modest 9,000 hectoliters. Over the past ten years, however, exports have tripled over mid-1970 levels and quintupled over 1950 levels. In 1984 they stood at just under 35,000 hectoliters and are expected to rise beyond 50,000 over the next fifteen years. At present, all classified growths and most of the better "petit chateaux" offer excellent values in overseas markets. Five countries—Belgium, the United States, Holland, the United States, and Switzerland—import more than 80 percent of total exports. Tiny Belgium, the recipient of 25 percent of all exports, is the leading importing country.

White wine can be marketed as "Graves Blanc" or "Graves Supérieures," the major difference being that the latter designation has a minimum of 12 percent alcohol, while the former has 11 percent. For both, the yield is limited to 40 hectoliters to the hectare, and the grapes are restricted to Sémillon, Sauvignon Blanc, and Muscadelle. While average production has doubled over the past forty years, the production of the lighter, more-accessible Graves Blanc has grown much faster than the more alcoholic Graves Supérieures.

As recently as forty years ago, twice as much white wine was produced

Table 11.2 Sale of Graves Rouge, 1982

Sale	Hectoliters	Percent	Sale	Hectoliters	Percent
Belgium	4.737	25.2	Denmark	920	4.9
United States	2,768	14.7	Canada	1.124	6.0
Holland	2,398	12.8	Other	1,571	8.4
United Kingdom	2,054	10.9	Total exports	18,780	100.0
Switzerland	2,033	10.8	France	42,797	69.5
West Germany	1,175	6.3			
			Total sales	61,577	100.0

Source: Conseil Interprofessionnel du Vin de Bordeaux.

as red, but today the gap has narrowly shifted in favor of red. Moreover, a good deal of it, made sweet to semi-sweet, suffered from overchaptalization (the addition of sugar to raise alcohol levels) and sulfurization (excessive amounts affects flavor and aroma), and was usually thin, unbalanced, maderized (oxidized), often woody and stemmy, while the drier versions were overly acidic. As consumer tastes changed from sweet to drier, fruitier, cleaner, and lighter wines, traditional white Graves failed to compete in international markets. As a consequence, white Graves is experiencing a consummate transformation. Muscadelle has declined from nearly 20 percent of total plantings to less than 5 percent, and Sémillon is declining as fast as Sauvignon Blanc is increasing. The historic semi-sweet and sweet libations now account for only 10 percent of total output, vs. 80 percent fifty years ago. As a result, exports of Graves Blanc and Graves Supérieures have doubled since 1978, a remarkable achievement after years of stagnation.

Over the past fifteen years, overall quality has improved not only because of changes in the encépagement. Improved vinification and storage techniques have produced wine that is not only less oxidized, but is crisper, fruitier, fresher, cleaner, lighter in color, and definitely early maturing. Very rarely will it age beyond the fifth year, and probably it is at its best between the second and fourth years. In a young wine, the crisp, acidic, and flavorful character of the Sauvignon Blanc dominates the flavor, but after several years of bottle-aging, the more-subtle, richer flavor and aroma of Sémillon take over and soften the wine.

Like red Graves, white wine is made in a number of different styles: from quick fermentation and early bottling, to slow wood-fermentation and extended wood-aging. It can be made from a Sémillon-dominated encépagement or from 100 percent Sauvignon Blanc, and its price can vary by as much as $50 between luxury quality and supermarket specials. Historically, the very best, from the traditional properties, was racy, hard, often steely, full-bodied, and given as much as three years of wood-aging. Today, more than 90 percent is vinified in stainless steel and receives no wood-aging at all. Among the more prestigious growths that produce old-fashioned white Graves are *Ch. Haut-Brion, Ch. Malartic Lagravière, Ch. Carbonnieux, Ch. Laville-Haut-Brion, Ch. Bouscaut, Ch. Couhins-Lurton,* and *Dne. de Chevalier.* Here, the wine ages in wood for six to eighteen months and differs sharply from that which is not subjected to wood-aging. It is darker in color, richer in aroma, fuller, more round and complex, better balanced, and appears to age far longer than stainless steel versions. A few growths such as *Ch. Bouscaut, Ch. Laville-Haut-Brion, Ch. Haut-Brion,* and *Dne. de Chevalier* also vinify in wood. *Ch. Rahoul* and *Ch. Fieuzal,* two nonclassified growths, also use oak to age their wines prior to bottling. The principal classified growths who do not vinify or age in wood are *Ch. Smith-Haut-Lafitte, Ch. la Tour Martillac,* and *Ch. d'Olivier*—three growths with above-average reputations.

As production shifted from semi-sweet and sweet wines to dry, exports of white Graves recovered from the depression of the 1960s but have not approached the volume levels of red Graves. Nevertheless, it is interesting to note that of all the Gironde appellations, the Graves Blanc and Graves Supérieures appellations collectively export a larger percentage (between 70 and 75 percent) of total sales than any other. Holland, the United States, and the United Kingdom collectively import more than three-quarters of total exports.

The Graves Classification of 1953 and 1959

With *Ch. Haut-Brion* the one notable exception, no Graves property was considered in the 1855 Classification. Nearly 100 years later, sufficient pressure was applied to the INAO that an "official" listing of red and white wine estates was produced in 1953, effective in 1955. This list, with a few minor technical and alphabetical changes, was reviewed and revised in 1959. From the very beginning, the ranking presented in Table 11.3 proved highly controversial. The determination of who was included" and who excluded was apparently based largely on reputation and little else. Of the more than three hundred individual exploitations, the INAO saw fit to recognize only sixteen.

The classified growths are all located in the six northernmost communes of the delimited area. Of the sixteen properties, six are located in Léognan, with seven other growths located in Pessac, Talence, and Martillac. The geographical distribution is peculiar. If the classification were simply based on the French notion of *terroir,* there ought to be more than forty additional properties classified, especially in view of the fact that the distribution of clay/gravel soils with associated limestone material often varies in haphazard fashion every 100 meters. As it happens, the classified growths produce less than 1 percent of all white wine and less than 8 percent of all red. With the possible exception of a dozen or so

Table 11.3 1953 Graves Classification		
Commune	Classified red wines	Classified white wines
Pessac	Ch Haut-Brion Ch. Pape-Clément	
Talence	Ch. la Mission Haut-Brion Ch. la Tour Haut-Brion	Ch. Laville Haut-Brion
Léognan	Dne. de Chevalier Ch. Malartic-Lagravière Ch. Carbonnieux Ch. d'Olivier Ch. Haut-Bailly Ch. de Fieuzal	Dne. de Chevalier Ch. Malartic-Lagravière Ch. Carbonnieux Ch. d'Olivier
Martillac	Ch. la Tour-Martillac Ch. Smith-Haut-Lafitte	Ch. la Tour-Martillac
Cadaujac	Ch. Bouscaut	Ch. Bouscaut
Villenave-d'Ornon		Ch. Couhins Ch. Couhins-Lurton (added in 1960)

properties from the ranks of the excluded, the remaining vineyards are little known; and no matter how good they may be, the consumer is reluctant to buy them.

The Producing Communes

Mérignac, Talence, and Pessac are the major western and southern viticultural suburbs of Bordeaux, the latter two containing five of the sixteen classified growths. Four of the five are huddled together in Pessac and Talence, with only *Ch. Picque-Caillou* located in the city of Mérignac. How long these rather small holdings can hold out against the onslaught of contemporary urban growth is hard to tell, making prognosis for future generations of wine drinkers grim. Over the past twenty years a number of properties, including the above-average *Ch. Fanning-Lafontaine,* have been swallowed up by the insatiable demand for urban development.

Functionally a part of Bordeaux proper, Pessac, a city of 60,000, totally engulfs three above-average properties whose total vineyard amounts to a mere 70 hectares. The principal property, *Ch. Haut-Brion,* is a 45-hectare property producing 12,000 cases of exquisite red wine, and from 3 hectares, an additional 1,300 cases of sublime white wine. The red wine is known for its dark color, superlative bouquet, and high extract matter. Not only is it intense in terms of richness, but its texture is pure silk, its flavor is pregnant with fruit, and its finish is both elegant and complex. It is probably the only first growth that is not currently overvalued and is consistently good in off vintages. *Ch. Pape-Clément,* a 27-hectare property, makes 12,000 cases. Considered the oldest vineyard in Graves, it dates back to the 14th century and was owned by the archbishop of Bordeaux who became pope in 1305. The wine, the product of a long fermentation and aged in wood for two years, is surprisingly soft, fruity, delicate, low in tannin, rich, supple and well scented. Although it exhibits bouts of inconsistency, it offers excellent value in good years. The vineyard makes fewer than 100 cases of a rare white wine, not commercially available. *Ch. les Carmes-Haut-Brion* is a small, obscure, 4-hectare vineyard that makes fewer than 2,000 cases of highly distinctive and unusual wine. Of all the major Graves properties, this estate contains the highest percentage of Cabernet Franc, a major contributing factor to its excellent color, suppleness, complexity, and pronounced bitter after-taste—an attribute that is not all together unpleasant. An underrated wine, distinguished and impeccably made, it offers outstanding value. The vineyard is named after the Carmelite order who owned the property from 1584 to 1789. *Ch. Picque-Caillou* is a 13-hectare property located west of Bordeaux in Mérignac. The wine, made from equal amounts of Cabernet Sauvignon and Merlot, is an absolutely first-class libation second only to the top appellation growths. It is consistently well made, full on the palate, delicate, supple, and extremely well flavored. Offering excellent value, the output is 4,600 cases, *Ch. Chêne-Vert,* owned by *Ch. Picque-Caillou,* is a small property producing fewer than 1,600 cases.

Plate 11.1   Ch. Pape-Clément, Pessac

Although legally distinct, it is thought that the label serves as the second wine of the larger property.

The suburb of Talence (36,000 residents) is known for 28 hectares of vineland and three properties owned by the Woltner family until 1983. *Ch. la Mission-Haut-Brion,* a 22-hectare property located on heavy gravel, produces 10,000 cases of rich, full, dark wine with a long penetrating bouquet, exquisite flavor, and long finish. It is very consistent and ages well. This former religious property, in terms of concentration, fullness, and amount of extract, is equal to *Ch. Haut-Brion,* its immediate neighbor and present owner. *Ch. Laville-Haut-Brion* is a 5-hectare property that makes 2,500 cases of white wine only. While it is widely considered a second to *Ch. Haut-Brion,* the wine often exhibits a flat and tired character that should certainly be lacking in a first-class wine. *Ch. la Tour-Haut-Brion,* an 8-hectare property making fewer than 3,000 cases, is considered the second label of *Ch. la Mission-Haut-Brion.*

The city of Gradignan (22,000 residents) is located 4 kilometers south of *Ch. Haut-Brion.* The tiny 4-hectare property of *Ch. Poumey* lies along the north bank of the meandering l'Eau Bourde. This little-known vineyard makes fewer than 1,500 cases of full-bodied, robust, red wine that is mainly exported to Holland and Belgium. Downriver from Gradignan is the modern industrial city of Villenave (22,000 residents), located on an old fluvial terrace overlooking the Garonne River. It is bounded by the l'Eau Bourde on the north and the l'Eau Blanche on the south. The area contains 50 hectares of vineland and four properties with a reputation. *Ch. Baret* is a stately 40-hectare property making 3,800 cases of red wine and 1,500 cases of white. The red is well made, dark in color, tannin-rich, fragrant, and much better than the white. The latter is ligh-bodied but in good vintages exhibits elements of elegance. *Ch. Pontac-Monplaisir,* a 14-hectare vineyard, makes 5,000 cases of good, sound, well-structured red wine and 1,800 cases of full-bodied and well-flavored white wine. A small portion of output is also bottled under the *Ch. Limbourg* label, a small vineyard acquired some time ago. Both wines offer excellent value and should not be missed. *Ch. Couhins,* owned by the Ministry of Agriculture, is a 10-hectare property located south of the city overlooking the l'Eau Blanche on sloping land with heavy accumulations of gravel. The vineyard makes approximately 1,000 cases of red and 1,500 cases of white wine. Despite exhaustive research and experimentation, the wines, both red and white, do not measure up to classified standards. *Ch. Couhins-Lurton* is a 2-hectare property making 1,000 cases of red and 300 cases of white, the latter made from 100 percent Sauvignon Blanc fermented in wood.

Canéjan, an obscure town of 3,500 residents, is located to the west of Gradignan and contains only one growth, *Ch. de Rouillac,* a property that once belonged to Baron Haussmann, the famous 19th-century urban planner. Long abandoned, the property was revived in 1971 and is currently making 2,500 cases of excellent red wine with a pronounced *terroir* character. The small town of Cadaujac, barely 4 kilometers south of Bordeaux, contains 64 hectares of vineland and one large property—*Ch. Bouscaut*. Located between *Ch. Couhins* and *Ch. Smith-Haut-Lafitte,* this impressive 40-hectare property was owned by an American syndicate from 1969 to 1980, when it was purchased by Lucien Lurton of *Ch. Brane-Cantenac*. During its American tenure, the property was well managed, producing uncommonly concentrated, well-structured, firm, long-lived, but often dull red wine (10,000 cases) from low-yielding vines. The Sémillon-dominated white wine (1,500 cases) was fresh, not given much contact with wood and, although full on the palate and well made, remained undistinguished. Recently, production for red and white wines has increased dramatically, but whether or not the quality levels of the past can be maintained remains to be seen.

The 7,000-resident town of Léognan, with 338 hectares, is the second-largest Graves vineyard after Portets. Although it does not contain any growths equal to *Ch. Haut-Brion,* the commune does have six of the thirteen red wine classified vineyards in the appellation and four of the nine white growths. Along with Langon, Martillac, and Portets, it is an area of recent vine expansion. Of the nearly two dozen properties, three-quarters are first-class estates producing quality wine equal to the classified growths of the Médoc.

All the principal properties are located on hillsides on both banks of the l'Eau Blanche, whose local relief fluctuates between 20 and 50 meters. The well-drained soils, composed primarily of gravel (with some sand), rest on a subsoil of clay and limestone. *Dne. de Chevalier,* a 38-hectare property making 5,000 cases of red and 750 cases of white wine, is located on the edge of a 50-meter plateau amid a forest overlooking the l'Eau Blanche and *Ch. de Fieuzal*. This is a superb but underrated growth that produces full-bodied, dark-colored, elegant, concentrated, yet supple red wine that ranks just below the greatness of *Ch. Haut-Brion*. Meticulously made, this wine offers extraordinary value and should be part of any serious cellar. The white wine is dominated by Sauvignon Blanc and is considered by many superior to all in the appellation, including the current leader. Although less round than *Ch. Haut-Brion* and *Ch. Laville-Haut-Brion,* it has a lean, steely, clean, and refreshing character that satisfies completely despite its grassy and herbal flavors. An old-fashioned wine, it is aged in wood for eighteen months and requires at least five years of bottle-aging to round out flavor and balance; it is a bold, highly fragrant and, in good vintages, an intensely complex wine. *Ch. Haut-Bailly* is a superb, well-drained 33-hectare property located east of Léognan on hilly terrain between *Ch. la Louvière* and *Ch. Larrivet-Haut-Brion*. It makes 9,000 cases of highly distinctive, earthy, and flavorful wines that have improved tremendously over the past ten years. Considered today among the top-flight properties making old-fashioned *vin de garde* wine, fully-bodied and concentrated in extract and sapor, this largely underrated wine offers outstanding value. The second label is *La Parde de Haut-Bailly*. Also under the same management are *Ch. du Mayne* in Barsac and *Dne. de Courbon* (white wine only) located in Toulenne. *Ch. Malartic-Lagravière*, a 20-hectare property located south of Léognan, produces 5,500 cases of red and 1,100 cases of white wine. The red is a classic, dark-colored, rounded, well-scented *vin de garde* with the capacity for extended cellaring. It is a very distinctive, big, and powerful wine whose complexity, color, and flavor are influenced by an unusually high percentage of Cabernet Franc. Lacking suppleness, the white, made from 100 percent Sauvignon Blanc, is a firm, austere wine that requires five to seven years to mellow; it is generally not considered equal to that of other producers with a similar reputation. *Ch. d'Olivier* is a 35-hectare property making 17,500 cases of red and white wine, equally divided. Known for its rich and big wines that require time, the red, unusual for its high Cabernet Sauvignon content, is excellent and reliable. Long considered second to the white, the red wine is now above average for the region, offering outstanding value. The white, made of classic proportions of 65 percent Sémillon, 30 percent Sauvignon Blanc, and 5 percent Muscadelle, is consistently above average, being one of the fullest of all Graves. Managerial, enological, and aging philosophies have recently changed for the better.

Ch. Carbonnieux, the largest producer among the classified growths, is a 200-hectare property making 26,000 cases of wine, of which slightly more red is produced than white. The latter, considered much the better, is now dominated by Sauvignon Blanc and made lighter and fruitier than formally. Receiving three months of wood-aging prior to bottling, it is fresh, clean, but often inconsistent and early maturing. The red is a one-dimensional, very popular wine, but herbal and grassy flavored, often acidic, inconsistent, and overrated. *Ch. de Fieuzal*, a 22-hectare property located along the south bank of the l'Eau Blanche, produces 7,800 cases of red and 575 cases of white wine. It is a newly refurbished and much-improved property currently making fresh and zesty white and full-bodied, concentrated red wines; the latter, hard and acidic in youth, require ten years to round out. Both wines offer good-to-excellent value. *Ch. la Louvière*, a 50-hectare property, produces 16,000 cases of red and 7,000 cases of white wine. Despite the rather high percentage of Cabernet Sauvignon, the red wine is surprisingly soft, supple, well balanced, and full-bodied. The white is light yellow in color, clean, refreshing, and well balanced. Both wines are expertly made, popular, and offer excellent value. The finest wine is bottled under the *Ch. la Louvière* label, while the second wine is marketed under individual vineyard names. *Ch. Larrivet-Haut-Brion*, adjoining *Ch. Haut-Bailly* from the south, is a 16-hectare property producing 7,500 cases of red and fewer than 600 cases of white wine. The red, one of the most underrated wines of Graves, is robust, chewy, dark in color, and magnificently flavored, offering excellent value. The white is refreshingly dry, fruity, lively, and hard to locate; like the red, it is consistently well made. *Ch. de France,* a 27-hectare property located downslope from *Dne. de Chevalier,* produces 7,500 cases of raspy, multiedged, flavorful, and chewy red wine from equal amounts of Merlot and Cabernet Sauvignon. This recently improved property consistently produces above-average, fruity wine that offers excellent value. *Ch. Haut-Bergey,* a 14-hectare property located just to the west of Léognan, makes 7,500 cases of red wine only. The underrated, full-bodied, well-scented and flavored wine offers considerable value. *Ch. la Tour-Léognan,* a 7-hectare property owned by *Ch. Carbonnieux,* makes 4,500 cases of red and 2,500 cases of white wine. Located downslope from *Ch. d'Olivier,* the property produces only average, nondescript appellation wine. *Ch. Gazin,* an obscure 12-hectare property located next to *Ch. Haut-Bergey,* currently makes above-average, full-bodied, well-structured, *vin de garde* wine. *Ch. le Sartre* is a 25-hectare property currently making 4,000 cases of light-bodied, fruity, and early maturing red wine. Newly refurbished, planted, and expanded by the owners of *Ch. Carbonnieux,* the chateau will increase both product and quality in the near future. *Ch. Brown-Léognan* is a 10-hectare property making excellent, full-bodied, dark-colored, and chewy wine with a penetrating bouquet and rustic flavor. *Dne. de Grandmaison,* a small 7-hectare property located downslope from *Ch. Carbonnieux* along the south bank of the l'Eau Blanche, produces fewer than 3,500 cases of good, solid, red wine only. *Ch. le Pape,* a small property of 9 hectares facing southeast toward Martillac on a minor gravel bank, makes 2,800 cases of above-average, full-bodied, well-flavored wine that offers good value. Minor quantities of less good white wine are also made.

Isle-St.-Georges, a village of 500 people located on the Garonne, contains more than 70 hectares of vineland and seventeen growers, three of whom produce more than half the output. The coarse, acidic red wine from the rich alluvial soils is used mainly for blending purposes. The village of St.-Médard contains 39 hectares of vineland and seven growers, one of which enjoys a superlative reputation for both red and white wine production. Composed of *palus,* the soils in the east and south are little used for vinegrowing. In the central and western sections, however, considerable gravel, clay, and limestone support a small, but viable, white wine interest. The principal property is *Ch. de Cruzeau,* a 36-hectare property located on heavy gravel, producing 16,400 cases of red and 3,800 cases of white wine. Both, well made for the mass market, offer good value.

The important 200-hectare, vine-clad village of Martillac contains two important classified and five popular, nonclassified properties. *Ch. Smith-Haut-Lafitte* is a large 54-hectare property producing 25,000 cases of red and nearly 6,000 cases of white wine. Owned by the negociant firm of Eschenauer, the 16th-century property is well situated on a large, well-drained *Gunzian* gravel bank, and contains magnificent cellars capable of holding 2,000 barrels of wine—perhaps the largest in the appellation. Significantly improved since the 1981 vintage, the red wine contains a high proportion of Cabernet Sauvignon, and because it is firm, bold, and muscular, it requires time to mature. Made entirely from Sauvignon Blanc, the white, fresh and zesty but lacking elegance, is a top-flight libation that many think is superior to the red. The estate is currently in top form, and both wines offer excellent value. *Ch. la Tour-Martillac* is a 23-hectare property owned by one of the finest winemakers of Bordeaux— Jean Kressmann. Annual production consists of 7,500 cases of red and 1,400 cases of white wine, both of which are made by traditional methods and require patience. The red is expertly made, complex, full-bodied, well flavored and scented, exhibiting uncommon delicacy and finesse. It is made from very old vines and requires at least ten years to mature fully. The white, made by an unusually long *cuvaison,* is barrel-aged, full-bodied, eminently flavorful, and often among the top four wines in the appellation. The second wines are *Ch. les Pault* and *Ch. la Grave Martillac. Ch. de Rochemorin* is a newly resurrected, 45-hectare property that makes 17,000 cases of red and 2,000 cases of white wine. After forty years of abandonment, the property is now producing well made, fruity, early maturing, modern-type wines. *Ch. la Garde,* a large 65-hectare property owned by the negociant firm of Eschenauer, produces 23,000 cases of red and 1,500 cases of white wine. *Ch. Haut-Nouchet* is a 12-hectare property located south of Martillac producing 6,000 cases. *Dne. de la Solitude* is a 23-hectare property owned by a religious order. Well sited southwest of Martillac, it produces 7,000 cases of red and 1,600 cases of white wine. The red is dark and intensely flavored with a long finish, while the white is much lighter and early maturing. Both are hard to find but well worth the effort. *Ch. Ferran,* a 15-hectare property, makes 3,000 cases of red and white wines, equally divided. The white is well made, fruity, crisp, and absolutely sublime; the red is well structured, soft, and mellow, yet offers a good measure of complexity. Both are of classed standards and offer excellent value.

Ayguemorte-les-Graves is a small village of 500 people located between St.-Médard and Beautiran. The soils, mainly *palus,* sand, and gravel, support fewer than 21 hectares of vineland and six growers, of which *Ch. St.-Gérôme* and *Ch. Boiresse* are the most important. The small town of Beautiran, located on the Garonne, contains 91 hectares of vineland and seven growers. The soils to the north, east, and south are all *palus,* but in a few places west of the town there is good gravel mixed with sand resting on a clay and sandy subsoil. There are two principal growths: *Ch. le Tuquet,* with its 28 hectares and stately 18th-century country manor house produces 17,500 cases of red and white wine. *Ch. de la Limagère* is a property making 9,400 cases of full-bodied, robust, spicy red wine, made primarily from Cabernet Sauvignon. The town of Castres (1,300 residents), along with Portets, is one of the four most-important winemaking communes south of Martillac. It is the site of a large concentration of gravel and sand resting on a subsoil of clay and sand with occasional limestone. There are 105 hectares of vineland and fourteen growers, of which two enjoy an excellent reputation. *Ch. Ferrande,* a highly under-rated 42-hectare property, is outstanding in the production of full-bodied, well-structured red wine that ranks with the very best in terms of scent and flavor. The white is crisp, well balanced, and flavored, offering excellent value. *Dne. Périn de Naudine* is a small 4-hectare property making 1,400 cases of full-bodied, well-structured, and flavored red wine.

The medium-sized town of Portets, with 488 hectares of vineland, is the largest wine-producing commune in Graves and the most important in the output of quality wine south of Martillac. The soils consist of a variable mixture of clay, sand, and gravel with appreciable limestone infusions in the subsoil in the western, hillier portion of the producing district. The commune contains nearly fifty growers, ten of which enjoy a good reputation. *Ch. de Portets,* a 44-hectare property located on a former Roman settlement, produces 6,200 cases of red and 1,100 cases of white wine; both of which are outstanding and offer excellent value. *Ch. Millet* is a little known, highly underrated 61-hectare property producing 4,500 cases of red and 2,500 cases of white wine. The red, widely exported, expertly made, and highly consistent, exhibits elements of complexity, an admirable scent, and a flavor that seems to lack the *terroir* individuality of most red wines. The white is a fresh, acidic, and fruity libation that is not as good as the red. *Ch. Rahoul* is a 15-hectare property making 6,000 cases of red and 1,200 cases of white wine. This recently expanded and refurbished estate, owned by Len Evans, an Australian, is currently producing full-bodied, stylish, and satisfying red wine. The white is dry, full-bodied, crisp, and refreshing. Both wines offer good value. *Ch. la-Tour-Bicheau,* a 20-hectare property, makes 6,000 cases of red and 1,100 cases of white wine, both of which are well made and early maturing. *Ch. la Vieille-France* is a 16-hectare property making 2,000 cases of red and 2,100 cases of white wine in addition to 3,000 cases of generic Bordeaux red. This former Ginestet estate has been partially replanted and its physical plant improved. The red wine is savory, concentrated in flavor, underrated, and offers exceptional value. Six other properties with average reputations are: *Ch. Cabannieux* (25 hectares, and known for well-flavored and scented wines); *Ch. Jean-Gervais* (30 hectares, making 13,000 cases of early maturing wines); *Ch. Pessan* (40 hectares, making 6,000 cases of early maturing, light to medium-bodied wines); *Ch. du Mirail; Ch. Doms;* and *Ch. du Grand-Abord.*

Located south of Martillac, La Brède, a small town of 2,400 residents, contains 105 hectares of vineland, three good growths, and twelve small, part-time growers, of which fewer than half bottle their own wine. The soil, composed of sand and gravel with sizable accumulations of clay mixed with limestone, rests on a subsoil of deep gravel, sand, and clay-conditions that are very favorable for the production of white wine. The three principal properties: *Ch. la Blancherie,* the top growth in the commune, is a well-managed property of 18 hectares producing 3,600 cases of red and 4,400 cases of white wine. *Clos Méric,* a 12-hectare property in which the vines are "ecologically grown," produces fewer than 2,000 cases of well-made red and white wines. *Clos Magneau,* a 23-hectare property, makes 6,500 cases of white and 200 cases of red wine. Lying next to the Garonne, the hamlet of Arbanats contains 100 hectares of vineland and eight growers. The soils are essentially *palus,* with only one small gravel *croupe,* west of Arbanats, containing scattered sand. The two main properties are *Ch. Tourteau-Chollet* and *Ch. Moron-Lafitte. Ch. Virelade,* a large 37-hectare property with a good reputation, is the principal growth in the village of the same name located on the Garonne near Cérons.

Nearly surrounded by pine and deciduous forest, the village of St.-Selve is, with 51 hectares of vineland, a minor viticultural outlier. Although the approximately twelve growers are nearly all part-time farmers, there is only one major, economically viable property—*Ch. de Bonnat,* a 16-hectare estate making above average red, and light-bodied white wines. St.-Morillon, a small village located on a gravel *croupe,* contains 74 hectares and thirteen growers, of which two enjoy a local and regional reputation: *Ch. Piron* and *Ch. des Gravettes.* The small village of Pujols, located on gravel and sand with a limestone subsoil, contains 107 hectares of vineland and twenty-seven growers, of which three are important: *Ch. St.-Robert, Ch. Graville-Lacoste,* and *Ch. Montalivet.* Toulenne is a large village located on the Garonne northeast of Fargues. While *palus* soil occurs along the river and sand in the western sections of the commune, the center portion contains one small gravel *croupe,* 54 hectares of vineland, and five properties of note: *Ch. de Cardaillan, Ch. Respide, Ch. Chicane,* and *Dne. de Courbon.*

Of the four Graves communes located along the Garonne east and south of Sauternes, Langon, with 220 hectares of vineland, is the largest. Of the nearly three dozen growers, eight enjoy a good reputation: *Ch. de Respide, Dne. de Gaillat, Ch. Chantelouiseau, Ch. Ludeman-la-Côte, Clos la Maurasse, Ch. Brondelles, Ch. Tour de Boyrein,* and *Ch. Lehoult.* The village of St.-Pierre-de-Mons, with 294 hectares, is the third-largest winemaking village in Graves. Of the nearly three dozen growers, three enjoy good reputations: *Ch. Toumilon, Ch. Magence,* and *Ch. les Queyrats.* The five southernmost winemaking communes of Graves are Budos, Guillos, Léogeats, Roaillan, and Mazèras; the first is the most important in hectarage, and the last two in quality production. The principal proper-ties are *Ch. de Budos, Ch. Boyrein, Ch. le Pavillon-de-Boyrein,* and *Ch. Roquetaillade-la-Grange.*

12

THE WINES OF CERONS, SAUTERNES, AND BARSAC

CERONS

CERONS is a little known but sizable 800-hectare viticultural region producing more than 35,000 hectoliters of wine annually. It fronts on the Garonne and adjoins Barsac/Sauternes, forming an enclave within the Graves appellation. Much more important in the 19th century than at present, its vineland declined from 1,600 hectares in 1873 to 644 in 1945. The area is heavily forested, with vineyards located in only three areas that contain significant gravel *croupes*. The area along the Garonne contains *palus* and is used only in the production of vermouth-type libations. Cérons consists of three important communes: Podensac (120 hectares), Cérons (310 hectares), and Illats (345 hectares). Located along the northern margins of Barsac and Sauternes, all three communes are historically associated with the production of half-dry, semi-sweet, and sweet white wine. The latter are rarely liquoreux, concentrated with the flavor and aroma of *botrytis,* memorable, or unpalatable; but neither have they generated a loyal following outside the immediate area, except for small quantities still shipped to Belgium and Holland.

Historically, the methods of vinification, field practices, and type of wine made were similar to Sauternes, with the following significant areas of departure. *Botrytis* is less common in intensity and geographical occurrence in this region; consequently, the wines are less luscious than Sauternes and significantly below the levels of Monbazillac, Cadillac, and Ste.-Croix-du-Mont. They are by no means light-weight libations without character, but neither are they substantial enough to compete in a shrinking sweet white market. Faced with declining sales, growers have switched from sweet to dry white grapes and, increasingly, to red wine production. With improved vinification techniques, the red and white wines are now cleaner, less sulfured, and very pleasant, offering good value in good vintages.

The Cérons appellation name can be used only for the production and sale of semi-sweet and sweet white wine, with the following restrictions: the sugar content must be at least 212 grams per liter, the minimum alcohol content 12.5 percent, and the yield restricted to 40 hectoliters per hectare, an appreciable increase from the 25 in Sauternes. In addition, while the same three white grape varieties are the same, the percentage of Muscadelle is quite high.

Sweet wine bearing the name of Cérons, however, is quite rare today. Of the nearly 800 hectares in production, 225 are planted in red grapes, 445 are used in the making of dry wine, and only about 100 are usually declared under the Cérons name, making fewer than 4,000 hectoliters of sweet wine annually. Most of it is consumed locally, with a good portion (some estimate as much as 10 percent of appellation total) going to the large Lillet firm located in Podensac. Three-quarters of all wine commercialized within the producing district is therefore marketed either as Graves or Graves Supérieures. Usually referred to as "Petit Graves," it is crisp, very fresh, fragrant, light-bodied, consumed young, and priced to sell quickly. Made from 65 percent Sauvignon Blanc, 25 percent Sémillon, and 10 percent Muscadelle, it is fermented in stainless steel and receives no barrel-aging. The red is a combination of Cabernet Sauvignon, Merlot, and a little Cabernet Franc and Malbec, but the tendency in recent years is to use more Merlot. It is very fruity, light-to-medium in body, low in acid, and very quaffable. Both Graves and Graves Supérieures benefited from the resurgence of lighter and drier wines, and have, over the past thirty years, changed the character of the region. Hectarage since 1955 has increased and probably will continue to increase in the near future; this sleepy, backwater appellation has suddenly become a hot property in the production of dry white and red wines.

Podensac, the largest of the three communes in Cérons, is located in the extreme northern portion of the district. It contains 120 hectares of vineland and nearly two dozen growers, of which five enjoy a good reputation. *Ch. de Chantegrive,* with nearly 60 hectares of vineland, is the most substantial and one of the most modern of all properties within the producing region. It makes 12,200 cases of full-flavored red wine (from 50 percent Cabernet Sauvignon, 40 percent Merlot, and 10 percent Cabernet Franc) and 5,500 cases of fresh, zesty white wine. *Ch. d'Anice,* and old property with a formidable social history produces 700 cases of red and 6,200 cases of crisp, well-flavored white wine. *Dne. de Brouillaou* is a small 4 hectare property making 1,200 cases of above-average-quality white wine only. *Ch. de Mauves,* a recently enlarged property located on the Graves border, produces 4,600 cases of full-bodied red and 2,500 cases of dry white wine. *Ch. Bédat,* located on the Graves border, is a small property making 2,600 cases of excellent red wine. *Ch. de Madère,* a small vineyard located in the northern portion of the commune, makes minute quantities of good, sound, robust red and 1,500 cases of fresh and crisp white wine.

The large village of Cérons contains 310 hectares of vineland and nearly four dozen growers, eight of which enjoy a good reputation. Over the past thirty years the percentage of red wine has increased from less than 10 percent to nearly 45 percent, and approximately 60 percent of all white wine is now made dry. The most important properties: *Grand-Enclos du Château de Cérons,* a 30-hectare property, is considered the finest producer in the commune. It is the only major estate producing nothing but white wine, most of which is dry. *Ch. de Cérons* is a 15-hectare property making 2,000 cases of red and 4,500 cases of white wine. The property also markets wine under the label of *Ch. de Calvimont,* the latter named after the legendary Marquis de Calvimont. *Clos du Barrail,* a large 27-hectare property, makes 8,500 cases of various styles of white wine. *Ch. Moulin-de-Marc* is a greatly expanded property that is now making 3,500 cases of red and 3,200 cases of white wine. This property makes above-average, full-bodied, robust, and well-flavored wines that offer excellent value. Other properties include *Ch. Haut-Mayne, Ch. de l'Emigré, Ch. Mayne-Binet, Ch. Ferbos, Ch. Sylvain,* and *Ch. Balestey.*

The village of Illats and its 345 hectares of vineyards lie on a large gravel *croupe* in the extreme southern portion of the Cérons appellation. Of the nearly four dozen growers, twelve enjoy good reputations. *Ch. Archambeau* is a 7-hectare property located on solid gravel/clay soil with soft and crumbly limestone rock in the subsoil. It produces 1,000 cases of firm, tannin-rich red and 3,000 cases of fresh, crisp, well-flavored, dry white wine, and both offer excellent value. *Ch. Hillot,* located west of Illats on an isolated gravel bank, makes 500 cases of red and 4,500 cases of excellent white wine. *Ch. d'Ardennes,* magnificiently situated on sloping ground, is a large, recently expanded, well-managed, 14th-century property that makes excellent wine (4,500 cases red and 3,500 cases white). *Dne. de Lionne,* the largest and one of the oldest properties in the region, is located northeast of Illats on the Cérons border. This well-maintained, 57-hectare vineyard makes 7,000 cases of excellent red and 14,000 cases of various types of white wine. *Ch. Peyragué* is a 21-hectare property with a good reputation that produces 4,500 cases of red and 3,000 cases of white wine. Other properties include *Ch. le Merle, Clos St.-Georges, Ch. de Navarro, Ch. Beaulac, Ch. la Hontasse, Ch. la Roche,* and *Ch. de Courrèges.*

SAUTERNES AND BARSAC

Located south of Bordeaux and surrounded by the Graves appellation, Sauternes is a pleasant, gently undulating landscape of scattered woods, grazing land, vineyards, and about two dozen dignified, affluent, and impressive wine-producing estates. The name Sauternes is reserved for sweet white wine originating in the communes of Sauternes, Fargues, Preignac, Bommes, and Barsac. The latter, with 761 hectares, is the largest, producing close to 40 percent of total output (actual production figures are obscured by the fact that growers here have a choice of using either the Sauternes or Barsac appellation). Of the five, Sauternes (because of *Ch. d'Yquem* and the prevalance of large amounts of *alios* and limestone-clay accumulations in the subsoil) is considered the finest commune, followed by Barsac, Bommes, Preignac, and Fargues. Containing more classified growths than any other, Barsac's wines tend to be less sweet, fresher, and more austere in flavor than the other four.

For the department of Gironde, sweet white wine amounts to 150,000 hectoliters, or 16 percent of total white wine production. Fully 70 percent of all sweet wine originates in Entre-Deux-Mers and along the north bank of the Gironde and Dordogne, while less than 30 percent comes from the famed Sauternes appellation. Table 12.1 indicates the approximate annual production and percentage of sweet white wine among the various Gironde appellations.

More than 2,000 hectares of vineland produce 45,000 hectoliters of wine, or approximately 2 and .8 percent of Gironde totals, respectively. Annual output is only 5 percent of the department's total white wine production, but despite the surprisingly small amount of wine produced, its reputation and asking price are second to none in France and the world. The appellation produces a rich, honeyed wine of incomparable quality that is widely imitated, with little success. The wine is sweet and golden yellow in color; the bouquet and flavor are powerful, haunting, spicy, and impregnated with multiple layers of perfectly balanced acid, sugar, and fruit essence. Chilled, it makes an ideal aperitif with Roquefort cheese, it further compliments rich, delicate patés, creamed sauces, and dried nuts; and its richness perfectly balances the fatness of duck. The wine is absolutely sensational with a Grand Marnier soufflé and makes an outstanding cooking wine. The nearby appellations of Cadillac, Cérons, Ste.-Croix-du-Mont, and Loupiac all produce the same type of wine but lack the intensity of flavor and bouquet of the finest Sauternes.

The history of Sauternes, although long and varied, has been less spectacular than areas to the north. Vinegrowing and winemaking were practiced in the 3rd century A.D., but significant plantings did not occur until the later medieval period. Barsac, because of its location on the

Table 12.1   AOC Sweet White Wine Production in the Gironde, 1980

Appellation	Hectoliters	Percent of total	Appellation	Hectoliters	Percent of total
Sauternes	26,899	18.0	Cérons	7,407	5.0
Barsac	13,739	9.2	Cadillac	2,551	1.7
Ste.-Croix-du-Mont	13,927	9.3	Other (estimated)	75,000	50.3
Loupiac	9,739	6.5	Total	144,262	100.0

Source: French Ministry of Agriculture.

Gironde, began to export wine to England in the 13th century. Its sizable
trade increased until the 16th century, when Holland replaced England as
the main importer. By the second half of the 18th century, winemakers
began to reduce the percentage of Muscat, to increase Sémillon, to pick
late, and to mature wine in wood and then bottle.

Historically, the region had few large estates, but during the 18th
century a number of large holdings emerged that set the standard for a
good deal of the Médoc. Production and exports, unfortunately severely
curtailed for more than a generation by the French Revolution, the
Jacobin dictatorship, and the rise of Napoleon, increased to record levels
after 1825, especially in the lucrative Russian, Polish, and Scandinavian
markets. During this period, a good deal of the former viticultural
hectarage was reclaimed and replanted, and large estates once again began
to appear on both banks of the Ciron River. Since then, Sauternes has
been plagued by rising costs and declining demand brought about by a
combination of international economic and political factors. Foremost
have been World War I, the Russian Communist Revolution of 1917, the
subsequent world depression, and the post–World War II west European
and American abhorance for sweet white wine—all of which, in combination, disrupted historic markets, reduced demand, and strained producer
profit margins. While dry white wine from the Gironde increased fivefold
during the past forty years, the production of Sauternes has remained
stable, and its share of total white wine production has declined sharply
(Fig. 12.1) As a result, a number of properties have discontinued
operations, at least two dozen have changed hands and, most important,
quality has suffered with the introduction of more mechanized and
simplified viticultural and vinification methods. It is obvious that everywhere in the Gironde, including neighboring Bergerac in the department
of Dordogne and the entire southwest, sweet white wine production is in
retreat. Nevertheless, as the price of Sauternes vineland deteriorated over
the past forty years, its speculative economic attributes have attracted a

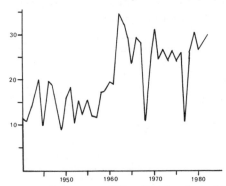

Figure 12.1   Sauternes: Wine Production, 1940–1983
(in thousands of hectoliters)

number of foreign interests, which added a good measure of renewed life and vitality to the physical appearance of the appellation.

While exports have exhibited a mild but steady decline over the past forty years, the aggregate number of cases (less than 180,000) represents about 1 percent or less of total Bordeaux exports, or less than 25 percent of all sweet white wine exports. For both Barsac and Sauternes, the chief export market is the United Kingdom, followed by Belgium, the United States, and Japan, the latter, becoming a principal player for expensive wines only within the past 15 years (see Table 12.2). Second to the United Kingdom is the collective market of Belgium, Holland, Luxembourg, West Germany, and Switzerland, which together imports more than 20 percent of all Sauternes-Barsac. The domestic market consumes more of the cheaper sweet wines of the Loire, but the overwhelming preference appears to be the VDN wines of the Midi, particularly those of Roussillon.

Microclimate, Vines and Wines

The quality of Sauternes is the result of a number of interesting combinations: soil, microclimate, grape varieties, and viticultural practices. The soil throughout the appellation is mainly gravel and sand over a clayey subsoil, except in Barsac and portions of Preignac where the topography is flatter and the soil mainly calcareous. The best sites are located on the higher hilly elevations, areas that not only benefit from the better water and air drainage but seem to prolong the duration of *botrytis* infection (a fungus that rots the grapes and is despised in all dry white and red wine regions, but is essential in the production of fine Sauternes). In sharp contrast, lowland areas contain more clay, are poorly drained, and produce lower-quality, rather tasteless, coarse wine. Quality properties also sit on an irregular layer of *le calcaire à astéries,* a degraded chalk that is sufficiently weak to allow excellent root penetration. Accentuating this excellent attribute, especially in Sauternes and Barsac, is the presence of a

Table 12.2   Sale of Sauternes, 1982

Sale	Hectoliters	Percent	Sale	Hectoliters	Percent
United Kingdom	4,520	36.5	West Germany	461	3.7
United States	2,243	18.1	Others	2,123	17.2
Belgium[a] & Holland	1,262	10.2	Total exports	12,379	100.0
Japan	1,010	8.2			
Switzerland	760	6.1	France	10,861	46.7
			Total sales	23,240	100.0

[a]Also includes Luxembourg.
Source: Conseil Interprofessionnel du Vin de Bordeaux.

subsoil that also contains heavy *alios* accumulations. The water table is quite high throughout the appellation, and the proportion of sand, gravel, clay, mica, and quartz fragments is extremely variable and locally very important. Except for Barsac where the vineyards are more contiguous, the rest of the producing district is hilly, with the individual vineyards isolated from each other by forest and pasture.

Marking the western limit of the appellation, the Ciron River, a tributary of the Garonne, diagonally cuts across the producing region to create an environment with a favorable microclimate. During the period of September–December the slow-moving Ciron attracts fog, which promotes the growth of *botrytis*. The ever-present fog is expressed as morning and evening mist, and its incidence, enhanced by humid air, is clearly a local phenomenon: no other appellation exhibits such a high frequency of occurrence and duration of fog as does Sauternes. The *botrytis* fungus attacks the skins, causing the individual grape berries to dehydrate, become darker, and wither, one by one, on the vine. *Botrytis* also promotes the secretion of gumlike substances that add glycerine, flavor, and bouquet to the wine. Yet the fungus does not spread consistently in the producing region nor throughout a particular vineyard necessitating many pickings or "sortings" during the course of grape maturation, as few as three in most vintages to as many as twenty in those properties wishing to produce the very best wine. One such property is *Ch. d'Yquem,* the foremost vineyard in the region, where each vine in a good *botrytized* vintage produces a scant 15 to 22 centiliters of wine. *Botrytis,* in appreciable amounts, occurs every three to four years, with one year in seven producing outstanding *botrytis* flavor and aroma. It is widely acknowledged that *botrytized* wine was not made until 1845–47.

Since the cost rises according to the number of "sortings" and reduced must content, the temptation to use unaffected grapes becomes a very important financial consideration. When the percentage of unaffected grapes increases, the wine lacks concentration, flavor, scent, sweetness, and long life. If not aged in wood, it is often watery on the palate, bland in taste, usually unbalanced, overly sulfured, and invariably appears as "negociant-blended wine," offering little value.

Sauternes is produced from only three grape varieties: Sémillon, Sauvignon Blanc, and Muscadelle. The first, because of its suppleness, fragrance, and excellent golden color and soft skin, seems to attract and benefit most from *botrytis* infection. As a consequence, it is the most important of the three and is highly localized in the Gironde, which contains three-quarters of all national plantings. Although no official formula exists for the production of Sauternes, Sémillon accounts for between 50 and 90 percent of the encépagement. The actual amount used is essentially a matter of the type of wine produced and the standards and reputation of the producing property. For the more-traditional estates, the percentage is higher, while for those properties making nouveau-type Sauternes (lighter and drier), the percentage is sharply reduced.

Sauvignon Blanc represents between 10 and 50 percent of the total blend. It is a well-flavored and scented, early maturing grape with a thick skin and much higher acid levels, but comparatively lower sugar levels, than either Sémillon or Muscadelle. Although less productive and more resistant to *botrytis*, it has become a prime player in the production of semi-sweet and half-dry Sauternes; as a consequence, plantings have recently increased.

The third and least-important grape variety, the Muscadelle, is a strongly scented and flavored grape whose wine is easily oxidized. Historically more important than today, it currently comprises 15 percent of the encépagement in only two properties and less than 5 percent in fifteen other classified properties. While more than 60 percent of all growers have discontinued plantings, this grape variety, with 65 percent of all national plantings in the Gironde, still shows a remarkable concentration.

Sauternes is made by allowing the grapes to hang on the vine as long as possible during the long, hot, and often sunny autumn months until they dry to the consistency of moldy raisins. Ideally, the grape berries should be picked one by one, thus prolonging the harvest by weeks and even months. When the grapes are pressed the must is exceptionally concentrated and reduced in volume by as much as 95 percent. Throughout the five communes, the yield is limited to 25 hectoliters per hectare, with the finest properties often yielding less than 10. Barsac adds one more qualifier if it chooses to use its name on the label; namely, that the must be the product of "late-picked" grapes harvested in successive "sortings" (this is one reason why most growers prefer to sell under the more-liberal Sauternes appellation name).

The wine quality is mainly a function of degree of *botrytized* infection, sugar content, and thoroughness in the discarding of waste matter prior to pressing. The final product is golden yellow in color, high in alcohol, and has at least 225 grams of unfermented sugar per liter. It is well balanced, velvety on the palate, with a long, lingering, and full *botrytized* flavor. The bouquet is honeyed, with elusive hints of spice, nuts, and ripe fruit; as it ages, the wine's color becomes progressively darker, its flavor more complex, and its nose more pronounced. Historically, bottling occurred only after a minimum of three years oak-aging and rarely did a good vintage mature quickly, which is to say, before its fifteenth birthday. As a consequence, Sauternes, rivaled in quality only by the finest Trocken-beerenauslese and Tokay Essencia, has often been called the "solar wine" or, as the country gentry are fond of saying, "extravagant perfection."

Sauternes is the costliest wine to make in France. It involves expensive labor, erratic vintages, the unpredictability of *botrytis* infection, and low yields (as low as 5 to 8 hectoliters to the hectare). Only *Ch. d'Yquem, Ch. Nairac, Ch. Climens, Ch. Coutet,* and a few others use new oak barrels each year, and only *Ch. d'Yquem* tolerates widely spaced, low-yielding vines, replacing them only after they reach thirty-five years.

Because of the exorbitant expense incurred in the production of Sauternes and its stable demand, growers have begun to compromise traditional viticultural, vinification, and aging practices. The tendency over the past forty years has been to increase yields, reduce the number of sortings, shorten fermentation time, and reduce or eliminate wood-aging. As a result the wines, lighter in concentration, flavor, and aroma, are often dull, nondescript, and only a shell of their former character. More than half of production offers hardly any value even when compared with Monbazillac, Loupiac, Cadillac, and Ste.-Croix-du-Mont. As a consequence, three distinct styles have developed over the past thirty years. The top tier, representing less than 1 percent of total production, is quality wine no matter what the cost. The very best mature after their fifteenth birthday, and at twenty evolve into rich, harmonious libations with extraordinary richness. The middle group of vignerons, unable to sustain the high cost of producing top-flight quality wines, aim at a less-sophisticated market. Their wines, the result of many shortcuts, are fresher with some (or no) wood-aging and only traces of *botrytized* flavor and aroma. They are responsible for 20 percent of the total output at best. The bottom tier, responsible for more than 75 percent of total output, makes wine with the least amount of sweetness and *botrytized* flavor— lighter in color, unbalanced, heavily sulfured, and overly chaptalized. Those that are sweet are cloying, heavy on the palate, lack freshness and bouquet, and taste worse than the less-sweet styles. Offering no value whatever, they appear to be debasing the good name of Sauternes and would probably be better if made into a dry wine.

Finally, due to the chronic nature of the stable Sauternes market, growers have begun deemphasizing *botrytis* grapes and sweet white wines and are producing ever-increasing amounts of dry white (with less Sémillon and more Sauvignon Blanc) and red wine. Although dry white wine has always been made in the region, output began to grow to significant levels only after 1960. Today nearly every major estate produces from 5 percent to as much as 35 percent of total output as dry white wine. In addition, at least ten major properties produce red wine. *Ch. Doisy-Védrines,* for example, produces as much red as sweet wine. Appearing to offer excellent possibilities, both the dry white and red are infinitely better than the bland and poorly made sweet white wines.

The Sauternes Classification

The official classification of the Great Growths of the Gironde also included a ranking of twenty-one Sauternes properties. The official 1855

Table 12.3   SAUTERNES-BARSAC VINTAGE CHART

1985	10–17	Late and uneven *botrytis* infection created a variable harvest; those properties picking late produced rich, flavorful wines.
1984	10–14	Small harvest of soft, early maturing wines.
1983	14–17	Average to above-average quality vintage; a number of excellent wines equal the 1976s and 1979s. *Botrytis* well developed with moderately high acid levels.
1982	9–14	Hot, dry summer with little humidity, uneven *botrytis* development, and lower acid levels than normal. Heavy fall rain produced little good wine – a small, expensive harvest of low acid, early maturing wines.
1981	8–13	Rain in September produced low levels of *botrytis*. Wines are firm and will outlast the 1980s and 1982s. Quantity below normal levels.
1980	7–13	Small harvest produced acceptable levels of *botrytis* but early maturing wines.
1979	12–17	Highly variable harvest – slightly higher in quality in Sauternes, but sweeter wines in Barsac. Much better than 1978 in terms of *botrytis* development, extract, and length finish.
1978	7–11	Thin, acidic, and hollow wines with little *botrytis*.
1977	4–8	Small harvest caused by severe spring frost produced a late vintage of light, unbalanced wines.
1976	14–18	Excellent vintage; perhaps not the equal of 1975, but more consistent.
1975	12–20	Outstanding vintage: full-bodied with considerable finesse and breeding marred only by variability. For the finest properties, the wine was very rich, concentrated, and long-lived. One of the best vintages in the past 50 years.
1974	0–5	Below-average, unsubstantial wines, little of which was bottled under château labels.
1973	6–10	Below-average vintage of light wines with little concentration and balance.
1972	0–2	Very poor.
1971	13–17	Above-average vintage with many excellent to outstanding wines, though less elegant and well balanced than the later 1970s. Concentration less than perfect, but long lasting.
1970	15–19	Large harvest, the very best growths making outstanding wines in terms of body, concentration, and elegance. One of the finest vintages within the past 25 years.

listing and the subsequent changes are indicated below and in Table 12.4. Over the past 132 years, the number of changes in name, dimension, and status have been rather formidable and include the following:

Ch. Bayle changed its name to *Ch. Guiraud.*
Ch. Broustet-Nerac has been divided into *Ch. Broustet* and *Ch. Nairac.*

Table 12.4 The Sauternes-Barsac Classification	
The 1855 Classification	Current Position
Name, Rank, and Commune	*Name and Rank*
Premier Cru Supérieur	*Premier Cru Supérieur*
Ch. d'Yquem (Sauternes)	Ch. d'Yquem (Sauternes)
Premiers Crus	*Premiers Crus*
Ch. Climens (Barsac)	Ch. Climens (Barsac)
Ch. Coutet (Barsac)	Ch. Coutet (Barsac)
Ch. Bayle (Sauternes)	Ch. Giuraud (Sauternes)
Ch. Peyraguey (Bommes)	Ch. Lafaurie-Peyraguey (Bommes)
	Clos Haut-Peyraguey
Ch. Vigneau (Bommes)	Ch. Rayne-Vigneau (Bommes)
Ch. Rabeaud (Bommes)	Ch. Rabaud-Promis (Bommes)
	Ch. Sigalas-Rabaud
Ch. Rieussec (Sauternes)	Ch. Rieussec (Sauternes)
Ch. Suduiraut (Preignac)	Ch. Suduiraut (Preignac)
Ch. Latour-Blanche (Bommes)	Ch. La Tour-Blanche (Bommes)
Seconds Crus	*Seconds Crus*
Ch. d'Arche (Sauternes)	Ch. d'Arche (Sauternes)
Ch. Broustet-Nérac (Barsac)	Ch. Broustet (Barsac)
	Ch. Nairac
Ch. Caillou (Barsac)	Ch. Caillou (Barsac)
Ch. Doisy-Daene	Ch. Doisy-Daëne
	Ch. Doisy-Dubroca (Barsac)
	Ch. Doisy-Védrines
Ch. Filhot (Sauternes)	Ch. Filhot (Sauternes)
Ch. Lamothe (Sauternes)	Ch. Lamothe Despujols (Sauternes)
	Ch. Lamothe-Guignard (Sauternes)
Ch. de Malle (Preignac)	Ch. de Malle (Preignac)
Ch. Mirat (Barsac)	Ch. Mirat (Barsac);
	part of Chateau Cantegril
Ch. Pexoto (Bommes)	Ch. Rabaud-Promis (Bommes)
Ch. Romer (Preignac)	Ch. Romer (Preignac)
	Ch. Romer-Du-Hayot (Preignac)
Ch. Suau (Barsac)	Ch. Suau (Barsac)

Ch. Doisy has been divided into *Ch. Doisy-Daëne, Ch. Doisy-Dubroca,* and *Ch. Doisy-Védrines.*

Ch. Lamothe has been divided into *Ch. Lamothe* (Despujols) and *Ch. Lamothe* (Guignard).

Ch. Latour-Blanche changed its name to *Ch. la Tour-Blanche.*

Ch. Mirat changed its name to *Ch. Myrat* and since 1976 has not produced any wine under its name.

Ch. Pexoto, like *Ch. Myrat,* is no longer producing wine under its name.

Ch. Peyraquey has been divided into *Ch. Lafaurie-Peyraquey* and *Ch. Clos Haut-Peyraquey.*

Ch. Rabaud acquired Ch. Pexoto and subsequently was divided into *Ch. Rabaud* and *Sigalas-Rabaud.*

Ch. Romer has been divided into *Ch. Romer* and *Ch. Romer-du-Hayot.*

Ch. Vigneau changed its name to *Ch. Rayne-Vigneau.*

Today, after all of the above revisions, there are twenty-seven classified properties producing between 15 and 25 percent of all wine marketed under the Sauternes-Barsac appellation names. In addition to the classified growths, more than 200 other properties collectively make more than 70 percent of all appellation wine, and despite their small size they have not banded together to found a cooperative. It is the wine of the small, often part-time grower that flows into the innocuous blends of the negociant.

The Producing Areas

The village of Barsac, with 2,000 residents, lies north of the Ciron River on a 10-meter former Garonne River terrace. It contains 761 hectares of vineland, about one-third of the appellation's total hectarage (more than any other commune). It contains seven classified growths (more than any other commune) and nearly eighty additional unclassified properties, of which about eighteen are important quality producers. Nearly two dozen small producers, all located essentially on *palus* soil near the Garonne, are not allowed to sell their wine under the appellation name but market it as plain Bordeaux or Bordeaux Supérieure.

Although the topography is less hilly than the other four communes to the south, the soils are highly variable: limestone dominates the subsoil, clay the surface soil, and near the Ciron and Garonne, heavy accumulations of alluvium are to be found. Because of the excellent permeability of the subsurface limestone, the surface soil is quite dry, which influences the character of the wine to be firm, less sweet, earthy, and more austere in flavor. The principal properties: *Ch. Climens,* a large 30-hectare property, is part of the huge stable of wine estates owned by Lucien Lurton. For decades it was considered the leading estate in Barsac, a claim now challenged by *Ch. Coutet.* The property is located on high ground (a major accomplishment in this rather flat region) in the southwestern portion of the producing area. Its historic reputation rested on consistency and a quality performance approaching greatness. Although not as concentrated as *Ch. d'Yquem,* it is elegant and quite refined, but in poor vintages it tends to be less smooth and with a marked "acid grip." The yield in recent years has increased from the historic figure of 10 to 15 hectoliters to the hectare, and the wine is apt to be more inconsistent than a first-growth property should be. Output exceeds 5,000 cases. *Ch. Coutet,* with 40 hectares and an annual production of 8,000 cases, is one of the largest properties in the appellation. The vineyard is located in the central portion of Barsac, but unlike *Ch. Climens,* its principal rival in the area, it is on lower ground closer to the Ciron. The wine, despite the presence of Muscadelle in the encépagement, is similar to the reputed leader; and more often than not in recent years, it has become the top growth in Barsac, being concentrated in flavor and bouquet, and offering outstanding value. A supreme libation called "Cuvée Madame" is made in limited quantities and only in exceptional years, the latter having the distinction of being a better-keeping wine than the normal bottling.

Ch. Broustet is a modest property of 16 hectares producing 3,000 cases of wine annually. This humble estate, owned by Eric Fournier of *Ch. Canon* in St.-Emilion, produces highly controversial, nontraditional dry white as well as sweet wines. The latter is well balanced, has a delightful bouquet, and has a honeyed flavor that is both clean and lingering on the palate. More important, the property consistently produces above-average-quality wine, a feature that few other properties, with the major exception of *Ch. d'Yquem,* are able to attain. The wine, hard to find but worth the search, offers outstanding value. The second label is called *Ch. de Ségur.* The dry wine is clean, flavorful, and absolutely refreshing. *Ch. Nairac,* an immaculate 16-hectare property located in the extreme northern portion of the producing area, makes 3,500 cases of traditionally made and rapidly improving Barsac. The fragmented property was long neglected until 1971, when an American acquired it and began a series of sweeping changes in an attempt to raise quality levels. After sixteen years of reform, the wine is just about to enter its golden years. It is well balanced, fruity, not overly sweet, has a good lingering finish, and takes at least seven years to begin the first phase of its maturity cycle. The wine ranks among the best, is hard to find, and offers excellent value.

Ch. Caillou, flanked by *Ch. Myrat* and *Ch. Climens* in the western portion of Barsac, is an 18-hectare estate with a veritable masterpiece of a chateau producing 4,500 cases annually. The wine, well balanced, early maturing, fruity, and not overly sweet, is marred only by inconsistency, a disconcerting fault that should not be part of any classified property. Also made are a dry white wine called "Dne. Sarraute Sec," a dry red called "Clos du Clocher," and minor quantities of an undistinguished rosé. The wine, mainly sold direct to private clients and at the property, is not readily available. *Ch. Doisy-Daëne,* well situated between *Ch. Climens* and *Ch. Coutet,* is a 14-hectare property making 4,000 cases of wine that has shown marked improvement in recent years. Until recently the wine was anything but distinguished and rarely sweet. Today it is made in a modern style—fresh, sweet, stylish, and with less than one year of wood-aging. A dry white called "Doisy-Daëne Sec," made from Sémillon, Sauvignon Blanc, Chardonnay, and Riesling, is most interesting, with quite a future if the owner wishes to pursue this new style. Also produced is a stylish, well balanced and flavored red wine called "Chantegril." *Ch. Doisy-Védrines,* located in the southernmost area of Barsac, is a 30-hectare property producing 4,500 cases of traditional but unspectacular Barsac. Although inconsistency is a major problem, the wine is often elegant, and in exceptional years it is very full and rich with the capacity to last beyond fifteen years. The property also makes a substantial red wine called "Ch. Latour-Védrines" (this wine now accounts for 20 percent of total output) made from 60 percent Merlot and 20 percent each of Cabernet Sauvignon and Cabernet Franc. A dry white, made from 100 percent Sauvignon Blanc, is known as "Chevalier de Vedrines." *Ch. Doisy-Dubroca,* the smallest of the classified growths of Barsac, contains less than 4 hectares of vineland that produce 1,500 cases of light, undistinguished wine. Although the wine appears to be made by traditional practices and is aged in wood for two years, it is no better than average, and often thin and overly acidic. *Ch. Suau,* a 7-hectare property located immediately south of the town of Barsac, makes 1,500 cases of good, and often, spectacular wine. It is one of the few Barsacs that is literally impossible to find, as most is sold to restaurants, private clients, or at the property. *Ch. Roumieu* is a 14-hectare estate producing 3,000 cases annually. This Bourgeois growth, considered one of the leading nonclassified estates, does not appear to have the financial viability to make old-fashioned, concentrated wine for a market that no longer demands a sweet wine. As a consequence, yields have increased, and although the wine is acceptable and technically flawless, it lacks the consistency and levels of concentration required of top-flight Barsacs.

Ch. Padouën is an 11-hectare property making 2,100 cases. Dating back to the early 18th century, the property has recently been purchased and rejuvenated by the Australian Len Evans. The quality has been upgraded, and it is a property to watch. *Ch. Piada-Clos du Roy,* a 27-hectare property, makes 3,000 cases of unexciting wine in most years, but above-average libations in good vintages. An unusual dry white called "Clos du Roy," made from a combination of Sauvignon Blanc and Riesling, seems to offer better financial possibilities than the traditional sweet wine of the region. *Ch. Cantegril* is a well-managed 20-hectare property making 4,600 cases of average appellation-quality wine. It claims second-growth status because it was once part of *Ch. Myrat.* Other properties are *Ch. Roumieu-Lacoste* (a well-maintained 15-hectare property that makes 2,000 cases), *Ch. Liot* (a large 38-hectare property that makes 8,000 cases of flavorful, well-flavored wine) offering outstanding value, *Ch. Guiteronde-du-Hayot* (a 25-hectare property making 7,000 cases of above-average-quality wine), *Ch. Pernaud* (a recently improved 20-hectare property that makes 4,000 cases of fresh tasting, fragrant, and stylish wine), *Ch. de Ménota* (a 16-hectare property producing 3,500 cases of average-quality wine); *Ch. du Mayne* (a 13-hectare property making 2,000 cases of excellent but not overly sweet wine, offering good value), *Ch. Simon* (a 10-hectare property making 1,800 cases of good, respectable Barsac), *Ch. Gravas* (a 26-hectare property well situated in the middle of the producing region, making 2,000 cases of average-quality wine); *Ch. de Rolland* (a 20-hectare property making 4,000 cases of average-quality wine).

Located south of Barsac, the large village of Preignac is the most physically varied of the five communes in the Sauternes appellation. It has *palus* soils along the Garonne, alluvial material along the Ciron, heavy gravel in the south, light sand and gravel in the west, and light gravel/soil material in the northeastern section. The commune contains 558 hectares of vineland, one first growth, two second growths, and more than fifty assorted properties, of which forty produce fewer than 1,000 cases annually. The commune's main growth is *Ch. Suduiraut,* a large 200-hectare estate making 12,500 cases. Despite its size and magnificent chateau, the wine, before recent years, was notoriously inconsistent, often lacking depth and sweetness, and outrageously overpriced. While prices at present have remained high, the wine is now more concentrated in extract, the color is deeper, and the flavor and bouquet are more expansive, in keeping with its first-growth status. Small quantities of red wine are produced under the "Ch. Castelnau" label.

Ch. de Malle, located on clay and gravel soil, is a beautiful, immaculate 54-hectare property currently making 5,400 cases of above-average wine worthy of its second-growth status. The vineyard has recently been replanted, and the facilities refurbished. The wine, despite lengthy wood-aging, remains fruity, is consistently well made, early maturing, and semi-sweet in character to accommodate contemporary tastes. The property also makes 6,500 cases of red wine, called "Ch. de Cardaillan," and 3,500 cases of a dry white wine, called "Chevalier de Malle," the latter made principally from Sauvignon Blanc. *Ch. Gilette* is a small but highly individualistic property making, but not bottling, its wine for twenty years or more. The wines are sweet, well made, and concentrated in extract, flavor, and bouquet. It is surprising that it is not as expensive as most classified growths. The wines of this property are not to be missed by those who love, understand, and appreciate well-aged Sauternes. Output is less than 3,000 cases.

Ch. Bastor-Lamontagne, a little-known property of 41 hectares, has long made above-average wine equal to the best second growths. Although not as refined and classy as the better-known properties, this well-managed property, owned by a financial corporation, offers excellent value. Output is approximately 9,800 cases. *Ch. Haut-Bergerson,* overlapping into Sauternes and Bommes, is a 20-hectare property making fewer than 2,500 cases of interesting and distinctive wine. Whatever this property lacks in repute it more than makes up in its production of full-bodied, luscious, well-structured libations with incredible fragrance and flavor. *Ch. St.-Amand* is a 20-hectare property located north of Preignac along the south bank of the Ciron. Made with a relatively large percentage of Sauvignon Blanc, this well-made wine is rarely encountered because a good portion of output is regularly sold to a prominent negociant. The distinctive and interesting wine is worth searching for; annual production is 4,000 cases. *Dne. d'Arche-Pugneau* is a newly improved 15-hectare property making 2,000 cases of good but unspectacular wine. *Ch. Voigny,* a greatly expanded property of 35 hectares, is currently making 5,500 cases widely available in the United States. Although much lighter in body, with little or no *botrytis* flavor, than second-growth properties, the wine appears to be consistently well made and offers good value. *Ch. du Mayne* is a recently improved and expanded property that makes 2,000 cases of good, sound wine. *Ch. du Pick,* a 23-hectare property, makes 2,600 cases of light, well-flavored, early maturing wine. Two other, smaller properties with a good local reputation are *Ch. les Remparts* and *Ch. Veyres.*

The village of Fargues, located east of Sauternes, contains 196 hectares of vineland, three classed and 30 additional properties, twenty-four of which produce the equivalent of fewer than 1,000 cases annually. Fargues lies on a hill along the right bank of a small stream of the same name. The entire commune, except for the forested and flatter northern portion, is quite hilly and is composed of clay and limestone soils with scattered gravel. The principal properties: *Ch. Rieussec* is a large property of 75 hectares producing 13,000 cases. Located on the same hill as *Ch. d'Yquem,* it is widely considered one of the top five growths in the appellation. The hill, of gravel and sand resting on sandstone, has high porosity and very dry soil conditions. Both sweet and dry wines, while highly variable in the past, have been more consistent in recent years. Characterized by rich flavors and outstanding balance, the wine is fruity, distinctive, long on the finish, with exceptional depth of flavor and fragrance. Except for fewer sortings, the wine is very traditional and often offers excellent value. In exceptional years, it can be magnificent, maturing only after fifteen to twenty years. The second label is *Clos Labere. Ch. de Fargues,* owned by *Ch. d'Yquem,* is a 10-hectare property currently making 2,000 cases of fine, delicate wine that is variable in average, but outstanding in excellent, vintages. This old 15th-century estate has a bright future under the able direction of its new owner. *Ch. Romer-du-Hayot,* with 62 hectares, makes more than 3,500 cases of non-oaky wine, the larger and finer of the two Romers. Recently improved, the wine is now more consistent than in the past—fresh, fruity, and early maturing. *Ch. Romer,* with a modest country house located in the northern portion of Fargues near *Ch. de Malle,* is a 14-hectare property making fewer than 1,200 cases of good, but not exceptional, sweet wine. *Ch. Barbier* is a 6-hectare property making 1,300 cases of good, sound, appellation-quality wine. As proprietors of *Ch. du Juge* in Cadillac, the owners are well known in the production of sweet wine.

Sauternes is a village of less than 600 inhabitants, 415 hectares of vineland, six classified growths, and twenty other properties, more than half of which make less than 900 cases annually. The soils along the Ciron River are humid and heavy with sand, but the slopes contain varying mixtures of clay and gravel, with many properties having iron-bearing gravel, a feature peculiar only to this area. The principal property and the most celebrated in the entire appellation is *Ch. d'Yquem,* a large 173-hectare estate (of which 120 are planted in vines) producing between 6,000 and 7,000 cases of absolutely marvelous wine. Considered the apotheosis of fine, sweet white wine, it commands extraordinary high prices and is unquestionably one of the premier wine estates in the world. The turreted medieval chateau and the surrounding vineyards are sited on a modest hill of 75 meters with excellent drainage. This superlative property rarely makes bad wine; it is full-bodied and has a beautiful color and a disposition that does not allow it to mature before its twentieth birthday, and often beyond. Grapes are not picked unless absolutely ripe, and then one by one, hence the high prices. Yields are the lowest in the

Plate 12.1   Ch. d'Yquem and its vineyards

appellation (between 5 and 10 hectoliters to the hectare), and the wine, although expensive, is worth the asking price. Not only is the wine most concentrated in flavor, highest in glycerine, and the silkiest in texture of any estate in Sauternes, but it is highly consistent, the product of dedicted fastidiousness and expertise. Small quantities of dry white wine made from equal amounts of Sémillon and Sauvignon Blanc are also made and labeled "Y".

Ch. Raymond-Lafon, a recently rehabilitated 15-hectare property located next to *Ch. d'Yquem,* makes 1,500 cases of very rich, unctuous wine that offers outstanding value. *Ch. Guiraud,* located on a minor hill south of *Ch. d'Yquem,* is a large 118-hectare property making 10,000 cases. Known as *Ch. Bayle* at the time of the 1855 classification, the property lapsed into disrepair after World War I, until the present Canadian owner, Frank Narby, purchased it in 1981. Progress during the past six years has been spectacular, and the wine, as a consequence, has improved enormously. Although not yet up to its potential, the wine is big, honeyed, and well above average. The estate also makes a good red wine from 15 hectares (50 percent Cabernet Sauvignon, 25 percent Malbec, and the remainder Cabernet Franc and Merlot) labeled "Pavillon Rouge de Ch. Guiraud." The dry white wine is labeled "Pavillon Sec de Ch. Guiraud."

Ch. Filhot, a 55-hectare property located in the extreme southern portion of the commune, produces 8,400 cases. Once belonging to the president of the Bordeaux parliament, it is an immaculate property with an aristocratic ambience. Today it is probably the best of the "new" style of Sauternes—early maturing, fruity, not overly sweet, light-bodied, palate-cleansing, and eminently refreshing. The wine, not aged in wood and neither elegant nor rich, is highly reliable. The estate also makes a good dry white called "Grand Vin Sec du Ch. Filhot." *Ch. d'Arche,* a 36-hectare property located on good gravel soil just north of the village of Sauternes, makes 4,500 cases of full, robust, concentrated wine that is inconsistent, but which in fine vintages can be exceptional. In those rare years, the estate ferments select quantities in wood, producing highly concentrated and well-flavored wine. *Ch. Lamothe* (Despujols) is an 8-hectare property that make 1,500 cases of light-bodied, early maturing, highly reliable wine that offers good value. *Ch. Lamothe* (Guignard) is an 11-hectare property located west of the village of Sauternes overlooking the Ciron. Despite its admirable location, the wine is unpretentious, rarely seen, and not up to second-growth-quality standards. Output is about 2,200 case.

The small village of Bommes, located north of Sauternes, contains 307 hectares of vineland, six classified growths, and thirty-six additional properties, thirty of which make fewer than one thousand cases of wine annually. The entire commune, composed of three hills, is drained by the Ciron. The soil, a variable mixture of pure gravel, sand, and clay, lies on top of a very hard and impermeable clayish subsoil. Lacking the element of austerity found in most Barsacs, the wines are plummy and smooth with few rough edges. The principal property, *Ch. Lafaurie-Peyraguey,* a 35-hectare property well situated in the center portion of the commune, makes 5,000 cases of reliable, well made, medium-bodied wine that often falls short of first-growth standards. As with all Cordier vineyards and wines, this 13th-century estate, one of the most beautiful and interesting in the area, is well managed. The technically flawless wine has recently been improved and, since it is moderately priced, offers excellent value. *Ch. Sigalas-Rabaud,* a 14-hectare property magnificiently situated on top of one of the highest hills in the area, makes 3,000 cases. Despite soils heavily impregnated with clay, the wine, not as dark, woody, or heavy on the palate as it once was, is now made in a lighter, more refreshing, less-sweet style. It often offers good value in above-average vintages. *Ch. Rayne-Vigneau* is a magnificent 90-hectare property situated on one of the most-spectacular exposures in all Sauternes. It produces 17,000 cases of good, light-bodied wine that is not only early maturing, but loosely knit, often flavorless, and lacking that special touch of sweetness to make it feel rich and substantial on the palate. The dry wine, called "Ch. Rayne-Vigneau Sec," is made principally from Sauvignon Blanc and appears to be the better of the two. *Ch. Clos Haut-Peyraguey,* a slightly smaller estate than its neighbors, makes 2,800 cases of light, not overly sweet, early maturing wine. Despite its excellent exposure on one of the highest hills in the commune, the quality of the wine in recent years has lacked complexity, and, on occasion, has been overly acidic.

Ch. la Tour-Blanche is a 65-hectare estate situated on a hill with well-drained soils that just begs for expert guidance. The Ministry of Agriculture, which keeps the property as a training school, has not maintained the illustrious reputation of the 19th century when it was considered second only to *Ch. d'Yquem.* The wine today, made in a modern, early maturing style lacking concentration and intensity, is light in color and not overly sweet. Although it lacks the elegance and consistency of a first growth, the wine is fresh, quite drinkable, and not overpriced. *Ch. Rabaud-Promis,* located next to Ch. Sigalas-Rabaud and well situated on the northernmost gravel bank in the commune, is a 30-hectare estate making 7,400 cases. Highly variable, the wine is light-bodied and early maturing. Two other properties of note are *Ch. Haut-Bommes* and *Ch. Mauras,* the latter making 4,000 cases of firm, full-bodied wine.

13

THE WINES OF ENTRE-DEUX-MERS

THE geographic region of Entre-Deux-Mers is a triangular peninsula bounded by the Dordogne on the north, the Garonne on the south, and the departments of Dordogne and Lot-et-Garonne along the eastern and southeastern margins. It measures 60 kilometers wide in the south, and from the northern tip near Ambès to the department of Lot-et-Garonne it is 110 kilometers long. With 42,000 hectares of vines, this large vineyard encompasses 46 percent of the viticultural landscape of the Gironde department, produces more than half of its wine, and more than three-quarters of all white wine. (The name is both a geographical entity and an appellation.) While the area contained more than 90,000 hectares before the *phylloxera* epidemic, the intensity of viticulture has diminished over the past 100 years: hectarage had been reduced to 60,000 by 1925 and to 49,000 by 1960, with further declines expected in the coming decades. Today it is an area of mixed agriculture with a number of specialties: horse and cattle breeding, vines, orchards, and garden crops.

Soils vary from alluvial accumulations along the floodplains to pure gravel, clay, and sand in scattered locations throughout the peninsula. Limestone is found only along the hilly north bank of the Garonne from Cénon to St.-Macaire. In general, valleys are given to cereal and animal husbandry, while the mild slopes containing limestone and gravel are covered with vineyards. The gravelly soils of Graves de Vayres and the limestone/clay uplands of the Premières Côtes de Bordeaux appellations appear to be the best areas for the production of red wines. The largest concentrations of limestone and gravel are found in Cadillac, Loupiac, and Ste.-Croix-du-Mont—three areas known for the production of sweet and semi-sweet white wines. More than half the vine hectarage of Entre-Deux-Mers is devoted to the production of inexpensive red, white, and rosé, and is the source of more than three-quarters of all wine sold under the regional banners of Bordeaux and Bordeaux Supérieur. Of the more than 2.5 million hectoliters produced annually, fewer than 500,000 are considered good enough to be labeled as above the generic designation.

Only the central region of the peninsula is allowed to produce dry white wine under the appellation name of Entre-Deux-Mers. While its boundaries were delimited in 1924, not until 1953 was the Entre-Deux-Mers appellation restricted to white wine whose residual sugar content is

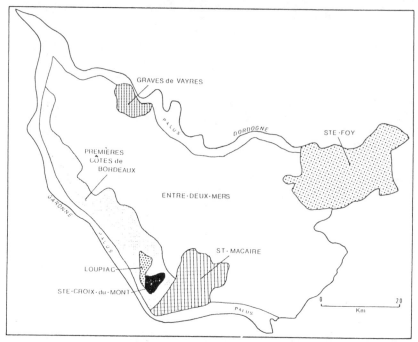

Figure 13.1   The AOC Appellations of Entre-Deux-Mers

less than 4 grams per liter. The recent but rarely used "Bordeaux Blanc Sauvignon" appellation is expected to become an important presence in the 1990s.

Although white wine production has been declining for the past forty years, red wine has been increasing but is not allowed to be officially classified as Entre-Deux-Mers. Less than 30 percent of the total red wine output is sold under the Premières Côtes du Bordeaux, Haut-Benauge, and Graves de Vayres appellations. Sold only as plain Bordeaux or Bordeaux Supérieur, the wine must contain at least 10 percent alcohol, and the yield is restricted to 50 hectoliters to the hectare. While technically sound and clean on the palate, the wines lack body, flavor, and aroma and offer little value.

The decidedly better white wines are now made drier than in the recent past. Mainly used in the production of generic Bordeaux, they are light in color and body, with a pleasant flavor and scent. Since the wines do not convey a prestigious image, they are widely sold as shippers' blends in 1.5 and 3 liter bottles. The principal varieties are Sémillon, Sauvignon Blanc, and Muscadelle, followed by four "lesser" grapes: Merlot Blanc, Colombard, Mauzac, and Ugni Blanc. Although variations exist, the usual mix of the encépagement is between 50 to 70 percent Sémillon and Muscadelle, with progressively smaller amounts of Merlot Blanc, Colombard,

Mauzac, and Ugni Blanc. Recently the trend has been to reduce the percentage of Mauzac, Colombard, Ugni Blanc, and Sémillon and to increase the amount of Sauvignon Blanc. In an attempt to regain former markets, vinification and distribution methods have improved radically over the past several decades. Cold fermentation in stainless steel, now standard practice, produces fresher, fruitier, and more fragrant wines; as a result, the area has attracted the attention of large negociant houses. Sovicop-Producta, for example, a holding company for several large cooperatives, is responsible for more than one-fifth of the peninsula's entire output of wine.

Of the more than 100 communes in the appellation, twenty-three collectively contain more than 12,000 hectares of vineland. The three largest communes are Sauveterre-de-Guyenne, Blasimon, and St.-Germain-du-Puch. While there has been a dramatic increase in size of average holdings, estate-bottled wine is rare, as most is made, bottled, and distributed by seventeen large cooperatives. The principal growths: In Ambares, the major property is *Ch. du Gua.* In St.-Loubès the major properties are *Ch. de Reignac* and *Dne. des Valentons-Canteloup.* The village of Beychac-et-Caillou is known for three properties with a good reputation for white and red wines: *Ch. la France, Ch. Quinsac,* and *Ch. Lesparre. Ch. Lamothe* is the principal growth in La Sauve, *Ch. de Camarsac* in Carmarsac, *Ch. Vieil-Hermitage* in Genissac, *Ch. du. Grand-Puch* and *Ch. Jonqueyres* in St.-Germain-du-Puch, *Ch. Arromans* in Moulon, *Ch. de Martouret* in Nérigean, and *Ch. Bonnet* and *Ch. Reynier* are two excellent growths in Grézillac. In the medieval town of Réole, the important and energetic negociant/grower firm of *Yvon Mau* has pioneered a new breed of Entre-Deux-Mers wines in foreign markets. It also owns the good, modest-sized *Ch. Ducla* in the village of St.-Exupéry. Soussac is the site of the excellent *Ch Launay* and the much smaller *Ch. Vrai-Caillou. Ch. de Goélane* (St.-Léon), *Ch. le Gay* (St.-Sulpice). *Ch. Canet* (Guillac), and *Ch. Fonchereau* (Montussan) are also reliable.

Premières Côtes de Bordeaux

Located on the right bank of the Garonne River, the Premières Côtes de Bordeaux appellation extends from the northern outskirts of the medieval village of Cénon in the north to St.-Maixant in the south. It is an area of many castles, country mansions, and historical monuments. In the southern portion it surrounds the two separate enclaves of Loupiac and Ste.-Croix-du-Mont.

Stretching for 60 kilometers, the producing district is very hilly with good, deep friable soils and a large number of microclimates. Located below the hillcrests on southerly and southwesterly aspects overlooking the Garonne, the best sites contain gravel and limestone soils. Downslope sites containing more clay and less stone and gravel are less good for the production of quality wine. The Garonne floodplain with its *palus* soils has little extensive vine cultivation.

While the cultivation of vines and the production of wine has continued in an uninterrupted manner since Roman times, this region's reputation for red, rosé, and white wine production has always been overshadowed by the more-famous names across the river. Historically, the unbottled wines were sold in bulk to Bordeaux negociants for use in blending their regional house styles. The red wines, known for their dark color and fruity bouquet, had limited appeal. More widely known than today, white wines, mostly semi-sweet and sweet, dominated production. They were popularly called "Vins de Côtes," and the red wines of the southern portion were confusingly labled as "Vins de St.-Macaire."

The appellation was officially defined in the late 1930s, but it required an in-migration of *pied noirs* (French immigrants) from Algeria in the 1960s to rekindle interest in the viticultural potential of the region. The *pied noirs* expanded estate-bottled wine, increased the hectarage from fewer than 4,000 hectares to more than 6,300, and publicized their product with a large measure of success. As a result, all wines have shown dramatic improvement in quality in recent years. See Figure 13.2 for production of red Premières Côte de Bordeaux.

The red, while coarse, has body and is well colored, flavored, and scented. It is becoming very popular and now accounts for more than half of total appellation output. Made from a variable mixture of Merlot Rouge, Malbec, Cabernet Franc, and Cabernet Sauvignon, it must contain at least 10.5 percent alcohol and the yield be limited to 40 hectoliters to the hectare. The wines sell well in the United Kingdom, West Germany, Holland, and Belgium, and are becoming fashionable with restaurants and tourists. The wine is good, technically sound, early

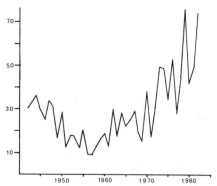

Figure 13.2   Premières Côtes de Bordeaux: Wine Production,
1940–1983
(in thousands of hectoliters)

maturing, and fresh on the palate; it can offer considerable value. The very best can age as long as eight years. While wood-aging is rare, prolonged skin contact is a standard feature, and the largest producers are increasingly interested in carbonic maceration.

White wine, made principally from Sémillon, Sauvignon Blanc, and Muscadelle, must have 11.5 percent alcohol and, as of 1981, a minimum of 4 grams of sugar per liter. The appellation produces more than 270,000 hectoliters of wine, of which less than half is allowed the Premières Côtes de Bordeaux designation. In general, red wines are produced in the northern section and white in the southern. The most important communes in the northern part include Quinsac, Cénac, Yvrac, and Ste.-Eulalie. The principal vinegrowing communes in the more-important southern portion include Cadillac, Gabarnac, St.-Maixant, Verdelais, Monprimblanc, St.-Germain-de-Grave, Béguey, Omet, Laroque, Rions, Cardan, Lestiac-sur-Garonne, Langoiran, Capian, and Haux.

Quinsac, with more than 215 hectares of vineland, is the principal wine-producing village of the northern portion, the home of the only cooperative and four above-average growths. *Ch. de Roquebert,* a 16-hectare estate with an excellent reputation, makes full-bodied, deeply colored red wine; *Ch. Bel-Air,* owned by the Borie family, makes soft, supple red and white wines; *Ch. Montaigne,* an old 18th-century property, makes full-bodied, well-structured red wine; and *Ch. Péconnet,* known for reliable white and red wines. The principal growths in the village of Camblanes-et-Meynac: *Dne. Pasquier* is widely considered one of the finest properties in the appellation; and *Ch. Lafitte, Ch. du Tasta, Ch. Brethous,*

Plate 13.1   The medieval walls of Cadillac

and *Dne. de Chastelet* all produce fruity, early maturing, light-bodied red wines. Yvrac, second to Quinsac in importance, contains 214 hectares of vineland and four important properties: *Dne. de Mirefleurs* is a large property making full-bodied, dark, tannin-rich red wine; *Dne. de Bouteilley,* dating back to the 17th century, is a large estate known for well-balanced, somewhat refined, well-flavored and scented wine; and *Ch. Lafitte-Laguens* and *Ch. Maillard* make light-bodied, fruity, early maturing wines.

South of Cambes, the wines change to white and are mainly semi-sweet. The production area includes twenty-one communes that collectively constitute about 80 percent of all hectarage in the Premières Côtes de Bordeaux appellation. The sweetest wines originating in the commune of Cadillac and surrounding areas are marketed under the semi-official designation "Cadillac." It is important to note that due to sluggish sweet wine sales, nearly all the important properties produce red wine.

The village of Baurech contains four important growths: *Ch. la Roche, Ch. Champcenetz, Ch. Gaussens,* and *Ch. de Beau-Rivage.* The small village of Tabanac is known for *Ch. Lagarosse, Ch. Bessan, Ch. la Clyde,* and *Ch. Lamothe.* The important village of Haux, situated on high ground north of Langoiran, contains the important growths of *Ch. Lamothe, Ch. Grava,* and *Ch. du Juge.* Overlooking the Garonne, the strategically located medieval village of Langoiran contains 400 hectares of vineland and three important growths: *Ch. du Biac, Ch. du Vallier,* and *Ch. Laurétan.* The latter, owned by the Cordier negociant firm, is a large 100-hectare property that also markets its wines under the *Ch. Tanesse* and *Ch. Gardera* labels.

Capian, with 514 hectares of vineland, is the largest wine commune in the appellation. *Ch. du Peyrat* and *Ch. de Caillavet* are the two best-known properties. In the village of Béguey, the two principal growths are *Ch. Reynon-Peyrat* and *Ch. Birot.* Lying along the northern borders of Loupiac and Cadillac, the hamlet of Omet contains two important properties, *Dne. de Poncet* and *Ch. la Bertrande,* known for the finest semi-sweet and dry wines of the appellation. Adjoining Loupiac, the important and charming town of Cadillac is known for the finest semi-sweet white wines of the appellation. The commune contains nearly 400 hectares of vineland and five above-average growths with the right to market their white wines under the communal name: *Ch. du Juge* (an 18,000 case property making outstanding, early maturing white wine), *Ch. Fayau* (a 38-hectare property known for reliability), *Ch. la Ferreyre* (a small but excellent producer), *Ch. Arnaud-Jouan* (large and consistent), and *Dne. de St.-Martin* (one of the oldest properties, offering considerable value). The village of St.-Maixant, the southernmost producing commune of the appellation, is known for three excellent growths: *Ch. Labatut, Ch. la Prioulette,* and *Ch. Malagar.*

Bordeaux Haut-Benauge

The 3,000-hectare Haut-Benauge vineyard is located east of the Premières Côtes de Bordeaux appellation. The area is heavily wooded, subject to frost, and dominated by the historic 13th-century Ch. Benauge. While the soils resemble those of Premières Côtes du Bordeaux, they contain less calcareous material and more clay, and are decidedly more productive. Nearly two-thirds of total output is white wine, the best being fresh, pleasant on the palate, and dry rather than semi-sweet. Although the bulk of production is marketed under generic Bordeaux designations, the best, when the yield is limited to 45 hectoliters to the hectare and when 70 percent or more of the encépagement consists of Sémillon, Sauvignon Blanc, and Muscadelle, is sold under the little-known name of Bordeaux-Haut-Benauge, a semi-official appellation. Although white wines dominate output, the finest wines are the recently much-improved reds.

The appellation is composed of nine communes, of which Soulignac, Targon, Ladaux, and Escoussans contribute more than 80 percent of the appellation's hectarage. While the bulk of growers are mostly part-time farmers owning fewer than 5 hectares, the tendency over the past thirty years is for increased farm consolidation. The principal properties are *Ch. Toutigeac, Ch. Pargade, Ch. Grand-Jean, Ch. Haut-Marchand, Ch. de Beauregard,* and *Ch. Martinon.*

Graves de Vayres

Graves de Vayres is situated on the northern portion of Entre-Deux-Mers along a bend of the Dordogne River, opposite Libourne and Fronsac. As the name suggests, this section of Entre-Deux-Mers contains large accumulations of gravel instead of the usual mix of clay and sand; as a consequence, the wines are marginally better than neighboring areas. Of the 1,000 hectares of vineland, approximately 450 (300 planted in white and 150 in red grapes) are considered good enough to carry the Graves de Vayres appellation name, or 20,000 out of the 50,000 hectoliters of wine produced annually. The two principal producing communes are Vayres and Arveyres, and despite the area's obvious physical advantages, hectarage has been reduced by half since 1945. Because of its supple, fleshy character, beautiful color, and fruity flavor, the red is widely acknowledged to be superior to the white. The latter, often too sweet and unbalanced, is not the equal of other producing regions and, as a consequence, is declining in importance.

Although wines were sold under the name of Graves de Vayres in the 19th century (official AOC status was granted in 1937), the area's growers did not make a determined effort to market their wines under the legal banner until 1966. The official requirements for white wine production set a minimum alcohol content of 10.5 percent and limit grapes to Sémillon, Sauvignon Blanc, Muscadelle, and Merlot Blanc, each with a maximum of 30 percent. Red grape varieties, not restricted by percentage, include Cabernet Sauvignon, Cabernet Franc, Merlot Rouge, Malbec, Carmenère, and Petit Verdot. While the minimum alcohol content is the same as for white wine, the yield is reduced from 43 to 40 hectoliters to the hectare. The principal properties include *Ch. Bel-Air, Ch. de Barre, Ch. Juncarret, Ch. Goudichaud, Ch. Gayat, Ch. du Lau, Ch. Tillède, Ch. Pichon-Bellevue,* and *Ch. Pontete-Bellegrave.*

Ste.-Croix-du-Mont and Loupiac

Ste.-Croix-du-Mont and Loupiac are two wine-producing enclaves of the long and diverse Premières Côtes de Bordeaux appellation. Collectively they contain 1,000 hectares of vineland and produce nearly 50,000 hectoliters of wine a year, half of which is entitled to the appellation names of Ste.-Croix-du-Mont and Loupiac. Dry white and red wines can be sold only under the two generic Bordeaux appellation names.

These two small appellations, lying on a series of hills composed of limestone and fossilized oyster shells (the latter more common in Ste.-Croix-du-Mont than in Loupiac), face Barsac and Sauternes across the Garonne. The best sites lie near the Garonne on low but steep hills with well-drained soils that contain limestone.

Historically, both were known for semi-sweet and sweet white wines much in the style of their more-famous neighbors across the river, but in general the wines are lighter in body, and less concentrated, balanced, and flavorful. Occasionally they do reach heights that rival Monbazillac and the lesser wines of Barsac and Sauternes. They are considerably better than the wines of Ste.-Foy and St.-Macaire and usually outperform those from Cadillac. At their best, they are supple, mellow, and improve in bottle for several years; but at their worse, they tend to be dark, light in body and concentration, overly sulfured, and lack *botrytized* flavor. Although the best estates do use small quantities of grapes blessed by *botrytis*, multiple pickings rarely occur, and as a result the wines are less intense in flavor, color, scent, and balance than in years past. A number of properties, able to afford the expense, maintain one or two hectares of very old Sémillon grapes and manage to produce wine that approaches the quality of middle-level Sauternes. Although the very best producers wood-age for as long as eighteen months prior to bottling, the wines rarely offer value except in the producing region.

The appellations have been in an economic crisis since the early 1930s when fashion began to shift from sweet to dry white wines. As a result, hectarage has steadily declined from more than 2,675 hectares in 1926 to 1,064 in 1983, a development that is not hard to understand. Market shrinkage has also been aggravated by depressed local economic conditions. The region contains few cities and, unable to hold its youthful population, it has become an area of chronic outmigration. Over the past seventy years, half the properties have changed ownership, 1,600 hectares have gone out of cultivation, and the slopes containing the finest vineyards have largely been abandoned due to the lack of available manpower. Today there are fewer than thirty full-time growers, and thirty more cultivate under the *métayage* (sharecropping) system on a part-time basis. The remaining 100 small growers are strictly weekend vinegrowers. The only cooperative, located in Ste.-Croix-du-Mont, ceased production in 1972. Apparently the only road to economic solvency is to sell direct (50 to 60 percent of all sales), an activity that is considered the largest underground economy in the region. The remainder is sold to negociants to make house blends or who act as shippers for château-bottled wine, exporting it mainly to Belgium, Holland, and the United Kingdom.

To accommodate the prevailing fashion for drier white and red table wines, red grapes are replacing white, Sémillon and Muscadelle are declining, and Sauvignon Blanc is increasing. As a result, an ever-increasing amount of production is vinified into dry white and red (50 percent), a development that is threatening the historical raison d'être of the two appellations. Holding stable since 1945, combined production varies between 15,000 and 35,000 hectoliters annually.

Vine cultivation in the commune of Ste.-Croix-du-Mont is quite intensive, since 60 percent of all arable land is devoted to grapegrowing. Of the 107 growers cultivating the 549 hectares, only fifteen produce more than 5,000 cases of wine, while twenty-five produce less than 1,000 (see Fig. 13.3). One of the two best sites is concentrated on the edge of the bluff overlooking the Garonne north and south of the town of Ste.-Croix; the second and the more important (it contains the largest accumulation of limestone in the producing area) lies in an irregular line on the plateau east of the town. The principal properties: *Ch. Bel-Air,* a 20-hectare property situated on high ground, is known for supple, well-balanced wine; *Ch. Loubens,* a beautiful 16th-century property, is considered the standard in the appellation; *Ch. de Tastes,* with an imposing, medieval castle, is known for small quantities of fragrant wine; *Ch. la Rame* is a recently improved and highly reliable property; *Dne. de*

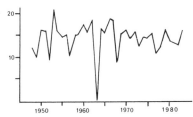

Figure 13.3   Ste.-Croix-du-Mont: Wine Production, 1948–1983
(in thousands of hectoliters)

Morange, a 17-hectare property, enjoys an excellent reputation; and *Ch. Lousteau-Vieil* is an excellent 10-hectare property making expensive wine. Other properties include *Ch. Crabitan-Bellevue, Ch. Crabitan, Ch. la Grave, Ch. des Mailles, Ch. de l'Escaley, Ch. de Verthueil, Ch. les Marcottes, Ch. Laurette, Ch. Lamarque, Ch. Roustit, Ch. du Mont, Ch. Laborie, Ch. Coulac, Ch. du Pavillon, Ch. Bertranon,* and *Ch. Bouchoc.*

Slightly smaller than Ste.-Croix-du-Mont, Loupiac, with 515 hectares of vineland, makes approximately 10,000 hectoliters of sweet white wine annually. Although the wines are somewhat less rich than those of Ste.-Croix-du-Mont, the appellation has an impressive history and a number of large estates with an international reputation. Of the sixty-eight growers in the appellation, eighteen make less than 1,000 cases, and only five, more than 10,000 cases. The best sites are located on high ground north and south of the town of Loupiac. The principal properties: *Ch. Ricaud,* dating from the 9th century, is one of the oldest and largest estates in the region. In addition to a dry wine made principally from Sauvignon Blanc, production includes an excellent, well-made, highly concentrated sweet wine made almost entirely from Sémillon. *Ch. Dauphine-Rondillon,* a well-managed property in the north-central plateau makes white and red wines. *Ch. Loupiac-Gaudiet,* a 12th-century property located on high ground, makes fresh, zesty sweet wine without Muscadelle. *Ch. Mazarin* dates from the 16th century and makes light-bodied wines. *Clos Jean* and *Ch. du Cros* are old properties that make solid and reliable sweet and dry wine. Other properties include *Ch. du Vieux-Moulin, Ch. la Nère, Ch. de la Yotte, Ch. Barbe-Maurin, Domaine du Noble, Ch. le Portail-Rouge, Ch. le Moyne, Ch. de Rouquette,* and *Ch. Miqueu Bel-Air.*

Bordeaux-St.-Macaire

Taking its name from the medieval walled town overlooking the Garonne River, St.-Macaire represents the southernmost appellation in Entre-Deux-Mers. Of the ten communes that comprise the sizable 2,300-hectare vineyard, four—St.-Macaire, St.-Pierre-d'Aurillac, St.-Martin-de-Sescas, and Caudrot—are arranged on a series of parallel hills along the Garonne; the rest are scattered inland amid woodland clearings. The best sites are the limestone bluffs near the Garonne and the dispersed, well-drained interior knolls. The high incidence of frost and the unpopularity of white sweet wine caused more than half of all vineland to be replaced by fruit orchards in the past sixty years. Approximately 40 percent of all arable land is devoted to viticulture, and the number of large properties is limited. More than two-thirds of all growers are part-time farmers, practically all of whom belong to cooperatives. The most-important producing villages and hamlets are St.-André-du-Bois, St.-Martial, St.-Laurent-du-Bois, Le Pian-sur-Garonne, and St.-Pierre-d'Aurillac.

Of the 2,300 hectares, slightly more than half are planted in red grapes whose wines are sold as plain Bordeaux. Wine to be labeled St.-Macaire must be white and made from the usual mixture of white Bordeaux varieties (a minimum of 90 percent Sémillon, Sauvignon Blanc, and Muscadelle), have 11.5 percent alcohol, and the yield be limited to 42 hectoliters to the hectare. Although considered far better than the red, the white, semi-sweet to sweet in character, is obscure in reputation and usually sold in bulk to negociants for blending purposes.

Ste.-Foy-Bordeaux

The appellation of Ste.-Foy-Bordeaux is located on the left bank of the Dordogne along the easternmost point of Entre-Deux-Mers. This white and red wine region contains 4,400 hectares and produces more than 150,000 hectoliters of wine annually, of which fewer than 10,000 hectoliters are allowed the Ste.-Foy appellation name. Of the more than twenty villages that encompass the geography of this producing region, the most important are Massugas, St.-Quentin-de-Caplong, Gensac, Pellegrue, Pineuilh, and Les Lèves-et-Thoumeyragues.

Although Ste.-Foy has been a separate appellation since 1928, its reputation has suffered because of its historic association with the semi-sweet and sweet wines of Bergerac, its next-door neighbor to the north. To suit contemporary tastes, the wines are now vinified much drier and fruitier. They are made from Sémillon, Sauvignon Blanc, and Muscadelle, with a maximum of 10 percent coming from Merlot Blanc, Mauzac, Ugni Blanc, and Colombard. The minimum alcohol content is 11 percent, and the yield is limited to 45 hectoliters to the hectare. The best sites are in scattered locations where the soil contains sufficient limestone to impart strength and flavor. At its best, the wine has a pale yellow color and a pleasant fragrance. All too often, however, the wines are flat, dull, somewhat bitter, and marred by a lack of balance.

Red wines, made from Cabernet Sauvignon, Cabernet Franc, Merlot Rouge, Malbec, and Petit Verdot, must contain a minimum of 10.5 percent alcohol. Considered secondary in quality to the white wine, they are coarse and lack finesse, flavor, and bouquet. Although the finest appellation is Ste.-Foy-Bordeaux, more than 95 percent of total output is sold under the generic Bordeaux appellation. Despite the presence of a number of large chateaux and an active land consolidation program, nearly all the wine is made by the four cooperatives in the appellation.

PART III

THE WINES OF THE SOUTHWEST

14

INTRODUCTION

THE southwestern vineyard, stretching from the southern extremities of the Massif Central to the Pyrénées Mountains, covers the whole of the ancient province of Gascony and all or part of ten departments. On the west it is flanked by the Gironde, the area with the highest concentration of AOC appellations, and along the eastern margins by Languedoc-Roussillon, the region with the largest wine production. The entire region in 1979 had 57,446 hectares in vines that produced 2.5 million hectoliters of wine, of which three-quarters was *vin ordinaire*. The area contains two major and six minor VDQS appellations producing 25,000 hectoliters, of which Côtes de Marmandais is the most important (see Fig. 14.1). There are also nine major *vin de pays* areas. Fifty-five percent of total AOC output is red wine, 4 percent is rosé, and 41 percent is white, half of which is either sweet or moelleux (mellow).

In terms of geography, the largest portion of the region is related to the solid 25-mile wall of mountains called the Pyrénées, whose rivers radiate outward toward the Bay of Biscay and the Gironde estuary. Five—the Baise, Save, Gers Gimone, and Ariège rivers—flow north to feed the Garonne, which in turn empties into the Gironde. Only the Adour, a rapidly flowing river fed by alpine waters, lies outside the Garonne drainage system. The entire region is sheltered by high mountains from rain-bearing winds, so that only a small area along the western margins of the Adour basin receives more than an average 1000 millimeters of rain per year. Precipitation is characterized by a spring maximum, with summer and fall distinguished by mild, dry weather—conditions very conducive for proper grape maturation. This ideal picture is reinforced by Foehn-type winds (hot, oppressive, and dessicating) during spring and summer, often spawning numerous thunderstorms. In late winter and early spring they melt snow and cause extensive flooding; in the fall, they encourage the formation of *botrytis cinerea*.

One-third of regional production occurs along the Tarn and Lot rivers—tributaries of the Garonne—found along the eastern edges of the producing district. This area is part of the southern margins of the Massif Central—a mass of ancient volcanic mountains alternating with rolling plateaus. The topographic feature of consequence here is the west-sloping Causse plateau. Lying on the edge of the hotter and more-arid Mediterra-

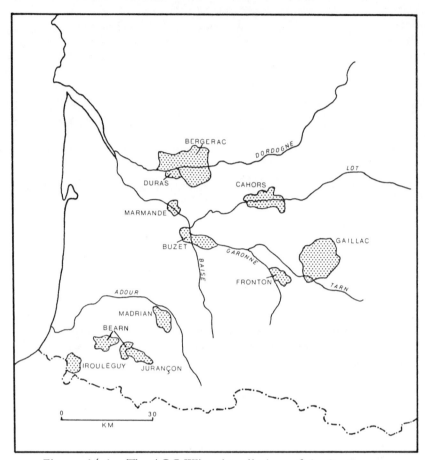

Figure 14.1   The AOC Wine Appellations of the Southwest

nean coast, this rocky and exposed limestone plateau is slightly more than 400 meters high. The numerous highland basins and river valleys between the Dordogne and Garonne rivers differ markedly in natural vegetation and economy from the hillier, more heavily forested regions of the south. This area and the Pyrénéean section are commonly referred to as the "high country."

Lying between these two mountain masses, the Garonne valley forms a corridor where the Canal du Midi links the Atlantic Ocean with the Mediterranean Sea. Along the alluvial banks of the Garonne, small quantities of insignificant wines are made. The other major river is the Dordogne, in the northern extremities of the region. It drains the western margins of the Massif Central and, along the lower portion of its course, manages to produce about 52 percent of all AOC wine in the southwest.

The southwest is a region of extensive cattle raising, mixed agriculture, and orchards. Here viticulture exhibits the greatest concentration along the lower Dordogne River, Gaillac, and Cahors. Despite its apparent opulence and present-day tranquility, a number of elements place the southwest in a category by itself. Less than 30 percent of the region is forested, and no more than 40 percent is considered suitable for commercial agriculture. Moreover, the southwest has the largest number of small and fragmented farms and the least amount of capitalization per hectare in all of metropolitan France. Toulouse and Carcasonne are the only sizable cities, and rural settlement is rather widely dispersed. The southwestern viticultural region, therefore, is not homogeneous; the wines of each district range through all shades of color and are characterized by a distinct flavor, bouquet, and aging capability. Of the thirteen major AOC appellations, Bergerac is the largest, followed by Cahors, Monbazillac, and Côtes de Bergerac.

History

A good portion of the region was settled in prehistoric times, and major Paleolithic settlements have been found in the Aveyron and Ariege river valleys. The first inhabitants known to us were the Liguri, followed by the Iberians, who came north across the Pyrénées. The entire area came under the domination of Rome in 56 B.C. For nearly 400 years after the fall of Rome, the region was an unstable frontier between Moor and Gaul, and was invaded by Visigoths, Moors, Franks, and Normans.

Located along the only main route between the Mediterranean Sea and the Atlantic, the southwest's gateway position has done little to generate economic development or political stability. Due to its relative isolation, its political and economic fortunes ebbed and flowed with the prevailing power of regional monarchs during the early Middle Ages. Albi, now the capital of the Tarn department, in the 12th century was the center of a Christian sect, the Albigenses, who were considered heretics by Rome. A crusade and a special inquisition ordered by Pope Innocent III put an end to the movement early in the 13th century. The Hundread Years' War in the 14th and 15th centuries was followed by devastating religious conflict between Catholics and Protestants in the 16th century. In 1607, Henry IV introduced some semblance of political and economic stability when he incorporated the entire region into the royal domain for the first time.

The religious wars helped to depopulate the country and thus interfered with the normal pace of economic growth and development. More than half of all towns and cities founded between 1150 and 1350 were bastide towns, so named after the Provençal word for "fortress." The counts of Toulouse founded many such bastides during the Albigensian Wars, thus giving the region a distinctive character. In a similar manner, Henry III and Edward I each created a line of bastides between the Garonne and Dordogne rivers.

Throughout this turbulent history, there were times when viticulture flourished. In 920, for example, the Archdeacon Benebert bequeathed land for vineyard development, and in the 11th century numerous Benedictine and Cistercian religious orders established extensive viticultural holdings. After the Hundred Years' War, vineyards again expanded, and wine exports became an important staple of the regional economy. As the trade quickened, the wines were hindered from reaching market by the downriver vignerons and negociants who imposed *maltotes* (illegal tolls) along the vast stretches of the Garonne and Dordogne— particularly the former. The bloody and burdersome struggles for free navigation to the Gironde lasted, in one form or another, until Napoleon put an end to the petty regional rivalries early in the 19th century.

The region's population and economic life expanded rapidly in the 17th century, only to decline early in the 18th. The Methuen Treaty of 1703 reduced the lucrative English trade until the defeat of Napoleon. Soon afterward, viticulture grew at unprecedented levels, particularly in response to British demand for full-bodied red wines. As a consequence, the wines of Cahors, Gaillac, and Madiran came to be known as *vins de medicine, vins de transport, vins de cargaison,* and *vins de conseine* because their dark color and high alcohol content amplified the feeble dimensions of Gironde "claret." By the middle of the century, the extensive vineyards of the southwest produced nearly 20 percent of all French wine, a figure never to be reached again (see Table 14.1). Thanks to *oidium* in 1855, rapid railroad construction (which gave greater economic advantages to other regions), *phylloxera,* and the feverish industrialization of the north, the vineyards of the southwest were placed in an unfavorable position. As a result, the region lagged behind the economic performance of the rest of the country, incomes fell, and economic stagnation became the order of the day.

The decline of viticulture was also caused by a long-standing history of

Table 14.1   Vine Hectarage in Southwest, Selected Years

Department	1979	1952	1935	1875	1816
Tarn-et-Garonne	6,379	20,449	23,046	39,430	25,000
Tarn	17,006	34,265	35,175	41,478	23,000
Lot-et-Garonne	8,859	32,321	37,155	75,900	60,000
Lot	4,503	11,498	13,496	63,900	40,000
Pyrénées-Atlantiques	1,812	9,428	9,712	14,780	11.000
Haute-Garonne	5,029	28,072	28,461	56,306	35,000
Dordogne	13,858	42,870	46,794	91,306	62,000
Total	57,446	178,903	193,839	383,100	256,000

Source: French Ministry of Agriculture.

excessive depopulation, leading to an aging remnant population, farm abandonment, and overall rural neglect. For nearly eighty years the region remained peripheral to the growing economic centers of the nation. The southwest had one-quarter the income of greater Paris, and the quality of health services and education was substantially less than desirable. Reflecting regional economic depression, viticulture declined from 193,839 hectares in 1935 to 57,444 in 1979.

In 1955, France created a series of development schemes to raise the levels of economic standards in the underdeveloped regions of the country. The main beneficiary regions were the Massif Central, the southwest, the Midi region of Mediterranean France, and a number of industrial centers in the north. The targets for sustained economic growth focused on the forces for urban growth, the introduction of new industries, promotion of agriculture, and improvements in the transportation network. Agricultural efficiencies have been realized through land consolidation, mechanization, establishment of cooperatives, and farmer-assistance programs. The overall effect has been to halt the deterioration in vine hectarage, to replace hybrid vines with superior stock, to improve vinification equipment and, hence, the quality of wine.

15

THE WINES OF THE SOUTHWEST

THE BERGERAC WINE-PRODUCING REGION

THE Bergerac wine region, just to the east of Castillon la Bataille, is an area of rounded, rolling hills with no sharp physical elements separating the "high country" of the interior from the alluvial plains of the Gironde. It is a region of fortresses, strongholds, castles and one major city of consequence—Bergerac (see Fig. 15.1). With 28,000 inhabitants, it is not only the largest city and the most important settlement, but is the regional center for the wine and tobacco industry (a local specialty). It owes its fame to Cyrano de Bergerac, the Hundred Years' War, and Monbazillac, the region's most famous wine.

Approximately 11,000 hectares of vines planted within AOC appellation boundaries support more than 2,500 growers, of whom more than half are part-time farmers owning fewer than 2.5 hectares of vineland.

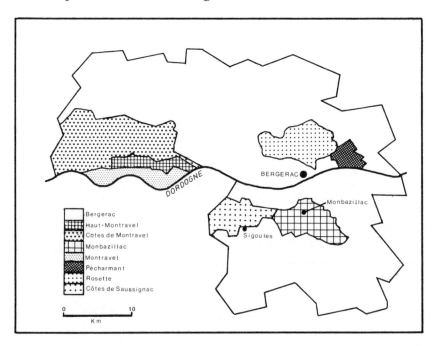

Figure 15.1 The AOC Wine Appellations of Bergerac

Table 15.1 Southwest Wine Production, 1980

Selected AOC appellation	Hectoliters	Percent of total
Bergerac Rouge	118,531	18.5
Bergerac Blanc	72,171	11.3
Côtes de Bergerac Rouge	18,666	2.9
Côtes de Bergerac Blanc	26,003	4.0
Montravel	18,832	2.9
Monbazillac	63,278	9.9
Pécharmant	5,469	.9
Côtes de Buzet Rouge	34,267	5.4
Côtes de Duras Rouge	18,475	2.9
Côtes de Duras Blanc	34,366	5.4
Cáhors Rouge	84,064	13.1
Côtes du Fronton Rouge and Blanc	33,004	5.2
Gaillac Rouge	26,190	4.1
Gaillac Blanc	28,064	4.4
Béarn Rouge	6,013	.9
Jurançon Blanc	15,109	2.4
Madiran Rouge	28,815	4.5
Other	8,011	1.3
Total	639,328	100.0

Source: French Ministry of Agriculture.

AOC wine production now exceeds more than 325,000 hectoliters, or about 50 percent of all wine made in the southwest (see Table 15.1). While viticulture dates back to Roman times, it was not until the end of the Hundred Years' War that vinegrowing and winemaking began to dominate the agricultural landscape. As in the Gironde and the lower Loire valleys, the Dutch demand for sweet white wine and *vin ordinaire* for distillation into brandy was for years a dominant element in the viticultural fortunes of the region. The viticultural outline of the region was clearly established by the middle of the 15th century; by the middle of the 18th, the wines of Bergerac came to be known as the "companion to Cyrano."

Vinegrowing prospered until the Bordeaux vignerons and shippers attempted to prevent the wines of the "high country" from being shipped through the port of Bordeaux. Bergerac was the forefront of innumerable wars, and its viticultural fortunes during the 16th and 17th centuries were long and brutal. After the elimination of the monarchy and the secularization of a good deal of ecclesiastical land, Bergerac thrived, and by the middle of the 19th century the region contained more than 50,000 hectares, producing 20 percent of Bordeaux's total annual production.

After the *phylloxera* epidemic, the better, higher-up, low-yielding slopes were abandoned for higher-yielding sites on floodplain soil. Wholesale stagnation, chronic outmigration, difficulty in selling sweet white wine, and fierce competition with the Gironde depressed prices, and reduced hetarage and production. For a short period after the formation of the European Economic Community, regional economic conditions worsened. Since Community wines must be labeled accurately as to origin, the dry red, white, and sweet wines of Bergerac were at a clear disadvantage since they were not well known outside the region.

The grape varieties of Bergerac, unlike any others in the southwestern vineyard, are overwhelmingly Bordeaux-type. The white grape that dominates hectarage, the Sémillon, is responsible for the production of semi-sweet or moelleux wine. It is planted widely in the Côtes de Bergerac, Haut-Montravel, Côtes Montravel, and in Monbazillac. When it is used for dry wine production, it cannot compete with Sauvignon Blanc, as it has a neutral aroma and flavor and reduced acid levels. The Muscadelle grape, because of its pronounced musky aroma, is judiciously used in both dry and sweet wines. But because it adds balance, flavor, and color, it is mainly used in the production of sweet wine. Yet the vine's low yield, susceptibility to *botrytis,* and *millerandage* (the irregular growth of berries) tend to counterbalance its advantages to the point that the vine is slowly losing ground to other, fresher, crisper, and higher-yielding vines. As the percentage of the Muscadelle decreases, that of Chenin Blanc, Ondec, and Sauvignon Blanc increases accordingly. The latter has a bouquet that is very much in vogue at the moment, and since it is equally good in the production of dry as well as sweet wine, its hectarage has been encouraged throughout the region.

Red wine grapes consist of the usual Bordeaux varieties—Merlot dominates hectarage and is the principal ingredient in all wine. Cabernet Franc, the second most-important red grape, is grown for suppleness, delicacy, and high yields. Cabernet Sauvignon and Malbec, long neglected, are again being replanted; small quantities of Fer Servadou are also found, as is the rare and obscure Perigord. The proportion of red vines has been increasing over the past 25 years and now amounts to around 43 percent of total hectarage, compared to 10 percent in 1955.

Monbazillac and Côtes de Saussignac

Historically, Monbazillac was second in popularity to Sauternes in the production of sweet white wine. It was very popular throughout France and particularly in Holland, where a large number of French Protestants migrated after the revocation of the Edict of Nantes in 1685. At different periods since that date, the Dutch import market has consumed more than 85 percent of production. Monbazillac, by a wide margin the larger appellation, is responsible for more than 50,000 hectoliters of wine, compared to less than 5,000 of Saussignac, whose wines are lighter in alcohol, color, bouquet, and extract. As a consequence, they mature much faster than those of its more-famous neighbor to the east.

Monbazillac, with 2,500 hectares of vineland, is the largest appellation south of the Dordogne River. Its vineyards lie on the largest concentration of chalk and sandstone within the entire Bergerac region; this, plus the presence of a microclimate that fosters *botrytis cinerea*, sets it apart from the Côtes de Saussignac and other white wine–producing appellations. Both are located on hills overlooking the Dordogne east of Port-Ste.-Foy-et-Ponchapt. Avoiding the heavy alluvial soil of the floodplain, vineyards lie along the slopes of the valley in those districts where the soil contains calcareous material.

Thirty years ago, Monbazillac produced more than twice its present production (see Fig. 15.2). Known throughout the country as the "poor man's Sauternes," it is made from the usual combination of Sémillon, Sauvignon Blanc, and Muscadelle. It is produced mainly in the communes of Monbazillac, Ponport, Rouffignac, Colombier, and St.-Laurent-des-Vignes.

Although considered the best sweet wine of Bergerac, Monbazillac falls short of the majesty that is Sauternes and Barsac, and is certainly not in the same league as the sweet rarities of the Loire and Alsace. It is less rich, usually overly sulfured, darkens rapidly, lacks an intense nose, and is deficient in the necessary acidity to "freshen" the palate. This does not mean that it is third-rate, only that if falls short of expectations when compared with the more-noble wines of the same class. While in times past Monbazillac of a good year was expected to last fifteen to twenty years, today nearly all is expected to be consumed within seven years. Historically, it was known for its deep golden color, "roasted" nose, and the flavor of overripe and *botrytized* grapes. Today, the alcohol content is

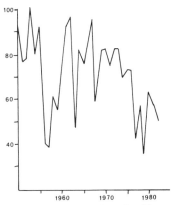

Figure 15.2   Monbazillac:
Wine Production, 1950–1983
(in thousands of hectoliters)

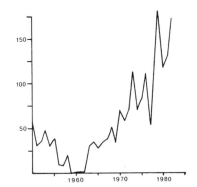

Figure 15.3   Bergerac Rouge:
Wine Production, 1950–1983
(in thousands of hectoliters)

reduced, the color is lighter, the nose is fresher and less heavy, and the range in style varies enormously by producer because no clear formula has been established for its production.

In addition to its reasonable price, the best Monbazillac is attractive because it is a sound, fast-maturing, sweet wine that is superb as an aperitif with fresh fruit or foie gras, and absolutely magnificent as a cooking wine. In those rare years when Monbazillac reaches extraordinary heights, its bouquet and taste are a cornucopia of honey and wild sweet scents. Monbazillac, with a touch of elegance, is a good value, as it sells for less than similar wines from Cérons and St.-Croix-du-Mont.

With sweet wines not in current fashion, more than 50 percent of production within the Monbazillac appellation today is Bergerac Sec, made from Sauvignon Blanc, Sémillon, Muscadelle and, in increasing frequency, Chenin Blanc. Made in the new style of low temperature and slow fermentation, minimum exposure to oxygen, absence of wood-aging, reduced sulfuring, and early bottling, Bergerac Sec is a delicious libation rivaling most dry wines of the Gironde. While most, if not all, major producers make respectable Bergerac Sec, the Union ds Coopéra-tives Vinicole de la Dordogne is responsible for nearly 50 percent of the regional production of wine, ranging from red and rosé, to dry and sweet white wines. The cooperative owns the *Ch. de Monbazillac,* a national monument that is open to the public. It is the largest producer of carefully made Monbazillac, intended for early consumption. Of the more than 100 producers of wine within the Bergerac region, about three dozen make reliable and acceptable wines. Two properties exhibiting consist-ency in the production of well-made and balanced wines are *Ch. Treuil-Nailhac* and *Repaire du Haut-Theulet.* Others include *Ch. le Tehulet, Ch. Ladesvignes, Ch. Vieux Vignobles de Repaire, Ch. de Thenoux, Ch. Pintoucka,*

Plate 15.1   Ch. Monbazillac

Ch. Peroudier, Ch. de la Fonvieille, Dne. de Tirecul, Ch. Sigalas, Dne. du Touron, Ch. Poulvère, Ch. le Fage, Ch. le Caillou, and *Ch. la Borderie.*

Montravel, Haut Montravel, and Côtes de Montravel

These three appellations, whose vines occupy bottom and sloping land on the north bank of the Dordogne, are all located downriver from Bergerac. The wines are all white, vary from dry to sweet, and must contain at least 11 percent alcohol. The best wine is the moelleux-type, which, in a good year, will exhibit balance, fruitiness, and depth of flavor. For the Haut Montravel and Côtes de Montravel designations, the only authorized varieties are Sémillon, Sauvignon, Blanc, and Muscadelle. For Montravel Sec, up to 25 percent Ugni Blanc is allowed as long as the percentage of Sauvignon Blanc remains the same. All three appellations produce about 30,000 hectoliters of wine annually, or about 5 percent of all AOC wine.

Nearly all the wine of Montravel is dry and characterized by a muted bouquet and a good dose of acidity, enabling nearly all of it to be blended with softer wines or to be sold as carafe libations in cafés. The same cannot be said of Haut Montravel and Côtes de Montravel, whose wine is softer, sweeter, better balanced, more fragrant, and by far superior. A major flaw of the wines in all three areas is that they can often be flat. More than 80 percent of all wine is produced by four aggressive cooperatives. Dependable Montravel producers include *Dne. de la Roche-Marot, Dne de Libarde, Ch. du Berny,* and *Dne. de Fonfrede.* For moelleux-type wines, *Ch. la Taye, Ch. de Michel de Montaigne,* and *Dne. de Hautes Roches* are above-average producers.

Pécharmant

Located immediately to the northeast of Bergerac, Pécharmant is the smallest geographical appellation. The vineyards, which are neither extensive nor contiguous, lie on chalky and gravelly slopes, face south, and produce a comparatively low yield of fewer than 10,000 hectoliters of red wine.

Made from varying perentages of Merlot, Cabernet Franc, Cabernet Sauvignon, and Malbec, the wines are dark, full-bodied, heavily scented, concentrated, and capable of aging for as long as seven years. The best communes are Creysse, Mouleydier, St.-Sauveur, and Lembras.

One of the two properties to enjoy an outstanding reputation is *Dne. du Haut Pércharmant* (a superlative growth, and one of the few making dark, full-bodied, unfiltered wine capable of extended cellaring), which rivals a number of the better growths of St.-Emilion. The other, much larger estate, *Ch. Tiregand,* make lighter, earlier maturing, supple wines with a good bouquet and excellent acid balance. Both properties offer remarkable value. Other important and consistently good properties are *Ch. Champarel, Clos Peyrelevade,* and *Dne du Grand-Jaure.*

Rosette

The Rosette appellation occupies a land surface that is twice the size of Pécharmant but produces only a fraction of the latter's output. Essentially a white wine region of average to common quality, the wines of note, which are produced along the eastern margins of the district but sold as Pécharmant, are red. Due to the minuscule output, and because of an effort to reduce the number of appellation designations, the Rosette appellation is rarely seen on labels.

Bergerac and Côtes de Bergerac

The Bergerac and Côtes de Bergerac appellations are regional wines emanating from an area that nearly engulfs all the preceeding appellations. To be so labeled, the grapes must originate within the confines of Bergerac on soil allocated to AOC status. The difference between the two appellations is largely one of alcoholic content (the Côtes de Bergerac has one percent more), but since both almost always reach the minimum 11 percent figure, the distinction is almost negligible. Both appellations have experienced dramatic growth within the last twenty years, particularly the Bergerac Rouge appellation, which grew from fewer than 2,000 hectoliters in 1959 to more than 189,000 hectoliters in 1979 (Fig. 15.3). The wines range from dark, full-bodied, well-structured libations to light rosé made from the carbonic maceration process. While the largest amount is undistinguished wine, that of the first category can compete in quality with that from Pécharmant. The difference between the full-bodied and the light-weight is not only fermentation and wood-aging, but the nature of the cépage. Light styles contain a much greater percentage of Merlot, Cabernet Franc, and Malbec, to the near exclusion of Cabernet Sauvignon. Bergerac Rosé, similar in color and intensity of fragrance to Beaujolais though more grassy and acidic on the palate, is currently the rage in the region; expectations are that by the end of the decade production will reach half that of Bergerac Rouge. Because the wine is not severely chaptalized, it offers an interesting alternative to Beaujolais in terms of quality, consistency, and value.

Bergerac Sec refers to dry wine from a mixture of Sauvignon Blanc and Sémillon, with varying proportions of other grapes added. Although little known, production has tripled within the last ten years to reflect a strong continuous demand. Perhaps the very best wine that the entire region is able to offer, it is clean, crisp and, since it is much less expensive than most equivalents from the Gironde, offers excellent value. Some of the best Sec comes from Haut-Montravel, Côtes de Montravel, and Rosette, with all three having the right to sell under their respective appellations, as well. The dry wines from the Côtes de Montravel can be quite delicate and go well with seafood or simply as an aperitif. The designation Côtes de Bergerac Moelleux is very confusing. It is a reference to the semi-sweet wines from the Côtes de Saussignac, Côtes de Montravel, Haut Montravel, and Rosette, all of which are light, flavorful wines meant to be well chilled and consumed while young.

As sparkling wine has again become fashionable, the region is attempting to increase production from highly acid, indigenous varieties growing in hilly locations throughout the appellation. Thus far, mousseux (sparkling) production has met with limited success. Producers within the wider Bergerac and Côtes de Bergerac appellations vary enormously in terms of consistency and style. Most producers will make wine that will accommodate the prevailing fashion, and they attempt to imitate the wines of Graves and Sauternes, rather than developing a unique regional or local style of their own.

All the following properties produce widely differing styles under the Bergerac and Côtes de Bergerac appellations. *Ch. Court-les-Mûts,* a well-mechanized 23-hectare property, makes full-bodied, well-structured red, rosé, and dry white, Saussignac, and sparkling wines. It is one of the few properties to export more than 50 percent of total output. Another property with a reputation for excellent wine production is *Ch. de Panisseau,* a 13th-century estate that makes above-average dry white (from 100 percent Sauvignon Blanc) and a well-flavored red (from equal amounts of Merlot, Cabernet Franc, and Sauvignon). Two small properties—*Ch. Puy-Servain* and *Ch. la Raye*—have well-established reputations for full-bodied *vin de garde* red wine. The Comte de Bosredon owns a small stable of properties that make red wine and dry and moelleux white: *Ch. du Chayne, Ch. Boudigand, Abbaye de St.-Mayne,* and *Ch. Bellingard* (for Monbazillac only). *Ch. de la Jaubertie* is known for reasonably dry, crisp white and full-bodied red wine. Both *Ch. Bellevue* and *Ch. le Rually* are known for full bodied red wine; the wines of *Ch. Michel de Montaigne* are reasonably good and quite popular, as the chateau is a national monument. *Ch. Thénac, Ch. de Perjan,* and *Ch. la Borderie* are all above average in quality. *Dne. Teylet Mausalet,* a small property, is known for its superlative and full-bodied red, crisp white, and small amounts of Monbazillac. While a good deal of regional production is for early drinking, *Dne. Constant* is highly regarded locally for well-aged wines— dry, moelleux, red, and Monbazillac. Finally, *Ch. le Caillou* enjoys a superlative reputation for above-average Sauvignon Blanc and full-bodied, dark, chewy, wood-aged red wine. Two properties with excellent white wine reputations are *Dne. de Combrillac* and *Abbaye de St.-Mayne.*

THE WINES OF CAHORS

After Monbazillac, the second most-notable wine of the southwest is the "black wine of Cahors," so-named after the medieval bastide town of Cahors. The wine and the town's fortified bridge—the Pont Valentre—are the pride and symbol of the region. Like many other cities of the southwest, Cahors was a defensive, river-meander site surrounded on three sides by the river Lot. The regional economy is one of mixed agriculture, and the Causse limestone plateau, which surrounds the incised valley of the Lot, is the nation's leading truffle region.

Although winemaking dates back to Roman times, the medieval church and the bishops of Cahors did much to foster grape growing and winemaking and, for a short time in the 7th century, owned most of the viticultural real estate in the region. After consolidation of the southwest into the royal domain, the wine, like most others in the region, found a ready outlet through the Garonne. Along with Sauternes and Barsac, Cahors became a major export to Russia, where it was adopted as the official communion wine of the Russian Orthodox church. The English trade was sizable, beginning with the exploits of the Black Prince, who was partial to the wines of Cahors as well as Gaillac. The wine was also popular in Austria, Holland, and Belgium.

During the last half of the 19th century, changing tastes, railroads, *oidium* and *phylloxera* devastated a good deal of the vineyards of Cahors. As detrimental as these events proved to be for the local economy, the *coup de grâce* was administered by national and international conditions—the industrialization of the larger cities in the north and the growth of overseas colonial opportunities—that syphoned off much of the younger population. The entire region, including viticulture, was economically depressed and suffered massive and chronic out-migration until the end of World War II. During this period, production declined from 127,418 hectoliters in 1857 to fewer than 9,000 in 1958. During the 1930s the wine became a *vin de pays*—forgotten, shunned by the finest restaurants, sold at rock bottom prices below that of bulk Midi, and viewed with suspicion.

Problems in post-*phylloxera* recovery centered around the region's inability to develop suitable rootstock to accommodate the finnicky Malbec vine. Those that were available proved incompatible, hindering the proper formation of berries after flowering. Since all other stocks grafted on new varieties made unpalatable wine, many hybrid vines were imported. By 1930 nearly 40 percent of all vine stock consisted of inferior grapes and, as a consequence, production and quality declined to catastrophic levels.

New direction, incentive, and organization arrived with the establishment of the Cave Coopérative les Côtes d'Olt in Parnac in 1947. Financial cash payments were made to vignerons, which allowed them to uproot hybrid and inferior vines and replace them with superior, classic grapes, a plan of action aided by the prevailing depressed land prices. Hectarage began to increase from fewer than 200 hectares in 1955 to more than 2,000 in 1980, a rate of growth unequalled anywhere else in the southwest. New varieties were introduced, including the Tannat for tannin and longevity and the Merlot for alcohol and sublety. Development progressed so smoothly that VDQS status was awarded in 1951, and despite the disastrous frosts of 1956 and 1957, the sense of determination and optimism continued until AOC status was granted in 1971. Production throughout the post–World War II period continued to increase rapidly, from fewer than 4,000 hectoliters in 1960 to more than 152,000 in 1982 (Fig. 15.4).

The Cahors vineyards lie 200 kilometers inland from the Bay of Biscay along the climatic divide between maritime and continental influences. Protected from cold, northerly winds by the Massif Central, the regional climate is as temperate as the Gironde, but with much less humidity and rainfall. The quality of the vintage depends primarily on the duration and persistency of warm and dry southeasterly winds from the Mediterranean during September and October; as a consequence, Cahors is one of the most reliable of all red quality wines of France.

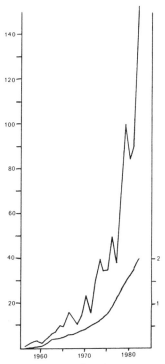

Figure 15.4   Cahors: Wine Production and Hectarage, 1951–1983
(in thousands of hectoliters and hectarage)

The producing area begins on the western margins of Cahors and continues for 50 kilometers along the meandering banks of the River Lot to Fumel. In between are the important producing communes of Pradines, Mercuès, Caillac, Parnac, Albas, Duravel, Puy-l'Evêque, Leygues, Anglars-Juillac, Prayssac, Belaye, Castelfranc, and Luzech. While a good portion of the vines is planted on inferior alluvial soil, the best sites face south at elevations close to 300 meters near the upper limits of the Causse plateau. Albas, in particular, contains superlative tracts of vineland on steep terraces. These terraces are comprised of red sand mixed with heavy accumulations of gravel and stone. Because the vines are very old and the plots are fragmented, hectarage is declining. The area of recent rapid expansion is the fertile and undulating country south of Parnac. Throughout the region, vineyards are neither extensive nor contiguous, but take the form of small plots intermingled with cornfields, vegetable gardens, and orchards. With rare exceptions, most vignerons are part-time farmers, the majority of whose holdings are in the process of enlargement and consolidation. Approximately 30 percent of the total hectarage consists of fields whose size exceeds 20 hectares, a rather high landholding size for the southwest. While slightly more than 2,000 hectares of land are planted within the Cahors appellation, an additional 2,000 have been authorized for future development.

Soils are mainly decomposed limestone with iron accumulations, thus providing a very fertile, reddish-colored soil capable of sustained yields. Along the terraces and bottomland within the Lot valley proper, the limestone subsoil is overlain by alluvial material of varying thickness, poor in organic matter and heavy in gravel, chalky stone, and quartz fragments. Here, yields are high and the quality of wine is less desirable. The best sites are on hilly terrain with thin, stony soil and as little clay as possible.

A true old-fashioned Cahors is nearly opaque, quite full on the palate, and loaded with tannin, and possesses a consistency bordering on viscous. With time, the color fades into a subtle brown-red, bottle aroma and bouquet develop, and the tannin diminishes in intensity. At its best after twenty years, the wine attains an element of refinement and is able to compete with any full-bodied red wine, except the finest growths of Bordeaux and Burgundy. Historically, the rather lengthy *cuvage* was a prime reason for the high extract and dark color. This, however, was the wine of olden days; today the tendency is for early consumption— certainly less than ten years, with a good portion ready within five years. That which is produced from grapes grown on the chalky plateau of the Causse has a deeper color and more tannin and tends to greater longevity.

Good Cahors is rustic, satisfying, and known for its distinctive odor and flavor of green olive. The very best can be absolutely superlative in its suppleness, complexity, and ability to marry well with food. Unlike Chianti, good Cahors is not heady, but is warm, generous, and always satisfying. It is an excellent restaurant wine since it is almost impossible for the wine lover to encounter a bad bottle. The very best is highly underrated and should be part of any serious cellar.

Cahors is a blended wine in which the largest player is Malbec, or Auxerrois, as it is known locally. Grown in widely diverse regions in western and southern France, it manages to rise to great heights only along a short stretch of the Lot. The vine is moderately vigorous, resistant to rot, gives good color and, a surprising characteristic, its thick skin is free of bitterness and astringency. Since it lacks finesse and refinement, other grapes are added to make up the deficiencies. Minute quantities of Jurançon Noir (also called Dame Noir) are added for bouquet; larger amounts of Merlot contribute finesse, fruit, aroma, and alcohol; and the Tannat, a Madiran grape, is used for tannin extraction and firmness. The formula for Cahors is not prescribed by law, so the final product varies enormously from producer to producer. Approximately 50 to 70 percent of the encépagement is Malbec, 20 to 30 percent is Merlot, Tannat is hardly ever less than 5 percent, Jurançon Noir can be as much as 10 percent, and Syrah (highly controversial in the region) no greater than 10 percent. When made from old Malbec, Tannat, and Jurançon Noir vines grown in upper, drier slopes, the wine is capable of extended life and remarkable bottle improvement.

Above-average-quality Cahors is the most expensive red wine of the southwest, two or three times that of Pécharmant, and twice the price of first-class Madiran. When produced by a reliable property, it is excellent value when it retails for less than the price of a fifth-growth Médoc. About 20 percent of all Cahors is sold by direct sale to tourists traveling south to Carcassonne, Spain, or to seasonal homes in the area. Estate bottling, for a quality region, is rather rare, but growing rapidly.

Approximately 40 percent of the regional wine output and more than 50 percent of AOC Cahors is the product of Cave Coopératives les Côtes d'Olt in Parnac, which produces, processes, and distributes more than 90,000 hectoliters of wine annually. It makes light, fast-maturing wines of average but consistent quality. Its premium label is "Caves du George V.," a slightly darker, fuller, and more flavorful wine than the average. Private producers make a wide assortment of styles and quality/price ranges. The house of Jean Jouffreau, considered one of the top three producers in the region, owns *Clos de Gamot* in Prayssac and makes wine in the traditional manner—dark, flavorful, spicy, and capable of extended bottle improvement. His *Ch. de Cayrou,* considered by many to be the better, is lighter and early maturing. Both wines are expensive by Cahors standards but worth seeking out.

In the same quality league is George Vigouroux, one of the most indefatigable proponents of Cahors. He owns *Ch. de Haute-Serre,* a well-run estate in Cieurac that is one of the few quality single vineyard wines. Historically, it was a medieval estate of 1,096 hectares situated in the heart of the Cahors producing district. After the onslaught of *phylloxera*, *Haute-Serre* was abandoned and eventually covered with scrub, juniper trees, and stunted oak. In 1970, a small portion was purchased by Vigouroux, who began a long, expensive rebuilding program. Considered one of the top five properties of the appellation, the estate covering 40 hectares is well situated above the prevailing channeled winds of the river valley and the persistent fog blanket that reduces effective and even ripening of most valley grapes. The soil is well drained, as it contains as much as four feet of stone near the surface. George Vigouroux also owns *Ch. de Mercuès,* once a former medieval fortress but now a stylish and expensive hotel perched on a hill and surrounded with woodland, scrub, mixed agriculture, and scattered vineyards. The label "Les Comtes de Cahors" is above average but lacks the consistency and depth of flavor of *Haute-Serre.* In addition to the two above-mentioned properties, Vigouroux has a thriving negociant business that exports more than 300,000 cases of wine annually. Furthermore, a good portion of his output is intended for the restaurant trade, of which "Cahors Gouleyant" and "Germain Vigouroux Vieille Reserve" are very popular. "Germain Vigouroux," a top-of-the-line wine, is vintaged and sold only by prestigious restaurants and a limited number of retailers. The firm also bottles wine under many other labels.

Established in the 1640s, Rigal et Fils, one of the largest growers and negociants, is known for average, early maturing wines. The firm distributes no fewer than eight different Cahors labels, plus a host of wines from Bergerac, Gaillac, Fronton, Madiran, Buzet, as well as a large amount of bulk, non-AOC table wine. The premium label is *Ch. St.-Didier,* a 70-hectare estate containing old vines. Surprisingly, its reputation is one of inconsistency despite its location on a mixture of gravel, calcareous, and sandy soils in Parnac, one of the best communes in the production of quality Cahors. *Caves St.-Antoine,* one of the largest negociants in Cahors, makes and distributes more than 450,000 cases of wine annually. The firm owns the excellent 52-hectare *Ch. de Chambert, Clos des Batuts,* and *Dne. du Single* properties.

The firm of *M. Baldès* makes average supple, early maturing wines in addition to the firmer, darker wine called Prince Probus. The showpiece of the firm, *Clos Triguedina,* is a superb single-vineyard wine made from 70 percent Malbec, 20 percent Merlot, and 10 percent Tannat, aged in oak for two years. The final product is dark in color, full of character, high in tannin, well flavored and scented, and capable of extended cellaring. *Dne. du Cedre,* another full-bodied, spicy, and plummy wine with individuality, offers excellent value. The firm of *André Bouloumié* enjoys the reputation for the "blackest" wines of the entire appellation. The *Les Cambous* label, while always reliable, is usually not ready to drink before its eighth birthday. Two properties known for full-bodied, flavorful and well-scented wines are *Dne. de Paillas* and *Dne. de la Pineraie.* Similar wines, but perhaps not as concentrated, are *Clos la Coutale, Metairie Grande du Theron, Dne. de Grauzils, Dne. de Quattre, Ch. Parnac,* and *Dne. de Peyrie.* The house of *Durou et Fils* also makes traditional wine that is dark, full-bodied, concentrated, and usually an excellent value. *Ch. de Caiz,* near Luzech, is similar in style but somewhat lighter in color and concentration.

THE WINES OF GAILLAC

Gaillac, the easternmost AOC vineyard of the southwest lying along the north side of the Garonne-Carcassonne gateway, is a supermarket area for all manner of wine. The vineyard is named after the principal city of the appellation, Gaillac, which is sited over a wide area along the narrow and swift-flowing Tarn River. The river is a tributary of the Garonne, which originates high in the mountains of the southern Massif Central.

Gaillac is one of the oldest French wine-producing areas and experienced early influence by the Phoenicians. The first major, modern viticultural impetus occurred in 920 when Archbishop Benebert donated vineland to the monks of Albi. Other religious orders arrived in 951 and 972, and by 1050 there where more than 900 hectares of planted vines, principally in Albi, Rabestens, Puycelei, Tonnac, Lupiac, and Cordes. The wines of the region acquired an element of celebrity in the 13th and 14th centuries when exports to England and Holland amounted to more than half of regional production. Henry III even kept his own wine merchant in residence in Gaillac to oversee the royal requirements.

With the outbreak of religious warfare between Protestants and Catholics, the Albigencian heresy, and political uncertainties mentioned earlier, the position of Gaillac proved untenable. Viticulture suffered, and the economic power of religious orders declined as many monasteries were abandoned. Regional security was gradually assured when bastide towns were established, and the area was finally incorporated with the rest of France. Viticulture was quickly reestablished, and by the end of the 18th century Gaillac imports to England exceeded 20,000 hectoliters, a considerable amount.

Gaillac has historically been in the forefront in the promulgation of wine legislation to regulate quality and production. The wines were so well known in the 13th century that counterfeiting became widespread, prompting the Count of Toulouse, Raymond VII, in 1221 to prohibit all foreign wine from entering the region prior to, during, and after the vintage in a futile attempt to prevent the harvest from being "stretched." Although appellation boundaries were not delimited until 1922, the various monastic orders generated some of the nation's oldest legal restrictions regulating the care of vineyards, winemaking, and wine selling. For example, the first laws to govern the quantity and type of fertilizers were enacted in 1288, and legislation affecting wine quality was enacted as early as 1378, with revisions in 1688 and 1748. The strong traditions of the region are illustrated by the fact that it has one of the oldest fraternal organizations in France—the Confrérie de la Dive Bouteille de Gaillac, first organized in 1529. In addition, the appellation has generated its own unique bottle for red wine and has preserved some of the oldest grape varieties in the country. A number of old-timers also claim that "claret," the notorious light-red wine of Bordeaux that was shipped to England in large quantities in the early days of wine exports, was actually invented for the English market by the vignerons of Gaillac, hence its name "The Pink City."

Widely diffused, with vineyards stretching along both sides of the Tarn and north of the bastide town of Cordes, are sixty villages producing varying amounts of red, rosé, white, and sparkling wine. The climate is the product of both marine west coast and Mediterranean influences. Winter is dominated by the prevailing westerlies, which are responsible for the dark, cloudy, and humid weather. Mediterranean weather arrives from the east and south during the early summer and lasts through November. Since it is characterized by high temperatures and low humidity levels, the maturation of the grapes and the vintage almost always take place under favorable conditions. The latter part of the growing season is influenced by a southerly wind called *vent du'auton,* a hot, dry air mass that accelerates berry maturation and is thus beneficial for viticulture.

Soils in the Gaillac appellation have been influenced by alluvial forces, primarily by the erosive forces of the Tarn River. Along the south bank lies a floodplain that is 7 kilometers wide. It contains small pebbles, fine loam, and sandy soil that is highly acidic, poor in organic matter, but fertile in minerals. Bordering the floodplain are a number of terraces, composed of sand, gravel, and medium-sized stones, that are little used for viticulture because the underlying clay layers inhibit drainage.

The main white grape varieties are a combination of Gironde favorites and exotic local celebrities. Among the latter is the Mauzac (a grape low in natural acidity but high in flavor and scent), which is responsible for semi-sweet, sweet, and dry, first-class white wine. The Len de l'El is widely used in blends to impart a dose of finesse and acidity to otherwise low-acid wines. Ondec, a variety destined for extinction, is an obscure grape known more for its low yields and irregular growing habits than for its wine quality. Among the Gironde grapes, the Sauvignon Blanc makes well-perfumed libations locally called *pierre à fue* (fiery stone), character-ized by spiciness and tartness—unusual features for this variety. Of lesser importance, the Muscadelle and Sémillon are used only in the making of sweet and semi-sweet wines.

Among the indigenous red grapes, the Duras is used for color extrac-tion, fruit, and tannin, while its first cousin, the hardy Braucol (also known as Fer Servadou and Petit Verdot), imparts tannin and longevity.

The Gironde varieties consist of Cabernet Sauvignon, Merlot, and Cabernet Franc, all widely planted and producing light-weight wines with no particular distinction. Two Rhône grapes, the Gamay and Syrah, have dramatically increased their hectarage share in recent years, the former being used almost exclusively for rosé wine. The other grapes considered current favorites are the Negrette, Malbec, and Portugais Bleu. Widely planted after the *phylloxera* outbreak, the indigenous and obscure varieties of Grand Noir, Jacquez, and Valdiquier have largely disappeared, as have the once-popular Durif and Alicante vines.

The Gaillac AOC appellation contains fewer than 1,400 hectares of vine, substantially less than the 16,000 hectares in existence in 1925. About half of production is red, 5 percent is rosé, and the remainder is composed of various types of white still and sparkling wines. Of the approximately 500 growers, 65 percent belong to cooperatives. For all appellation wine the alcohol content must be at least 10.5 percent, and since 1969 all commercial wines shipped out of the region must be subjected to an official tasting. The Gaillac appellation produces fewer than 65,000 hectoliters of wine in an average year.

Historically, Gaillac was a white wine region based on the Mauzac grape variety, which produced a highly fragrant and popular sweet and semi-sweet wine. Today, the Mauzac-dominated white wines are noticeably lighter in body, drier, less concentrated, refreshing, and very appealing. They are rich in aroma, have good color and plenty of fruit, and are surprisingly quaffable, marred only by low acid levels. What distinguishes superior from average bottles is the amount of Len de l'El in the final blend, with 20 percent being considered ideal.

The white wine of repute is Gaillac Premières Côtes, an appellation engaged in the production of grapes from the best communes of "inner Gaillac"—Broze, Cahuzac-sur-Vère, Castanet, Cestayrols, Fayssac, Montels, and Gaillac. The yield per hectare is limited to 40 hectoliters, and alcohol must be at least 12 percent. The wine is flavorful and with sufficient acidity to make a most refreshing beverage. Production has declined to insignificant levels, however, because the appellation is little known and, hence, hard to sell (nearly all is sold as plain Gaillac).

Made by the *méthode champenoise,* sweet, semi-sweet, but rarely brut, Gaillac Mousseux is rather light in body, delicate, and well flavored. Like Blanquette de Limoux, it is not chaptalized or subject to *dosage,* as is the case with Champagne and other sparkling wines. Made almost entirely from Mauzac grapes, the best producing region lies near Albi, the birthplace of Toulouse-Lautrec. Although technically flawless, Gaillac Mousseux is rarely a good value outside its region of production. Recently there has been a sharp increase in the production of pétillant, or perlé, wine, also made from Mauzac. Producers with a reputation in the production of mousseux are the Coopérative at La Bastide-de-Levis *Jean-Cros, Ch. Clares, Dne. de Labarthe, Ch. Lastours,* and *Dne. Clement Termes.*

Among red wines, the most important in terms of quantity is Gaillac Rouge, a dark, ruby-colored libation known for its pronounced nose and body when it contains a high percentage of Braucol. It is very coarse when young, but after several years of bottle-aging it tends to round out and attain a good degree of suppleness. The very best has high tannin levels and needs at least five years to mature. Since there is no formula for its production, styles vary widely according to the type of grapes used. Gaillac Primeur Rouge, made primarily from Gamay, is rounder, darker in color, and has more substance than Beaujolais Nouveau, its nearest competitor. It is not exported in large quantities but offers excellent value within the producing district, although rarely in other parts of the country. Gaillac Rosé, made primarily from Gamay with a touch of Syrah, is a beautiful cherry-colored wine that is well perfumed and the current rage in the southwest, particularly in Toulouse and Carcassonne. Recently a formidable trade has arisen in the export (primarily to the United Kingdom, the Low Countries, and West Germany) of *Vin du Pays du Tarn,* a blended regional wine made both dry and semi-sweet, in all three colors.

Production is dominated by two large and one small cooperative, all of which make a wide assortment of appellation and regional wines. In addition, nearly eighty small to medium-sized private producers are responsible for about 40 percent of total regional production. Of the total, three firms with above-average reputations specialize in the making of full-bodied red wines. *Dne. de Pialentou, Ch. de Rhodes, La Croix St.-Salvy, J. Aakser, J. Couderc,* and *A. Geddes* all specialize in classic *vin de garde* red Gaillac. *Jean Albert* heads the long list of vignerons producing multiple types of wine, particularly in the production of light, early maturing red wines and soft, fruity whites. The firms of *R. Assie, Ch. Clares, Jean Cros, Mas d'Aurel, Dne. des Bouscaillons,* and *Guy Laborie* are less fine but reputable.

THE WINES OF BEARN

The vineyards of Jurançon, Irouléguy, and Béarn occupy the western portions of the Pyrénées, often called *Eskual Herria,* or "Basque Country," especially the region between Pau and Bayonne. To these three districts we add the non-Basque wine region of Madiran, which lies just below the crest of the large alluvial fan between Pau and Tarbes. All the above contribute less than 12 percent of the total wine production in the southwest.

In the center of French Basque country, the ancient province of Béarn lies on the foot of the Pyrénées on what used to be the northern extension of the Navarre kingdom. From Pau, the capital and largest city, to the southwest sits the most famous vineyard of the region—Jurançon. To the west, on the Spanish border, is the minor viticultural site of Irouléguy.

The Béarn vineyard is contiguous to Jurançon along the latter's western border, while several kilometers due north, but on lower ground, is the most celebrated red wine district of the Pyrénées—Madiran.

In the middle of the 19th century, the vineyards of Béarn were more extensive: estimates range from 14,000 to 25,000 hectares, figures that are substantially greater than the meager plots of today. Despite the heavy toll of *phylloxera,* depopulation, and weak prices, the area has experienced a viticultural resurgence during the last twenty-five years, with hectarage increasing from 1,500 in 1960 to 2,300 in 1984.

Historically, the wines of Jurançon and Madiran were Swedish favorites. They continue to be so, perhaps because Pau was the birthplace of General Bernadotte, the founder of the reigning Swedish dynasty. Unlike the wines of the Garonne and the Dordogne, which had to find an outlet through the ports of the Gironde, the wines of Béarn were shipped directly to northern Europe through Bayonne and Biarritz. Today, Basque wines suffer from a lack of recognition and are rarely encountered outside the region, despite their very competitive prices.

Jurançon

The scattered vineyards of Jurançon, a 600-hectare region and the birthplace of Henry IV of Navarre, sit on steep hills above Pau. Although vines are indigenous to the area, large-scale commercial plantings first occurred during the medieval ages when religious orders, particularly the Abbey of St.-de-Bigorre, became the largest vineyard owners. It is curious that Jurançon and other viticultural areas in the high Pyrénées were little affected by Roman influence. The Jurançon vineyard is a delimited area only for above-average sweet white and average dry white wines. Production is limited to approximately 17,000 hectoliters, and as exports out of the region are limited, the wines are rather rare and expensive. The best sites lie scattered along an east-west limestone ridge west of Pau and Gan. The villages known to produce the best wines are Gan, Monein, Uzos, Mazeres, Rotignan, Aubertin, Laroin, Gelos, Lostro-Sire, and St.-Faust.

The classic sweet Jurançon is made from Gros and Petit Manseng—local, late-ripening vines that have adapted well to the stony, glacial, acidic soils and higher elevations of the region. Although both varieties resist disease and attract *botrytis* well, the Petit Manseng appears to be superior to the higher-yielding Gros Manseng. Not only does it contain smaller berries and higher acid levels, but it yields highly concentrated must and intensely aromatic wine. Other exotic vines include Camerlet, Lauzet, Cruchen, Arrouyat, and Courbu. The first two produce minuscule yields of spicy flavored wine, while the Courbu is known for low acidity but supple, round wine. Folle Blanche and Picpoul are cultivated for the local carafe trade.

Jurançon wines, unique in flavor and aroma, offer a good deal of finesse, refinement, and elegance. The very best are semi-sweet to sweet without being cloying, age well beyond four and as long as twenty-five years. The wine is usually bottled after two years in wood, and has the ability to withstand rough handling. Exceptional Jurançon is made only from grapes affected by *botrytis* and has an alcohol content of 15 percent or more. Locally it is compared with Sauternes, but is less elegant, lighter in body, and not a formidable competitor.

Often labeled "Blanc de Blanc," a dry white, made from Gros Manseng, Courbu, Camerlet, and Lauzet, is fruity, fresh, light in body, and eminently drinkable. Jurançon Mousseux Brut is made from unripened grapes but is inferior to neighboring sparkling wines. Jurançon Rouge, made from Tannat and other grapes, is tasty but marred by high acid levels and a lack of balance.

Due to chronic out-migration and the high cost of labor, the wines are rather expensive in relationship to their quality. The very best are also *recherché*, as the French are fond of saying. Estate-bottling is equally rare, with only a handful of private producers attempting to maintain the Basque tradition that is Jurançon. Among the most important is *Cru Lamouroux*, a 6-hectare 120-year-old property jointly owned by J. Chigé and R. Ziemek. They both make dry and semi-sweet wines; the latter, aged in wood for eighteen months, is a full-bodied, alcoholic wine with considerable staying power. Another excellent producer of dry and sweet wine is *Alfred Barrère. Dne Guirouilh,* a good-sized estate with a national reputation, consistently makes above-average dry and sweet wines. Four additional, less well known but excellent properties are *Clos Cancaillau, Clos-Uroulat, Dne. Cauhape,* and *Clos Mirabel.* Ninety-five percent of all growers in the appellation are members of the Coopérative Vinicole de Gan-Jurançon, the largest producer of wine in the appellation. It makes a complete line of *vin de pays* (its staple business) under the Pyrénées Atlantique designation, and nearly all Juraçon, most of which is dry. This surprisingly full-bodied, strongly flavored, and scented wine offers excellent value. The Jurançon Moelleux is golden yellow to amber in color, rich, unctuous, smooth, and well scented.

Irouléguy

The wines, red, rosé and white, are marketed as Vins d'Irouléguy. The grapes, as one would suspect, are mainly Basque and consist of Gros and Petit Manseng, Courbu, and Tannat. Bordeaux vines, principally Sémillon, Malbec, Cabernet Sauvignon, and Sauvignon Blanc, have been added recently.

Although flavorful and dry, the wines are acidic and often lack sufficient alcohol and balance. An undetermined number of hectares (the total is thought to be less than 100) surround the villages of Irouléguy (the principal center), Jaxu, Ossès, Bidarray, St.-Etienne-de-Baïgorry,

and St.-Jean-Pied-de-Port. Production is usually less than 3,500 hectoliters annually, and a small cooperative is responsible for the entire output.

Béarn

Lying to the west of Jurançon, the fewer than 1,250 hectares remaining
within the appellation produce red and white wines similar to those of its
more-famous neighbor to the east. Unable to produce the rich, concentrated white wines of Jurançon nor the dark, full-bodied wines of
Madiran, Béarn has been selling its wine as carafe, or to be blended into
innocuous *vin de pays*. Made from Gros Manseng and Pacherenc, white
wines with no appreciable character dominate total output.

Madiran

The superb 20,000-hectoliter red wine region of Madiran, long obscured
by Armagnac and Bordeaux, is as good as or superior to Cahors and a good
number of fifth-growth Médoc estates. Fifteen main communes—Portet,
Crouseilles, Lembaye, Audie, Diusse, Maumusson, Viella, Conchez,
Montpezat, Mont-Disse, Aubous, Moncaup, Madiran, Tadousse-Ussau,
and Soublecause—produce the bulk of total output. They are all located
on gentle slopes separated by streams running along the Ger plateau.
North of Madiran is the large viticultural area of Armagnac, whose wines
are used mainly for the distillation of fine spirits. What little wine
remains is distributed by a large cooperative and consumed locally.

Produced from fewer than 1,200 hectares, wine output has increased
from less than 2,000 hectoliters in 1954 to more than 22,000 in 1981.
Madiran is a full-bodied red wine that is well flavored and balanced and
offers excellent value. It is never bad, but it is also never great; instead it
remains consistently above average in quality.

Historically, 70 percent of the encépagement was composed of Tannat,
a grape contributing tannin and color, but due to its lack of fragrance it
now accounts for less than 50 percent of the blend. As the percentage of
Tannat decreased after 1975, that of Cabernet Franc increased to more
than one-third. Vines contributing less than 15 percent of the mixture
include Fer Servadou (locally known as Pinenc and Couhabort) and
Cabernet Sauvignon. Although the finished product is dark, high in
tannin, astringent, and rough in its youth, it softens with extended oak-
and bottle-aging. It is marred only by a weak nose and a short finish, a
fault that has largely been corrected by the recent addition of Cabernet
Sauvignon. A superlative vintage is one in which the Tannat matures late,
thus avoiding an overly acidic must and producing wine that is very
similar in character to Cahors. Fermentation can take as long as two
weeks, and a year's aging in oak casks is considered a minimum prior to

bottling. Good Madiran requires at least five years of bottle-aging to mature fully.

Union de Producteurs Plaimont, the largest single producer of wine in the region, consists of 1,250 members and controls more than 2,000 hectares of vineland. It makes about one-third of all Madiran, a small amount of red and white Côtes de St.-Mont, and large quantities of red, rosé, and white Côtes de Gascogne Vin de Pays. The *Coopérative Vinicole du Vic-Bilh Madiran-Crouseilles* makes, principally from Tannat and Cabernet Sauvignon, one of the finest red wines of the southwest. The two finest private properties—*Ch. Montus* and *Ch. d'Audie*—are both known for outstanding *vin de garde* wines, good enough to be part of any serious cellar. Small amounts of excellent estate-produced wine comes from *Ch. d'Peyros* (for smooth, Bordeaux-type wine), *Dne. Barrejat* (for supple, elegant wine), *Dne. de Teston* (for well-flavored, supple wine), *Dne. Pichard* (for exceptionally balanced wine), *Ch. du Perron* (for full-bodied, well-structured wine), *Vignobles Laplace* (for heavy, dark, long-maturing wine), *Ch. de Gayon* (for spicy, well-flavored and scented wine), and *Dne. de Maouries* (for well-made, round, *vin de garde* wine).

Small amounts of white wine are made from Petit and Gros Manseng, Bresparo, Courbu, Arrufiat, Sémillon, Sauvignon Blanc, and Plant de Grève, and called Pacherenc du Vic-Bilh (after a range of local hills). The commune with the best reputation is Portet. The wine varies from very dry to sweet, the latter produced only when weather permits the formation of *botrytis* and, hence, very rare. Once bottled it will continue to improve for twenty-five years, acquiring a smokey flavor not too dissimilar to that of Madeira. Very unusual and distinctive in taste and flavor, both the dry and sweet versions offer excellent value. Among the best producers are *Vignobles Laplace* (known for rich, marvelously flavored wines); *Ch. d'Audie* (known for superb dry, fresh, well-scented and flavored wines); *Dne. Bouscasse* (for medium-bodied, fresh, vigorous, well-flavored wines); and *Dne. de Teston* (for dry, steely, aperitif-type wines).

Côtes de Buzet

Côtes de Buzet is a newly furbished 2,500-hectare AOC vineyard located north of Armagnac along the south bank of the Garonne River. It produces, primarily from Bordeaux grape varieties, more than 30,000 hectoliters of agreeable, medium-bodied, well-balanced red wine and small quantities of rosé and white wine. The most-important producing areas, all located on hillsides or former river terraces (on limestone or alluvial soil) are Nérac, Sait-Leon, Montesquieu, Damazan, Lavardac, Buzet, Xaintrailles, and Espiens.

Not only were the vineyards of Buzet hit hard by *phylloxera,* but the economic circumstances pertaining to the production and sale of red wine from the region were particularly disastrous. Côtes de Buzet wine simply did not sell once the Bordeaux appellation prohibited the addition of Buzet to improve the light-colored "Claret" after 1911. Sales declined, and the only alternative was to produce the cheapest possible grapes with the highest possible yields for brandy distillation. During the early part of this century, hectarage was reduced to less than 3,000 commercial hectares (down from 6,500 hectares in 1870), practically all subjected to the production of *vin ordinaire*. The deterioration of wine prices led to neglect and eventual abandonment of almost the entire vineyard during the economic depression of the 1930s. By 1937, several hundred hectares were officially classified as VDQS. But since 1973, when AOC status was awarded, production and hectarage have expanded dramatically in partial reaction to increased tourist traffic and to aggressive promotion by the local cooperative.

The most important wine is red (98 percent of total output), usually made from a combination of Merlot (40 percent), Cabernet Sauvignon (30 percent), and Cabernet Franc (30 percent). The wines are wood-aged for at least twelve months and are surprisingly vinous, well-flavored and scented, and can improve for as long as five years. In addition to the three grape varieties mentioned above. Here, Gamay, Merille, Jurançon Noir, and Alicante Bouschet are also cultivated. The minute quantities of dry white wine are made from Sémillon, Sauvignon Blanc, and Muscadelle.

Production is dominated by the large Caves Réunis des Côtes de Buzet, one of the most technologically efficient cooperatives in the southwest region. It has 118 members, makes more than two-thirds of the appellation's wine, and exports nearly 100,000 cases annually to Holland, Belgium, and West Germany. The wine is always well made, supple, soft, without excessive tannin, and not overly dark in color. From old vines and exceptional sites, the cooperative produces a premium "Cuvée Napoleon," one of the better wines of the southwest. It has excellent depth of flavor, a beautiful color, and outstanding balance; it improves for ten years in the bottle, offers superb value, and is a good alternative to Bordeaux.

The cooperative also vinifies, ages, and bottles three estate wines. *Ch. de Gueyze* is a 75-hectare vineyard entirely located on gravel with a limestone subsoil. From equal amounts of Cabernet Sauvignon, Cabernet Franc, and Merlot, it produces a smooth, elegant, and well-flavored wine. *Ch. de Bouchet,* containing more Cabernet Sauvignon, is a firm, meaty, tannin-rich, and well-structured wine that can age beyond its fourth birthday. Located in the commune of Montesquieu, the wine of *Dne. Roc de Caillou,* made primarily from Merlot, is the most fragrant of the three.

In addition to the large cooperative, about a dozen private growers make a wide assortment of wines in varying degrees of quality. Leading the list is *Ch. Pierron,* a medium-sized producer of dark, heavily scented, wood-aged wine. *Dne. des Cramais* and *Dne. des Guignards* are two estates with excellent local reputations for consistency and fair value. Smaller and less distinguished, *Ch. de Padère* is known for light-colored, weak-flavored red wine.

Côtes du Fronton

Located west of Gaillac and just north of Toulouse is the obscure but above-average red wine region of Fronton. The producing region is located on old, stony Tarn River terraces whose soils are dry, poor in fertility, but high in iron and quartz. The most important wine-producing communes are Campsas, Nohic, Fabas, Canals, Bouloc, Fronton, and Villaudric. The appellation, producing more than 40,000 hectoliters of AOC wine from 1,150 hectares, enjoys an excellent local and regional reputation. The wine is a blend of the local Negrette (a grape variety that produces very dark, firm, tanin-rich, well-flavored and scented wine) and Cabernet Sauvignon, Cabernet Franc, Malbec, and Syrah. The Negrette, forming at least 50 percent of the blend, has adapted well along the hilly exposures between the two principal communes of the producing region—Fronton and Villaudric. Small quantities of white wine, primarily from Mauzac, Sauvignon Blanc, and Sémillon, are also made.

The two principal cooperatives—Caves Coopératives Côtes du Fronton, and Villaudric—account for more than 90 percent of production. While both make acceptable Fronton "Rouge" and Rosé," their main business is the production of regional, non-appellation wine. Of the two, Fronton, with an annual output of more than 80,000 hectoliters and exports of 450,000 cases, is much larger. Private producers with a reputation for consistent, above-average-quality wine production include *Ch. Bellevue La Forêt, Ch. Montauriol, Dne. de Bel-Air, Ch. Cransac, Dne. Ferran,* and *Dne. de la Colombière.* The largest property in the region is *Ch. Bellevue La Forêt,* a 125-hectare immaculate and well-managed property that makes 80,000 cases of outstanding, highly distinctive wine. Although fruity, supple, and early maturing, the wine contains more than the minimum percentage of Negrette (along with Gamay, Syrah, Cabernet Sauvignon, and Cabernet Franc), and thus manages to produce a highly flavorful and distinctive red wine that should not be missed. The property also makes an interesting white wine from Colombard.

Côtes de Duras

Between the Côtes du Marmandais and Bergerac appellations is the important AOC Côtes de Duras viticultural district that is responsible for more than 60,000 hectoliters of wine from 1,800 hectares of vineland. Slightly more than half of production is dry white wine very similar to that produced in Entre-Deux-Mers and Bergerac. While the Ugni Blanc, Sémillon, Colombard, and Mauzac dominated production in the past, the

Sauvignon Blanc appears to have captured an ever-increasing percentage of total hectarage in recent years. The wine is well made, but it lacks character, balance, and consistency. The recently improved red wine, made from Bordeaux varieties, has doubled its output over the past ten years. It is more distinctive than the white and offers better value.

Although both wines are as good as those found in the Entre-Deux-Mers and Bergerac regions, the area's relative isolation and historic obscurity preclude easy sales. Moreover, as the holdings are small and tended on a part-time basis by growers, the vines cannot compete effectively with plums, tobacco, and corn. Yet the wines do offer excellent value within the district.

The local Duras Coopérative Cellar vinifies and distributes more than three-quarters of production. Approximately 50 percent of output is sold in plastic-lined cardboard containers.

Other Producing Vineyards

The southwest portion of France contains two important and six minor VDQS appellations. A VDQS region near the Gironde border, Côtes du Marmandais, produces red and white wines, with the former the better of the two. Bordeaux-type grapes have replaced indigenous varieties, making fruity, soft, and well-scented wines very much in the new style of the Gironde. White wines are not particularly gifted with desirable qualities, yet their production is a rather sizable 25,000 hectoliters and appears to be growing, due to demand for café and container wines. The second most-important VDQS appellation is Côtes de St.-Mont, a 12,000 hectoliter vineyard (awarded VDQS status in 1981) located in the southwest corner of the Gers department. Straddling both banks of the Adour River, the small but sprawling vineyard includes the important villages of Plaisance, Aignan, Riscle, and St.-Mont. Red wine dominates and is made from Tannat (70 percent), Fer Servadou, Cabernet Franc, Cabernet Sauvignon, and Merlot. Although the wine resembles Madiran, it is lighter in color and body and lacks the flavor and aroma of its more-famous neighbor. Small quantities of white wine are made from Gros Manseng, Arrufiac, and Clairette.

The six minor VDQS appellations are Tursan, Lavilledieu, Côtes du Brulhois, Vins d'Entraygues, Vins d'Estaing, and Vins de Marcillac. Tursan, located in the department of Landes close to Madiran, is a small, obscure, 5,000-hectoliter red and white wine appellation. A light, feeble rosé, dominates production. Lavilledieu is a tiny 75-hectoliter red wine appellation lying near the confluence of the Tarn and Garonne rivers producing red wine from Negrette and Bordeaux grape varieties. The most recent VDQS vineyard is the small, 1,500-hectoliter red wine appellation of Côtes du Brulhois. It adjoins the Côtes de Buzet vineyard, but its wine, despite its resemblance, is not the equal.

INDEX

Fayssac, 261
Francs, 145
Fronsac, 105–8
Fronsadais, 105

Gabarnac, 231
Gaillac viticultural region, 244,
  259–62
Gaillan, 190
Gan, 263
Gardégan, 144
Gelos, 261
Gensac, 237
Gironde-Dordogne viticultural region,
  96–108
  Blaye, 72, 96–100
  Bourg, 96, 97, 100–103
  Canon–Fronsac, 106
  Coutras, 103, 104–5
  Cubzac, 103–4
  Fronsac, 105–8
  Fronsadais, 105
  Guîtres, 103, 104–5
  Libournais, 108
Gorges, 10, 15
Gradignan, 194, 201
Grand Crus classification, 149–55
Graves viticultural region, 69, 70, 71,
  76, 93, 146, 192–207
  Ayguemorte-les-Graves, 205
  Barsac, 192, 203, 210–12, 213–14,
    219–22
  Beautiran, 205
  Budos, 193, 207
  Cadaujac, 194, 202
  Canejan, 201–2
  Castres, 205–6
  classifications of 1953 and, 1959,
    198–99
  Gradignan, 194, 201
  Guilles, 207
  Isle-St.-Georges, 204
  La Brède, 206–7
  Landiras, 193
  Langon, 193, 202, 207
  Léogeats, 207
  Léognan, 193, 194, 202
  Martillac, 193, 194, 198, 202,
    204–5
  Mazèras, 207
  Mérignac, 193, 199
  Pessac, 193, 194, 198, 199–201
  Portets, 193, 202, 206
  producing communes, 199–207
  red wines, 195–97, 198

St-Pierre-de-Mons, 193, 207
St.-Selve, 207
Talence, 193, 194, 198, 199, 201
Villenave, 194
vineyard types, 184
white wines, 197–98
Gros Plant du Pays Nantais, 18–19
Guillos, 207
Guîtras, 72, 103, 104–5

Haie-Fousassière, 10, 15
Haut Montravel, 253
Haute et Basse-Goulaine, 10
Haute-Goulaine, 15
Haut-Médoc, 180–88
  Arcins, 185, 186
  Avensan, 187
  Blanquefort, 187
  Castelnau, 187
  Cissac, 182–83
  Cussac, 185–86
  Lamarque, 185, 186
  Le Pian, 187
  Le Taillan, 187
  Ludon, 187
  Macau, 187
  Parempuyre, 187
  St.-Laurent-et-Benon, 180, 184–85
  St.-Sauveur, 183–84
  St.-Seurin-de-Cadourne, 180–82
  Vertheuil, 182
Haux, 231
Huismes, 48

Illats, 208, 210
Indre-et-Loire, 7
Ingrandes-de-Touraine, 51
Irouléguy, 262, 264–65
Isle-St.-Georges, 204

Jasnières, 53
Jau-Dignac, 188
Jaxu, 264
Jurançon, 262, 263–64

La Brède, 206–7
La Chapelle-Basse-Mer, 15
La Chapelle-Heulin, 15
La Chapelle-sur-Loire, 51
La Dervinière, 48
La Haie-Fousassière, 15
La Haie-Foussière, 10
La Regrippière, 15
La Roche-Clermault, 48
Labarde, 170, 175

CHATEAU POUGET

GRAND CRU CLASSÉ

MARGAUX

Appellation Margaux Contrôlée

1970

P. GUILLEMET, PROPRIÉTAIRE A CANTENAC (GIRONDE)

MIS EN BOUTEILLES AU CHATEAU

IMP. CH. DESTOUT - BORDEAUX

Château Saint Pierre

SEVAISTRE

S. JULIEN-BEYCHEVELLE

GRAND CRU CLASSÉ

MM. Van den Bussche Propres

1970

MÉDOC

Appellation Saint-Julien contrôlée

GRAND VIN

CHATEAU
LYNCH ⚜ BAGES

GRAND CRU CLASSÉ

PAUILLAC
MÉDOC

1969 — APPELLATION PAUILLAC CONTROLÉE

J.C. CAZES, PROPre

MISE EN BOUTEILLE AU CHATEAU

CHATEAU

Prem
Appell

Mis en bouteilles au Château

E. CHARUIS - BORDEAUX

GRAND VIN DE GRAVES

1983
CHÂTEAU
LA LOUVIÈRE

MIS EN BOUTEILLE AU CHATEAU

GRAVES
LÉOGNAN

APPELLATION GRAVES CONTRÔLÉE

75cl

ANDRÉ LURTON
PROPRIÉTAIRE-VITICULTEUR A LEOGNAN — GIRONDE
PRODUCE OF FRANCE

MICHEL SIMON / FROSSAC

IMP VIGNES ET CELLIER

1967

CHATEAV
SMITH HAVT LAFITTE

MARTILLAC

®

APPELLATION GRAVES CONTRÔLÉE

GRAND CRU CLASSÉ

*LOUIS ESCHENAUER S·A·PROPRIETAIRE
A MARTILLAC · GIRONDE · FRANCE*

Mise en bouteilles par

LOUIS ESCHENAUER S. A. · BORDEAUX

DÉPOSÉ

PRODUCE OF FRANCE